LATIN AMERICAN STUDIES
A Basic Guide to Sources

Contributing Editors

Carole Travis
Roger R. Macdonald
Ann E. Wade

Contributors

Laurence Hallewell

Alan Biggins
Chris Clark
Harold Colson
Tim Connell
Paula A. Covington
Hilda Cuthell
Martha Davidson
Carl W. Deal
John East
James Elliott
Betty D. Fathers
Gillian Furlong
Paul Goulder
Brigid M. Harrington
Margaret Johnson

Peter T. Johnson
Peter Ward Jones
Sara E. Joynes
David Newton
John R. Pinfold
Barbara J. Robinson
Michael Rogers
Patricia A. Semple
Gillian Shaw
Noel Treacy
John Wainwright
Purabi Ward
Geoffrey West
Gayle A. Williams
Christine Younger

LATIN AMERICAN STUDIES
A Basic Guide to Sources

Second Edition

Revised and Enlarged

Robert A. McNeil, *Editor*

Barbara G. Valk, *Associate Editor*

SCARECROW PRESS
Metuchen, N.J. & London
1990

‡ 19739669

*Prepared under the auspices of
Standing Committee of
National and University Libraries
Advisory Committee on
Latin American Materials*

Library of Congress Cataloging-in-Publication Data

Latin American Studies : a basic guide to sources / Robert A.
McNeil, editor, Barbara G. Valk, associate editor. — 2nd ed., rev.
and enl.   p.   cm.
    Rev. ed. of: Latin American bibliography / by Julia Garlant ...
[et al.].
    Includes index.
    ISBN 0-8108-2236-9 (alk. paper)
    1. Latin America—Bibliography.   I. McNeil, R. A.   II. Valk,
Barbara G.   III. Title: Latin American bibliography.
Z1601.L324   1990
[F1408]
016.98—dc20   89-34133

Contents

Non-Print Sources

Specialised Information

Research and Career Development

Preface

Latin America has become, over the past twenty years, a major subject for research in all parts of the English-speaking world. Courses and study programmes in the history, geography, politics, literatures, economy and social development of the region have proliferated, at undergraduate as well as postgraduate levels. Moreover, the events of the last decade in Argentina, Central America, Chile and the Falkland/Malvinas Islands have encouraged increasing numbers of students to take an intelligent interest in the affairs of the subcontinent.

While courses in Latin American bibliography—by which is meant the systematic study of sources of information and research on the region—form an integral part of academic programmes in Latin American studies at most major North American universities, they remain far less common in the UK and much of Europe. And the need is still felt, in both hemispheres, for a basic textbook in research methods for students commencing their study of the area.

In 1986, the Advisory Committee on Latin American Materials (ACOLAM) of the Standing Conference of National and University Libraries (SCONUL) determined, as part of its bibliographical programme, to sponsor a new edition of *Latin American Bibliography: A Guide*, edited by Laurence Hallewell (London: SCONUL Latin American Group, 1978). As Dr Hallewell himself felt unable to take on the task, an editorial board was formed under my chairmanship, and work commenced in 1987 on updating the articles that made up the earlier text. It soon became evident, however, that a more radical revision would be necessary to encompass the enormous advances made in Latin American studies over the last fifteen years. New chapters were suggested, the alphabetical arrangement of the original edition was, with some regret, abandoned in favour of a more strictly form-based approach, and the scope was widened to take more account of Latin American studies as practised outside the UK. Several librarians based in the US were invited to contribute to the work, and Barbara G. Valk of the University of California, Los Angeles, generously agreed to serve as Associate Editor. The book that has resulted is, in almost all respects, a new work—although it is one that could not have existed without the pioneering labours of Laurence Hallewell and his original team of collaborators.

My first and principal acknowledgment is therefore to Laurence Hallewell, who not only acquiesced in the dismemberment and reconstruction of his classic text, but actively assisted in the process, and remains the largest single contributor. I should also like to thank those contributors to the first edition—Julia Garlant, Maria Landau, Elizabeth Long, Bernard Naylor, Patricia Noble, Robin Murray Price, Colin Steele and Sarah Tyacke—who were unable to help with the revision but were happy to allow their original contributions to be modified. And a special debt is owed to all the members of ACOLAM, and in particular to Chris Hunt, the Chairman, for their support and encouragement during what turned out to be a longer process than any of us had envisaged.

On a more personal level, I should like to thank Chris Anderton for his help and advice in the book's planning stages; Jim Ballantyne and William Vernon Jackson for their expert knowledge; my colleagues at the Bodleian Library, and in particular Margaret Robb, Joanna Dodsworth and Judy Howe, for their continued support; the Reverend Stephen Cope for his assistance in preparing a publishable text; Scarecrow Press for their patience, not to mention their forbearance when confronted with a manuscript full of British spellings and punctuation; Colleen Trujillo for her technical advice; and all the contributors for their time, their skills and their good temper. My principal debt, however, is to Barbara Valk, the Associate Editor, for her firm and unimpeachable judgment, her editorial expertise and her determination to make the book as good as possible.

RAM

Introduction

Latin American Studies is a form-based, introductory guide to research on Latin America in the social sciences and humanities. It is designed to serve both as an adjunct to formal university courses in Latin American bibliography and research methods and as a basic handbook for other researchers embarking on investigations involving the region. Its purpose is to describe the many types of resources and research techniques available for the study of Latin America, to identify major reference works in the field, and to lead the reader from the publications cited to more exhaustive sources of specialised information in each of the areas examined.

Scope

The term 'Latin America' is here interpreted in its broadest sense: geographic coverage encompasses all of the Western hemisphere from the United States–Mexico border region to Tierra del Fuego, including the Caribbean islands. Some sources are also listed referring to Hispanic populations in the United States. Cited materials include items written in English, Spanish, Portuguese and other Western European languages, and date from the earliest printed sources still in use to works in progress at the time of publication.

The book was prepared in Great Britain, but a concerted effort has been made to address the research requirements of readers throughout the English-speaking world; to this end, more than a quarter of the contributors—including the Associate Editor—were drawn from librarians and subject specialists working in the United States, and all chapters include both British and North American components.

The volume was compiled primarily in 1987 and 1988, and was revised early in 1989. While it is the nature of any printed reference source to become obsolete almost before it appears, close attention has been paid to combining classic works of continuing value with ongoing, frequently-updated current publications and databases to alleviate the problem.

Arrangement

The book is divided into six main parts. The first part identifies leading Latin American library collections in Great Britain, Europe and the United States and archival collections worldwide. It attempts to facilitate access to the collections by explaining the organisation of library catalogues and classification schemes, and by listing a number of published catalogues and guides to the holdings of major repositories. Also offered are suggestions for obtaining materials through photocopying services, inter-library loans or direct purchase.

The second part lists and describes the major bibliographies available in the field. An introductory chapter gives complete citations for many of the key publications mentioned throughout the volume, and identifies other general works of importance to Latin American research. Specialised sources are cited in the three following chapters: 'Subject Bibliographies' includes materials on particular topics; 'National Bibliographies' identifies the book production from and about particular countries or regions; and 'Personal Bibliographies' traces works by and about individual authors.

The next part includes seven chapters giving information on other kinds of printed sources essential to researchers, from dictionaries and encyclopaedias to newspapers and periodicals. An examination of non-print sources—databases, microforms, sound recordings and visual materials—follows. Thereafter, the book deviates from its form-based approach to address specific types of information— biographies, legal materials, statistics and the like—which can be found in many different types of sources.

The final part of the work focuses on career preparation and professional development. Among the topics discussed are research centres and academic programmes for Latin American studies, scholarship opportunities, language courses, avenues for study abroad, societies and associations and professional conferences. The section concludes with advice concerning travel in and correspondence with Latin America, and some thoughts on possible careers for Latin American specialists.

Following the text is a brief guide to sources for identifying acronyms and abbreviations, accompanied by a list of those that appear in the book. Two indexes facilitate access to the information presented: a subject index including references to institutions as well as topics, and an author-title index of reference sources, interfiling the names of personal authors, editors. compilers and revisers with full-title references to all cited materials.

Authorship

Latin American Studies is a work of collective authorship, prepared by thirty-six librarians and subject specialists, but drawing on the advice and experience of many more. The contributors, both named and unnamed, include representatives of some of the major Latin American collections in Great Britain and the United States. Each chapter bears the initials of the writer or writers primarily responsible for its contents. It should be remembered, though, that the task of editing the whole volume has involved a certain amount of rearrangement to avoid overlapping treatment of the same topic, and as a result many of the contributors have influenced more chapters than they have signed. The presence of the Editor and Associate Editor, moreover, is in evidence thoughout the work, and it is they who take ultimate responsibility for any omissions, inaccuracies or inconsistencies in the final text. Perfection is an ongoing process, and the editors will be delighted to receive notifications of errors or suggestions for improvement from any interested reader.

Robert A. McNeil
Bodleian Library
University of Oxford

Barbara G. Valk
Latin American Center
University of California, Los Angeles

Libraries and Their Use

Library Resources on Latin America

Library facilities for Latin American studies vary considerably, ranging from large, well-established collections in universities to small and comparatively recently formed collections in independent organisations. Finding out what is available and where can be a daunting proposition for the researcher, given that there are about 200 significant collections of Latin Americana in the UK alone, around 300 more on the continent of Europe, and countless others in the US and Latin America itself.

In Latin America proper there is regrettably no equivalent to the well-established interdisciplinary professional organisations that have done so much to benefit academic programmes and library collections in Europe and the United States; nor have there been any surveys on the subject. As a result, collections specialising in Latin America or the Caribbean are more difficult to identify. The major libraries of Latin America can, of course, be traced through the frequently revised publication:

> *World Guide to Libraries/Internationales Bibliotheks-Handbuch.* 8th ed. Munich: K. G. Saur, 1987.

In addition, the more important libraries are regularly listed in such directories as the annual *World of Learning* (London: Europa Publications, 1947—). There is nonetheless a very real need for a comprehensive and detailed guide to library resources in the region. Until this need is met, a handy introduction to sixteen Latin American libraries may be found in:

> STEELE, Colin. *Major Libraries of the World.* London: Bowker, 1976. Gives the full address, with notes on access and opening hours, and a brief account of the major holdings of each library listed. Many of the minutiae are, however, now out of date.

For European collections, a useful new guide to what is available and where to find it is:

> MACDONALD, Roger and Carole TRAVIS. *Libraries and Special Collections on Latin America and the Caribbean: A Directory of*

European Resources. London: Athlone Press, 1988. Provides
detailed descriptions of collections and their accessibility, with
a comprehensive index enabling the researcher to establish
where relevant material is located.

There is no exact equivalent covering the US; for students in North
America the best substitutes are general guides to Latin American
studies programmes such as BRAY (see below, p. 12) or HARO (see
UNIVERSITIES AND RESEARCH CENTRES, p. 312), or guides to
individual collections, where they exist; some are listed below on pp.
13–14.

Having established which collections are potentially useful, the
student is faced by the question of access, and all the other problems
involved in becoming familiar with a new library. There are a few
useful hints which are worth noting, whichever library you are using.

When you intend to visit an unfamiliar library it is usually helpful
to write or telephone in advance; the staff will be able to advise you
whether or not your planned visit is worthwhile and alert you to any
special admissions procedures. Most libraries are prepared to admit
bona-fide researchers as readers, but rarely grant immediate borrowing privileges.

Do not be afraid to ask the library staff for assistance—that is
what they are paid for—but do try to find out whether there is
someone specially appointed to look after the Latin American
materials. Most of the major US Latin American collections, and
many European ones, have Latin American bibliographers who
routinely assist researchers when they require help. When using
libraries in Latin America, a letter from one's own university or
research centre confirming one's credentials as a scholar is often very
helpful.

Try to be specific and precise in asking for information. It will be
helpful if you can keep a record of the books and periodicals you
have already consulted, so that the reference staff do not have to go
over the same ground again.

It is worth noting that although a library may be open until late
in the evening and at weekends, in many libraries professional staff
may well be present only during 'office hours' from Monday to
Friday. Complicated queries are best presented on weekdays, and
well before five o'clock!

Many libraries provide coin-operated photocopying facilities; if
you intend to photocopy considerable amounts of material, you
would be well advised to equip yourself with a wide selection of coins.

Further hints on library use may be found in two recent publications:

BEASLEY, David. *How to Use a Research Library*. New York: Oxford University Press, 1988. Based on the collections of the New York Public Library, but applicable anywhere.

MANN, Thomas. *A Guide to Library Research Methods*. New York: Oxford University Press, 1987.

Libraries in Great Britain

University Libraries

The Parry Report of 1964 recommended the establishment of centres for Latin American studies at five UK universities (see UNIVERSITIES AND RESEARCH CENTRES, p. 307). Special funds were made available for library development, and over the years some impressive facilities for Latin American studies have been created in the following libraries, building upon existing strengths:

Cambridge University Library (West Road, Cambridge CB3 9DR. Telephone: 0223 333000).

Glasgow University Library (Hillhead Street, Glasgow G12 8QE. Telephone: 041–339 8855).

Sydney Jones Library, University of Liverpool (P.O. Box 123, Liverpool L69 3DA. Telephone: 051–709 6022, ext. 3122).

University of London Library (Senate House, Malet Street, London WC1E 6BT. Telephone 01–636 4514).

Bodleian Library, University of Oxford (Broad Street, Oxford OX1 3BG. Telephone 0865 277000).

None of these libraries has a comprehensive collection covering all aspects of Latin America: each will display its particular area of interest, emphasising certain disciplines or countries. In the past, however, the libraries and universities have collaborated to ensure that no area or topic is completely neglected. Nor is it safe to assume that the Latin American collections of each university will be concentrated in the central library: in London, much material can be found in the libraries of University College and King's College, while Oxford has a special library in the Taylor Institution for the study of foreign literatures, including those of Latin America.

Cambridge and Oxford have the additional advantage of being copyright libraries, entitled to claim free copies of any work published in the British Isles; as a consequence, both collections are very large.

While several of the universities have Centres or Institutes of Latin American Studies, these act in most cases as coordinating bodies, housing only small working collections for student use and leaving the bulk of the Latin American holdings to the major university libraries. The Institute of Latin American Studies in London has a special role, in that it houses the British Union Catalogue of Latin Americana (see UNION CATALOGUES AND UNION LISTS, pp.63-64), and has built up a large collection of reference material and bibliographical guides.

In addition to the five Parry Centres, there are other university collections with major holdings of Latin American materials. Notable among them are the University of Essex Library (Wivenhoe Park, Colchester CO4 3UA; telephone 0206 873333), which has built up a large research collection; and the library of the Institute of Development Studies at the University of Sussex (Andrew Cohen Building, Falmer, Brighton BN1 9RE; telephone 0273 606261), specialising in economic, social and political science. University collections elsewhere tend to be smaller, simply reflecting the requirements of any of the academic staff who have an interest in the region.

Polytechnic Libraries

The Frewen Library of Portsmouth Polytechnic (Cambridge Road, Portsmouth PO1 2ST; telephone 0705 827681) has developed a substantial collection of materials complementing the institution's interdisciplinary course in Latin American studies for undergraduates. Two other, smaller, public sector collections worthy of note are at Wolverhampton Polytechnic (Robert Scott Library, The Polytechnic, St. Peter's Square, Wolverhampton WV1 1RH; telephone 0902 313005) and Ealing College of Higher Education (St. Mary's Road, Ealing, London W5 5RF; telephone 01-579 4111); in both places the material supports modern language courses offered.

The British Library

The British Library is a national collection, comprising several divisions containing different classes of material. The divisions most relevant to Latin American studies are listed below.

British Library, Humanities and Social Sciences (Great Russell Street, London WC1B 3DG; telephone 01-323 7676). This is frequently still referred to by its old designation, the British Museum Library. Here are the largest and most significant holdings on Latin America in the UK, the result of more than two centuries of collecting. All British publications are received and added to stock automatically; in addition, the Library attempts to develop and maintain a general collection on all topics and periods. Mexico and Brazil are especially well represented, and there is a noteworthy collection of government publications. All materials must be consulted in person, *in situ*; the published author and subject catalogues are well known, and can be found in most research libraries.

British Library Newspaper Library (Colindale Avenue, London NW9 5HE; telephone 01-200 5515). This division currently receives about 80 Latin American newspapers, and holds over 900 more dead titles. There is an eight-volume published catalogue (1975).

British Library Document Supply Centre (Boston Spa, Wetherby, West Yorkshire LS23 7BQ; telephone 0937 843434). Intended as a back-up to the central collections, this division acquires all periodicals cited in the indexing and abstracting services used by specialists in the field, and makes either the originals or photocopies available through inter-library loan. Serial titles held can be traced through the *Keyword Index to Serial Titles* (see INTER-LIBRARY LENDING, p. 73).

Science Reference and Information Service (25 Southampton Buildings, Chancery Lane, London WC2A 1AU; telephone 01-323 7494). This is the science and technology counterpart of the old British Museum Library, dealing with inventions, engineering, technology and business; one feature is an extensive collection of Latin American patent and trade mark journals (see PATENTS AND TRADE MARKS, p. 287). Another branch (covering life sciences, earth sciences and mathematics) can be found at 9 Kean Street, London WC2B 4AT; telephone 01-323 7288.

Special Libraries

The largest specialised library in the British Isles on Latin America, Spain and Portugal is the Library of the Hispanic and Luso-

Brazilian Council at Canning House (2 Belgrave Square, London
SW1X 8PJ; telephone 01–235 2303). Open to the general public, it
has a fine collection of recent English language publications on the
region and older material in all languages. More information about
Canning House may be found in the chapter on SOCIETIES AND
ASSOCIATIONS (p. 334). Many UK libraries specialising in other
disciplines try to collect comprehensively in their chosen field of
interest, and consequently hold Latin American materials on a
variety of topics from Administration to Zoology. Full details of
such collections can be found in the guide by MACDONALD and
TRAVIS, cited above.

Libraries in Europe

Material on Latin America is to be found in all European countries,
though the coverage and the range and depth of the collections vary
considerably. There are a number of university centres and institutes
which concern themselves with problems of the Third World and
developing countries; these can be a fruitful source for the student
seeking ephemera and 'grey literature'.

It is, of course, not practical to list here all the relevant collections
on the continent of Europe. The following, however, deserve a
special mention. It should be noticed that the telephone numbers
given do not include the internal or international access code for the
country concerned; from abroad, the country code must always
come first (see CONTACTS WITH LATIN AMERICA, p. 346).

France

One of the major libraries in the world, with the right to a legal
deposit copy of all French publications, is the Bibliothèque Nationale
(58 rue de Richelieu, 75084 Paris Cedex 02; telephone 47 03 81 26).

This great collection has an estimated 120,000 items relevant to
Latin America, and attempts to cover all the countries in the region.
The collections have been documented in three articles by Prof.
William Vernon Jackson of the University of Texas at Austin:

> JACKSON, William Vernon. 'Bibliographic Tools and Tech-
> niques for the Study of Latin American Resources at the
> Bibliothèque Nationale.' In *Reference Services and Library Educ-
> ation: Essays in Honor of Francis Neal Cheney.* Lexington, MA:
> D.C. Heath, 1982.

JACKSON, William Vernon. 'L'étude des fonds latino-américains de la Bibliothèque Nationale, XIXe et XXe siècles.' *Revue de la Bibliothèque Nationale* 9 (1983), pp. 29-41.

JACKSON, William Vernon. *Resources for Brazilian Studies at the Bibliothèque Nationale.* (Austin, TX, 1980).

The Bibliothèque et Centre de Documentation of the Institut des Hautes Etudes de l'Amérique Latine at the Université de Paris III (28 rue Saint-Guillaume, 75007 Paris; telephone 222 35 93 ext. 48) holds France's largest collection of Latin American materials outside the Bibliothèque Nationale, and specialises in the social sciences and the humanities. Not far away there is a collection of some 15,000 volumes specialising in the politics and government of Latin America, at the Services de Documentation of the Fondation Nationale des Sciences Politiques (27 rue Saint-Guillaume, 75341 Paris Cedex 07; telephone 1 260 39 60).

Mexico and Mexican history are the main foci of interest in the 20,000-volume collection at the Bibliothèque 'Benito Juárez' of the Maison du Mexique (9C Boulevard Jourdan, 75014 Paris; telephone 5 89 77 56).

Outside Paris, the departments and institutes of several French universities have collections of Latin American material: two of these are the Bibliothèque de Documentation Internationale Contemporaine at Nanterre (BDIC, Centre Universitaire, 92001 Nanterre Cedex; telephone 47 21 40 22), with some 35,000 volumes concentrating on social, political and economic aspects of the twentieth century; and the University of Toulouse Le Mirail (5 allées Antonio Machado, 31058 Toulouse Cedex; telephone 61 41 11 05). The latter university has four separate collections in institutes which between them cover social, economic, geographic, historical and literary aspects of Latin America.

Federal Republic of Germany

The Ibero-Amerikanisches Institut Preussischer Kulturbesitz (1000 Berlin 30, Potsdamer Strasse 37; telephone 30 26 65) is the largest library in Europe specialising in Latin American materials. The collections include over 570,000 volumes, 14,000 periodical titles and 48,000 maps, as well as substantial holdings of press cuttings and audio-visual materials. Although the collection covers all disciplines, it is strongest in the fields of ethnology and archaeology.

Three major collections are to be found in Hamburg, led by the Ibero-Amerikanisches Forschungsinstitut of the University (2000 Hamburg 13, Von Melle-Park 6 VI; telephone 40 41 23 27 54/48 01), whose well-established collection concentrates on language and literature. A library specialising in political, social and economic materials can be found at the Institut für Ibero-Amerika-Kunde (2000 Hamburg 36, Alsterglacis 8; telephone 40 41 20 11), while the library of the Institut für Wirtschaftsforschung Hamburg (2000 Hamburg 36, Neue Jungfernstieg 21; telephone 40 3 56 21) is strong in economics and the social sciences.

As in France, many collections of Latin Americana of varying sizes can be found in the libraries of university departments and institutes. Among them is Cologne University's Iberische und Lateinamerikanische Abteilung des Historischen Seminars (5000 Köln 41, Albertus-Magnus-Platz; telephone 22 14 70 24 46), which has a collection specialising in colonial history, particularly of Mexico and the River Plate region.

Of the state libraries, the Bayerische Staatsbibliothek (8000 München 22, Ludwigstrasse 16; telephone 89 21 98 3 22) has extensive research facilities, and its Latin American holdings are estimated at over 55,000 items, mainly in the humanities and social sciences.

German Democratic Republic

The teaching of Latin American studies in the DDR is particularly strong in Rostock, where the Universitätsbibliothek (Wilhelm-Pieck-Universität, 2500 Rostock, Universitätsplatz 5; telephone 81 36 94 31) has a 40,000-volume collection, with special strengths in philosophy, ideology, economics, history, languages and literature.

Italy

The Biblioteca Nazionale Centrale 'Vittorio Emmanuele II' (Viale Castro Pretorio 105, 00185 Roma; telephone 4989) is a legal deposit library for all Italian publications. The Latin American holdings are estimated at some 50,000 volumes. Also in Rome is the Istituto Italo-Latinoamericano (26 Piazza G. Marconi, 00144 Roma), a general library of around 60,000 volumes focusing on scientific, technical, social and cultural aspects of Latin America.

Netherlands

The Centrum voor Studie en Documentatie van Latijns Amerika (Centro de Estudios y Documentación Latinoamericanos, or CEDLA) has, since 1964, built up a 20,000-volume collection on the social sciences, anthropology and history of Latin America (Bibliotheek CEDLA, Keizersgracht 395-397, 1016 EK Amsterdam; telephone 20 5253248 or 5253242). In addition, the Royal Institute of Linguistics and Anthropology Library (Koninklijk Instituut voor Taal–, Land– en Volkerkunde, P.O. Box 9515, Reuvensplaats 2, 2300 RA Leiden; telephone 71 148333, ext. 4025) has a comprehensive collection of material on Surinam, the Netherlands Antilles and other Caribbean territories. This library also maintains a union catalogue of Caribbeana (see UNION CATALOGUES AND UNION LISTS, p. 64).

Portugal

The University Library at Coimbra (Biblioteca Geral, Universidade de Coimbra, Praça da Porta Verrea, 3049 Coimbra Codex; telephone 39 25541/2) serves as a national library and receives by legal deposit all Portuguese publications on Latin America; its subject bias favours the humanities.

Excellent holdings of colonial documents on Brazil are to be found in the Arquivo Histórico Ultramarino (formerly 'Colonial') in Lisbon (Calçada da Boa-Hora 30, 1300 Lisboa Codex). The Archive also maintains a supporting library for the use of researchers. More manuscript material on Brazil may be found in the Biblioteca Nacional (Campo Grande 33, 1751 Lisboa Codex), together with wide coverage of secondary and periodical literature on the nineteenth and twentieth centuries.

Spain

The largest collection of printed materials on Latin America to be found in Spain is in the Biblioteca Nacional (Paseo de Recoletos 20, 28001 Madrid; telephone 1 275 68 00). Comprehensive coverage is attempted on the contemporary period in the fields of the humanities. A major specialised collection is the Biblioteca Hispánica of the Instituto de Cooperación Iberoamericana (Avenida Reyes Católicos 4, 28040 Madrid; telephone 1 244 06 00 ext. 393). This library, too, has excellent holdings on contemporary Latin America, and covers most subject areas, with a bias toward the humanities.

A significant repository of material on the discovery, conquest and independence of Spanish America, including maps and manuscripts, can be found in the Biblioteca del Museo Naval (Montalban 2, 28014 Madrid; telephone 1 221 04 19 and 222 65 10, ext. 1022). The University also has a major library specialising in American history (Universidad Complutense, Biblioteca del Departamento de Historia de América, Ciudad Universitaria, 28003 Madrid; telephone 1 449 65 00, ext. 38).

Outside Madrid, two universities having significant collections on Latin America are in Seville (San Fernando 4, 41004 Sevilla) and Santiago de Compostela (Biblioteca Universitaria, Travesía de Fonseca, Santiago de Compostela; telephone 9 56 38 33). The great Spanish archives of Seville and Simancas are treated under MANUSCRIPTS AND ARCHIVES (see pp. 24–25).

Sweden

The library of the Latinamerika-Institutet (S-106 91 Stockholm; telephone 8 162887) has collected over 35,000 volumes dealing with the history, economics, politics, social anthropology and sociology of Latin America.

Libraries in the United States

Owing to its proximity and its cultural, political and economic impact upon the United States, Latin America is the most intensively studied foreign area in US colleges and universities. It is not surprising, then, that the leading library collections on the region have grown and flourished as integral parts of formal academic programmes. The most useful current directory of Latin American studies programmes and libraries in the United States is:

> BRAY, David B. and Richard E. GREENLEAF. *Directory of Latin American Studies in the United States*. New Orleans, LA: Tulane University, Roger Thayer Stone Center for Latin American Studies, 1986. Provides a brief description and volume count of library collections that support university courses.

This directory identifies 110 academic programmes in Latin American studies that form the backbone of Latin American library resources in the United States; forty-one of these institutions have more than twenty affiliated Latin Americanist faculty members, and are supported by strong library resources. Libraries at twenty-seven of the institutions, however, are especially worthy of mention: all maintain Latin American collections in excess of 100,000 volumes, and most, while maintaining a broad current collection policy, also provide an array of special collections and opportunities for research. Specific areas of strength in these collections are not widely known, however, and there has been no successful national effort to describe them by subject content and quality rather than by quantity. One learns of their strengths only through use, and through the advice of experienced colleagues.

Typically, the more comprehensive collections acquire primary works in the humanities and social sciences from throughout the region. All focus greater attention on the major publishing countries (Brazil, Mexico and Argentina), but some concentrate as well on one or more specific regions (such as the non-English-speaking Caribbean, Central America, the Andean region or the Southern Cone) reflecting institutional teaching and research interests. Most of the libraries also offer access to special materials such as maps, music, photographs and machine-readable data files. They subscribe to the most important journals and to some newspapers, and collect selectively important government documents and the publications of international organisations.

Guides to Collections

Several leading libraries have published guides to their collections. Among them are UCLA, Princeton and Indiana University. These three guides not only offer a key to bibliographic and other research materials in the collections, but are also excellent sources for developing research strategies in using Latin American resources in any library collection.

LAUERHASS, Ludwig, Jr. *Library Resources on Latin America: Research Guide and Bibliographic Introduction.* Los Angeles, CA: UCLA Latin American Center and University Library, 1978.

STEIN, Barbara. *Latin America: A Guide to Selected Reference Sources, Bibliographies and Introductory Texts in the Princeton University Library.* Princeton, NJ: Princeton University Library, 1977.

READ, Glenn F. *Latin American Bibliography: A Syllabus.* Bloomington, IN: Indiana University, Latin American Studies Program, School of Library and Information Science, 1983.

The Benson Latin American Collection at the University of Texas at Austin and the Tulane University Latin American Collection have each published an excellent series of subject guides to their holdings. Students and researchers, especially those new to the field, should spend time with these guides as well as with the more extensive published catalogues produced by a number of major libraries (see PUBLISHED LIBRARY CATALOGUES, p. 46).

There are, in addition, a few guides to specific regions and subject areas that describe the holdings of major libraries throughout the country. Although now rather outdated, they can still prove very useful. Preeminent among them is the splendid:

BARTLEY, Russell H. and Stuart L. WAGNER. *Latin America in Basic Historical Collections: A Working Guide.* Stanford, CA: Hoover Institution, 1972. Goes beyond academic collections to include holdings in special libraries, museums and archives throughout the world. Features a superb bibliography of published sources and guides to collections.

A second and more specialised work is:

JACKSON, William Vernon. *Library Guide to Brazilian Studies.* Pittsburgh, PA: University of Pittsburgh Book Center, 1964. An excellent tool for locating Brazilian materials in academic and other research libraries in all fields, but especially in the social sciences and humanities. Although it is dated, no other single guide of this quality exists for other countries.

There are, unfortunately, too few of these guides to provide adequate coverage of the available library resources in the United States. In a paper presented in 1980 to the XXV Seminar on the Acquisition of Latin American Library Materials (SALALM), Dan Hazen recognised this lacuna, noting: 'Within Latin American librarianship, we have only impressionistic information with regard to which institutions have built major collections in which countries and disciplines. The statistics and descriptive accounts upon which we could base effective resource sharing are notably absent.' ('Major Latin American Collections in Private Institutions: New Roles and Responsibilities in the 1980s.' In *Library Resources on Latin America: Final Report and Working Papers.* Madison, WI: SALALM, 1981, p. 240).

In an effort to deal with this problem, SALALM has taken two initiatives. The first is the development of a Latin American Conspectus, or a map of collections in the United States and

Canada, as part of the North American Collections Inventory Project (NCIP) currently being sponsored by the Association of Research Libraries (ARL). When libraries are able to describe their holdings within the 700 or more Library of Congress subject classifications that have been selected for Latin America, this conspectus will provide an excellent automated online guide to library holdings. The second SALALM initiative is the establishment, now under way, of a Task Force on Standards for Developing and Maintaining Latin American Research Collections beyond the Twentieth Century.

Meanwhile, in the continuing absence of precise descriptive data, we must rely on such published reports as are available. Essential sources of information on collections throughout the world are to be found in the monographs of the SALALM Bibliography and Reference Series, in the annually-published *Papers* of the organisation, and in the G. K. Hall catalogues of major Latin American collections.

Academic and National Libraries

The first useful documentation of major Latin American collections in US academic libraries was published by Marietta Daniels Shepard in the 'List of Books Accessioned' by the Columbus Memorial Library in 1956. A third and final edition of this work, prepared by Kent Miller and Gilberto Fort in 1970, provides a helpful basis for measuring the growth of major collections listed in later surveys.

According to Miller's 1970 survey, 41 academic, special and public libraries reported having more than 25,000 volumes in their Latin American collections. Of that number, three libraries reported holdings of more than 50,000 volumes, three others reported more than 100,000, and the Library of Congress outdid the rest with holdings of more than 500,000 volumes. While no doubt other libraries at the time might with justice have claimed larger numbers of relevant volumes, the survey shows that relatively few of the more comprehensive collections we know today were then in existence.

Growth in these and other collections since 1970 has been impressive, as recorded in BRAY's more recent survey (cited above) and by data collected by Carl Deal in 1988. By that year, 27 libraries included Latin American holdings in excess of 100,000 volumes. The largest and most comprehensive is still, of course, the Library of Congress collection in Washington, DC, with more than a million relevant items; this collection is discussed below. Next largest are the University of Texas at Austin and the University of California at Berkeley, each supporting collections in excess of 500,000 volumes, and Yale University and the University of Illinois at Urbana-Champaign, which both maintain collections of more than 300,000 volumes. More than 200,000 volumes can be found in libraries at Columbia, Cornell, Indiana, Tulane, UCLA and the Universities of Wisconsin-Madison, New Mexico, Pittsburgh, Virginia, Arizona, Kansas, Miami, North Carolina and Florida. Libraries containing more than 100,000 volumes exist at Princeton, Arizona State and Stanford, the University of Southern California, the University of California at San Diego, the Universities of Chicago and Wisconsin-Milwaukee and the American University in Washington, DC. The New York Public Library has the largest and most significant coverage of the region outside an academic library after the Library of Congress.

One must be careful, however, also to consider the special collections that may be available on these and other campuses. For example, collections on Chicano studies are particularly strong at UCLA, Stanford, Texas and Santa Barbara, and Berkeley's strengths are supplemented by the printed and manuscript resources of the Bancroft Library. Likewise, research at Stanford might involve the use of the Library of the Hoover Institution on War, Revolution and Peace as well as the University Library proper. Other important specialised collections include the Lilly Library at the University of Indiana, a major centre for materials from the colonial period; the Oliveira Lima Library at the Catholic University in Washington, considered one of the finest collections of Luso-Brazilian materials in the US; and the library of the Centro de Estudios Puertorriqueños at Hunter College, the leading interdisciplinary collection on Puerto Rico and its émigré populations in the Caribbean and the US.

The massive Latin American collection of the Library of Congress, containing as it does (in addition to books and periodicals) extensive holdings of manuscripts, maps and atlases, microforms, newspapers, photographs, films and music, is the world's largest repository on the region. The collection supports the activities of the Hispanic Division, which houses a users' reading room, publishes bibliographic guides to the collections as well as the annual *Handbook of Latin American Studies*, carries out an active acquisitions programme and conducts other substantive bibliographic projects.

While no library can claim comprehensive coverage of such a vast area as Latin America, the Library of Congress comes closest to the ideal. Its acquisitions efforts are supported not only by direct purchases through its very effective Hispanic Acquisitions Program but also through its heavy reliance on the Library's Gifts and Exchange Program. In addition, a Brazil Office was established in 1966 as part of the Library's National Program for Cataloging and Acquisition (NPAC). The *Library of Congress Accessions List, Brazil,* published bi-monthly, has provided access to materials often previously unobtainable in the United States.

Other Libraries

There are many public and special libraries throughout the country that offer significant opportunities for research and study on Latin America. Among public libraries, those of New York and Boston are the strongest. The New York Public Library (NYPL) is noted for its extensive research collections, which include manuscripts and government documents, as well as for its very broad current coverage of books, newspapers and periodicals from the area. (A G. K. Hall catalogue offers a description of its holdings on the history of the Americas). The Boston Public Library and NYPL were, for many years, the only public libraries participating in the Latin American Cooperative Acquisition Plan (LACAP), the major acquisitions vehicle for many research libraries from 1962 to 1970.

The Center for Research Libraries in Chicago (CRL) is another leading repository, particularly for works in microformats, which include among other items newspapers filmed for its Foreign Newspaper Microfilm Project, foreign dissertations and official publications and journals supplied by the Latin American Microforms Project (LAMP). Loan of these materials can be arranged through any of the 125 libraries that support the CRL programmes, and researchers should certainly avail themselves of any available institutional privileges.

The Columbus Memorial Library of the Organization of American States (OAS) has the second largest Latin American collection in Washington, DC, after the Library of Congress. It houses extensive holdings of periodicals, current newspapers and OAS documents, as well as monographs in many subject areas. Another important special library in Washington is that of the Inter-American Development Bank (IADB or IDB), which is very strong in socioeconomic materials. Any Latin Americanist working in the Washington area should not fail to consult:

GROW, Michael. *Scholars' Guide to Washington, DC, for Latin American and Caribbean Studies.* Washington, DC: Smithsonian Institution, 1979.

Other special libraries likely to be of importance for Latin American researchers are: the Los Angeles County Law Library, for legal materials; the Newberry Library in Chicago, for its emphases on colonial Mexico and Brazil, on indigenous peoples of the Americas (the Edward E. Ayer collection) and on Portuguese history and overseas expansion (the William E. Greenlee collection)—the latter two collections have published catalogues from G. K. Hall; the Genealogical Society of Utah library in Salt Lake City, for its vast microfilm holdings of Latin American civil and church records related to genealogical research; and the John Carter Brown Library at Brown University, for its collections of early colonial imprints. Further special collections focusing on Latin America may be located through the use of BARTLEY (cited above) or through such works as:

ASH, Lee and William G. MILLER. *Subject Collections: A Guide to Special Book Collections and Subject Emphases as Reported by University, College, Public and Special Libraries and Museums in the United States and Canada.* 6th ed. New York: Bowker, 1985.

RRM/CWD

Manuscripts and Archives

Archives are not always easily accessible, or indeed freely available, to all. It is therefore advisable to consult one of several published guides before embarking an any research visit, whether in the UK or abroad. It is also wise to investigate local conditions in advance, as they can vary considerably from place to place, and to become adequately acquainted not only with the Spanish (or Portuguese) language, but also with early forms of handwriting.
The most useful general guide to archives is:

International Directory of Archives. London: Mansell, 1976. Broad coverage of archive repositories and their holdings. Includes such useful practical information as opening hours and conditions of access.

More specifically on Latin America, there are:

BARTLEY, Russell H. and Stuart L. WAGNER. *Latin America in Basic Historical Collections: A Working Guide*. Hoover Institution Bibliography Series, 51. Stanford, CA: Hoover Institution, 1972. Although the best coverage is of the US (107 institutions), Canada, Latin America, the West Indies, Europe, Australia, Japan and the Philippines are also included. The description of private, municipal, national and government archives is particularly rewarding. There is an extensive bibliography, and a brief note on social science data archives in the US.

GROPP, Arthur E. 'Bibliografía de fuentes archivísticas relacionadas con Ibero-América: catálogos, guías, índices, inventarios, listas y publicaciones periódicas.' *Anuario de Estudios Americanos* 22 (1965), pp. 919–973.

Unesco and the International Council of Archives have sponsored a series of guides to Latin American materials in the archives of foreign countries. Volumes published to date cover Belgium (1967), Denmark (1968), France (1984), East Germany (1971), West Germany (1972), Great Britain (1973), Italy (1976), The

Netherlands (1968), Spain (1966–1969), Sweden (1968) and the
Vatican (1970). Fuller details are given below in the sections on
individual countries and areas. From 1968 to 1976 the journal
History (London: Historical Association, 1912—) included a series of
general guides, 'Libraries and Archives for Historians', but the
coverage was essentially limited to European institutions.

For a helpful guide to handwriting, see:

> MILLARES CARLO, Agustín and José Ignacio MANTECÓN.
> *Album de paleografía hispanoamericana de los siglos XVI y XVII*. 3
> parts. Mexico City: Pan-American Institute of Geography
> and History, 1955.

The rest of this chapter is devoted to a listing of selected sources
available for the location of Latin American archives in individual
countries or regions. In virtually every case the sources refer to
manuscript material physically located in (rather than concerning,
or originating from) the area mentioned. The only exception is the
treatment of the codices of Mesoamerica, which for convenience are
dealt with under Mexico. The British Isles are discussed first,
followed by the rest of Europe and the Americas.

Great Britain and Ireland

The general guides, both now somewhat out of date, are:

> WALNE, Peter. *A Guide to Manuscript Sources for the History of
> Latin America and the Caribbean in the British Isles*. London:
> Oxford University Press, 1973. Produced for the Unesco
> project.

> RAIMO, John W. *A Guide to Manuscripts Relating to America in
> Great Britain and Ireland*. Rev. ed. London: British Association
> for American Studies, 1979. A revision of the guide edited by
> B. R. Crick and M. Alman, originally published in 1961.

The most up-to-date guide to the holdings of individual repositories
(though not designed to be used purely for subject access) is:

> FOSTER, Janet and Julia SHEPPARD. *British Archives*. London:
> Macmillan, 1982. Rev. ed., 1989.

The Royal Commission on Historical Manuscripts maintains an
ongoing index, currently being computerised, of accessions to
repositories, and keeps copies of available handlists of collections.

All of these can be consulted at the Commission's offices (Quality House, Quality Court, Chancery Lane, London WC2A 1HP). Most archive repositories have some form of finding-aid to their holdings, but (as previously mentioned) researchers should address the archivist of the establishment concerned as to conditions of access before setting out on an investigation.

For guides relating to specific collections, there are:

OLIVEIRA LIMA, Manuel de. *Relação dos manuscriptos portuguezes e estrangeiros de interesse para o Brazil, existentes no Museo Britannico de Londres.* Rio de Janeiro: Companhia Typ. do Brasil, 1903. Reprinted from the *Revista Trimestral do Instituto Histórico e Geográfico Brasileiro* 65:2 (1902), pp. 5–139. This work is an update of earlier listings by Frederico Francisco de la Figanière and Francisco Adolfo Varnhagen.

GAYANGOS Y ARCE, Pascual de. *Catalogue of the Manuscripts in the Spanish Language in the British Museum.* 4 vols. London: British Museum, 1875–1893; reprinted, 1976.

GRAJALES RAMOS, Gloria. *Guía de documentos para la historia de México existentes en la Public Record Office de Londres, 1827–1830.* Mexico City: Pan-American Institute for Geography and History, 1967. Includes Foreign Office records.

COSTELOE, Michael P. *Mexico State Papers, 1744–1843: A Descriptive Catalogue of the G. R. G. Conway Collection in the Institute of Historical Research, University of London.* London: Athlone Press, 1976. Contains a few manuscripts.

PRICE, Robin Murray. *An Annotated Catalogue of Medical Americana in the Library of the Wellcome Institute for the History of Medicine.* London: Wellcome Institute, 1983.

A more general guide is:

GRAJALES RAMOS, Gloria. *Guía de documentos para la historia de México en archivos ingleses, siglo XIX.* Mexico City: UNAM, 1969.

Europe

THOMAS, Daniel H. and L. M. CASE. *The New Guide to the Diplomatic Archives of Western Europe.* Philadelphia, PA:

University of Pennsylvania Press, 1975. A revision of their
original guide of 1959.

GOMEZ CANEDO, Lino. *Los archivos de la historia de América:
período colonial español*. 2 vols. Mexico City: Pan-American
Institute of Geography and History, 1961.

The Pan-American Institute is also responsible for the series,
Misiones Americanas en los Archivos Europeos, begun in 1949. The
volumes
give details of various modern expeditions to European archives in
search of materials relating to individual Latin American countries.

For information on records held in European repositories relating
to the Caribbean, see the general section on Latin America and the
Caribbean, below.

Belgium

LIAGRE, Leone and Jean BAERTEN. *Guide des sources de l'histoire
d'Amérique Latine conservées en Belgique*. Brussels: Archives Gener-
ales du Royaume, 1967. Produced for the ICA/Unesco
project.

Denmark—See Sweden

France

OZANAM, Didier. *Les sources de l'histoire de l'Amérique Latine: guide
du chercheur dans les archives françaises*. Volume 1: Affaires
étrangères. Paris: Institut des Hautes Etudes de l'Amérique
Latine, 1963.

DIAS, Cícero. *Catálogo de documentos referentes ao Brasil coligidos ...
nos Arquivos Nacionais de Paris*. Brasília: Comissão de Estudo dos
Textos de História do Brasil, 1975.

*Guide des sources de l'histoire de l'Amérique Latine et des Antilles dans
les archives françaises*. Paris: Archives Nationales, 1984. Produced for the ICA/Unesco project.

Germany

*Übersicht über Quellen zur Geschichte Lateinamerikas in Archiven der
Deutschen Demokratischen Republik*. Potsdam: Staatliche Archiv-
verwaltung, 1971. Produced for the ICA/Unesco project.

HAUSCHILD-THIESSEN, Renate and Elfriede BACHMANN. *Führer durch die Quellen zur Geschichte Lateinamerikas in der Bundesrepublik Deutschlands.* Veröffentlichungen aus dem Staatsarchiv der Freien Hansestadt Bremen, Bd. 38. Bremen: Schunemann, 1972. Produced for the ICA/Unesco project.

Italy

BURRUS, Ernest J. 'Research Opportunities in Italian Archives and Manuscript Collections for Students of Hispanic American History.' *Hispanic American Historical Review* 39:3 (August 1959), pp. 428–463.

PASZTOR, Lajos. *Guida delle fonti per la storia dell'America Latina negli archivi della Santa Sede e nelle archivi ecclesiastici d'Italia.* Collectanea Archivi Vaticani, 2. Vatican City: Archivio Vaticano, 1970. Produced for the ICA/Unesco project.

LODOLINI, Elio. *Guida delle fonti per la storia dell'America Latina esistenti in Italia.* Pubblicazioni degli Archivi di Stato, 88. Rome: Ministero per i Beni Culturali e Ambientali, 1976—. Produced for the ICA/Unesco project. To date, only the first volume has appeared, covering archives in Rome.

Netherlands

ROESSINGH, M. P. H. *Guide to the Sources in the Netherlands for the History of Latin America.* The Hague: Algemeen Rijksarchief, 1968. Produced for the ICA/Unesco project.

Portugal

PESCATELLO, Ann. 'Relatorio from Portugal: The Archives and Libraries of Portugal and Their Significance for the Study of Brazilian History.' *Latin American Research Review* 5:2 (Summer 1970), pp. 17–52.

'Inventário dos documentos relativos ao Brasil existentes na Biblioteca Nacional de Lisboa.' *Anais da Biblioteca Nacional* (Rio de Janeiro) 93 (1973), pp. 1–256.

BOSCHI, Caio César. 'O Brasil nos arquivos e bibliotecas de Portugal: levantamento bibliográfico crítico.' *Revista de Historia* (São Paulo) 51 (1975), pp. 343–400.

Spain

General guides to Spanish archives include:

RODRÍGUEZ MARÍN, Francisco. *Guía histórica y descriptiva de los archivos, bibliotecas y museos arqueológicos de España: sección de archivos.* Madrid: Revista de Archivos, Bibliotecas y Museos, 1916 [i.e. 1921].

Guía de los archivos de Madrid and *Guía de los archivos de Barcelona.* Madrid: Dirección General de Archivos y Bibliotecas, 1952.

More specifically on Latin American materials, there are:

BURRUS, Ernest J. 'An Introduction to Bibliographic Tools in Spanish Archives and Manuscript Collections Relating to Spanish America.' *Hispanic American Historical Review* 35:4 (November 1955), pp. 443–483.

Guía de fuentes para la historia de Ibero-América conservadas en España. 2 vols. Madrid: Dirección General de Archivos y Bibliotecas, 1966–1969. Produced for the ICA/Unesco project, this does not totally supersede:

TUDELA DE LA ORDEN, José. *Los manuscritos de América en las bibliotecas de España.* Madrid: Cultura Hispánica, 1954.

CORTÉS ALONSO, Vicenta. *Archivos de España y América, materiales para un manual.* Madrid: Universidad Complutense, 1979.

The greatest collections of official archives relating to Spain's former colonies are located in Seville (the Archivo General de Indias) and Simancas (the Archivo General de Simancas, or Archivo Histórico Nacional). The Seville archive has produced catalogues of around 40,000 *legajos* (bundles of manuscripts) pertaining to the administration and commerce of the Indies. There are many publications relating to this collection, among which are:

NAUMAN, Ann K. 'The Archivo General de Indias.' *Archives* 15:68 (1982), pp. 216–223. A good general description with a detailed bibliography.

TORRE REVELLO, José. *El Archivo General de Indias de Sevilla: historia y clasificación de sus fondos.* Publicaciones del Instituto de Investigaciones Históricas, 50. Buenos Aires: Peuser, 1929.

PEÑA Y DE LA CÁMARA, José de la. *Archivo General de Indias de Sevilla*. Madrid: Junta Técnica de Archivos, Bibliotecas y Museos, 1958.

HANKE, Lewis and Celso RODRÍGUEZ. *Guía de las fuentes en el Archivo General de Indias para el estudio de la administración virreinal española en México y en el Perú, 1535–1700.* 3 vols. Lateinamerikanische Forschungen, Bd. 7. Cologne: Bohlau, 1977.

BALLESTEROS-BERETTA, Antonio. 'Juan Bautista Muñoz: la creación del Archivo de Indias.' *Revista de Indias* 2:4 (1941), pp. 55–95.

The archives of Simancas are described in:

Guía del Archivo General de Simancas. Madrid: Dirección General de Archivos y Bibliotecas, 1958.

Sweden

MÖRNER, Magnus. *Fuentes para la historia de Ibero-América: Escandinavia*. Stockholm: Riksarkivet, 1968. Covers mainly Sweden, but has a short appendix (in English) dealing with the Danish national archives.

Yugoslavia

GAVRILOVIC, Stoyan. 'Hispanic American History Research Opportunities in Yugoslav Archives.' *Hispanic American Historical Review* 42:1 (February 1962), pp. 37–50.

North America

A major general guide to US archives, prepared under the auspices of the National Historical Publications and Records Commission, is:

Directory of Archives and Manuscript Repositories in the United States. 2nd ed. Phoenix, AZ: Oryx Press, 1988.

Specifically for Latin American materials, there are:

HILTON, Ronald. *Handbook of Hispanic Source Materials and Research Organizations in the United States.* 2nd ed. Stanford, CA: Stanford University Press, 1956.

JACKSON, William Vernon. *Latin American Collections.* Nashville, TN: Vanderbilt University Bookstore, 1974. Discusses 13 major US collections in some detail.

Guides to individual collections include:

ULIBARRI, George S. and John P. HARRISON. *Guide to Materials on Latin America in the National Archives of the United States.* Washington, DC: National Archives and Records Service, 1974. Produced for the ICA/Unesco project.

SPELL, Lota M. *Research Material for the Study of Latin America at the University of Texas, Austin.* Austin, TX: University of Texas Press, 1954; reprinted, Westport, CT: Greenwood Press, 1970.

SZEWCZYK, David M. *A Calendar of the Peruvian and Other South American Manuscripts in the Philip H. and A. S. W. Rosenbach Foundation, 1536–1914.* Philadelphia, PA: Rosenbach Foundation, 1977.

SZEWCZYK, David M. *The Viceroyalty of New Spain and Early Independent Mexico: A Guide to the Original Manuscripts in the Collection of the Rosenbach Museum and Library.* Philadelphia, PA: Rosenbach Museum and Library, 1980.

Specific areas and topics are covered in:

MARCHANT, Alexander. *Boundaries of the Latin American Republics: An Annotated List of Documents, 1493–1943.* Washington, DC: Department of State, 1944.

INGRAM, Kenneth E. *Manuscripts Relating to Commonwealth Caribbean Countries in United States and Canadian Repositories.* St. Lawrence, Barbados: Caribbean Universities Press, 1975.

Latin America and the Caribbean

A classified archival bibliography is now an annual feature of the *Boletín Interamericano de Archivos* (Córdoba, Argentina: Centro Interamericano de Desarrollo de Archivos, 1974—). Volume 4 (1977) includes reports of surveys of South and Central American archives carried out in 1972 and a valuable section devoted to replies to a questionnaire on archival organisation and facilities sent to Latin American and Caribbean countries in 1975. Volume 5/6 (1978–1979) reviews the international and South American organisations and associations of archivists.

Basic information on the archives of almost all the Caribbean countries (including Mexico, Guatemala and Colombia) is available in the *Report of the Caribbean Archives Conference, University of the West Indies, 1965* (Kingston: Government Printer, 1965). Included is information on Caribbean records held in European repositories. This report is supplemented by *Caribbean Archives* (Basse-Terre, Guadeloupe, 1973—), the bulletin of the Caribbean Archives Association.

The major remaining general works are as follows:

GROPP, Arthur E. *Guide to Libraries and Archives in Central America and the West Indies, Panama, Bermuda and British Guiana.* New Orleans, LA: Middle America Research Institute, 1941; republished, Ann Arbor, MI: University Microfilms, 1970.

HILL, Roscoe R. *The National Archives of Latin America.* Cambridge, MA: Harvard University Press, 1945. Covers the national collections of twenty countries, describing their establishment, history, buildings, directors, publishing and contents.

DE PLATT, Lyman. *Genealogical Historical Guide to Latin America.* Detroit, MI: Gale Research, 1978. Includes full descriptions of the Latin American archives of interest to genealogists.

MENDOZA L., Gunnar. *Situación actual de los archivos latinoamericanos: manual de información básica.* Washington, DC: Reunión Interamericana sobre Archivos, 1961.

MILLARES CARLO, Agustín. *Los archivos municipales de Latinoamérica: libros de actas y colecciones documentales, apuntes bibliográficos.* Maracaibo: Universidad del Zulia, 1961.

MORALES, Enrique L. 'Estado actual de los archivos en Latinoamérica.' *Boletín de la Escuela Nacional de Bibliotecarios y Archivistas* (UNAM) 5:8 (April 1961–August 1962), pp. 45–72.

SECKINGER, Ron L. 'A Guide to Selected Diplomatic Archives of South America.' *Latin American Research Review* 10:1 (Spring 1975), pp. 127–153.

TEPASKE, John J. *Research Guide to Andean History.* Durham, NC: Duke University Press, 1981. A very detailed guide, covering Bolivia, Chile, Ecuador and Peru.

Argentina

Two important journals are the *Revista del Archivo General de la Nación* (Buenos Aires: AGN, 1971—) and the *Boletín Interamericano de Archivos* (cited above). Issue number 6 (1977) of the *Revista* is devoted mainly to reporting on the first National Archives Congress in Argentina (pp. 67–181).

The Archivo General de la Nación has also issued two useful indexes in its collection Auxiliares heurísticos:

Indice temático general de unidades archivonómicas del período colonial —Gobierno. Buenos Aires: AGN, 1978.

Indice temático general de unidades archivonómicas del período nacional —Gobierno. Buenos Aires: AGN, 1977.

Brazil

MIGUEIS, Maria Amélia Porto et al. *Guia preliminar de fontes para a história do Brasil: instituições governmentais do Município do Rio de Janeiro.* Rio de Janeiro: Fundação Getúlio Vargas, 1979.

Chile

EYZAGUIRRE E., Juan. 'Guía de los archivos de Chile.' *Boletín Interamericano de Archivos* 3 (1976), pp. 160–187.

See also TEPASKE, above, in the general section on Latin America and the Caribbean.

Colombia

Colombia is included in the *Report of the Caribbean Archives Conference* (cited above). Much of the archival materials specifically covering the independence movements in Greater Colombia can be found in the archives of Simón Bolívar and Francisco de Miranda; they are identified and reproduced in:

BLANCO, José Félix, and Ramón AZPURÚA. *Documentos para la historia de la vida pública del Libertador de Colombia, Peru y Bolivia.* 14 vols. Caracas: Opinión Nacional, 1875–1878; republished, Caracas: Presidencia, 1978.

MIRANDA, Francisco de. *Colombeia.* Edited by Josefina Rodríguez de Alonso. Caracas: Presidencia de la República, 1978—. Still in progess. This is a new, greatly expanded edition of the old *Archivo del General Miranda* (1929–1950).

Commonwealth Caribbean

In addition to the *Report of the Caribbean Archives Conference* mentioned above, the following guides are available:

BAKER, E. C. *A Guide to Records in the Leeward Islands*. Oxford: Blackwell, 1965.

BAKER, E. C. *A Guide to Records in the Windward Islands*. Oxford: Blackwell, 1968.

CHANDLER, M. J. *A Guide to Records in Barbados*. Oxford: Blackwell, 1965.

INGRAM, Kenneth E. *Sources of Jamaican History, 1655–1838: A Bibliographical Survey with Particular Reference to Manuscript Sources*. 2 vols. Zug: Inter-Documentation Company, 1976.

Cuba

The *Boletín del Archivo Nacional* began publication in 1902 and has been published regularly ever since, except for a ten-year gap from 1965. Two catalogues have been published dealing with foreign materials:

FRANCO, José L. *Documentos para la historia de México (existentes en el Archivo Nacional de Cuba)*. Publicaciones, 53. Havana: Archivo Nacional, 1961.

FRANCO, José L. *Documentos para la historia de Venezuela existentes en el Archivo Nacional de Cuba*. Publicaciones, 51. Havana: Archivo Nacional, 1960.

Mexico

A good introduction to the Mexican Archivo General de la Nación and its collections is given in the *Boletín del Sistema Nacional de Archivos*, numbers 2 and 3 (November–December 1983 and January–February 1984). The Archivo is becoming increasingly well catalogued. The basic guides are:

CIVEIRA TABOADA, Miguel and María Elena BRIBIESCA. *Guía descriptiva de los ramos que constituyen el Archivo General de la Nación*. Mexico City: AGN, 1977.

Guía general de los fondos que contiene el Archivo General de la Nación. Mexico City: AGN, 1981.

Much more detail is given in the Archivo's Serie: Guías y Catálogos (1977—), of which upwards of a hundred volumes have already been published. The codices of Mexico—probably the most celebrated Latin American manuscripts in existence—are covered extensively in:

Handbook of Middle American Indians. Edited by Robert Wauchope. Volumes 14 and 15: Guide to Ethnohistorical Sources, parts 3 and 4. Edited by Howard F. Cline. Austin, TX: University of Texas Press, 1975. Many of the articles are written by John B. Glass.

Other general guides to the codices are:

AZCUE Y MANCERA, Luis. Códices indígenas. Mexico City: Orion, 1966.

GUZMÁN M., Virginia and Yolanda MERCADER M. Bibliografía de códices, mapas y lienzos de México prehispánico y colonial. 2 vols. Colección Científica, 79. Mexico City: Instituto Nacional de Antropología e Historia, 1979.

LEÓN-PORTILLA, Miguel and Salvador MATEOS HIGUERA. Catálogo de los códices indígenas del México antiguo. Suplemento al Boletín Bibliográfico. Mexico City: Secretaría de Hacienda y Crédito Público, 1957.

The latest work on the subject comes from a publishing house that has produced facsimile editions of many of the codices in European libraries:

ANDERS, Ferdinand and Maarten JANSEN. Schrift und Buch im alten Mexiko. Graz: Akademische Druck, 1988.

Further helpful catalogues and bibliographies can be found in:

GLASS, John B. Catálogo de la colección de códices. Mexico City: Instituto Nacional de Antropología e Historia, 1964. A catalogue of the collection of the Museo Nacional de Antropología in Mexico City.

ROBERTSON, Donald. Mexican Manuscript Painting of the Early Colonial Period: The Metropolitan Schools. New Haven, CT: Yale University Press, 1959.

Puerto Rico

CASTRO, María de los Angeles. *Los primeros pasos: una biblio-grafía ... [y] guía descriptiva de los fondos documentales existentes en el Centro de Investigaciones Históricas.* Río Piedras, PR: Universidad de Puerto Rico, 1984.

Venezuela

MILLARES CARLO, Agustín. *Estudio bibliográfico de los archivos venezolanos y extranjeros de interés para la historia de Venezuela.* Biblioteca venezolana de historia, 10. Caracas: Archivo General de la Nación, 1971.

The Academia Nacional de la Historia also publishes a series, Archivos y Catálogos, which includes:

BOSSÍO PENSO, Bertalibia. *Archivo de la Academia Nacional de la Historia.* Serie Archivos y catálogos, 3. Caracas: ANH, 1984.

See above, under Colombia, for further archival collections relating to the independence period in Venezuela.

Asia and Oceania

Collections in Australia, Japan and the Philippines are covered in BARTLEY and WAGNER; see above, p. 19.

GF

Library Catalogues

Catalogues and indexes can come in many physical forms: cards in drawers, slips in sheaf binders, computer (online or printout), microfiche, even occasionally printed books. Within the catalogue, books, manuscripts, microforms and other materials may be organised under author, subject or title. There are, however, only two ways in which the material may be arranged: alphabetical or classified. Author catalogues are virtually always arranged alphabetically; subject catalogues can also be alphabetical by subject heading, but are frequently arranged in classified (numerical) order, according to the classification method favoured by the library concerned. For an introduction to these mysteries, see LIBRARY CLASSIFICATION SCHEMES (p. 40); for information on what published catalogues exist, see PUBLISHED LIBRARY CATALOGUES (p. 46). This chapter will introduce library catalogues in general, arranged by author, title or subject.

Alphabetisation

Alphabetical order is so pervasive in research tools that it is surprising how unaware students often are of its possible pitfalls. Alphabetisation, for example, comes in two styles, depending on the value given to blank spaces between words. If you ignore the spaces and file letter-by-letter, then New York will file after Newark; if you count them as coming alphabetically before 'A' (as most catalogues, indexes and filing systems do), then New York will come first. The decision particularly affects the order of Spanish language compound surnames: it will determine whether 'Echeverri Ortiz, Sancho' comes before or after all the 'Echeverría' entries. When you fail to find something in a catalogue that is new to you, always be sure that you have not mistaken the style of alphabetical order used.

Abbreviations and numbers usually file as if spelled out in full in the appropriate language. 'St. Louis' files as 'Saint Louis', 'Sta. Cruz' as 'Santa Cruz'. In title catalogues you should expect to find a book entitled *D. Pedro II* under 'Dom Pedro Segundo', and

Guillermo Thorndike's work on the Pacific War entitled *1879* under 'Mil ochocientos setenta y nueve'—though some computerised catalogues may file numerals in a separate sequence before (or after) the regular alphabetical sequence. In established manual catalogues 'McIntyre' or 'M'Neil' are generally filed as 'MacIntyre', 'MacNeil' (to keep all the Macs together), but in automated catalogues there is an increasing tendency to file exactly as spelled.

Spanish language indexes and library catalogues in Spanish-speaking countries will of course follow the Spanish practice of alphabetisation: this treats 'N' with a tilde (Ñ, ñ) and the digraphs 'CH' and 'LL' as separate letters, following 'N', 'C' and 'L' respectively. Thus, a South American gazetteer will have 'Cuzco' before 'Chaco' and 'Antigua' before 'Añatuya'. Portuguese alphabetisation follows the English practice.

Author Approach

Hunting for a book in an author catalogue can become irksome when the catalogue is large and the name a common one, particularly if you do not know the full forename. In such cases, it may save time to find out the author's full name first from a biographical dictionary or directory (see BIOGRAPHIES, p. 267). Spanish American and Brazilian names present their own special problems, which are discussed below.

Spanish and Spanish American Personal Names

A Spanish speaker will generally have at least two surnames. A married woman will have her father's surname followed by her husband's, sometimes separated by *de*—for example, 'Rafaela Contreras de Darío'. Anyone else, male or female, will generally take the father's surname followed by the mother's, with or (more usually) without a connecting *y*: 'Ramon Menéndez Pidal'; 'Marcelino Menéndez y Pelayo'.

The second surname is frequently dropped in normal usage; 'Fidel Castro [Ruz]', 'Victoria Ocampo [de Estrada]'. Occasionally it is the father's name that is dropped, especially when it is a common one: 'Federico [García] Lorca', 'Gustavo Adolfo [Rodríguez] Becquer'—and frequently in the case of wives: 'Eva [Duarte de] Perón'. Library catalogues may or may not persist with the the full legal form in such cases.

The usage frequently causes confusion among library cataloguers, especially when the middle one of three names could equally well be a second forename or first surname: 'Alonso Piñeiro, Armando', 'Martínez, Pedro Santos'. Most modern library catalogues will, however, give copious cross-references to enable you to track down the author you want. It should be noted that Spanish indexes frequently impose their own rule on foreign authors, with confusing results: 'Allan Poe, Edgar', 'Hickling Prescott, William' and the like.

Portuguese and Brazilian Personal Names

Until the beginning of this century the Portuguese method of organizing surnames was much the same as the Spanish practice, detailed above. Present practice (which did not become general until the 1950s) is to file the author under the last element of the name other than a soubriquet (see below): thus, 'Silva, Arthur da Costa e', 'Lobato, Jose Bento Monteiro'. An apparent exception to this rule is 'Castelo Branco, Humberto'—'white castle' is logically a single element, and is always treated as such.

The soubriquets of relationship (*Filho, Júnior, Net(t)o, Sobrinho*) were until recently ignored, except in the rare cases where they had become genuine surnames. Today they are generally added to the heading, but the author is filed under the name that precedes the soubriquet: 'Café Filho, João', 'Coelho Netto, Henrique'.

An older custom, which persists in many catalogues and indexes, was to attempt to discover and conform to the author's personal preference, as for example, 'Machado de Assis, Joaquim Maria' ('Machado' was his mother's name). A still older custom was to arrange by *first* (i.e., Christian) name, a practice frequently found in nineteenth-century indexes, and still persistent in parts of Brazil. Given the social importance of Christian names in Brazil, this was a very practical arrangement.

Unfortunately, whichever heading rule is chosen by a particular catalogue, complications remain: many Portuguese speakers use forms quite different from their full legal names, and some libraries prefer the latter. So be prepared to look for Lins do Rêgo under 'Cavalcanti', and Juscelino Kubitschek under 'Oliveira'. Even when a catalogue accepts the short everyday form, it may still insist on expanding names that lack any surname at all (e.g., Washington Luís, who will probably be found under 'Souza') or any forename (e.g., Barbosa Lima Sobrinho). Names consisting of one Christian name and one soubriquet (e.g., Adonais Filho) may have to be searched for under the unused surname (in this case 'Aguiar') or may even be filed under the soubriquet. National heroes universally known by nicknames (Pele, Tiradentes, Aleijadinho) may well also be listed under their surnames ('Nascimento', 'Silva Xavier', and 'Lisboa' respectively). Of course there should be cross references, but some libraries (and indexes) can be lax in this respect.

A final complication is the spelling. Orthographic reform has been going on in Portuguese continually since 1910, but individuals (and their publishers) have different ideas as to how far it should apply to personal names. So always try both 'Beça' and 'Bessa', 'Corrêa' and 'Correia', 'Melo' and 'Mello', 'Morais' and 'Moraes', 'Luís' and 'Luiz', 'Queirós' and 'Queiroz', and so forth. Brazilian libraries and reference works tend to prefer the modernized spelling; British and American library catalogues seem to persist with whichever form was used in the author's first book acquired by that particular library!

Prefixes

Almost all prefixes in Spanish and Portuguese—*de, del, de la(s), de los, do(s), da(s)*—are ignored in filing when they occur at the beginning of the surname (unless of course they have linked up with the name, as in the case of 'Degregori, Carlos Iván'). Some Spanish indexes ignore them for the purpose of alphabetization even when they appear in the middle of a name. There is, unfortunately, less consistency with Italian prefixes such as *di, lo* or *della*, found in some Argentine, Brazilian and Uruguayan names.

Multiple Authorship

Works written by two or three authors in collaboration ('joint authorship') are normally catalogued under the author first named on the title-page; it is thus better to know his name in full than to have only the bare surnames of both (or all) of the writers involved.

A work made up of clearly differentiated contributions by several writers (such as this one) constitutes 'multiple authorship'. These works are frequently still to be found in catalogues under the editor, although according to the new *Anglo-American Cataloguing Rules* (AACR2) they should be entered under title. More and more libraries are now adopting AACR2, but not all are applying the rules retrospectively. Conference papers, by contrast, are usually

listed under the name of the conference or the organizing body (see
SOCIETIES AND ASSOCIATIONS, p. 328).

Societies and Institutions

A corporate body is often treated as the author of works issued in its
name or by its authority, and usually appears in the catalogue under
its full official name. Practice varies when the official name exists in
more that one language (e.g., 'Organization of American States' or
'Organización de los Estados Americanos'), and it is advisable to
check under both forms. See ACRONYMS AND ABBREVIATIONS (p.
357) for help if you do not know the full form of any name.

Earlier practice (still much in evidence in library catalogues)
made a distinction between societies, which were entered directly
under their names, and institutions, defined as physical entities with
a fixed abode, which were catalogued under their locality—for
instance, 'Bogotá. Universidad de los Andes', or 'Buenos Aires.
Biblioteca Nacional'. As so often happens, inconsistencies abound.
The concept of 'locality' is a vague one: should the University of
Sussex be entered under Sussex (the county), Brighton (the nearest
large town) or Falmer (where it actually is)? And government-
funded or government-administered bodies are sometimes treated as
departments of state and entered directly under the name of the
country: 'Venezuela. Instituto Autónoma Biblioteca Nacional', or
'Brazil. Instituto Brasileiro de Geografia e Estatística'. For more
about the citation of officially published or sponsored material see
OFFICIAL PUBLICATIONS (p. 199) and LAW AND LEGISLATION (p. 283).

Title Approach

Knowing only the title of a work is probably the commonest source of
frustration involved in using a library catalogue. While libraries are
increasingly adopting automated catalogues which can be searched
by title, depressingly large numbers still have only author and
subject catalogues. Author catalogues do almost always include
some title entries—for anonymous works, often for works of multiple
authorship, and sometimes for works with especially distinctive titles.
Title entries are also made for periodicals, although these may be in
a separate catalogue.

When title entries are made, some traditional libraries prefer to
file them under the first *significant* word (variously defined), but the
usual practice is to file under the first word following an initial

article. This rule may, of course, be breached through ignorance; the Portuguese articles 'o' and 'a' are frequently not perceived as such.

When you know only the title, and have looked for it in vain in the catalogue, you may (with much patience and some luck) track down the work and its author through a published bibliography. Where to look will depend on the language of the book, and its place and date of publication. *Whitaker's Books in Print* (previously *British Books in Print*), published annually in volume form and monthly on microfiche, includes title entries for all books currently available in the UK. The US equivalent is the annual *Books in Print*, published by Bowker; this is in three multi-volume sections, listing books by author, title and subject. An additional volume gives publishers' addresses. For Latin America as a whole there is *Libros en venta*, published irregularly (the last edition appeared in 1988). It is produced by Melcher Ediciones in San Juan, Puerto Rico, in conjunction with the monthly listing of new books, *Fichero Biblio-gráfico Hispanoamericano*; both works include title indexes. Several Latin American countries have now started to produce their own annual lists of books in print under the stimulus of the International Standard Book Number system (see NATIONAL BIBLIOGRAPHIES, p. 118); these generally have title-indexes.

For non-current books, searching by title is a slower process. Catalogues of other libraries may be helpful if they are automated or available in printed form (see PUBLISHED LIBRARY CATALOGUES, p. 46). If these are no help, then the researcher will be reduced to checking laboriously through the cumulative volumes of national bibliographies. The *British National Bibliography* has been listing UK publications since 1950; for earlier British titles and US materials back to 1928 there is the *Cumulative Book Index*, published in New York by the H. W. Wilson Company, which attempts (in monthly parts with annual cumulations) to cover English language publications throughout the world. For other countries, see again NATIONAL BIBLIOGRAPHIES.

Subject Approach

Most UK and US libraries have separate author and subject catalogues, although works about a person, institution or organization are sometimes filed in the author catalogue along with any works by them. Biographies of and critical works on the author of *El Gaucho Martín Fierro* will thus be found in the author catalogue under 'Hernández [Pueyrredón], José', next to editions of the text itself.

The subject catalogue may be arranged in classified or alphabetical order; the former is more common in Britain, the latter in the United States. Both have their advantages and disadvantages, as is explained below. When you first use the subject catalogue of a particular library, it is a good idea to ask the staff to explain its finer points to you; be wary of over-reliance on posted notices ('How To Use This Catalogue') which must be brief and can be misleading.

The classified catalogue is arranged according to the method of classification employed by the particular library (see LIBRARY CLASSIFICATION SCHEMES, p. 40), and needs an alphabetical key (usually called the 'Subject Index' or 'Subject Guide') to help the researcher locate the information required. There is a natural temptation to go directly from the subject index to the shelves, overlooking the fact that the classified catalogue will be much more informative than the actual shelf arrangement. A book that covers several topics can be on the shelves in only one place, while a good subject catalogue will have an entry for the work under each topic.

The alphabetical subject catalogue is an American idea, and virtually all libraries that employ it use headings from the *Library of Congress Subject Headings* (11th ed.; Washington, DC: Library of Congress, 1988), sometimes adapted to local needs. This means that American English is the norm, and speakers of English outside the US will have to adapt to 'Corn' instead of 'Maize', 'Eminent domain' in place of 'Compulsory purchase' and so on. Good catalogues will provide cross-references, but always be prepared to look under synonyms for the heading you require. Referring to the published list of headings is the best way to start a subject search, and will certainly help to identify appropriate terms related to your topic.

Some North American (and a few British) libraries integrate their alphabetical subject and author catalogues into one sequence, which is then known as a 'dictionary catalogue'. This can be convenient, but it produces its own problems: it may not be clear, for instance, why official publications of 'Washington (State)', for instance, precede works about 'Washington D.C.'—and why both come before 'Washington County (Arkansas)' but after 'Washington, George'.

The most common mistake in using an alphabetical subject catalogue or the index to a classified catalogue) is to choose too broad a heading; a reader wanting something on coffee in São Paulo may tend to look under 'Agriculture—Brazil' rather than under 'São Paulo (Brazil : State)— Industries' or 'Coffee—Brazil—São

Paulo (State)'. The important thing is to think creatively about possible subject terms; there will usually be more than one appropriate heading to try, sometimes alternative, sometimes complementary, for the materials you need. One search might lead you to try both 'Agriculture—Mexico' and 'Haciendas—Latin America'; another might require 'Argentine poetry' and 'Heroes in literature'.

Broader or narrower terms can be helpful if you are having difficulties in identifying your subject: try searching, for example, 'Caribbean area—Economic conditions' instead of 'Barbados', or 'Indians of Mexico—Games' instead of just 'Games'. You may sometimes also have to reverse headings ('Censuses—Peru' instead of vice versa).

Libraries with computerised catalogues may have the capability of searching by keywords; this makes the task easier, as instead of having to search on the basis of a standard list of subject terms you can retrieve sources through any significant word in the title. You may also be able to combine terms—for example, 'Textile industry' with 'Labor dispute'—for more rapid searching.

LH/RAM

Library Classification Schemes

It is not, of course, necessary to know the history or the underlying assumptions of a particular classification scheme in order to find a book on a shelf, or even to browse through the titles in a particular section. Hopefully, all schemes will ensure that the books on, say, the social organisation of the Mapuche Indians of Chile, or the problems of the Colombian coffee industry, are in the same area of the library; if you have difficulty in finding them, the staff will be happy to show you in which corner to look. But it is undeniable that a working acquaintance with the principles and conventions of the scheme your library uses will greatly increase your ability quickly to identify and locate the materials you need, and to take full advantage of the facilities offered. This chapter is designed for readers who are sufficiently interested in the subject to take this plunge.

Shelf Arrangement

There are four major ways of arranging books by subject; all are numerical or alphabetical in nature, and all are ultimately American in origin. The classification system used for shelf arrangement may also be the basis for the organisation of the library's subject catalogue, especially in the UK (see LIBRARY CATALOGUES, p. 32), and the same schemes are occasionally employed for the organization of files of documents or published bibliographies.

Unfortunately, the physical order of books on a shelf can display only a single linear relationship, and there will inevitably be a physical scattering of subjects that some readers would regard as closely related. The economic history of South American railways, for instance, will probably be some distance from works on their engineering. The Dewey classification scheme splits up the literary work of individual authors so as to keep together all works in the same literary genre (novels, essays, plays and so forth). By contrast, the Library of Congress scheme keeps each author's whole body of work together, adjacent to critical writings on it, but separates the bibliographies, which all go together at the very end of the classification. And most schemes fail to hold together works concerning a particular locality: books on various aspects of São Paulo, for example, will be found with economic history, social history, coffee, the Jesuits, railways or whatever.

It should also be remembered that not all of a library's holdings will be kept in the main classified sequence. Rare books, reference works, oversize books, pamphlets, newspapers and periodicals are all likely to have their own separate sequences. Material in non-book formats (discs, films, maps, microforms, videos) will almost certainly be kept apart. There is even the possibility that the library will have changed from one classification scheme to another without reclassifying earlier stock; in such a case there will always be a separate arrangement of material acquired before the changeover. Always consider this possibility in an unfamiliar library that appears to have few older books (or no new ones) on your subject.

Dewey Decimal Classification

The Dewey Decimal System ('Dewey') was invented in 1876 by a young American college librarian, Melville Dewey (afterwards, Melvil Dewey—he championed spelling reform). His scheme is virtually universal in Anglo-American public libraries, and is still fairly common in academic libraries, especially in Spanish-speaking America. The classification is not ideal: despite a century of use and development, it remains rooted in the religious, national, social, philosophic and scientific world-view of a late nineteenth century Yankee Presbyterian. But its notation and underlying principles are simple and logical. There are ten main classes, divided decimally and always expressed with a minimum of three digits:

> 000 General works
> 100 Philosophy
> 200 Religion
> 300 Social sciences
> 400 Linguistics
> 500 Pure science
> 600 Technology
> 700 Art and recreation
> 800 Literature
> 900 Travel, biography and history

Within the Dewey system for instance, Spanish language is 460, Spanish literature 860, Spanish drama 862; Portuguese literature is

869, and Portuguese drama 869.2. Detailed subdivision can produce excessively long numbers: a work on household refuse disposal in Grenada, for example, would be classified at 628.45729845; successive digits mean 'technology', 'engineering', 'sanitation', 'public cleaning', 'refuse disposal', 'America', 'Central America and the Caribbean', 'West Indies', 'Eastern Caribbean', 'Windward Islands' and 'Grenada'.

Library of Congress Classification

In the 1890s the Librarian of Congress, under pressure to have his vast collections arranged by subject, reluctantly agreed to let his staff classify them, provided that the results were 'nothing like Dewey'. This they did—or rather, each of more than twenty subject division heads constructed his own classification along broadly similar lines. The result was the Library of Congress Classification ('LC'), a twenty-volume scheme so monumental, and so impressive in its detail, that it has been adopted by nearly all the major research libraries in North America (whence it has spread to Mexico) and many in Britain. Conceived at the high-water mark of Western and US expansionism, and to cover a collection of mainly US books, its basic, unspoken assumptions can be as intrusive as those of Dewey. Western hemisphere history, for instance, is divided into class E (general works, and general histories of the USA) and class F (local history of the United States, with, at the tail-end, the history of the rest of the Americas). Also, when a subject is divided geographically, Mexico nearly always comes before general works on Latin America, to bring it next to the US. The basic classes are:

A General works	M Music
B Philosophy and religion	N Art
C Auxiliary sciences of history	P Philology
D Old World history	Q Science
E American history	R Medicine
F American local history	S Agriculture
G Geography and anthropology	T Technology
H Social sciences	U Military science
J Constitutional law	V Naval science and
K Law	shipbuilding
L Education	Z Bibliography

All of these (except E, F and Z) have further letter subdivisions; for instance:

AE Encyclopedias
AM Museums
AP General periodicals
AS Academies and learned societies
AY Yearbooks and almanacs

The next stage of subdivision is by classes numbered 1 to 9999, arranged arithmetically rather than decimally. Sometimes decimals are used, but merely as a way of squeezing in more than 9999 subdivisions. Thus, within class HE (transport and communications) the 5600s are dedicated to 'automotive transport', of which HE 5644 to 5649 cover 'automotive transport in the Caribbean'. In order to insert the US Virgin Islands and the Leewards and Windwards between HE 5648 (Puerto Rico) and HE 5649 (Trinidad), they are allocated the numbers HE 5648.3, HE 5648.7 and HE 5648.9 respectively.

Further subdivision can take place after a decimal point, by means of letters followed by numbers used decimally. Thus, under F 1234 (the Mexican Revolution) we find a work on Amado Aguirre at F 1234.A238 shelved before one on General Felipe Angeles at F 1234.A56. If the full Library of Congress practice is followed (not often the case in UK libraries), the same sub-arrangement method is then repeated to arrange works in the same class number by their authors, or (in the case of literary works) by one author's individual titles. Unfortunately, not even all this elaboration always manages to bring works on the same subject together, and at times the arrangement can be frankly unhelpful.

A further problem with this classification is that cataloguers and classifiers, being human, make mistakes and fail to be consistent; and unfortunately any error made by the Library of Congress is automatically repeated by practically every major North American library, since they all employ computer link-ups to make use of LC cataloguing copy. Thus, for instance, half the works in the ABC/Clio Press World Bibliographical Series are classified in class Z (bibliography) and the other half in classes D to F (history of individual countries).

And if American and Canadian libraries are too conformist, those in the UK are too individualistic. Whatever classification scheme a British library adopts, chances are that it will have decided that a little tinkering will make it better. Often it does, but this also means that the more familiar you become with Library of Congress (or any other classification), the more perplexed you may be on visiting a new library when you find what they have done with it.

Universal Decimal Classification

Early in this century two optimistic Belgian gentlemen contemplated the creation of a classified file of every article from every learned and scientific journal in the world. The scheme came to nothing (two German invasions in twenty-five years did not help the project), but in the course of their endeavours they produced the Universal Decimal Classification ('UDC'). It started out as a Europeanised Dewey, but they made it a thousandfold more flexible by introducing a series of punctuation marks and other symbols to combine different sections of the classification in a way reminiscent of a child's erector set. Thus, whereas Dewey occasionally uses the figure '6' to denote sometimes Spain and sometimes the Spanish language, UDC has a convention that parentheses enclose an indication of location, and an equals sign precedes a language; so '(4)' always means Europe, '(46)' is always Spain, '= 6' is always Spanish, and similarly, '(469)' is Portugal, '= 69' is Portuguese. The result is ingenious, adaptable and efficient. Displayed on the spines of books, however, it looks incredibly complicated, and until you learn the ordinal values ascribed to all the signs and symbols you cannot understand the filing order.

In the UK this classification system is in very wide use in technical and scientific libraries, but is seldom met with elsewhere. In North America it is virtually unknown. On the continent of Europe its use is much greater, and the Latin Americanist is likely to come upon it in Spain and in Brazil. Just as Dewey is popular in Spanish America because it has been published in Spanish, so UDC has been adopted in many Brazilian libraries simply because (unlike Dewey and LC) it exists in a Portuguese version.

Bliss Classification

The Henry E. Bliss classification ('Bliss') was invented in the 1930s, and its planning thus benefited from the experience of the earlier schemes. The notation consists almost entirely of letters, giving it a base of 26 instead of Dewey's ten numerals. This means that the Bliss subject notation as it actually appears on the spines of library books is brief—often only three letters; it is easy to remember, and easy for the library staff to shelve in the correct place. It came into existence when most US and UK libraries were already too committed to LC or Dewey to make any change, and is thus still practically unknown in the United States, its inventor's home country. It has, however, been taken up by a group of British enthusiasts, who have worked to keep it updated (coincidentally anglicising it in the process). Experience has shown, moreover, that it is far and away the easiest scheme for the ordinary library user to understand. Unfortunately, most of the enthusiasts are from college, rather than university or public, libraries: few British research libraries have adopted the system, and the only place the Latin Americanist is likely to encounter it is in the University of London's lending library for students at Senate House.

Accession Numbers, Call Numbers and Shelfmarks

The classification number as used in most UK libraries does no more than indicate the subject of the work. When there is a need to identify individual copies, a simple running number is generally assigned to each book in order of acquisition or accession; this is known as the 'accession number'. By contrast, US practice is to elaborate the classification number to individualise each work and each edition thereof. If, despite every trick of the classifier's trade, two items end up with the same class number—as, for instance, if both the New York and London editions of Vargas Llosa's *War of the End of the World* were published in the same year—then the volumes would simply have to be distinguished alphabetically at the end: PQ 8498.32.A65G8131984a, and PQ 8498.32.A65G8131984b. The individual parts of a multi-volume work would be further identified by the addition of 'v1', 'v2' etc., and if more than one copy of the same edition were owned, the class number would end in 'c1', 'c2' and so on. The result is a number totally individualising each item in the library. Such a number is, in library jargon, a 'call number' or 'shelfmark'.

LH

Published Library Catalogues

Published library catalogues are a bibliographical source, in that they help the researcher to trace what publications exist and to check references for items that are already known. At the same time, they provide a fixed location for each item, and can thus be a great help if a photocopy or inter-library loan is needed, or in planning a research visit. As with bibliographies, however, the student's first requirement is to know which published library catalogue to consult. Union catalogues can provide a starting point: for US libraries, the *National Union Catalog*; for UK libraries, the *British Union Catalogue of Latin Americana*, either on fiche or by means of a telephone call or a personal visit to the Institute of Latin American Studies of the University of London. These and other resources are discussed in the chapter, UNION CATALOGUES AND UNION LISTS (p. 62).

Many of the major libraries whose catalogues are discussed here are also mentioned in the chapter on LIBRARY RESOURCES ON LATIN AMERICA (p. 3); if a visit to any of them is contemplated, it is worthwhile checking in advance to see if the catalogue has been published.

This chapter includes catalogues of special subject collections, but not of special materials such as newspapers or manuscripts; these are discussed elsewhere in the book as appropriate. Some libraries also publish short lists of their holdings in particular subjects as guides for their own readers: some of these are listed on p. 14. Finally, it should be noted that the catalogues of national libraries are supplemented to some extent by current national bibliographies, which record additions to their stock; details of Latin American examples will be found under NATIONAL BIBLIOGRAPHIES (pp. 119-126).

The published library catalogue as we know it today owes much to the industry of the Boston publishing house of G. K. Hall in the 1960s and 1970s. Earlier in the century, only a few major, traditional libraries (such as the Bibliothèque Nationale in Paris and the Library of Congress in Washington, DC) continued the nineteenth century practice of producing printed catalogues of their collections. Most of the the G. K. Hall catalogues were produced by xeroxing records, sometimes selectively, from card catalogues; this frequently involved having several columns of entries to a page, and it is sometimes difficult to follow the alphabetical sequence exactly. Some are dictionary catalogues, listing personal and corporate authors, titles and subject headings in one sequence; more are main entry catalogues, listing materials by author, or by title if the author is lacking. Most catalogues have a short introduction explaining the scope, catalogue rules and layout used.

Printed catalogues are expensive to acquire, and while those of the national collections are usually available in most large reference libraries, others can be found only in the largest or most specialised collections. Some catalogues originally published in book form have been reissued on microfilm or fiche at a lower cost, and have thus attained wider availability.

Increasingly, catalogues are 'published' as computerised bibliographic databases, accessible from terminals or micro-computers in the library itself, in other libraries, and occasionally in the researcher's own home. Catalogues available in this way usually have a better coverage of recent publications than of older ones, whose records are often still held in traditional card or guard-book catalogues. Major UK library catalogues being produced in database form are discussed below; the practice is so widespread in the United States that readers are advised to consult in advance with libraries they may wish to visit to determine whether the catalogue is available to the public online (see also the chapter on UNION CATALOGUES AND UNION LISTS, p. 62). Some libraries having an automated catalogue cannot allow the reader online access. In such instances printout or microfiche lists are generally produced from the database for the use of readers, or for gift or sale to other libraries.

The following brief description of major published library catalogues is arranged by geographical area, starting with the catalogues of North American collections and proceeding via the UK and Europe to Latin America. It concludes with a few catalogues of the collections of international organisations.

United States

The holdings of the Library of Congress in Washington, DC, form a major part of the *National Union Catalog* (see p. 62). There is a *Shelflist of the Library of Congress* on microfiche (Ann Arbor, MI: UMI, 1979), arranged by subject classification with an accompanying users' guide. An additional aid is:

Cumulative Title Index to the Classified Collections of the Library of Congress, 1978. 132 vols. Arlington, VA: Carrollton Press, 1979–1982.

All these are, however, to a large extent superseded by the *Main Catalog of the Library of Congress, 1890–1980*, published on microfiche by K. G. Saur of Munich. All titles catalogued by the Library between those dates are listed by subject, title, series and author in one alphabetical sequence.

No special catalogue has been issued of the Library of Congress's Hispanic holdings, though the largest and smallest areas of Latin America have been treated in two specialised listings:

JACKSON, William Vernon. *Catalog of Brazilian Acquisitions of the Library of Congress, 1964–1974.* Boston, MA: G. K. Hall, 1977.

LARSON, Everett E. *A Selective Listing of Monographs and Government Documents on the Falkland (Malvinas) Islands in the Library of Congress.* Washington, DC: Library of Congress, 1982.

The Library's office in Rio de Janeiro has since 1975 issued *Library of Congress Accessions List: Brazil*, a comprehensive and current bimonthly source of information on the publications acquired by the office and forwarded to Washington, DC. Most (but not all) of this material will subsequently appear in the Library's catalogue. Recently catalogued Latin American material is also included in the *Bibliographic Guide to Latin American Studies* (see below), except when the Library's holdings overlap those of the University of Texas at Austin. The Library of Congress catalogue is available from 1968 in computerised form under the name LCMARC (Library of Congress Machine Readable Catalog). It is maintained in three files, covering 1968–1976, 1977–1983 and 1984 onwards.

Probably the largest published catalogue in the G. K. Hall series contains the collections of the New York Public Library:

Dictionary Catalog of the Research Libraries, 1911–1971. 800 vols. Boston, MA: G. K. Hall, 1979. Supplemented by *Dictionary Catalog of the Research Libraries, January 1972–July 1981* and *Interim List: Titles Catalogued August 1981–March 1985.*

The Library's Reference Department has also compiled two specialised catalogues of interest to Latin Americanists:

Dictionary Catalog of the History of the Americas. 28 vols. Boston, MA: G. K. Hall, 1961. With *Supplement* (9 vols.; 1974). Also available on microfilm.

List of Works Relating to the West Indies. New York: The Library, 1912.

Two other general catalogues of interest to the Latin American researcher are those of the University of California, Los Angeles, and of the University of California, Berkeley. These were both published by G. K. Hall in 1963: UCLA's as *Dictionary Catalog of the University Library, 1919–1962* (129 vols.), and UCB's (including the holdings of the Bancroft Library) as *Author-Title Catalog* (115 vols). An earlier catalogue of the Berkeley collections is:

Spain and Spanish America in the Libraries of the University of California: A Catalogue of Books. 2 vols. Berkeley: The Library, 1928–1930; reprinted, New York: Burt Franklin, 1969. Volume 1 covers the General and Departmental Libraries, volume 2 the Bancroft Library.

A later catalogue of the Bancroft alone was published by G. K. Hall:

The Bancroft Library, University of California, Berkeley: Catalog of Printed Books. 22 vols. Boston, MA: G. K. Hall, 1964. Supplements appeared in 1969 (6 vols.), 1974 (6 vols.) and 1979 (5 vols.). Also available on microfilm.

Among the catalogues of US Latin American collections, that of the University of Texas at Austin must be the most comprehensive:

Catalog of the Latin American Collection. 31 vols. Boston, MA: G. K. Hall, 1969. Supplements appeared in 1971 (5 vols.), 1973 (3 vols.), 1975 (3 vols.) and 1977 (3 vols.); the last was issued as *Catalog of the Nettie Lee Benson Latin American Collection, General Libraries, University of Texas* after the collection had been renamed. The main volumes and first three supplements of the dictionary catalogue are all also available on microfilm. Further supplementary lists have appeared annually from 1979 in two or three volumes under the title *Bibliographic Guide to Latin American Studies* (Boston, MA: G. K. Hall, 1979—). This includes entries for additional items acquired by the Library of Congress.

Another important collection is recorded in:

Catalog of the Latin American Library of the Tulane University Library, New Orleans. 9 vols. Boston, MA: G. K. Hall, 1970. Supplements followed in 1973, 1975 and 1978, all on microfilm.

Generally speaking, Mexico is very well represented in US library catalogues. The Bancroft, Tulane and Texas collections are all particularly strong in Mexican materials, and several specialist catalogues of other libraries also exist. Examples are:

VALENTINO RAMÍREZ, Pablo. *Bibliografía mexicana de la Universidad de California en San Diego.* Mexico City: Instituto Nacional de Antropología e Historia, Departamento de Investigaciones Históricas, 1976.

DAVIDSON, R. and C. JOINER. *Mexico in the University of New Mexico Libraries: A Guide to Special Materials and Older Works.* Albuquerque: University of New Mexico, Zimmerman Library, 1976.

There is also a recent listing from Yale, which reflects that collection's strength in Mexican and Peruvian items:

WILSON, Lofton et al. *Guide to Latin American Pamphlets from the Yale University Library: Selections from 1600–1900.* 7 vols. New York: Clearwater Press, 1985.

Material for Luso-Brazilian studies is collected in two specialist listings, in addition to its coverage in the general catalogues:

The Catalog of the Oliveira Lima Library. 2 vols. Boston, MA: G. K. Hall, 1970. This collection is held at the Catholic University of America in Washington, DC.

GILLETT, Theresa and Helen McINTYRE. *Catalog of Luso-Brazilian Material in the University of New Mexico Libraries.* Metuchen, NJ: Scarecrow Press, 1970.

Colonial Latin America, with Spain and Portugal, are the subjects of:

Catalogue of the Library of the Hispanic Society of America. 20 reels of microfilm. Boston, MA: G. K. Hall, 1962. With a 1970 supplement (4 reels).

The Caribbean area is the particular strength of two major collections having published catalogues:

Catalog of the Latin American Collection, University of Florida Libraries, Gainesville. 13 vols. Boston, MA: G. K. Hall, 1973. With a 1980 supplement (7 vols.).

Catalog of the Cuban and Caribbean Library, University of Miami, Coral Gables. 6 vols. Boston, MA: G. K. Hall, 1977.

There are also catalogues of specialised subject collections that contain significant holdings of Latin American material. Among these are:

Research Catalog of the American Geographical Society. 15 vols. Boston, MA: G. K. Hall, 1962. With a *Map Supplement* (1962), and subsequent updating volumes (1972, 1974 and 1978). The Latin American materials are found in volumes 6 and 7.

Dictionary Catalog of the Edward E. Ayer Collection of Americana and American Indians, The Newberry Library, Chicago. 8 vols. Boston, MA: G. K. Hall, 1961. Supplements appeared in 1970 (3 vols.) and 1980 (4 vols.).

Dictionary Catalog of the American Indian Collection, Huntington Free Library and Reading Room, New York. 4 vols. Boston, MA: G. K. Hall, 1977.

Dictionary Catalog of the Missionary Research Library, New York. 17 vols. Boston, MA: G. K. Hall, 1968. Also available on microfilm.

United Kingdom

The most comprehensive general catalogue published in book form and including Latin American material is that of the British Library (Humanities and Social Sciences) in London. The full citation of the latest form of the printed catalogue is:

The British Library General Catalogue of Printed Books to 1975. 360 vols. London: Bingley, and Munich: K. G. Saur, 1979–1988. The main set has six supplementary volumes. Subsequent volumes, issued by Saur alone, cover 1976–1982 (50 vols., 1985), 1982–1985 (26 vols., 1986) and 1986–1987 (22 vols., 1988). The period 1976–1985 is also available as a microfiche set (London: BL Publications, 1986) with supplements.

The earlier edition of the catalogue is, however, the one still held by many libraries: this is the *General Catalogue of Printed Books* of what was then the British Museum Library, covering holdings up to 1955 in 263 volumes (London: Trustees of the British Museum, 1959–1966). Supplements (89 volumes in all) brought the record up to 1975. There is a subject index to the collections, starting in 1881, entitled *Subject Index of Modern Books Acquired by the British Museum Library*. A series of volumes was issued for each five or ten year period up to 1975. This has now been continued by *The British Library General Subject Catalogue, 1975–1985* (75 vols.; London: K. G. Saur, 1986), which is also available on microfiche as *Subject Catalogue of Printed Books, 1975–1985* (London: BL Publications, 1985).

The Library's catalogues of modern accessions are maintained on BLAISE (British Library Automated Information Service), a bibliographic database. BLAISE-LINE's BNBMARC file contains records for all British publications back to 1950, and the HSS file contains records for BL Humanities and Social Sciences material since 1976. This is an important source for Spanish and Portuguese language material, as well as for US publications. In the future the Library will be giving priority to providing online access to its catalogues. The two files already mentioned are accessible through JANET (Joint Academic Network). The pre-1976 catalogues are also being entered into a database, and will be available on CD-ROM from 1989 and online in the early 1990s.

The British Library Document Supply Centre at Boston Spa produces a catalogue of the material it makes available for inter-library loan. This is *Books at Boston Spa* (London: BL Publications, 1980—), with bi-monthly updates; it is available as the DSC file on BLAISE-LINE. It is, however, not strong in foreign language materials.

Most of the other UK research libraries supporting strong Latin American holdings have not published their catalogues, although attempts are being made to make them accessible through automation. It is hoped that the catalogue of pre-1920 holdings of the Bodleian Library, Oxford, will soon be available on CD-ROM, and its catalogue of post-1988 accessions will eventually be accessible online, together with catalogue records from other Oxford libraries, including that of the Taylor Institution. The main catalogue of Cambridge University Library also remains unpublished, although post-1977 records have been entered on a database, and a microfiche catalogue has been generated. The University of London produced a computerised union catalogue of the acquisitions of its constituent schools and colleges from 1979 to 1988, available on BLAISE as the

UOL file, and also on fiche. There is a separate microfiche catalogue of the central University of London Library. The University is currently introducing a new automated system for its catalogues, and primary access will, it is hoped, be online. Other libraries with significant Latin American collections, including those of Liverpool and Glasgow Universities and Portsmouth Polytechnic, have at least some of their catalogue records in databases. The intention is that all of these catalogues be widely available online not only within the institutions but also to other centres of research through tele-communications networks.

One important UK library catalogue available in book form is that of the British Library of Political and Economic Science (BLPES) at the London School of Economics. The original compilation covered its holdings up to 1929, together with those of some other major London libraries:

> *London Bibliography of the Social Sciences.* 4 vols. (London: London School of Economics and Political Science, 1931). Supplements have appeared regularly, and are currently published annually by Mansell. Now contains the holdings of the BLPES and the Edward Fry Library of International Law.

Another institution of the University of London has also published its catalogue: this is the Institute of Commonwealth Studies (368 microfiches; Cambridge: Chadwyck-Healey, 1979). It is just one of several catalogues of London libraries notable for the Caribbean materials they contain. Another is:

> *Subject Catalogue of the Library of the Royal Commonwealth Society.* 7 vols. (Boston, MA: G. K. Hall, 1971. With a *Supplement* (2 vols., 1977).

This does not totally replace the earlier catalogue of the same library:

> LEWIN, Evans. *Subject Catalogue of the Library of the Royal Empire Society, Formerly Royal Colonial Institute.* 4 vols. London: The Society, 1930-1937. Caribbean materials appear in volume 3.

More Caribbean material, as well as items of interest for UK–Latin American relations, can be found in:

> *Catalogue of Printed Books in the Library of the Foreign Office.* London: His Majesty's Stationery Office, 1926.

Catalogue of the Foreign Office Library, 1926–1968. 8 vols. Boston, MA: G. K. Hall, 1972.

Catalogue of the Colonial Office Library. 15 vols. Boston, MA: G. K. Hall, 1964. With a supplement (1967).

In 1968 these two libraries were merged. Subsequently there appeared:

Catalogue of the Colonial Office Library (Foreign and Commonwealth Office), London. 2 vols. Boston, MA: G. K. Hall, 1972. Contains accessions of 1968–1971.

Foreign and Commonwealth Office: Accessions to the Library, May 1971–June 1977. 4 vols. Boston, MA: G. K. Hall, 1979.

An important library for Latin America, Spain and Portugal is that of Canning House in London. Its catalogue was published in two parts:

Canning House Library: Hispanic Council. 4 vols. Boston, MA: G. K. Hall, 1967.

Canning House Library: Luso-Brazilian Council. Boston, MA: G. K. Hall, 1967. Supplements to both parts were issued in 1973.

Finally, two highly specialised catalogues of interest to the Latin Americanist are:

THOMAS, H. *Short-Title Catalogues of Portuguese Books and of Spanish-American Books Printed before 1601 now in the British Museum.* London: Quaritch, 1926. Describes 54 early Latin American books. Reprinted and issued in one volume with an equivalent work on early Spanish books (London: BM Publications, 1966).

PRICE, Robin Murray. *An Annotated Catalogue of Medical Americana in the Library of the Wellcome Institute for the History of Medicine: Books and Printed Documents, 1557–1821, from Latin America and the Caribbean Islands, and Manuscripts from the Americas, 1575–1927.* London: The Institute, 1983.

France

One of the most important general national library catalogues is that of the Bibliothèque Nationale (BN) in Paris, now published on microfiche by Chadwyck-Healey France. The fiche set comprises the

Catalogue général des livres imprimés, Catalogue général des livres imprimés, 1960–1969, and the previously unpublished card catalogue covering 1897–1959. Additionally, there is a new and rapidly-growing database of catalogue records for post-1970 acquisitions. The BN has also published two specialised catalogues of interest:

BARRINGER, Georges. *Catalogue de l'histoire d'Amérique.* 8 vols. Paris: Bibliothèque Nationale, 1887–1911. The last three volumes are concerned with Latin America.

SIMON, Nicole. *Le fonds cubain de la Société de Géographie: inventaire.* (Paris: Bibliothèque Nationale, 1986).

A substantial accessions list is the semi-annual *Acquisitions récentes* of the Bibliothèque de l'Institut des Hautes Etudes de l'Amérique Latine of the Université de Paris III. This library belongs to the Réseau Documentaire Amérique Latine, which issues the semi-annual *Bulletin Bibliographique Amérique Latine* (Paris: Recherches sur les Civilisations, 1982—). Only about a fifth of the entries in it are for books: the rest cite periodical articles, theses and research reports. The principal objective of the Réseau Documentaire Amérique Latine is to disseminate French language publications on Latin America throughout the world.

Germany

The most comprehensive European catalogue of Latin Americana is:

Schlagwortkatalog des Ibero-Amerikanischen Instituts Preussischer Kulturbesitz in Berlin/Subject Catalog of the Ibero-American Institute Prussian Cultural Heritage Foundation in Berlin. 30 vols. Boston, MA: G. K. Hall, 1977. Contains indexes of geographical names, place names listed under their respective countries and of persons listed by profession, and a general sequence arranged under German subject headings (with English and Spanish indexes to them).

Netherlands

The Centro de Estudios y Documentación Latinoamericanos of the University of Amsterdam (CEDLA) first published its catalogue, without a title, in 1968, with supplements in 1969 and 1970. These were followed by *Catalogus 1965–1971* (3 vols., 1972), with

supplements covering 1972–1975. Since 1975 regular updates have been issued on microfiche, generated from a computer database. Recently the catalogue has incorporated the holdings of the University Library in Leiden and the Faculty of Arts in Utrecht to become virtually a union catalogue.
For the Netherlands Antilles, there is:

NAGELKERKE, Gerard A. *Literatuur-overzicht van de Nederlandse Antillen vanaf de 17e eeuw tot 1970: literatuur aanwezig in de Bibliotheek van het Koninklijk Instituut voor Taal–, Land– en Volkenkunde te Leiden.* Leiden: Bibliotheek KIT, 1973. The KIT Carabaische Afdeling now also publishes the *Centrale Catalogus Caraibiana* on microfiche (see UNION CATALOGUES AND UNION LISTS, p. 64).

A catalogue rich in Latin American political material is:

Alfabetische catalogus van de boeken en brochures van het Internationaal Instituut voor Sociale Geschiedenis. 12 vols. Boston, MA: G. K. Hall, 1970. With a supplement (2 vols., 1974).

Spain

The Biblioteca Nacional's main catalogue is now available on fiche:

Biblioteca Nacional, Madrid: Catálogo general de libros impresos. Approximately 4,600 microfiches. Cambridge: Chadwyck-Healey, 1989. Available in two parts, covering pre-1982 imprints and books added 1982–1987 respectively, with a printed guide.

There is also a catalogue of its Latin American materials:

CUESTA, Luisa. *Catálogo de las obras iberoamericanas y filipinas de la Biblioteca Nacional de Madrid.* Madrid: Biblioteca Nacional, 1953.

An older Spanish catalogue, with emphases on Cuba and Puerto Rico, is:

Museo-Biblioteca de Ultramar en Madrid: catálogo de la biblioteca. Madrid: Minuesa de los Rios, 1900.

Further information on the same collection can be found in:

CUESTA DOMINGO, Mariano and Nieves SÁENZ GARCÍA. 'Fondos de la Biblioteca de Ultramar en el Museo de América de Madrid.' *Historiografía y Bibliografía Americanistas* 24 (1980), pp. 127–187. Lists the 850 most interesting books in the Museum (pp. 131–187).

Italy

One of the great collections of material on Columbus and the other early explorers of America is documented in:

Catalogo della Raccolta Colombiana, Civica Biblioteca Berio, Genova/ Catalog of the Columbus Collection, Berio Civic Library, Genoa. Boston, MA: G. K. Hall, 1963. Also available on microfiche.

An earlier catalogue of the same collection is:

CERVETTO, Luigi. *Catalogo delle opere componente la Raccolta Colombiana esistente nella Civica Biblioteca Berio di Genova.* Genoa: Pagano, 1906.

Caribbean Area

A major collection, which now forms part of the National Library of Jamaica, is treated in:

The Catalog of the West India Reference Library. 6 vols. Millwood, NY: Kraus International, 1980. This collection was initially part of the Public Library of the Institute of Jamaica (though, as the title suggests, the coverage is not restricted to Jamaica).

Several earlier catalogues were also based on the holdings of this library, most notably three by the same author:

CUNDALL, Frank. *Bibliotheca Jamaicensis: Some Account of the Principal Works on Jamaica in the Library of the Institute.* Kingston: Institute of Jamaica, 1895; reprinted, New York: Burt Franklin, 1971.

CUNDALL, Frank. *Bibliographia Jamaicensis.* Kingston: Institute of Jamaica, 1902. Supplements to this and the above work were issued in 1908.

CUNDALL, Frank. *Bibliography of the West Indies Excluding Jamaica.* Kingston: Institute of Jamaica, 1909; reprinted, New York: Johnson Reprint Corp., 1981.

From Barbados comes:

Moss, S. G. *Books on the West Indies or by West Indian Writers Held in the Richard B. Moore Library, Barbados*. St. Michael: Author, 1986. Documents a collection focusing on the history of the black race.

A very rich collection of materials on Haiti is documented in:

LOWENTHAL, Ira P. and Drexel G. WOODSON. *Catalogue de la collection Mangonès, Pétionville, Haïti*. New Haven, CT: Yale University, Antilles Research Program, 1974.

Mexico and Central America

The Mexican national collection is covered by:

Catálogo Oficial, Biblioteca Nacional de México. 39 reels of microfilm. Mexico City: UNAM, Instituto de Investigaciones Bibliográficas, 1982. Also available on microfiche.

Older catalogues of the same library, general and special, include:

VIGIL, Jose M. *Catálogo de la Biblioteca Nacional de México*. Mexico City: Secretaría de Fomento, 1889–1894. With *Primeros suplementos* (1895).

Catálogo especial de las obras mexicanas o sobre México, Biblioteca Nacional. Mexico City: García Cubas, 1915.

VALTON, Emilio. *Impresos mexicanos del siglo XVI ... en la Biblioteca Nacional de México, el Museo Nacional y el Archivo General de la Nación*. Mexico City: Universitaria, 1935. Gives detailed descriptions of 75 items.

YMHOFF CABRERA, J. *Catálogo de incunables de la Biblioteca Nacional de México*. Mexico City: UNAM, 1968. Fifteenth century material only.

Another important Mexican library is documented in:

Catálogo de la Biblioteca Nacional de Antropología e Historia. 20 reels of microfilm. Boston, MA: G. K. Hall, 1972.

The catalogues of the central and departmental libraries of the Universidad Nacional Autónoma de México (UNAM) are all maintained on the online database, LIBRUNAM, and have been accessible in the UK and the US through DIALOG. This collection is also available on microfiche, and has been distributed widely inside the country.

Guatemalan and other Central American publications figure in:

Catálogo de la Biblioteca Nacional. Edited by Rafael Arévalo Martínez. Guatemala: Biblioteca Nacional, 1932.

The Belize national collection is covered by a succession of catalogues, the earliest of which is:

A Bibliography of the National Collection in the Central Library, Bliss Institute, Belize. Belize: British Honduras Library Service, 1960. Subsequent editions were issued under slightly different titles up to the fourth (1977), with a 1979 supplement.

An essential tool for the study of the Panama Canal is:

Subject Catalog of the Special Panama Collection of the Canal Zone Library-Museum, Balboa Heights: The History of the Isthmus of Panama as It Applies to Interoceanic Transportation. Boston, MA: G. K. Hall, 1964. Covers the planning and construction of the Canal together with other projects. Also available on microfilm.

South America

The Argentine national library produced a series of published catalogues at the turn of the century:

Catálogo metódico de la Biblioteca Nacional, seguido de una tabla alfabética de autores. 7 vols. Buenos Aires: Coni, Biblioteca Nacional, 1893–1931.

Another major national resource is documented in:

Argentine Bibliography: A Union Catalogue of Argentine Holdings in the Libraries of the University of Buenos Aires. 7 vols. Boston, MA: G. K. Hall, 1980.

A substantial catalogue of a wide range of Brazilian materials can be found in:

Catálogo da Biblioteca do Senado Federal. 5 vols. Brasília: Senado Federal, Subsecretaria da Biblioteca, 1975.

A good collection of Colombian material is listed in:

Catálogo de la Biblioteca Luis-Angel Arango: Fondo Colombia. 4 vols.
Bogotá: Banco de la República, 1972.

Early printing in the same library is the focus of:

*Incunables de la Biblioteca Luis-Angel Arango del Banco de la
República.* Bogotá: Arco, 1982.

Early materials in the national collection of Ecuador can be traced
through:

*Incunables y libros raros y curiosos, siglos XV, XVI, XVII y XVIII:
sección llamada Hispanoamérica.* Quito: Biblioteca Nacional, 1959.

The major catalogue from Paraguay lists Paraguayan books in the
Biblioteca Central of the Universidad Nacional:

GONZÁLEZ PETIT, E. R. de and R. E. MOREL SOLAECHE.
Bibliografía de obras paraguayas. Asunción: Universidad Nacional, 1982.

The national collection of Peru is covered by:

*Catálogo de autores de la Colección Peruana, Biblioteca Nacional del
Perú.* 6 vols. Boston, MA: G. K. Hall, 1979.

Another important (but expatriate) Peruvian collection is treated
in:

RENÉ-MORENO, Gabriel. *Biblioteca peruana: apuntes para un
catálogo de impresos.* 2 vols. Santiago: Biblioteca del Instituto
Nacional, 1896; reprinted, Naarden, Netherlands: Van
Bekhoven, 1970. An inventory of books taken from Peru by
the Chilean Army in the 1880s.

The national library of Venezuela has produced:

Catálogo de la Sección de Bibliografía Nacional, Biblioteca Nacional.
Caracas: Biblioteca Nacional, 1921. A second edition appeared in 1930.

International Organisations

The Latin American and Caribbean holdings of the library of the
International Monetary Fund and the World Bank are included in
the first volume of:

The Developing Areas: A Classed Bibliography of the Joint Bank-Fund Library. 3 vols. Boston, MA: G. K. Hall, 1976.

The collections of the Pan-American Institute of Geography and History are recorded in two works:

Vivo, Jorge F. *Catálogo de la Biblioteca, 1930–1939.* Tacubaya: Instituto Panamericano de Geografía e Historia, 1940.

Jordan, Fernando. *Catálogo de la Biblioteca, 1940–1944.* Mexico City: Instituto Panamericano de Geografía e Historia, 1945.

AEW

Union Catalogues and Union Lists

A union catalogue lists the holdings of a number of autonomous libraries or various branches of a single library system, and indicates where each item is held. Union catalogues (like all catalogues) can exist in a number of different forms: cards, microfiche/film, printed or online; for some of the latter, see also DATABASES, p. 229.

Union lists are usually printed, and also cover a group of libraries, but are narrower in scope than union catalogues. They may be limited to works on a particular subject area, or to materials of a given type (censuses or periodicals, for example). Though always bibliographically useful, published union lists tend to become less helpful with the passage of time for information on locations and holdings, as items are added to or removed from collections. Particularly vulnerable in this respect are union lists of periodicals and newspapers. Both these types of material are prone to erratic publishing histories, and the physical bulk of newspapers when acquired in paper form makes them an early target for disposal in libraries with space problems. For these reasons, an ongoing flexible union catalogue, either on cards or online, is a more effective vehicle; changes are easily recorded, resulting in more reliable location information.

Union catalogues and lists spring from a need to share information about scarce and scattered resources. The field of Latin American materials is particularly problematic—short print runs, poor distribution facilities, inadequate national bibliographic control and difficulties of communication all contribute to the scarcity of information on books and periodicals emanating from the region.

Union Catalogues

No specialised union catalogue for Latin America exists in the United States. Its place is filled, however, by the massive:

> *National Union Catalog* (NUC). 754 vols. London: Mansell, 1968–1981. The main set covers pre-1956 imprints; a supplement was published covering the years 1956 through 1967

(Totowa, NJ: Rowman and Littlefield, 1970–1972); further printed supplements were issued to 1982, cumulated five-yearly to 1978 and annually thereafter; from 1983 NUC exists only on microfiche. Contains all Library of Congress records, together with titles reported by some 500 other North American research libraries. Gives at least one location for each cited item; frequently there are several.

In addition, large automated library databases such as OCLC or RLIN, formed primarily for the purpose of cooperative cataloguing, now perform the secondary function of providing locations for the materials they contain. Some have even, in effect, become international union catalogues: OCLC, for instance, includes the Latin American holdings of Essex University Library and the Wellcome Institute in London, as well as those of many strong Latin American collections inside the United States.

There are three Latin Americanist union catalogues currently available for consultation in Europe: the *British Union Catalogue of Latin Americana* (BUCLA) in the UK, the *Centrale Catalogus Caraibiana* (CCC) in the Netherlands, and *Documentación Latinoamericana* in West Germany.

British Union Catalogue of Latin Americana (UK, 1967–1988)

BUCLA was established at the Institute of Latin American Studies of the University of London (ILAS), in recognition of the Institute's national role as the UK's central documentation centre in the field of Latin American studies. The aim was to compile, collate and publish information on the Latin American holdings of all British research libraries. A total of 94 national, university, polytechnic, college, special, embassy and public libraries contributed to the catalogue (a full list of contributors is available from the ILAS library). Attempts were made where possible to include retrospective holdings as well as current acquisitions. ILAS provided accomodation for the catalogue and the staff to service it until September 1988, when BUCLA was closed for financial reasons. While its future is at present unclear, the whole catalogue (1967–1988) remains available for consultation in card form at the Institute, and has been published (to 1987) on microfiche by the Inter Documentation Company (PO Box 11205, 2301 EE Leiden, Netherlands).

Coverage is as broad as possible: the catalogue cites materials published on or in all countries south of the Rio Grande, including the Caribbean, regardless of language. All fields and disciplines of Latin American studies are covered, as are works published inside the region on non-Latin American topics. All forms of printed material are included: monographs, pamphlets, periodicals, newspapers and government publications.

BUCLA registers some 370,000 locations of about 203,000 items; Library of Congress cards are also included for titles for which no location has yet been traced in the British Isles. Arrangement is in a single alphabetical sequence (filed letter-by-letter); entry is generally by author, but is by title for periodicals or works produced under editorial direction. There is no subject access. Explanatory notes are provided for users at the Institute, setting out some of the finer points on form of entry and arrangement. For further information, one should contact The Librarian, ILAS, 31 Tavistock Square, London WC1H 9HA. Location information is also given by telephone (01-387 4055) or post, and personal callers are welcomed at 35 Tavistock Square (the nearest Underground stations are Russell Square, Euston and Euston Square).

Centrale Catalogus Caraibiana (The Netherlands, 1978—).

Maintained by the Royal Institute of Linguistics and Anthropology in Leiden, the CCC covers social science subjects relating to the Caribbean Islands, Surinam, Guyana, French Guiana and Belize, together with a selection of materials on Central America, Mexico, Venezuela and Colombia. Although founded comparatively recently, the catalogue contains the retrospective holdings of its twenty contributing university and special libraries, thirteen of which contribute on a regular basis. Between them, these libraries comprise all the relevant collections in the country. A wide range of material is included: books, periodical titles (though not newspapers), periodical articles and government publications. CCC takes the form of a card catalogue arranged by author, and is also published on fiche with annual cumulations in author, classified subject (their own classification) and country sequences. At the end of 1987, the catalogue contained some 45,000 titles.

Requests for bibliographical and location information are accepted by post, telephone (71-148333, ext. 4144) and in person. For further information one should contact the Documentalist, Royal Institute of Linguistics and Anthropology, Department of Caribbean Studies, P.O. Box 9515, 2300 RA Leiden, The Netherlands.

Dokumentationsdienst Lateinamerika/Documentación Latinoamericana (West Germany, 1968—)

This catalogue is maintained by the Deutsches Übersee-Institut in Hamburg, and covers the countries of Latin America from the Rio Grande to Tierra del Fuego, including the Caribbean Islands, in the fields of sociology, politics and economics. It contains books, periodical titles and articles and government publications. Founded in 1968, the catalogue contains only materials acquired after that date. Some 72 libraries contribute: these include national, government and university libraries, together with other libraries belonging to the Asociación Alemana de Investigaciones sobre América Latina. Coverage, though impressive, does not claim to be exhaustive, and there are some major libraries which do not contribute. The 72,000 titles (and 360,000 locations) currently included are arranged by author, alphabetical subject, country and organisation sequences. Available only as a card catalogue from 1968 to 1985, it has been made accessible online from 1985.

Requests for bibliographical and location information are accepted by letter, telephone (040 35 62–581), or in person. Further details are available from The Librarian, Deutsches Übersee-Institut, Übersee-Dokumentation Referat Lateinamerika, Neuer Jungfernstieg 21, 2000 Hamburg 36, West Germany.

Union Lists

As indicated above, most published union lists deal with newspapers, periodicals or government publications. The major titles are listed in other appropriate chapters of this volume: see NEWSPAPERS AND NEWS MAGAZINES (pp. 189–190), PERIODICALS (pp. 213–215/p), CENSUSES (p. 278) and INTER-LIBRARY LENDING (pp. 73–74).

CT

Copyright and Photocopying

Copyright is simply the right of an author, artist or composer to profit from, or control the use of, his or her own creations. Unfortunately, the law of copyright is far from simple; it varies from country to country, depending on each government's adherence (or non-adherence) to the Berne Convention of 1886 or the Universal Copyright Convention of 1952, together with their various revisions. Practice also varies widely: in many countries, for example, the protection of the copyright laws can only be obtained by registering a literary or artistic work in the appropriate government office, while in the British Commonwealth copyright is deemed to be intrinsic in any written work. In the United States, copyright is intrinsic only until publication, at which time the work must be registered in order to receive copyright protection.

Most nations have at least one copyright or depository library with the entitlement to receive free of charge all domestic publications ('legal deposit'). In the United States this is the Library of Congress, in which 'two complete copies of the best edition' of all published works and sound recordings, registered or not in the Copyright Office, must be deposited. The UK equivalent is the British Library in London (formerly the British Museum Library), which receives one copy of all British and Irish publications. The copyright privilege has also been extended to five other libraries in the British Isles: the Bodleian Library in Oxford, the University Library in Cambridge, the National Library of Scotland in Edinburgh, the National Library of Wales in Aberystwyth and the library of Trinity College, Dublin. By contrast, in many parts of Latin America, even despite the presence of depository libraries, the law of legal deposit is not strictly enforced.

The area in which copyright is most likely to impinge on the student or researcher is in the field of photocopying or documentary reproduction; how far does the copying of part of a published text infringe the rights of its creator? In recent years the situation has also been complicated by the problems created by computer technology —software, databases and the problems of downloading and reformatting of data. Many libraries are employing these and other means of reproduction with the aim of preserving or replacing the older and more fragile items in their stocks. Neither in the US nor in the UK does the law specifically speak to these issues, which will no doubt be the principal concerns of copyright in the twenty-first century. This chapter, however, will concern itself exclusively with the issues raised by the practice of documentary reproduction, as employed by students and researchers.

Almost all libraries nowadays possess some means of repro-graphic copying; most will also have microform reader/printers that can produce full-size hard copy from microfilm and microfiche. In the last twenty years, photocopying has emerged as a simple and accurate alternative to hours of note-taking, and thus has been a great boon to students and researchers. Publishers and authors, however, see the matter differently; many have come to regard virtually every act of copying as an infringement of their rights and an unacceptable loss of income. In many countries the law has come to a compromise by allowing the photocopying of single copies of short extracts from a copyright work for private study ('fair use', or 'fair dealing'). But how short is short? Definitions and codes of practice vary from country to country and are sometimes impossible to ascertain fully. All this can lead to libraries' having to limit photocopying and requiring users to sign indemnity guarantees. Moreover, most libraries quite legitimately refuse to submit old, rare or fragile volumes to the strains and stresses of the photocopier.

The following sections will attempt to explain the rules of copyright as they are applied and interpreted in the UK and the US. Lack of space, and vagaries of law and interpretation, make it impossible to lay down rules for the other countries where the researcher might be working. And it must be stressed that the information given here is intended only as a guide; it cannot be expected to agree with the regulations of every library, nor should it be cited to unimpressed librarians as an excuse to copy more than is allowed.

UK Practice

The Copyright Act currently in force in the United Kingdom was passed in 1956, and is now widely accepted as being in need of replacement; a Royal Commission (the Whitford Commission) reported on the subject as long ago as 1977. The British government has announced its intention to legislate on the matter, but the exact provisions of the new law are as yet unclear. Any new legislation is likely to be more restrictive than the 1956 provisions, which have resulted in the current practices, as explained below.

Copyright in books comes in two categories: the literary and artistic copyright in the text, which belongs to the author and his heirs, and copyright in the typographical arrangement, which belongs initially to the publisher. These are quite distinct: the literary copyright lasts for a period of 50 years from the author's death (or 50 years after publication in the case of posthumous works), while the typographical copyright lasts for 25 years from the date of first publication.

With regard to the photocopying of works still in copyright, the 1956 act permits 'fair dealing with a literary, dramatic or musical work for the purposes of research or private study.' Non-profit libraries are permitted under certain conditions to supply single copies of copyright material to their users, provided that no more than 'a reasonable proportion' of the work is reproduced. Multiple copying is not permitted. Unfortunately, the act does not define either 'fair dealing' or 'a reasonable proportion', and most academic libraries work on the basis of principles laid down in 1970 by the British Copyright Council (representing the authors and publishers) in a pamphlet entitled *Photocopying and the Law*.

These rules, as generally applied, lay down different standards for periodicals and monographic works. In the case of periodicals or serials—including annually-published works—a student may be supplied with a single copy of a single article from any one issue of a periodical. In the case of monographic works, the permissible amount is a single copy of a single extract not exceeding 4,000 words, *or* a series of extracts (of which none exceeds 3,000 words) to a total of 8,000 words, provided that in no case the total amount copied exceeds ten per cent of the whole work. It should also be stressed that in the case of a collection of articles, essays or poems by different authors published together as a book, each item has to be regarded as a separate copyright work. This leads to a strange situation: when an article is published in a festschrift or a symposium only one tenth is available for copying, but if the same article were to appear in a periodical it could legally be photocopied in full.

In practice, many libraries simply allow their readers access to an unsupervised, usually coin-operated, copier, beside which is a notice laying down the copyright restrictions, and trust the individual's respect for the law. Other libraries do not permit unsupervised copying: the reader must submit an application form which includes a signed indemnity, and the library will carry out the photocopying up to the legal limit. In recent years the British Copyright Council (still representing the copyright-owners) has expressed its dissatisfaction with the practices set out above, and is making efforts to restrict the reproduction of copyright material. Its case is set forth in *Reprographic Copying of Books and Journals* (London: British Copyright Council, 1985), and will no doubt be considered in any future legislation.

US Practice

The US copyright law is a good example of attempts by lawmakers to create a balance between individual needs and the public good—trying, in effect, to make most of the people happy most of the time. The law was first decreed in 1790 (based on a 1710 statute of Queen Anne), and has evolved through various revisions, amendments and reinterpretations. The most recent revision (*US Code*, Title 17) was passed in 1976 and went into effect in 1978. Librarians and publishers registered almost immediate dissatisfaction with the law, particularly the areas of least precision, which were thus most open to different interpretations. By the law, US practice was brought more into line with that of the signatories of the Berne Convention: legal protection was provided for unpublished as well as published works; rights were extended to the consumers of intellectual property by codifying the doctrine of 'fair use'; and the duration of copyright protection was changed from 28 to 50 years after the author's death.

In practice, US library patrons are not required to sign indemnity guarantees for copyright purposes. Copying machines are placed in unsupervised locations, so that librarians cannot see what is being copied, and the required copyright notice is posted nearby. As long as the copying is 'unsupervised' in this way, the individual patron (rather than the library) carries the burden of responsibility for complying with the law. 'Fair use', although undefined and perhaps undefinable, is applied to non-profit, spontaneous copying by individuals of small portions of most works not in the public domain: examples could be 250 words of a poem, up to 2,500 words of an article or essay, or one illustration. Certain reference works, such as encyclopaedias, dictionaries and the like, are seen as virtually inviting the library user to copy small portions for the purpose of study and research. Unpublished works such as manuscripts, letters and diaries may not in general be reproduced except for preservation, security and research purposes.

In the matter of educational use of copying, however, the law shows itself much more liberal than UK legislation. Isolated copying by scholars, teachers and 'special users' is accepted as part of the educational process. Educators and scholars may thus make a single complete copy of most works for research purposes and, in special circumstances, even multiple copies for classroom use. In case of doubt, the most thorough interpretations of the law can be found in:

JOHNSTON, Donald F. *Copyright Handbook.* 2nd ed. New York: Bowker, 1982.

A copy of this text can be found in most US library reference departments.

RAM/BJR

Inter-Library Lending

Most countries in the Western world have highly developed inter-library lending systems, by which material may be obtained from other libraries near and far for use locally. The following account is based on the British system, which has the benefit of a national coordinating body (the British Library Document Supply Centre, or BLDSC, in Boston Spa, Yorkshire). Elsewhere, this is by no means always the case: in the US, for example, inter-library lending is organised mostly as a library-to-library transaction, with no centralised clearing system, though machinery for cooperation does exist in the form of the Center for Research Libraries, and within regional systems such as the MINITER system (based at the University of Minnesota) or among the nine campuses of the University of California. Moreover, because of the size and scope of the major US research collections, librarians in the United States have much less occasion than their colleagues in the rest of the world to make use of the international loan system. Nevertheless, most of the advice given here is applicable, *mutatis mutandis*, to other systems—though it should perhaps be stressed that this article is in no way intended as a substitute for the help and advice of a trained librarian in your own library. Most UK and US universities and research institutions have departments established specifically to handle inter-library loans, and the responsible staff will inevitably know much more of the local and individual circumstances than can possibly be explained here.

Most disappointments with the inter-library lending system occur not because the works fail to arrive, but because they do not arrive in time to be of use. Some delay is inevitable, so required reading should be planned well in advance and all library needs made known as soon as possible. The following hints should also help to speed things up.

Bibliographical Information

Always note where your reference came from. If the source is something at all unusual, make a photocopy of the reference; in the case of all foreign requests the International Federation of Library Associations (IFLA—the coordinating body for international loans) will insist on some proof of this sort that the required material really exists. If at all possible, obtain full bibliographical details: author or editor (unless it is a periodical); title (as given on the title-page, not the cover or spine); city or town where the work was published; publisher and date of publication. For a book published in the current year, and for any periodical, include the month as well as the year and the volume number, where applicable. The problem of tracing the author when only the title is known is dealt with under LIBRARY CATALOGUES (p. 36); periodical citation is discussed under PERIODICALS (p. 208).

Remember that the most common reason for a library's failing to locate an inter-library loan request is that you have given a mistaken or unusual style of author heading. This applies particularly to works of joint, multiple or corporate authorship. Libraries themselves are unfortunately not consistent in dealing with these: depending on the circumstances of publication and the idiosyncrasies of the individual library's catalogue, a set of conference papers, for example, may be recorded under its own title or that of the conference (in English or in the language of the country where it was held); under the sponsoring organization; under the editor or compiler of the published papers; or under the name of whomever happens to have written the first paper in the book. Fortunately, matters are improving: the new *Anglo-American Cataloguing Rules* (AACR2) are encouraging more and more libraries to standardize their form of heading—generally under the title. For the moment, however, the safest procedure is to check and follow the form of heading used in the *British National Bibliography* (for a UK public-ation) or in the *National Union Catalog* (for a North American, Latin American or other foreign publication). Even then, if the BNB or NUC heading seems in any way unusual or perverse, point out any alternative heading to the library staff when you hand in your request.

If the work exists in several editions, decide whether you need a particular one; if not, give details of the first (or earliest acceptable) edition and add '...or any later ed.'

Locations

You will speed up your request considerably if you can mark it with the name of a library or libraries that you are sure possess the item and will lend it (but see below, Unwilling to Lend).

In the UK book locations can be traced only through cooperative cataloguing databases and through the *British Union Catalogue of Latin Americana* (BUCLA). This last is available at the Institute of Latin American Studies of the University of London, and has also been published on microfiche by the Inter Documentation Company (IDC) of Leiden. If you cannot obtain access to a copy of the fiche, you can visit, write or telephone the Institute (or ask your local librarian to do so), to find out if there are any locations recorded for the item you seek. The address and telephone number may be found in the chapter on UNION CATALOGUES AND UNION LISTS (p. 64).

Locations of periodicals and serials can be found in the following general works:

British Union Catalogue of Periodicals (BUCOP). 4 vols. London: Butterworths, 1955–1958. Cumulated *Supplements* bring the work up to 1980).

Serials in the British Library. London: British Library, 1981—. A quarterly record of all new serial titles acquired by the London-based reference collections of the British Library.

Current Serials Received. Boston Spa: British Library Document Supply Centre, 1989. Published annually.

Keyword Index to Serial Titles (KIST). Boston Spa: British Library Document Supply Centre, 1989. This is a microfiche index by keyword to the current and dead periodical holdings of the BLDSC, the Science Reference and Information Service, the Science Museum Library, and Cambridge University Library. Work is proceeding to input the holdings of other libraries. Cumulated annually.

The most thorough list of this kind for Latin American titles available in Britain is the old but still frequently useful series Latin American Serials, compiled by the Committee on Latin America (COLA). The three-volume series consists of:

PORTER, K. I.. *Latin American Economic and Social Serials.* London: Bingley, 1969.

KOSTER, Christopher J. *Latin American History with Politics: A Serials List.* Farnborough: Gregg International, 1973.

HALLEWELL, Laurence. *Latin American Serials 3: Literature with Language, Art and Music.* London: COLA, 1977.

For books and serials held in the US, locations can be traced through databases such as the Online Computer Library Center (OCLC) and the Research Libraries Information Network (RLIN), through the *National Union Catalog* and, for periodicals, through:

> TITUS, Edna Brown. *Union List of Serials in Libraries of the United States and Canada.* 3rd ed. 4 vols. New York: H. W. Wilson, 1965. Lists holdings as of 1949.

> *New Serial Titles.* Washington, DC: Library of Congress, and New York: Bowker, 1973—. Titles for 1950–1970 are contained in four volumes, with a subject-index (1975). The Library of Congress publishes monthly supplements to the main work which cumulate annually and quinquennially.

Submitting the Request

If you have discovered a location or locations, you can now submit your request, giving all the locations you have found with their sources. In the UK, time will be saved if you make your request at a university library; universities can cut through inter-library loan procedures in ways not permitted to public or special libraries. The reverse is frequently true in the United States: public library systems in many large US cities have highly developed inter-library lending networks, which can be speedier in their services than busy university libraries. Remember that the library which holds the work you want may well, as a condition of the loan, not allow its property to be lent for home reading, so make your request in a library where it is convenient for you to spend time consulting the work.

The optimum time for a request where you supply a location is two to three weeks, though if the work happens to be out on loan when the request is received you can assume another two to four weeks waiting time.

No Location Found

If none of the UK sources mentioned above supply a location, there is a chance that the title is not held anywhere in the British Isles. If the work is still in print, it may be possible to persuade your library to purchase it. Most libraries have established procedures by which readers may suggest books for purchase, but it is also a good idea to speak to a senior librarian in the acquisitions section, who may be able to give you an idea as to whether your request is likely to be acceded to. If the work has to be ordered from Latin America, it may well take some time to arrive; count on months rather than weeks.

If it appears that purchase is impossible or will take too long, you can now hand in an inter-library loan request, stating that no locations have been traced (and listing the sources checked). The request will then be forwarded to the British Library Document Supply Centre at Boston Spa. They may still have the item in their own stock (particularly if it is published by an American university press), or they may find a location in their own nationwide union catalogue. This is an enormous file which covers libraries only selectively, and which by reason of its sheer size can never be completely up-to-date. If it is found there, the book should arrive within four weeks, if there is no waiting list; 50% of requests are filled within six days. Otherwise there is an outside chance that BLDSC itself may decide to buy a copy, which will take somewhat longer.

International Loan

If BLDSC has no record of your title and no wish to purchase it, about two months will be spent trying likely libraries in the UK. If this proves unsuccessful, the remaining possibility is to try overseas— though under the IFLA scheme international loan may not be used to supply material still in print. When you made your original request, you may have been asked whether in the event of a failure to locate a copy in this country you wanted an international loan to be attempted. BLDSC will now check back to your library to make sure you wish them to proceed with an international search. There may well be a further delay before the application is finally made.

Once the wheels are set in motion, the time taken to arrange an international loan depends on which foreign country is involved and the efficiency of their own inter-library loan system. For Latin American materials, BLDSC usually asks the United States first— invariably so, if a location is given in NUC, OCLC or RLIN—but may also try the country of origin. The wait is quite unpredictable: one month has been known, five to six months is more usual, and anything up to three years is possible.

Charges

The work involved in checking loan requests and identifying locations frequently involves the borrowing library in considerable expense; in addition, the BLDSC and many loan sources in the US make a charge for the use of their facilities, a charge which likewise falls on the borrowing library. As a result, many libraries have reluctantly decided to pass some of these costs on to the reader by charging him or her for the use of the inter-library loan service. While this may have the beneficial effect of concentrating the researcher's mind on essentials, it can also lead to frustration: payment is made in advance, and does not always ensure a successful outcome. So before embarking on a long and possibly expensive series of inter-library loan requests, you should consult carefully with the responsible staff member in your library. It may save you a considerable amount of money.

Periodical Articles and Short Extracts

If you are trying to obtain a particular article in a periodical, do not request the whole volume. The article may exist as an offprint, and be treated as a monograph in library catalogues. Libraries are also often willing to supply a photocopy of an article even when they are not prepared to lend the periodical itself (see below Unwilling to Lend). Similarly, if you are interested in one small part or chapter of a monograph, it may prove easier to obtain a photocopy of the required extract than to borrow the whole work. More information about photocopying is given under COPYRIGHT AND PHOTOCOPYING (p. 66).

Newspapers

With periodicals it is generally easier to obtain a copy of one article than to borrow a whole issue; with newspapers, paradoxically, the reverse is the case. When libraries obtain their newspapers in microform (as many do) it is more convenient for them to lend a whole reel or fiche (including several issues of the journal) than to track down and copy the exact page and column—assuming that they have been given the correct reference. More and more UK libraries are now acquiring newspapers from Latin America on microfilm, and in the US there are impressive collections available for loan from the Center for Research Libraries in Chicago. For more details see NEWSPAPERS AND NEWS MAGAZINES (p. 190).

Unwilling to Lend

Some libraries do not lend material at all. Others impose varying degrees of restriction on what may be lent. Anything classified (however arbitrarily) as a 'reference book' is usually excluded, as are particularly rare, valuable or fragile items. Works too bulky for parcel post (certain atlases or census returns, for example) are also likely to be restricted. Many libraries refuse to lend periodicals, especially the unbound issues of the current year, and periodical parts are specifically excluded from the IFLA international loan scheme. Readiness to supply photocopies of extracts and periodical articles will be affected by the individual library's obligations under the laws of copyright, which will also affect their willingness to lend theses and dissertations (see COPYRIGHT AND PHOTOCOPYING, p. 66, and THESES AND DISSERTATIONS, p. 221).

In such cases, the only way to see the material may be to visit the library concerned in person. Conditions under which the relevant UK and European libraries admit casual visitors, their opening hours and their lending practices are described in:

MACDONALD, Roger and Carole TRAVIS. *Libraries and Special Collections on Latin America and the Caribbean: A Directory of European Resources.* London: Athlone Press, 1988.

See also LIBRARY RESOURCES ON LATIN AMERICA (p. 73).

LH/HC

Booksellers

It is probably impossible to count the number of book dealers worldwide who take an interest in Latin American materials. Two useful general directories are:

> *International Book Trade Directory*. New York: Bowker, 1979.

> *International Directory of Booksellers*. 1st ed. London: Library Association, and Munich: K. G. Saur, 1978.

Both sources list dealers by country and town. There is also a Latin American equivalent, which includes publishers and distributors:

> *La empresa del libro en America Latina*. 2nd ed. Buenos Aires: Bowker, 1974.

In addition, there are two useful published listings of booksellers who specialise in new and antiquarian Latin American materials, compiled from different sides of the counter:

> BLOCK, David and Howard KARNO. *Directory of Vendors of Latin American Library Materials*. 3rd ed. Bibliography and Reference Series, 22. Madison, WI: SALALM, 1988.

> *List of Booksellers Dealing in Latin Americana and Caribbeana*. Edited by Carole Travis. 2nd ed. London: Institute of Latin American Studies Library, 1987.

BLOCK and KARNO's work is based on information provided by the dealers themselves, while TRAVIS's pamphlet derives from comments supplied by a group of British specialist librarians.

It is important to remember that the addresses and telephone numbers of booksellers frequently change, and all the above directories are thus likely to date quickly. In addition, it must be stated that the dealers mentioned in the remainder of this chapter constitute a brief and personal selection—which is therefore to be treated with caution.

ISBNs and ISSNs

An increasing number of countries participate in the system of International Standard Book Numbers, designed primarily to facilitate the computerization of book ordering. These numbers refer to specific editions—thus, the paperback and hard cover versions of the same text will have distinct ISBNs. They are included for each citation in many dealers' catalogues and lists of books in print, and book orders can generally be facilitated by quoting the ISBN along with the author, title, publisher and date. So far, ISBNs are in general use in the UK, North America and much of Europe; in the last few years they have also appeared in Mexico, Argentina, Colombia, Venezuela, Costa Rica and Brazil. Doubtless the remaining nations of Latin America will adopt the scheme eventually.

There is a corresponding system of International Standard Serial Numbers for periodicals, though the system is applied differently: all issues of each periodical carry the same ISSN.

Books in English

Your local university or other bookshop (in the UK or the US) should be able to obtain any current book published in either country. It is worth remembering that, owing to international bargaining over rights, a text may have one publisher for the UK and another for the US, and possibly a third for Australia or Canada. The appropriate publisher can be traced through national bibliographies or lists of books in print (see NATIONAL BIBLIOGRAPHIES, p. 118). If a local bookshop proves unsatisfactory, materials can be ordered by post from many dealers. For UK materials, a widely used book dealer is:

> W. Heffer and Sons, Ltd.
> 20 Trinity Street
> Cambridge CB2 3NG

and for US publications:

> Blackwell North America
> 1001 Friesmill Road
> Blackwood, NJ 08012

Books in Spanish and Portuguese

Local Suppliers

There are several booksellers in the UK who specialise in new Latin American books. The best known are:

> The Dolphin Book Co. (Tredwr), Ltd.
> Tredwr, Llangranog
> Llandyssul, Dyfed
> Wales SA44 6B4
>
> Grant and Cutler, Ltd.
> 55-57 Great Marlborough Street
> London W1V 2AY

In the US, dealers have tended to specialise further in a single country or a group of countries; these are listed, and usefully indexed, in BLOCK and KARNO (cited above). Central American materials are dealt with by:

> Libros Centroamericanos
> P.O. Box 2203
> Redlands, CA 92373

Books from Bolivia, Colombia, Ecuador and Venezuela can be obtained from a Bolivian dealer who retains a foothold in the US:

> Editorial Inca
> P.O. Box 164900
> Miami, FL 33116

For Cuban materials, there is a specialist dealer in New York:

> Ediciones Vitral
> P.O. Box 20043
> Greely Square Station
> New York, NY 10001

Books from these and all other parts of the region can usually be obtained from the following two dealers, both of whom also specialise in antiquarian materials:

> Howard Karno Books, Inc.
> P.O. Box 2100
> Valley Center, CA 92082-9998

Libros Latinos
P.O. Box 1103
Redlands, CA 92373

Customers should appreciate that it is good business practice for firms to include in their catalogues some items which are not always in stock; and that it is impossible for any one firm to carry the entire book production of Latin America!

Purchasing Direct

From time to time you may find that a particular work you need cannot be obtained locally. In this case your only recourse is to locate a dealer in the country of publication who is prepared to ship a copy to you. Books purchased in this way may at first sight seem to cost less than those ordered through a UK or US dealer, who will himself have taken care of any problems of shipping, customs clearance, or currency conversion. The fact is that any savings to be made by dealing direct can easily be offset by the extra time and labour involved, unless you are able to place substantial (or at least regularly continuing) orders. Exporting books in single-copy lots from Latin America has in the past been a slow and expensive business, beset by customs and currency regulations. To simplify matters, however, more and more Latin American dealers are now prepared to price their materials in US dollars or sterling, and many even have bank accounts in the US or the UK, making payment much less of a problem. Thus, when buying books directly from Latin America, it is important to comply to the letter with the dealer's instructions about payment, and not to keep him waiting for his money (working capital in the book trade is always short), nor to begrudge him his mark-up over the original published price. Booksellers willing to cope with all the problems of supplying books from Latin America need all the help we can give them.

A mine of useful advice for working with bookdealers can be found in a recent SALALM publication:

ILGEN, William D. and Deborah JAKUBS. *Acquisitions Manual: Guidelines for Librarians, Bookdealers and Publishers.* Bibliography and Reference Series, 21. Madison, WI: SALALM, 1988. Contains hints of value to all book-purchasers.

When you need to contact a dealer in Latin America, your best course is probably to discuss the matter with an experienced librarian in your university library's foreign purchasing department.

Failing that, you might care to choose a supplier from the following list, which has deliberately been kept as brief as possible, and should be used in conjunction with the listings of BLOCK and KARNO and TRAVIS (see above). In this list one supplier is suggested for each major country or area; all have proved reasonably efficient in handling orders for new books, and in many cases for tracing older material. Most of these booksellers issue regular lists of new books.

Argentina: Fernando García Cambeiro
Cochabamba 244
1150 Buenos Aires

Bolivia: Los Amigos del Libro
Casilla 450
Cochabamba

Brazil: Mrs Susan Bach
Rua Martins Ferreira 32
22271 Rio de Janeiro

Caribbean Area:
Alan Moss
4 Hopefield Heights
Paradise Heights
St. Michael
Barbados

Central America:
Literatura de Vientos Tropicales
Apartado 186
Código 1017
San José 2000
Costa Rica

Chile: Herta Berenguer L.
Correo 9
Casilla 16598
Santiago de Chile

Colombia: Libros de Colombia
Apartado Aéreo 12.053
Transversal 39 no. 124-30
Bogotá

Ecuador: Libri Mundi
          Juan Leon Mera 851
          Casilla 3029
          Quito

Mexico: Books from Mexico
          Apartado Postal 22-037
          Delegacion Tlalpan
          14000 México DF

Peru: E. Iturriaga y Cia., SA
          Jirón Ica no. 441
          Casilla 4640
          Lima 1

Uruguay: Librería Linardi y Risso
          Juan Carlos Gomez 1435
          Montevideo

Venezuela: Soberbia, CA
          Residencia Celta III Local 1
          Calle Pedroza
          La Florida
          1050 Caracas

For general notes on corresponding with Latin America, see the chapter on CONTACTS WITH LATIN AMERICA (pp. 345–348).

A considerable amount of material of Latin Americanist interest is also published in Spain and Portugal. Helpful local suppliers are:

Spain: Leon Sánchez Cuesta
          Apodaca 1
          28004 Madrid

Portugal: Livraria Portugal
          Rua do Carmo 70-74
          1200 Lisboa

Periodicals

Hints on periodical purchase are given in the chapter on PERIODIC-ALS (p. 219). Generally speaking, they can be acquired through many of the bookdealers mentioned above, from a subscription agent or direct from the publisher—frequently the easiest way. Preferential subscription rates are often available for professors or students, and sometimes for individuals in general (as opposed to institutions). It is also advisable to pay the extra for airmail delivery: many publishers' wrappings are too flimsy to stand up to the repeated handling involved in sea-mail, and the non-arrival of an issue can be reported much more promptly.

Prices

Prices can differ considerably from one supplier to another, and there may be occasions where an individual dealer seems out of line for a particular item. It should be remembered, however, that many overseas suppliers will add freight and insurance costs to the list price, while others quote an inclusive price. The more expensive firms may also provide a higher standard of service, involving frequent book lists, a rapid turnaround on orders and sympathetic treatment of claims— advantages which compensate for their higher mark-up.

RAM

Bibliographies

General Bibliographies

The section of this book dealing with bibliography—the foundation-stone of serious research in any subject—is divided into three major chapters. SUBJECT BIBLIOGRAPHIES deals with locating books on or about a particular topic; NATIONAL BIBLIOGRAPHIES enables the researcher to trace the bibliographic production emanating from a specific country or region and, to a lesser extent, materials concerning individual countries but originating elsewhere; and PERSONAL BIBLIOGRAPHIES treats the problems involved in finding books by and about individuals, and, more specifically, literary figures. Bibliographies of particular types of research resource will be found elsewhere in the work, under the appropriate chapter headings.

This introductory chapter gives full citations for many of the major works mentioned throughout the book; it also includes references to other important materials that happen to fall into none of the specific bibliographical areas treated elsewhere. It should be remembered that the following lists are not intended to be a comprehensive bibliography of bibliographies: they are merely a guide to some of the more useful general research sources. Actual research methods are treated more fully in the three subsequent chapters.

Bibliographies of Bibliographies

The major interdisciplinary bibliography of separately published bibliographies is now somewhat dated, but still useful for historical information:

> BESTERMAN, Theodore. *A World Bibliography of Bibliographies.* 4th ed. 5 vols. Lausanne: Societas Bibliographica, 1965–1966. Cites bibliographies on all subjects published through 1963, with some later additions.

This can be supplemented by the following index, which attempts to include all bibliographies, whether published separately or included in books or journals:

Bibliographic Index. New York: H. W. Wilson, 1938——. Published three times a year with annual cumulations.

These and the following works should help to initiate the researcher into the reference chain that leads from research guides ('bibliographies of bibliographies of bibliographies') through bibliographies of bibliographies and, hopefully, down to bibliographies of materials pertaining to the topic under consideration.

FOSTER, David William and Virginia Ramos FOSTER. *Manual of Hispanic Bibliography.* 2nd ed. New York: Garland, 1977.

WOODS, Richard D. *Reference Materials on Latin America in English: The Humanities.* Metuchen, NJ: Scarecrow Press, 1980. Arranged alphabetically by author with a subject index.

GEOGHEGAN, Abel Rodolfo. *Obras de referencia de América Latina.* Buenos Aires: Unesco, 1965. Arranged by subject with an author index.

SABOR, Josefina Emilia. *Manual de fuentes de información.* 2nd ed. Buenos Aires: Kapelusz, 1967. Emphasis on Argentina.

There are many specialist bibliographies of bibliographies in the Latin American field, but one set of publications stands head and shoulders above the rest:

GROPP, Arthur E. *A Bibliography of Latin American Bibliographies.* Metuchen, NJ: Scarecrow Press, 1968. Intended as an update of the work of the same title by C. K. JONES (Washington, DC: Government Printing Office, 1942; reprinted New York: Greenwood Press, 1969), this in fact almost doubles the number of references provided in the earlier work. Includes monographs only, published through 1964.

References to bibliographies published in periodicals were reserved for the companion work:

GROPP, Arthur E. *A Bibliography of Latin American Bibliographies Published in Periodicals.* 2 vols. Metuchen, NJ: Scarecrow Press, 1976. Includes periodical literature only, published through 1965.

Supplements have been issued regularly to keep the work up-to-date:

GROPP, Arthur E. *A Bibliography of Latin American Bibliographies: Supplement.* Metuchen, NJ: Scarecrow Press, 1971. Monographs only, 1965–1969.

CORDEIRO, Daniel Raposo. *A Bibliography of Latin American Bibliographies: Social Sciences and Humanities.* Metuchen, NJ: Scarecrow Press, 1979. Includes monographs, 1969–1974, and periodical literature, 1966–1974.

PIEDRACUEVA, Haydée. *A Bibliography of Latin American Bibliographies, 1975–1979: Social Sciences and Humanities.* Metuchen, NJ: Scarecrow Press, 1982. Includes monographs and periodical literature.

LOROÑA, Lionel V. *A Bibliography of Latin American Bibliographies, 1980–1984: Social Sciences and Humanities.* Metuchen, NJ: Scarecrow Press, 1987. Includes monographs and periodical literature.

Annual updates, also edited by LOROÑA, are published by the Seminar on the Acquisition of Latin American Library Materials (SALALM) in its Bibliography and Reference Series, under the title *A Bibliography of Latin American and Caribbean Bibliographies.*

Retrospective Bibliographies

The longest-established (and the longest) bibliography of Americana in general, still frequently cited, is:

SABIN, Joseph. *Bibliotheca Americana: A Dictionary of Books Relating to America, from Its Discovery to the Present Time.* Continued by Wilberforce Eames and completed by R. W. G. Vail. 29 vols. New York: Author, 1868–1892, and Bibliographical Society of America, 1928–1936; reprinted, Amsterdam: Israel, 1961–1962. A pioneering bibliography of the Americas, listing well over 100,000 items.

SABIN has also been reprinted in a handy compact edition, reduced photographically to fit into two volumes (New York: Mini-Print, c.1965). One drawback to the work's consultation was for a long time the lack of indexes; this has now been remedied by:

MOLNAR, John Edgar. *Author-Title Index to Joseph Sabin's Dictionary of Works Relating to America.* 3 vols. Metuchen, NJ: Scarecrow Press, 1974.

A major work of revision is now under way:

THOMPSON, Lawrence Sidney. *The New Sabin*. Troy, NY: Whitston, 1974——. A mammoth attempt to re-describe every one of the books listed in SABIN together with other relevant materials, all indexed by title, subject, joint authors, institutions and agencies.

A not dissimilar work to SABIN, though much shorter and limited to Spanish America, is:

MEDINA, José Toribio. *Bibliotheca Hispano-Americana, 1493–1810*. 7 vols. Santiago: Author, 1898–1907; reprinted, Amsterdam: Israel, 1958–1962. 8,500 titles arranged chronologically. An adjunct to MEDINA's bibliographies of the individual nations of Spanish America (see below under NATIONAL BIBLIOGRAPHIES, pp. 136–139).

Current Bibliographies

For current materials on Latin America in the humanities and social sciences the basic source, and easily the most comprehensive annotated bibliography for the region, is:

Handbook of Latin American Studies (HLAS). Edited by Dolores Moyano Martin. (Cambridge, MA: Harvard University Press, 1936——). Annual. An annotated guide to books, articles and essays on Latin American studies, produced by the Hispanic Division of the Library of Congress. Moved from Harvard to the University of Florida at Gainesville (1948–1978), and is currently published in Austin by the University of Texas Press. Since 1965 alternate volumes have covered the humanities and the social sciences. There is an *Author Index* to the volumes for 1936–1966 (Gainesville, FL: University of Florida, 1968).

For the last decade there has been another regular, annual listing of new publications from and about Latin America:

Bibliographic Guide to Latin American Studies. (Boston, MA: G. K. Hall, 1978——). A cooperative effort between the Benson Latin American Collection of the University of Texas at Austin and the Library of Congress in Washington, DC. Provides subject, author and title listings of recent acquisitions by these two libraries. Valuable for identifying recent books published in Latin America.

The principal research tool for identifying materials published in periodicals is the *Hispanic American Periodicals Index* (HAPI), cited in full in the chapter on PERIODICALS (p. 216).

Language and Country Bibliographies

There are many general bibliographies of Latin American and Hispanic studies limited to materials produced in a particular country or area, or in a particular language or group of languages. Among the listings of English language sources are:

> BAYITCH, Stoyan A. *Latin America and the Caribbean: A Bibliographical Guide to Works in English*. International Legal Studies, vol. 10. Coral Gables, FL: University of Miami Press, 1967. Emphasises law and the social sciences.

> HUMPHREYS, R. A. *Latin American History: A Guide to the Literature in English*. London: Oxford University Press, 1958. Interprets 'history' in a very wide sense, to include most of the social sciences.

Others restrict themselves further to particular periods:

> ALBERICH, José. *Bibliografía anglo-hispánica, 1801–1850: ensayo bibliográfico de libros y folletos relativos a España e Hispanoamérica impresos en Inglaterra en la primera mitad del siglo diecinueve*. Oxford: Dolphin, 1978.

> WILGUS, A. Curtis. *Latin America, Spain and Portugal: A Selected and Annotated Bibliographical Guide to Books Published in the United States, 1954–1974*. Metuchen, NJ: Scarecrow Press, 1977.

Bibliographies also exist for specific types of material, such as translations:

> SHAW, Bradley A. *Latin American Literature in English Translation: An Annotated Bibliography*. New York: New York University Press, 1976.

New books on the region appearing in the UK and North America are given annotated listings in the semi-annual publication:

> *British Bulletin of Publications on Latin America, the Caribbean, Portugal and Spain*. London: Hispanic and Luso-Brazilian

Council, 1949—. Also includes (unannotated) citations of articles in general periodicals and newspapers.

Some of the foreign language materials most often encountered are cited in another SALALM publication:

WOODBRIDGE, Hensley C. and Dan NEWBERRY. *A Basic List of Latin American Materials in Spanish, Portuguese and French.* SALALM Bibliography and Reference Series, 2. Austin, TX: SALALM, 1975. A brief, annotated list of essential works.

Spain is, of course, one of the principal European centres of Latin Americanist research. Many fairly recent sources are cited in:

Bibliografía americanista española, 1935–1963. Seville: Comité Organizador del XXXI Congreso Internacional de Americanistas, 1964.

A major centre for Latin American historical research in Spain has traditionally been Seville, with its transatlantic connections, the Archivo de Indias, the Universidad Hispalense and the Escuela de Estudios Hispano-Americanos (EEHA). A valuable and comprehensive listing of all relevant publications emanating from these and other institutions is included in:

CALDERÓN QUIJANO, José Antonio. *El americanismo en Sevilla, 1900–1980.* Seville: EEHA, 1986.

For more current materials from Spain, there is the important periodical *Historiografía y Bibliografía Americanistas* (Seville: EEHA, 1971–1987). Before its emergence as a separate work, this appeared from 1954 to 1969 as a section of *Anuario de Estudios Americanos* (Seville: EEHA, 1945—); from 1987 it reverted to being a supplement of the same journal. Nor should one forget Sylvia-Lyn HILTON's series of bibliographical articles, 'El americanismo en España', which have been appearing annually since 1982 in *Revista de Indias* (Madrid: Consejo Superior de Investigaciones Científicas, 1940—).

The major source for French titles on the region is:

LAMBERT, Michel. *Bibliographie latino-américaniste: France, 1959–1972.* Mexico City: Institut Français d'Amérique Latine, 1973. This can be supplemented for more recent material by *Bulletin Bibliographique Amérique Latine* (Paris: Recherches sur les Civilisations, 1982—).

Belgian publications are listed in:

Amérique Latine: essai de bibliographie des ouvrages belges, 1875–1962. Brussels: Commission Belge de Bibliographie, 1965.

The Soviet Union, Eastern Europe and other parts of the world are covered in:

OKINSHEVICH, Leo. *Latin America in Soviet Writings: A Bibliography.* Edited by Robert G. Carlton. 2 vols. Baltimore, MD: Johns Hopkins Press for the Library of Congress, 1966.

SABLE, Martin H. *Latin American Studies in the Non-Western World and Eastern Europe: A Bibliography on Latin America in the Languages of Africa, Asia, the Middle East and Eastern Europe, with Transliterations and Translations in English.* Metuchen, NJ: Scarecrow Press, 1970.

Finally, materials published in Latin America can usually be traced through:

Libros en venta en Hispanoamérica y España. 4th ed. 3 vols. San Juan, PR: Melcher, 1988. Revised editions appear every three to four years. The 1988 edition is the first to include a subject index.

Current publications from the region can frequently be found in *Fichero Bibliográfico Hispanoamericano* (New York, 1961—), now published eleven times a year by Melcher Ediciones in San Juan.

TC/RAM

Subject Bibliographies

Introduction

Most research involves the need to compile a bibliography on the subject; the methods and sources will vary depending on the subject area and the resources available within the particular field. The research will also be affected by the strength of the library collections available, the time period and subject being researched and the degree of comprehensiveness you wish to achieve in your research. Given such variables, there is no single course to follow. A basic research strategy for locating important books and articles is outlined below, but it is strongly advised that you consult your library's Latin American bibliographer early on for suggestions regarding the most efficient approach to your particular research topic.

Identifying a Bibliography

Identifying a bibliography of books, articles, essays, pamphlets and so forth on your subject can be a tremendous timesaver, and is often a good beginning point. If a bibliography cannot be identified through the library's subject catalogue, a researcher may turn to a number of publications that serve as subject indexes to bibliographies. The standard general source for locating Latin American bibliographies is:

> *Bibliography of Latin American and Caribbean Bibliographies.* Madison, WI: SALALM, 1986—. Annual. Cites bibliographies appearing either as books or as articles in journals. Five year cumulations have been published by Scarecrow Press.

Two journals that regularly publish bibliographical essays and reviews of the literature on Latin American topics are the *Latin American Research Review* (Albuquerque, NM: University of New Mexico, 1965—) and the *Inter-American Review of Bibliography/Revista Interamericana de Bibliografía* (Washington, DC: Organization of

American States, 1951—). These bibliographical reviews are often timely and fairly comprehensive; they are regularly indexed in the annual *Bibliography of Latin American and Caribbean Bibliographies* and *Hispanic American Periodicals Index* (HAPI). These sources may be supplemented by the *Bibliographic Index* (New York, H. W. Wilson, 1937—), published three times a year with annual cumulations. For locating earlier bibliographies on Latin American subjects, one should refer to Arthur GROPP's *A Bibliography of Latin American Bibliographies* (1968) and *A Bibliography of Latin American Bibliographies Published in Periodicals* (1976), together with their supplements (see pp. 88–89). Library catalogues, annual bibliographies and indexes and broad subject bibliographies, included below in this chapter, may also lead to other bibliographies tailored to your topic.

Extending the Search

While a good published bibliography is an invaluable resource, it may be more selective than you wish (for example, limited to English language sources, or to manuscripts in a particular archive) and will almost certainly need updating (the date of stated coverage is generally at least a year or two prior to its date of publication). In order to obtain thorough, up-to-date coverage of the topic, you will thus need to go beyond the sources listed in published bibliographies.

The library catalogue is the first step. Many researchers understandably experience problems in using catalogues because they vary so widely from one library to another, despite the fairly universal use in North America of Library of Congress subject headings. The vagaries of subject catalogues and their use are discussed in full in the chapter LIBRARY CATALOGUES (p. 32).

Because many libraries lack detailed subject catalogues, published catalogues of the collections of specialised libraries can be extremely useful. Specialised libraries usually have stronger collections, and also provide increased access to their resources by a greater degree of subject indexing in their catalogues. Printed catalogues of this kind may help, for instance, to identify essays in books or articles in journals held by the researcher's own library, as well as more specialised Latin American publications which could be borrowed. Some of the printed catalogues are valuable for researching a particular subject or country—the University of Texas's *Catalog of the Latin American Collection*, for example, is particularly strong in Mexican acquisitions (for further details, see the chapter, PUBLISHED LIBRARY CATALOGUES, p. 46).

One of the most useful subject catalogues is the recent annual publication, *Bibliographic Guide to Latin American Studies* (Boston, MA: G. K. Hall, 1978—). A cooperative effort between the Library of Congress and the Benson Latin American Collection of the University of Texas at Austin, the catalogue provides subject, author and title listings of recent acquisitions by these two great libraries. It is particularly useful for identifying recent books published in Latin America, and can serve as a helpful substitute in libraries without their own subject catalogues.

Another good source for tracing books by subject is RLIN (Research Libraries Information Network), an online catalogue of the holdings of a number of large American libraries offering keyword and subject access. Unfortunately, RLIN is available to researchers directly at only a limited number of libraries; however, the Latin American bibliographer may be able to conduct a search of the files for you upon request. (See also DATABASES, p. 229).

The annual *Handbook of Latin American Studies* (Cambridge, MA: Harvard University Press, 1936—) forms an essential part of the research strategy. Interdisciplinary in scope, it includes annotated citations to key books, articles and essays, and provides the researcher with the most comprehensive subject bibliography for Latin American studies. Produced by the Hispanic Division of the Library of Congress and edited by Dolores Moyano Martin, it is currently published by the University of Texas Press at Austin. Alternate volumes cover the humanities and the social sciences. There is an *Author Index* to the volumes for 1936–1966 (Gainesville, FL: University of Florida, 1968).

A new work, due to appear in 1990, is intended to serve as a beginning point for students and scholars conducting research on topics in the social sciences and humanities:

COVINGTON, Paula Anne. *Latin American and Caribbean Studies: A Critical Guide to Research Sources.* (Westport, CT: Greenwood Press, forthcoming 1990). A collection of subject biblio-graphies compiled by specialist librarians, each of which is preceded by a general article discussing major works and research trends on the subject written by a leading scholar in the field.

The principal source for locating periodical articles on Latin American topics is the *Hispanic American Periodicals Index* (HAPI; see p. 216). Published annually, it is the most comprehensive source for periodicals on Latin American topics worldwide and is particularly useful for periodicals published in Latin America.

You may want to supplement your search with other disciplinary periodical indexes, such as the *Social Sciences Index* (New York: H. W. Wilson, 1974—); the *Public Affairs Information Service Bulletin* (PAIS) (New York: Public Affairs Information Service, 1915—); its companion publication, *Foreign Language Index* (New York: Public Affairs Information Service, 1972—); or the *MLA International Bibliography* (New York: Modern Language Association of America, 1922—). These sources include articles on Latin American topics appearing in journals of a broader scope, and some of them are updated quarterly or more frequently.

Tables of contents of journals too recent to be covered by periodical indexes appear in contents-listing publications, such as *Contents of Periodicals on Latin America* (Miami, FL: University of Miami, Graduate School of Interamerican Studies, 1983—), *Current Contents: Social and Behavioral Sciences* (Philadelphia, PA: Institute for Scientific Information, 1969—), *Current Contents: Arts and Humanities* (Philadelphia, PA: Institute for Scientific Information, 1979—), and *ABC Pol Sci: Advance Bibliography of Contents: Political Science and Government* (Santa Barbara, CA: ABC/Clio, 1969—). Many computerised abstracts and indexes are also available in both online and compact disc formats. Check with your library to determine the availability of such services, which can provide you with a quick, up-to-date bibliography on many subjects. See also the chapter on DATABASES (p. 229).

The remainder of this chapter consists of brief introductions to the bibliography of a few major areas of study. The sources included are, of necessity, highly selective: in most cases they identify only a few general bibliographies and basic source works, with occasional hints on how best to approach the subject. In some cases, where it seemed that more extensive coverage was required, additional sources are provided. For information on new publications and advice on the most appropriate research sources and methods, you are once again advised to consult with the subject specialist or Latin American bibliographer in your library.

PAC

Agriculture

As literature on agriculture is normally organised by commodity rather than by country, material on Latin America tends to be scattered. Information, particularly on the scientific and technical aspects, can be located from primary sources such as books, periodicals and conference proceedings, from secondary sources such as abstracting and indexing services in printed form or as computerised databases. Published reports from organisations, both national and international, involved in the agriculture of Latin America may also provide material of interest.

Primary Sources

Two comprehensive general reference books are:

> BLANCHARD, J. Richard and Lois FARRELL. *Guide to Sources for Agriculture and Biological Research*. Berkeley, CA: University of California Press, 1981. Arranged in broad subject fields; the section on 'Abstracts and Indexes, General Bibliographies' contains a regional breakdown including Latin America, and has some very useful bibliographies.

> *Information Sources in Agriculture and Food Science*. Edited by G. P. Lilley. London: Butterworths, 1981. The chapter on tropical agriculture is of particular relevance to Latin America.

The most up-to-date materials are likely to appear as journal articles, reports or conference proceedings. Periodicals can be located through *Ulrich's International Periodicals Directory*, but the best access to recent information is through indexing and abstracting services.

Secondary Sources

International periodical abstracting and indexing services relevant to agriculture include :

> *Indice agrícola de América Latina y el Caribe*. San José: Centro Interamericano de Documentación e Información Agrícola, 1975—. Continues *Bibliografía agrícola latinoamericana*, 1966–1974.

> *Agrindex*. Rome: Food and Agriculture Organization, 1973—.

> *Abstracts on Tropical Agriculture*. Amsterdam: Koninklijk Instituut voor de Tropen, 1975—.

> *Bibliography of Agriculture* Phoenix, AZ: Oryx Press, 1942—.

Also useful are the 50 or so titles published by the Commonwealth Agricultural Bureau International at Wallingford in its series CABI Abstracts. Sources of purely national coverage are listed in BLAN-CHARD above. Much of this material is available on computer and can be searched online: one database is AGRICOLA, run by the National Agricultural Library of the US Department of Agriculture (Beltsville, MD), which also produces bibliographies of current interest.

Organisations

Of the many organisation actively involved in agriculture, the important ones relevant to Latin America include the Food and Agriculture Organization of the United Nations (FAO), the Inter-American Information System for Agricultural Science (AGRINTER), the Centro Interamericano de Documentación e Información Agrícola (CIDIA), the Centro Internacional de Agricultura Tropical (CIAT), the Centro Internacional de Mejoramiento de Maíz y Trigo (CIMMYT), the Instituto Interamericano de Cooperación para la Agricultura (IICA) and the Asociación Interamericana de Bibliotecarios y Documentalistas Agrícolas (AIBDA). Further details can be obtained from the principal directories (see HANDBOOKS, GUIDES AND DIRECTORIES, p. 162). Access to their publications is best obtained through library author catalogues.

PW

Anthropology

The standard textbooks on Amerindian life and culture are:

STEWARD, Julian Haynes. *Handbook of South American Indians*. 7 vols. Washington, DC: Government Printing Office, US Bureau of American Ethnology, 1946–1959; reprinted, New York: Cooper Square, 1963.

Handbook of Middle American Indians. Edited by Robert Wauchope. 16 vols. Austin, TX: University of Texas Press, 1964–1976.

The most comprehensive bibliography of the subject is now nearly thirty years old, and does not cover the whole of Latin America:

O'LEARY, Timothy J. *Ethnographic Bibliography of South America.*
New Haven, CT: Human Relations Area Files, 1963. Ex-
cludes Panama and points north, as well as the Caribbean
Islands.

This can be supplemented by the the semi-annual *Boletín Bibliográfico
de Antropología Americana* published in Mexico City by the Comité de
Antropología of the Pan-American Institute for Geography and
History from 1937 to 1979; in 1980 it was superseded by the *Boletín
de Antropología Americana.* A more general, but very complete listing
is the useful annual *International Bibliography of Social and Cultural
Anthropology/Bibliographie internationale d'anthropologie sociale et culturelle*
(London: Routledge, 1958—).

There are several bibliographies available covering individual
countries and areas, of which a good example is:

MARTÍNEZ, Héctor et al. *Bibliografía indigena andina peruana,
1900–1968.* Lima: Centro de Estudios de Población y Desarrollo, 1969.

For a comprehensive guide to Mexicans in the United States, there
is:

ROBINSON, Barbara J. and J. C. ROBINSON. *The Mexican
American: A Critical Guide to Research Aids.* Greenwich, CT: JAI
Press, 1980.

RAM

Art and Architecture

Listed below are the basic general sources for the study of Latin
American art history. Unless stated otherwise, all of them encompass the pre-Columbian period to the present, and include information on architecture and folk arts as well as painting, drawing
and (usually) sculpture.

Encyclopaedias

The *Encyclopedia of World Art* in 16 volumes (New York: H. W.
Wilson, 1959–1983) is a useful introductory source for major artists,
artistic forms and movements and national art histories. The only
encyclopaedia that is devoted entirely to Latin America is:

Enciclopedia del arte en América. Edited by Vicente Gesualdo. 5
vols. Buenos Aires: OMEBA, 1968. Two volumes cover art

history arranged by country, and the remaining three contain biographies of individual artists, arranged alphabetically.

Handbooks and Guides

The most recent and thorough bibliographic guide is:

Handbook of Latin American Art/Manual de arte latinoamericano: A Bibliographical Compilation. Edited by Joyce Waddell Bailey. 3 vols. Santa Barbara, CA: ABC/Clio, 1984—. Volume 1, in two parts, contains general references and material on nineteenth and twentieth century art (11,000 references), while volume 2 (1986) covers the colonial period (5,200 references); volume 3 (forthcoming) will deal with ancient art. Extensively indexed.

Much older, but still useful for historical information, is:

Guide to the Art of Latin America. Edited by Robert C. Smith and Elizabeth Wilder. Washington, DC: Hispanic Division, Library of Congress, 1948.

The best general introductory texts are probably:

KUBLER, George and Martin SORIA. *Art and Architecture in Spain and Portugal and Their American Dominions, 1500–1800.* Harmondsworth: Penguin Books, 1959. A basic survey with more than 400 illustrations, extensive footnotes, a bibliography and indexes of names, places and monuments.

CATLIN, Stanton L. and Terence GRIEDER. *Art of Latin America Since Independence.* New Haven, CT: Yale University Press, 1966. Exhibition catalogue, with high quality plates and excellent short introductory essays. Also contains a useful bibliography and biographical entries on 275 artists, indexed by country.

DE SA REGO, Stella M. *Modern Brazilian Painting: A Curriculum Guide.* Albuquerque, NM: University of New Mexico, Latin American Institute, 1986.

Bibliographies and Indexes

The most complete ongoing bibliographical source for recent information on Latin American art and artists is the semi-annual:

Répertoire international de la littérature de l'art (RILA). Williams-town, MA: College Art Association of America, 1975—. Indexes books, articles, exhibition catalogues, proceedings and doctoral dissertations from western Europe and the US (10,000 items annually). Available online from 1986 on DIALOG under the title Art Literature International.

Plans are currently underway to combine RILA (now part of the Getty Museum Art History Program) with the long-established *Répertoire de l'Art et l'Archéologie* (Paris, 1910—). The combined publication will be expanded to include materials published in Latin America and elsewhere.

Two other good sources for journal articles are the *Art Index* (New York: H. W. Wilson, 1933—) and the *Hispanic American Periodicals Index* (see p. 216). Information on all aspects of post-1800 art, architecture and design can be found in the semi-annual *Artbibliographies Modern* (Santa Monica, CA: ABC/Clio, 1969—).

Latin American art of the twentieth century (including sculpture and photography) is covered by an unannotated bibliography of books, exhibition catalogues and serial titles (but not articles):

> FINDLAY, James A. *Modern Latin American Art: A Bibliography.* Art Reference Collection, 3. Westport, CT: Greenwood Press, 1983.

Catalogues

> *Catalogue of the Library of the Museum of Modern Art, New York.* Volume 14: Latin American Archive. Boston, MA: G. K. Hall, 1976.

BGV

Economics

A basic guide to the literature of economics is:

> *Information Sources in Economics.* Edited by John Fletcher. 2nd ed. London: Butterworths, 1984. Contains chapters on libraries and literature searches, types of resources and specific branches of economics. Prepared by a team of UK librarians and economists.

Another comprehensive reference work is:

Encyclopedia of Economics. Edited by Douglas Greenwald. New York: McGraw Hill, 1982. Contains around 300 articles on concepts, institutions and historical events, but no biographical entries.

Current bibliographical material may be found in the annual *Bibliographic Guide to Business and Economics* (Boston, MA: G. K. Hall, 1975—), a dictionary catalogue of all the relevant materials catalogued during the year by the Research Libraries of New York Public Library, with additional entries from the Library of Congress; and in the annual *International Bibliography of Economics/Bibliographie internationale de science économique* (London: Routledge, 1954—). The PAIS publications listed below in the Social Sciences section will also be found useful.

For Latin American materials, two dated but still useful guides are:

Economic Literature of Latin America: A Tentative Bibliography. 2 vols. Cambridge, MA: Harvard University Press, 1935–1936. Prepared by the Bureau for Economic Research in Latin America, and arranged geographically by country or region.

Wirtschaft und Entwicklung Lateinamerikas. 3 vols. Hamburg: Institut für Iberoamerika-Kunde, 1967.

A newer, annotated guide to the economic history of the region, organised on the same lines as GRIFFIN's guide to the historical literature (cited below under History), is:

CORTES CONDE, Roberto and Stanley J. STEIN. *Latin America: A Guide to Economic History, 1830–1930.* Boston, MA: G. K. Hall, 1977. Includes a general bibliography covering the whole region, followed by separate sections for Argentina, Brazil, Chile, Colombia, Mexico and Peru.

Discussions of various information sources on Latin American economic conditions can also be found in *Latin American Economic Issues: Information Needs and Sources: Papers* of SALALM XXVI, 1981 (Madison, WI: SALALM, 1984).

RAM

Education

A general introduction to educational research can be found in:

WOODBURY, Marda. *A Guide to Sources of Educational Information.* 2nd ed. Arlington, VA: Information Resources, 1982.

and an impressive overview of current scholarship is contained in:

The International Encyclopedia of Education: Research and Studies. 10 vols. Oxford: Pergamon Press, 1985.

Probably the best retrospective bibliography of education in general is the published catalogue of the Teachers College Library of Columbia University:

Dictionary Catalog of the Teachers College Library. 36 vols. Boston, MA: G. K. Hall, 1970. Contains more than 400,000 items; three supplements were published covering 1970–1976 accessions (1971–1977, 17 volumes in all), and the catalogue is now continued by the annual *Bibliographic Guide to Education* (Boston, MA: G. K. Hall, 1979—).

The major regional bibliography is:

LAUERHASS, Ludwig, Jr. and Vera Lúcia Oliveira de Araujo HAUGSE. *Education in Latin America: A Bibliography.* Los Angeles, CA: UCLA Latin American Center, and Boston, MA: G. K. Hall, 1980.

RAM

Government and Politics

An essential introduction to the study of political science is:

Information Sources in Politics and Political Science: A Survey Worldwide. Edited by Dermot Englefield and Gavin Drewry. London: Butterworths, 1984. A basic reference work, with chapters on available resources, approaches to the study of politics and government and area-based sources. Restricted to English language materials, but nonetheless comprehensive.

The current South American dimension is well covered in:

Latin American Politics: A Historical Bibliography. Clio Bibliography Series, 16. Santa Barbara, CA: ABC/Clio, 1984. Abstracts more than 3,000 items published between 1973 and 1982 dealing with twentieth century Latin American and Caribbean politics.

This can be supplemented by the annual *International Bibliography of Political Science/Bibliographie internationale de science politique* (London: Routledge, 1954—), and, for periodical articles, by *ABC Pol Sci: Advance Bibliography of Contents: Political Science and Government* (Santa Barbara, CA: ABC/Clio, 1969—). Further references can be traced through the PAIS publications cited below under Social Sciences.

A good introductory historical text is:

SKIDMORE, Thomas E. and Peter H. SMITH. *Modern Latin America*. Oxford: Oxford University Press, 1984.

This may be supplemented by:

ROSSI, E. E. and J. PLANO. *The Latin American Political Dictionary*. Santa Barbara, CA: ABC/Clio, 1980.

Major topics in Latin American political science are dealt with in more specialised bibliographies, of which the following are good examples:

Agrarian Reform in Latin America: An Annotated Bibliography. Compiled by the Staff of the Land Tenure Center Library. Madison, WI: University of Madison-Wisconsin, Land Tenure Center, 1974.

CHILCOTE, Ronald H. *Revolution and Structural Change in Latin America: A Bibliography on Ideology, Development and the Radical Left, 1930–1965*. 2 vols. Hoover Institution Bibliographical Series, 40. Stanford, CA: Stanford University, 1970.

TRASK, David F. et al. *A Bibliography of United States–Latin American Relations since 1810*. Lincoln, NB: University of Nebraska Press, 1968. This has been supplemented by:

MEYER, Michael C. *A Supplement to A Bibliography of United States–Latin American Relations since 1810*. Lincoln, NB: University of Nebraska Press, 1979.

RAM

History

The major bibliographies for Latin American history are:

GRIFFIN, Charles C. *Latin America: A Guide to the Historical Literature*. Austin, TX: University of Texas Press for the Conference on Latin American History, 1971. Well-annotated entries, prepared by specialist scholars, for more than 7,000 works on general and specialised topics. The cutoff date for inclusion was 1966.

WERLICH, David P. *Research Tools for Latin American Historians: A Select, Annotated Bibliography.* New York: Garland, 1980. 'A classified, annotated bibliography of almost 1,400 reference works, compendiums of source materials and periodicals useful to Latin American historians.'

Older materials are well covered in:

WILGUS, A. Curtis. *The Historiography of Latin America: A Guide to Historical Writing, 1500–1800.* Metuchen, NJ: Scarecrow Press, 1975. Organised in three sections, covering the sixteenth, seventeenth and eighteenth centuries, each subdivided by area; discusses the work of more than 1,000 historians.

For the nineteenth and twentieth centuries, a later work is of use:

THOMAS, Jack Ray. *Biographical Dictionary of Latin American Historians and Historiography.* Westport, CT: Greenwood Press, 1984. Alphabetical arrangement, with useful bibliographical references under each entry. Extensively indexed.

For materials in Spanish on the colonial period, the best source is still probably:

SÁNCHEZ ALONSO, Benito. *Fuentes de la historia española e hispanoamericana: ensayo de bibliografía sistemática...* 3rd ed. 3 vols. Madrid: Consejo Superior de Investigaciones Científicas, 1952. 1st ed. published 1919.

Two basic historical texts, obviously destined to hold the field for the foreseeable future, both commenced publication in the the same year:

The Cambridge History of Latin America. Edited by Leslie Bethell. 8 vols. Cambridge: Cambridge University Press, 1984—. Written by an international team of historians, with bibliographical essays of major importance designed to update GRIFFIN (see above). Five volumes have been published to date, covering the colonial period (1-2), the Independence period to c.1870 (3) and c.1870–c.1930 (4-5).

New Iberian World: A Documentary History of the Discovery and Settlement of Latin America to the Early 17th Century. Edited with commentaries by John H. Parry and Robert G. Keith. 5 vols. New York: Times Books, 1984. Translations, 'ruthlessly excerpted', of original texts and documents; the volumes cover: 1, The Conquerors and the Conquered; 2, The Caribbean; 3, Central America and Mexico; 4, The Andes; 5, Coastlines, Rivers and Forests.

There is no wholly satisfactory one-volume history of Latin America, but the two listed below are useful, considering their dates:

HERRING, Hubert. *A History of Latin America, from the Beginnings to the Present.* 3rd ed. London: Cape, 1968. 1st ed. published 1955.

COLLIER, Simon. *From Cortés to Castro: An Introduction to the History of Latin America, 1492–1973.* London: Secker and Warburg, and New York: Macmillan, 1973. Readable and thought-provoking, but follows a non-chronological arrangement.

RAM

Linguistics

American Spanish

A selection of references to bibliographies of works on the Spanish of South, Central and North America will be found in:

BACH, Kathryn F. and Glanville PRICE. *Romance Linguistics and the Romance Languages: A Bibliography of Bibliographies.* London: Grant and Cutler, 1977. Annotated.

WOODBRIDGE, Hensley C. *Guide to Reference Works for the Study of the Spanish Language and Literature and Spanish American Literature.* New York: Modern Language Association of America, 1987.

Sections devoted to the language of Spanish America will be found in several bibliographies of Hispanic linguistics, notably:

HUBERMAN, Gisela Bialik. *Mil obras de lingüística española o hispanoamericana: un ensayo de síntesis crítica.* Madrid: Plaza Mayor, 1973.

The most exhaustive specialised bibliographies are:

SOLÉ, Carlos Alberto. *Bibliografía sobre el español en América, 1920–1967.* Washington, DC: Georgetown University Press, 1970.

NICHOLS, Mary Wallis. *A Bibliographical Guide to Materials on American Spanish.* Cambridge, MA: Harvard University Press, 1941.

For a comprehensive classified bibliography on Spanish as spoken in the United States, covering all the main Hispanic ethnic groups, see:

TESCHER, Richard V. et al. *Spanish and English of United States Hispanos: A Critical Annotated Linguistic Bibliography.* Arlington, VA: Center for Applied Linguistics, 1975.

Brazilian Portuguese

Major bibliographies of the Portuguese language in Brazil are:

DIETRICH, Wolf. *Bibliografia da língua portuguesa do Brasil.* Tübingen: Günter Narr, 1980. Annotated.

HOGE, Henry W. *A Selective Bibliography of Luso-Brazilian Linguistics.* Milwaukee, WI: University of Wisconsin-Milwaukee, 1966.

Indian Languages

Greatly to be recommended for the classification of the indigenous languages of South America, with extensive bibliographies, are:

TOVAR, Antonio. *Catálogo de las lenguas de América del Sur: enumeración con indicaciones tipológicas, bibliografía y mapas.* Buenos Aires: Sudamericana, 1961. Continued in a *Suplemento* by Consuelo Larrucea de Tovar (Florence: Valmartina, 1972).

LOUKOTKA, Čestmír. *Classification of South American Indian Languages.* Los Angeles, CA: UCLA Latin American Center, 1967.

Creole Languages

REINECKE, John E. *A Bibliography of Pidgin and Creole Languages.* Honolulu: University Press of Hawaii, 1975.

Current Bibliography

Keeping up with the current critical output on Latin American linguistics involves a regular check of serial bibliographies, of which the most important for Hispanic and Amerindian languages is:

> *Bibliographie linguistique.* Utrecht: Spectrum, 1949–1978; Dordrecht: Nijhoff, 1980—. Published annually (with a time lag of around three years) by the Comité International Permanent des Linguistes.

A current bibliography of Pidgin and Creole studies is provided in the thrice-yearly *Carrier Pidgin* (Stanford, CA: Stanford University Press, 1973—).

These may be supplemented by the *MLA International Bibliography* (New York: Modern Language Association of America, 1922—), as well as by such general works as the *Hispanic American Periodicals Index* (HAPI).

JW

Literature of Brazil

The most comprehensive histories of Brazilian literature are:

> ROMERO, Silvio. *História da literatura brasileira.* 5th ed. 5 vols. Rio de Janeiro: José Olympio, 1953–1954. First published in 1888, but still invaluable.

> COUTINHO, Afrânio. *A literatura no Brasil.* 3rd ed. 6 vols. Rio de Janeiro: José Olympio/EDUFF, 1986. Good bibliography.

Amongst dictionaries of Brazilian literature, the following are handiest for reference use:

> PAES, José Paulo and Massaud MOISÉS. *Pequeno dicionário de literatura brasileira.* São Paulo: Cultrix, 1967.

> FOSTER, David William. *A Dictionary of Contemporary Brazilian Authors.* Tempe, AZ: Arizona State University, 1981.

For biographical emphasis, see the *Dicionário literário brasileiro ilustrado* of Raimundo de MENEZES (see below under PERSONAL BIBLIOGRAPHIES, p. 146).

Of the bibliographies, one stands out above all others:

CARPEAUX, Otto Maria. *Pequena bibliografia crítica da literatura brasileira.* 3rd ed. Rio de Janeiro: Letras e Artes, 1964. Excellent general and personal bibliographies, including primary and secondary sources; deficient only in its index.

Also recommendable are:

TOPETE, José Manuel. *A Working Bibliography of Brazilian Literature.* Gainesville, FL: University of Florida Press, 1957.

HARMON, Ronald M. and Bobby J. CHAMBERLAIN. *Brazil: A Working Bibliography in Literature, Linguistics, Humanities and the Social Sciences.* Tempe, AZ: Arizona State University, 1975.

ZUBATSKY, David. *Latin American Literary Authors: An Annotated Guide to Bibliographies.* Metuchen, NJ: Scarecrow Press, 1986.

GALANTE DE SOUSA, José. 'Bibliografia.' In *Introdução ao estudo da literatura brasileira,* edited by José Brito Broca. Rio de Janeiro: Instituto Nacional do Livro, 1963, pp. 75–241.

An important bibliography of works published in Brazil up to 1808 is:

MORAES, Rubens Borba de. *Bibliografia brasileira do período colonial.* São Paulo: Instituto de Estudos Brasileiros, 1969.

A useful books-in-print for modern Brazilian literature is the list entitled *Literatura brasileira* (São Paulo: Nobel, 1985), including 3,000 titles extracted from the *Catálogo brasileiro de publicações* (see p. 121). It is not clear if this will be updated.

Other relevant reference works will be found in the chapter PERSONAL BIBLIOGRAPHIES (p. 140).

JW

Literature of Spanish America

The quantity and diversity of Spanish American literature and of attendant literary criticism make a brief bibliographical introduction impossible. However, a starting point is:

BRYANT, Shasta M. *A Selective Bibliography of Bibliographies of Hispanic American Literature.* 2nd ed. Austin, TX: University of Texas, Institute of Latin American Studies, 1976.

Among bibliographies, the following are useful:

CARRERA ANDRADE, Jorge. *Bibliografía general de la literatura latinoamericana*. Edited by Hector Luis Arena. Paris: Unesco, 1972.

FLORES, Angel. *Bibliografía de escritores hispanoamericanos, 1609–1974*. New York: Gordian Press, 1975.

RELA, Walter. *Guía bibliográfica de la literatura hispanoamericana desde el siglo XIX hasta 1970*. Buenos Aires: Casa Pardo, 1971.

This is supplemented by another work of the same author:

RELA, Walter. *Spanish American Literature: A Selected Bibliography/Literatura hispanoamericana: bibliografía selecta, 1970–1980*. East Lansing, MI: Michigan State University, 1982.

A country-by-country introduction to Latin American literature is provided by:

Handbook to Latin American Literature. Compiled by David William Foster. New York: Garland, 1987.

Foster is also the compiler of several bibliographical guides to individual countries, including Argentina and Mexico (see pp. 148–149).

Among the many general histories of Latin American literature, the following can be recommended:

ANDERSON-IMBERT, Enrique. *Historia de la literatura hispanoamericana*. 2nd ed. Mexico: Fondo de Cultura Económica, 1954. This work has been translated into English as *Spanish-American Literature: A History* (Detroit, MI: Wayne State University Press, 1963).

MADRIGAL, Luis Iñigo. *Historia de la literatura hispanoamericana*. 3 vols. Madrid: Cátedra, 1982—. Two volumes published to date.

GALLAGHER, D. P. *Modern Latin American Literature*. London: Oxford University Press, 1973. Does not attempt to be comprehensive, but is full of insights.

Other reference works on Latin American literature are discussed in the chapter, PERSONAL BIBLIOGRAPHIES (p. 140).

GW

Literature of the West Indies

A general history of and introduction to Commonwealth Caribbean writing can be found in:

KING, Bruce. *West Indian Literature*. London: Macmillan, 1979. Contains a general history, followed by chapters on eight major writers.

DANCE, Daryl Cumber. *Fifty Caribbean Writers: A Bio-Bibliographical Critical Sourcebook*. Westport, CT: Greenwood Press, 1986.

Among the available bibliographies are:

MERRIMAN, S. E. and J. CHRISTIAN. *Commonwealth Caribbean Writers: A Bibliography*. Georgetown: Guyana Public Library, 1970.

ALLIS, Jeannette B. *West Indian Literature: An Index to Criticism, 1930–1975*. Boston, MA: G. K. Hall, 1981.

More current material may be traced via the 'Annual Bibliography of Commonwealth Literature' published in the December issue of the *Journal of Commonwealth Literature* (London: Heinemann, 1965—), currently published in Oxford by Hans Zell.

RAM

Music

Bibliography

The most useful general guide to literature on Latin American music will be found in:

MARCO, Guy A. et al. *Information on Music: A Handbook of Reference Sources in European Languages*. Volume 2: The Americas. Littleton, CO: Libraries Unlimited, 1977.

For current material, *RILM (Repertoire international de la littérature musicale) Abstracts of Music Literature* (New York: International Association of Music Libraries, 1967—) provides a comprehensive bibliography of both books and periodical literature with short abstracts. It is well indexed, but has at present a six-year time lag.

Although now twenty-five years out-of-date, the following work remains a basic tool:

CHASE, Gilbert. *A Guide to the Music of Latin America.* 2nd ed. Washington, DC: Pan American Union, 1962; reprinted, New York: AMS Press, 1972.

A briefer, but more recent, listing is:

KUSS, Malena. 'Toward a Comprehensive Approach to Latin American Music Bibliography: Theoretical Foundations for Reference Sources and Research Materials.' In *Latin American Masses and Minorities: Their Images and Realities: Papers* of SALALM XXX, 1985. Madison, WI: SALALM, 1987, vol.2, pp. 615–663.

For the Caribbean, two important resources are:

STEVENSON, Robert M. *A Guide to Caribbean Music History.* Lima: Ediciones Cultura, 1975.

STEVENSON, Robert M. 'Caribbean Music History: A Selective Annotated Bibliography.' *Inter-American Music Review* 4 (1981), pp. 1–112.

Encyclopaedias and General Works

The major current musical encyclopaedia is:

The New Grove Dictionary of Music and Musicians. Edited by Stanley Sadie. 20 vols. London: Macmillan, 1980. This has useful articles under individual countries and musicians, covering both art and folk music, as well as a general article 'Latin America'. There are good bibliographies.

The best general introduction to Latin American music, with further bibliographical guides, is:

BÉHAGUE, Gérard Henri. *Music in Latin America: An Introduction.* Prentice-Hall History of Music Series, 11. Englewood Cliffs, NJ: Prentice-Hall, 1979.

The standard source for bio-bibliographical information on Latin America composers is still in progress:

Compositores de América: datos biográficos y catálogos de sus obras. Washington, DC: Pan-American Union (now Organization of American States), 1955—.

Individual countries have the following national encyclopaedias:

ARIZAGA, Rodolfo. *Enciclopedia de la música argentina.* Buenos Aires: Fondo Nacional de las Artes, 1971.

Enciclopédia da música brasileira: erudita, folclórica e popular. São Paulo: Art Editora, 1977.

OROVIO, Helio. *Diccionario de la musica cubana, técnico y biográfico.* Havana: Letras Cubanas, 1981.

The most comprehensive work covering Mexico is:

ESTRADA, Julio, ed. *La música de México.* Mexico City: UNAM, Instituto de Investigaciones Estéticas, 1984—. Part 1, 'Historia,' is in 5 volumes, part 2 consists of a 'Guía bibliográfica' (689 items) by Sylvana Young Osorio, and part 3 is a four-volume anthology. The set is to finish with a 'Diccionario de música y músicos mexicanos'.

Periodicals

The three main current journals, all with strong review sections, are:

Inter-American Music Review. Edited by Robert Stevenson. Los Angeles, CA: Theodore Front, 1978—.

Revista de música latinoamericana/Latin American Music Review. Edited by Gérard Béhague, Austin, TX: University of Texas Press, 1980—. This is effectively the successor to:

Anuario interamericano de investigación musical/Yearbook for Inter-American Musical Research. Edited by Gilbert Chase. New Orleans, LA: Tulane University; subsequently, Austin, TX: University of Texas, 1965–1975.

Revista musical chilena. Santiago: Universidad de Chile, 1945—.

For periodical indexing services, in addition to the *RILM Abstracts of Music Literature* (see above), the *Music Index* (Detroit, MI: Information Coordinators, 1949—) is issued in monthly parts (well up-to-date) with annual cumulations, which are several years in arrears. The *Hispanic American Periodicals Index* (HAPI) covers all three of the journals listed above.

PWJ

Science and Technology

The amount of scientific literature published in and about Latin America is substantial. This is perhaps to be expected in areas such as natural history, as the unique fauna and flora of Southern and Central America have long attracted scholarly attention (*Ulrich's International Periodicals Directory* lists eleven current Latin American serials in the field of botany alone). It is, however, less widely realised that much original research in areas of advanced technology is now being conducted in Latin American countries, most notably Brazil.

Scientific indexing and abstracting journals indigenous to Latin America tend to be slow in publication, short-lived, and rarely available in overseas libraries. The researcher is thus usually restricted to the large international bibliographic services, and coverage of Latin American publications in these is usually poor: the *Science Citation Index*, for example, indexes almost 3,400 scientific serials published worldwide, of which only 14 (0.4%) originate in Latin America.

Fortunately, there is a large body of scientific literature relating to Latin America published in North America and Europe, so a search of the standard bibliographic tools, or the corresponding online databases, will not necessarily prove as unrewarding as the foregoing comments might suggest. The number of scientific and technical bibliographic works is of course legion, and the uninitiated will find the first volume of A. J. WALFORD's *Guide to Reference Material* (4th ed.; London: Library Association, 1980) as good a starting point as any.

For those wishing to pursue their bibliographical researches further, GROPP's *Bibliography of Latin American Bibliographies* and its supplements, together with the annual SALALM *Bibliography of Latin American and Caribbean Bibliographies* (see pp. 88–89) may help to identify more specific bibliographic tools in the relevant field.

An important non-bibliographic reference work, suggesting useful contacts for the researcher, is:

Science and Technology in Latin America. Edited by Christopher Roper and Jorge Silva. London: Longman, 1983. Provides information on government bodies, research institutes, associations and universities engaged in scientific activity in each of the Latin American and Caribbean countries.

JE

Social Sciences

The classic general bibliography is:

WEBB, William H. et al. *Sources of Information in the Social Sciences: A Guide to the Literature.* 3rd ed. Chicago, IL: American Library Association, 1986.

Unfortunately this work is generally cursory in its coverage of Latin America. A better regional treatment is given in:

DELORME, Robert L. *Latin America: Social Science Information Sources, 1967–1979.* Santa Barbara, CA: ABC/Clio, 1981.

DELORME, Robert L. *Latin America, 1979–1983: A Social Science Bibliography.* Santa Barbara, CA: ABC/Clio, 1984.

Regular listings of new sociological materials can be found in several continuing publications. The major international bibliography is:

International Bibliography of Sociology/Bibliographie internationale de sociologie. London: Routledge, 1952—. This is one of several annual bibliographical cumulations prepared on behalf of Unesco by the International Committee for Social Science Information and Documentation and issued under the general title *International Bibliography of the Social Sciences.* Others are listed above under Anthropology, Economics and Politics and Government.

Essential for US coverage is:

Public Affairs Information Service Bulletin. New York: Public Affairs Information Service, 1915—. Generally known as PAIS, this source indexes by subject current literature relating to economic and social conditions. Monthly, with annual cumulations that include an author index. A *Cumulative Subject Index to the PAIS Annual Bulletin, 1915–1974* is also available (15 vols.; Arlington, VA: Carrollton Press, 1977–1978).

An essential companion to the *PAIS Bulletin* is:

Foreign Language Index. New York: Public Affairs Information Service, 1972—. Having commenced with a volume covering 1968–1971, this is now a quarterly publication, the fourth issue of the year being an annual cumulation. It is an index to foreign-language materials in the fields of economic and public affairs, arranged by subject with an author index. Coverage of Spanish-language material is extensive.

Other important sources are:

Social Sciences Index. New York: H. W. Wilson, 1975—. Currently provides cover-to-cover indexing of 353 English language periodicals. Includes book reviews.

Social Sciences Citation Index. Philadelphia, PA: Institute for Scientific Information, 1966—. A sophisticated aid to periodical use, indexing all the published works cited or referred to in each article. This enables the researcher to see how the works he or she is concerned with have been employed in the investigations and arguments of other writers. Also employs an ingenious form of keyword indexing (the 'Permuterm' subject index): by looking up each significant word one can see if any other word of interest has appeared in conjunction with it in an article title.

London Bibliography of the Social Sciences. London: London School of Economics and Political Science, 1931—. Currently published by Mansell. See also PUBLISHED LIBRARY CATALOGUES (p. 53).

Finally, the classic work of general reference for all social sciences is:

International Encyclopedia of the Social Sciences. Edited by David L. Sills. 17 vols. New York: Macmillan, 1968. With *Biographical Supplement* (1979).

RAM

National Bibliographies

To find materials covering particular countries one should use a combination of the techniques described in this book. The first step is to look in the subject catalogue of one's own library. It may then be necessary to go to another library known to have strong holdings on the country concerned. Check in advance to see if that library's catalogue has been published, and if so, study it before visiting (see the chapter on PUBLISHED LIBRARY CATALOGUES, p. 46). Other useful information can be found in bibliographies having a national or regional focus. This chapter is arranged in four sections: the first lists bibliographies of bibliographies, and the second gives information on current national bibliographies, where they exist. Subsequent sections deal with retrospective, country-specific bibliographies and bibliographies of early printed books.

Bibliographies of Bibliographies

The best way to identify an appropriate or likely-looking bibliography is to consult a bibliography of bibliographies. There are several that cover the whole of Latin America, and some information on these can be found in the chapter on GENERAL BIBLIOGRAPHIES (p. 87). Some examples having a national focus are:

GEOGHEGAN, Abel Rodolfo. *Bibliografía de bibliografías argentinas, 1807–1970.* Buenos Aires: Casa Pardo, 1970. Lists 452 works.

SILES GUEVARA, Juan. *Bibliografía de bibliografías bolivianas.* La Paz: Universidad Mayor de San Andrés, 1983.

BASSECHES, Bruno. *A Bibliography of Brazilian Bibliographies.* Detroit, MI: Blaine Ethridge, 1978. Very wide in its coverage.

GIRALDO JARAMILLO, Gabriel. *Bibliografía de bibliografías colombianas.* 2nd ed., revised by R. Pérez Ortiz. Bogotá: Instituto Caro y Cuervo, 1960. Includes relevant general bibliographies.

FERNÁNDEZ ROBAINA, Tomás. *Bibliografía de bibliografías cubanas, 1859–1972*. Havana: Biblioteca Nacional José Martí, 1973.

FLORÉN LOZANO, Luis. *Bibliografía de la bibliografía dominicana*. Ciudad Trujillo: Roques Roman, 1948.

MILLARES CARLO, Agustín and José Ignacio MANTECÓN. *Ensayo de una bibliografía de bibliografías mexicanas*. Mexico City: Oficina de Bibliotecas, Departamento del Distrito Federal, 1943. A volume of *Adiciones* was published in 1944.

LOSTAUNAU RUBIO, Gabriel. *Fuentes para el estudio del Perú: bibliografía de bibliografías*. Lima: Herrera Márquez, 1980.

MUSSO AMBROSI, Luis Alberto. *Bibliografía de bibliografías uruguayas*. (Montevideo, 1964).

In addition, a bibliography of Ecuadorian bibliographies can be found on pp. 9–25 of the *Anuario bibliográfico ecuatoriano, 1976–1977* (Quito: Universidad Central del Ecuador, 1978), and M. R. ARGUETA has published a 'Bibliografía de bibliografías hondureñas' in *Revista de la Universidad*, a journal of the Universidad Nacional Autónoma de Honduras (6:21 (1984), pp. 55–62). The Anglophone West Indies are covered by:

JORDAN, Alma and Barbara COMISSIONG. *The English-Speaking Caribbean: A Bibliography of Bibliographies*. Boston, MA: G. K. Hall, 1984.

Current National Bibliographies

Current bibliographies are essential for identifying and tracing new publications of interest. They can also be important sources of information on older material, as many have been published continuously over a period of time. 'A current national bibliography is a mirror that ... should reflect the interests and unique characteristics of a country ... [and] serves to present the history of the nation as it records its publishing output. By looking at current national bibliographies from years past, one is able to interpret literary, social, political and technological emphases as well as cultural trends that are of historical importance to the life if the nation' (Barbara L. BELL. In *An Annotated Guide to Current National Bibliographies*. Alexandria, VA: Chadwyck-Healey, 1986, p. xix).

Ideally, a national bibliography should be a record of all current publishing in the country concerned, issued at regular intervals, and distributed quickly to subscribers. It should be compiled according to internationally recognised standards of book description, and the arrangement should be a logical one, explained in an introduction.

In practice, these standards cannot always be met. Where a national bibliography exists, it is usually compiled by a national library or national bibliographic agency, and its comprehensiveness and currency will depend on the efficiency of the local system of legal deposit (see COPYRIGHT AND PHOTOCOPYING, p. 66). Standard commercial publications usually prove easier to acquire and record than privately published or non-commercial material, however important this latter may be for the researcher. Many existing national bibliographies started only in the last few decades, and some have been suspended for varying periods of time; in these cases, volumes have sometimes appeared retrospectively to fill the gaps.

All of these difficulties have affected the national bibliographies of Latin America. The laws relating to the legal deposit of publications have not been strictly enforced, and many bibliographies appear irregularly, several years after the date of publication of the items they contain. In some countries, there is no national bibliographic agency to compile a bibliography, and the task has been assumed by another institution, or even a private individual. While valiant efforts are made in these cases, the situation is far from ideal. In some countries the book trade is sufficiently organised to issue reasonably comprehensive national lists, frequently linked to the allocation of international standard book numbers (ISBNs) to publishers and individual titles. In other countries, the only available information on national book production may come from lists issued by individual booksellers.

It should also be remembered that in the case of many Latin American nations a significant proportion of their citizens reside abroad, voluntarily or otherwise. In these cases, the national bibliography may or may not record their publications, and it may be necessary to consult special lists of exile writings.

The following list tries to identify the major attempts at current national bibliography in Latin America. More general information may be found in the work by Barbara L. BELL, quoted above, and in:

Domay, Friedrich. *Bibliographie der nationalen Bibliographien.* Hiersemanns bibliographische Handbüche, Bd. 6. (Stuttgart: Hiersemann, 1987).

Argentina

Argentina does not currently produce a national bibliography, although several examples have appeared in the past, for varying periods. The longest running was probably the *Boletín bibliográfico argentino*, later the *Boletín bibliográfico nacional*, issued by the Comisión Nacional de Cooperación Intelectual and covering the years 1937–1963. For information about recent material one has to rely on *Libros argentinos ISBN*, published by the Cámara Argentina del Libro (1984—). The annual volumes are supplemented by bi-monthly listings in *LEA: Libros de Edición Argentina* (1983—).

Bolivia

Bolivia has been well served by the bookseller and bibliographer Werner Guttentag Tichauer, who has produced the annual *Bio-bibliografía boliviana* (previously *Bibliografía boliviana*) regularly since 1962. It is published in Cochabamba by Guttentag's bookstore, Los Amigos del Libro.

Brazil

The Biblioteca Nacional in Rio de Janeiro issued a *Boletim bibliographico* irregularly from 1918 to 1938, recommencing in 1953 (as *Boletim bibliográfico*) and continuing to 1982, with a gap for 1968–1972. The years from 1983 are covered by the *Bibliografia brasileira*, also issued by the Biblioteca Nacional, on magnetic tape and microfiche. It meets many of the criteria for national bibliographies set out above, but is rather late in appearing. Commercial publications are also included in the monthly microfiche *Catálogo Brasileiro de Publicações* (CBP), produced by Livraria Nobel of São Paulo.

English-Speaking Caribbean

The *Bibliografía actual del Caribe/Current Caribbean Bibliography/Bibliographie courante de la Caraïbe* was first issued by the Caribbean Commission in 1951, and has since changed publisher several times. Based on information gathered from libraries in the region and in the US, it covers books about the area as well as those published locally. At present it is far from current, and may have ceased publication.

The principal current bibliography is:

The CARICOM Bibliography: A Subject List of Current National Imprints of the Caribbean Community Member Countries. Georgetown: Caribbean Community Secretariat, 1977—. Collects data from the national bibliographies of Barbados, Guayana, Jamaica and Trinidad and Tobago, and seeks and publishes information from the remaining countries of the Caribbean Community. Material not produced for the book trade is included. Unfortunately, the work's currency leaves something to be desired: at present it is about three years in arrears.

The semi-annual *Bibliography of the English-Speaking Caribbean: Books, Articles and Reviews in English*, by Alvona ALLEYNE and R. NIEMEYER (Parkersburg, IA: Caribbean Books, 1978—) includes all materials on the Caribbean, whether published in the region or not.

Many of the individual countries have their own national bibliographies, usually published quarterly with annual cumulations. Examples are:

National Bibliography of Barbados: A Subject List of Works Deposited with the National Library Service ... and of Works of Barbadian Authorship Printed Abroad. Bridgetown: National Library Service, 1975—.

Bermuda National Bibliography: A List of Additions to the Bermuda Library. Hamilton: Bermuda Library, 1984—. Includes books about Bermuda published abroad.

Guayanese National Bibliography. Georgetown: National Library, 1974—.

The Jamaican National Bibliography. Kingston: National Library of Jamaica, 1975—. This is a continuation of:

The Jamaican National Bibliography, 1964–1974. Millwood, NY: Kraus International, 1981. Produced by the Institute of Jamaica.

Trinidad and Tobago National Bibliography. St. Augustine: University of the West Indies Library and Port of Spain: Central Library of Trinidad and Tobago, 1975—.

French-Speaking Caribbean

Notes Bibliographiques Caraïbes commenced publication in 1977, and has since continued irregularly. Containing articles as well as bibliographies, it is currently produced by the Association des Archivistes, Bibliothécaires et Documentalistes Francophones de la Caraïbe, based at the Bibliothèque Centrale de la Guadeloupe. For Haiti, see below.

Chile

The Biblioteca Nacional in Santiago de Chile has a long tradition of producing a national bibliography, partly as a result of the efficiency of the legal deposit laws. The *Anuario de la prensa chilena* appeared with reasonable regularity over the years 1886–1975, and a retrospective volume covering 1877–1885 was published in 1952. From 1975 it was replaced by the *Bibliografía chilena*, which is running about three years in arrears.

Colombia

The *Anuario bibliográfico colombiano* (Bogotá: Instituto Caro y Cuervo, 1951—) has a reasonably thorough coverage, although it has difficulty in keeping up to date.

Costa Rica

The *Anuario bibliográfico costarricense* (San José: Biblioteca Nacional) began with the year 1956 and continued to 1974. It has now been replaced by the annual *Catálogo nacional ISBN* (1983/1984—), produced by the Centro de Documentación y Bibliografía of the Biblioteca Nacional. The same institution published in 1984 a retrospective cumulation in *Bibliografía costarricense, 1937–1945*.

Cuba

The *Bibliografía cubana* (Havana: Biblioteca Nacional José Martí, 1968—) began with the years 1959–1962, and has progressed rapidly to the present. The coverage is thorough, and the distribution widespread and efficient. Volumes have also been issued for earlier periods: 1900–1916, 1917–1920 and 1921–1936 have so far been covered.

This supplements and partially overlaps with:

PERAZA SARAUSA, Fermín. *Anuario bibliográfico cubano.* Havana, 1937—. Appeared (with slight variations in the title) until 1970; from 1953 the cover title was *Bibliografía cubana.* The 1959 volume was the last to appear in Cuba: 1960 was published in Medellín, Colombia, and subsequent parts were published in Gainesville, Florida, where some earlier issues were also reprinted. The three volumes for 1966–1968 were published by the University of Miami Press at Coral Gables as *Revolutionary Cuba: A Bibliographical Guide.* The author died in 1969, and his widow published the final volume as *Bibliografía cubana, 1970,* no. 34 in the series.

Dominican Republic

The first national bibliography, *Boletín bibliográfico dominicano,* appeared in Ciudad Trujillo (Santo Domingo) in 1945; with the 1947 issue the name was changed to *Anuario bibliográfico dominicano.* Nothing more was published until 1978 when the *Anuario* reappeared under the aegis of the Biblioteca Nacional. Publication has continued sporadically, with the aim of including works about the country published abroad in addition to the national bibliographic production.

Ecuador

National bibliography started in Ecuador with the *Bibliografía ecuatoriana* (Quito: Universidad Central del Ecuador, Biblioteca General, 1975—). After the first few issues, the publishers joined forces with the Banco Central del Ecuador to produce the *Anuario bibliográfico ecuatoriano* for 1976/1977 (also called *Bibliografía ecuatoriana* no.8/9). The years 1979–1981 were covered by *Ecuador: bibliografía analítica,* prepared by the Centro de Investigacion y Cultura of the Banco Central, and from 1982 the same institution has continued publishing the *Anuario bibliográfico ecuatoriano.*

Guatemala

The *Indice bibliográfico guatemalteco* has appeared sporadically since 1951, published by the Biblioteca Nacional and the Biblioteca de la Universidad de San Carlos de Guatemala.

Haiti

There is no official national bibliography, but its purpose is served by the *Dictionnaire de bibliographie haïtienne* by Max BISSAINTHE (see below under Retrospective Bibliographies).

Honduras

The *Anuario bibliográfico hondureño, 1961–1971* appeared in 1973, and subsequent issues have covered 1981–1983. The first volume was published by the Biblioteca Nacional; later volumes by the Banco Central de Honduras. Another bibliography with the same name, prepared by Mario ARGUETA, commenced publication in 1980 (Tegucigalpa: Universidad Nacional Autónoma de Honduras).

Mexico

The Biblioteca Nacional and the Instituto de Investigaciones Bibliográficas of UNAM jointly publish *Bibliografía Mexicana*, which appeared six times a year from 1967 to 1980, and monthly from 1981. It is intended to be current, though there is some time lag. 1967 also saw the start of the *Anuario bibliográfico*, developed as a more permanent and comprehensive record of Mexican publishing. The first issues, covering the years 1958–1960, were published by the Biblioteca Nacional; from 1961, the task was taken over by the Instituto de Investigaciones Bibliográficas. The time lag is presently around twenty years.

Paraguay

Paraguay has no official national bibliography, but five years of editorial activity were covered in a recent work:

> KALLSEN, Margarita. *Paraguay: cinco anos de bibliografía, 1980–1984.* Asunción: Cromos, 1986.

Peru

Since 1978 the Biblioteca Nacional in Lima has published, with varying frequency, *Bibliografía nacional*. It is reasonably current, including periodical articles and material from or about Peru, or written by Peruvians abroad. Its predecessor was the *Anuario bibliográfico peruano*, also produced by the Biblioteca Nacional, which aimed to be a comprehensive and enduring record of literary production from 1943 onwards. It has appeared irregularly, and presently has a time lag of seven to nine years.

Puerto Rico

The *Anuario bibliográfico puertorriqueño*, covering 1948 onwards, is published by the Biblioteca de la Universidad de Puerto Rico at Río Piedras. The coverage is comprehensive, though it suffers a time lag of ten years or more.

Uruguay

The *Anuario bibliográfico uruguayo* began in 1946, and has continued to date (except for a gap from 1950 through 1967) with reasonable coverage and currency. In recent years it has included works by Uruguayans living abroad. Some of the missing years are filled by *Bibliografía uruguaya*, covering 1962–1977 in three parts (six volumes), issued by the Biblioteca del Poder Legislativo in Montevideo.

Venezuela

The Biblioteca Nacional in Caracas is responsible for all three forms of national bibliography so far produced in Venezuela. The first, the *Anuario bibliográfico venezolano*, covered the years 1942–1977; this was replaced by the *Bibliografía venezolana*, treating the years from 1980. The latter has a broad scope, including works published outside the country by Venezuelans and about Venezuela, but its currency leaves a lot to be desired. From 1987 the Agencia Nacional del ISBN, based in the Biblioteca Nacional, has issued the *Boletín ISBN Venezuela*, which is intended to be a current listing.

Retrospective Bibliographies

There are several general retrospective bibliographies that record publishing activity over a particular span of years. Examples cover the whole of Latin America (see the chapter, GENERAL BIBLIO-GRAPHIES, p. 87), groups of countries, and most, if not all, individual nations. These sources can compensate to some extent for the shortcomings in the national bibliographies, in addition identifying publications about the country concerned which were published abroad. The following section gives a representative selection of these; generally excluded are bibliographies covering material on a particular city or region of the country concerned, works on a particular subject or group of subjects, and lists treating particular types of material covered elsewhere in this book. Bibliographies of a country's early publications, covering the first years of printing, are listed in the next section.

Among regional bibliographies, having a wider than national scope but not covering the whole subcontinent, there is a recent, and timely, example for Central America:

> TORRES-RIVAS, Edelberto. *Para entender Centroamérica: resumen bibliográfico, 1960–1984.* San José: Instituto Centroamericano de Documentación e Investigación Social, 1985. Lists by country books and journal articles in the social sciences and the humanities.

The US–Mexican border region is covered by:

> VALK, Barbara G. *BorderLine: A Bibliography of the United States–Mexico Borderlands.* Los Angeles, CA: UCLA Latin American Center, 1988.

An older bibliography covers the Andean nations:

> WATSON, Gayle H. *Colombia, Ecuador and Venezuela: An Annotated Guide to Reference Materials in the Humanities and Social Sciences.* Metuchen, NJ: Scarecrow Press, 1971.

Several important works cover the Caribbean region, though each one has notable exclusions:

> COMITAS, Lambros. *The Complete Caribbeana, 1900-1975: A Bibliographic Guide to the Scholarly Literature.* 4 vols. White Plains, NY: Kraus International, 1977. Excludes Haiti and the Spanish Caribbean.

The Commonwealth Caribbean is covered by:

> HUGHES, Roger. *The Caribbean: A Basic Annotated Bibliography for Students, Librarians and General Readers.* London: Commonwealth Institute Library Services, 1987.

Two older, but still important, listings are:

> CUNDALL, Frank. *Bibliography of the West Indies excluding Jamaica.* Kingston: Institute of Jamaica, 1909; reprinted, New York: Johnson Reprint Corp., 1981. Lists material published in the area and Parliamentary Papers concerning the region (including Central America).

BROWN, Ann Duncan. *British Possessions in the Caribbean Area: A Select List of References.* Washington, DC: Library of Congress, Division of Bibliography, 1943.

The Dutch Antilles in general are covered by:

HISS, Philip Hanson. *A Selective Guide to the English Literature on the Netherlands West Indies, with a Supplement on British Guiana.* New York: Netherlands Information Bureau, 1943.

NAGELKERKE, Gerard A. *Netherlands Antilles: A Bibliography, 17th Century to 1980.* The Hague: Royal Institute of Linguistics and Anthropology, Department of Caribbean Studies, 1982.

The individual countries of Latin America are also covered in the World Bibliographical Series, published in Santa Barbara and Oxford by ABC/Clio Press. These give precedence to material in English; the following volumes have appeared so far:

Barbados (vol. 76, 1987)	*Haiti* (vol. 39, 1983)
Belice (vol. 21, 1980)	*Jamaica* (vol. 45, 1984)
Bolivia (vol. 89, 1988)	*Mexico* (vol. 48, 1984)
Brazil (vol. 57, 1985)	*Nicaragua* (vol. 44, 1983)
Chile (vol. 97, 1988)	*Panama* (vol. 14, 1982)
Dominica (vol. 82, 1987)	*Paraguay* (vol. 84, 1987)
Guatemala (vol. 9, 1981)	*Puerto Rico* (vol. 52, 1985)

Trinidad and Tobago (vol.74, 1986)

Listed below are a selection of the major country-specific bibliographies.

Argentina

Argentina, 1875–1975: población, economía, sociedad: estudio temático y bibliográfico. Mexico City: UNAM, 1978. Historical in focus, but invaluable for its broad coverage of the social sciences.

Belize

MINKEL, C. W. and R. H. ALDERMAN. *A Bibliography of British Honduras, 1900–1970.* East Lansing, MI: Michigan State University, 1970.

Bolivia

RENE-MORENO, Gabriel. *Biblioteca boliviana: catálogo de la sección de libros y folletos.* Santiago: Gutenberg, 1879. A catalogue of the compiler's own impressive collection, with 6,815 entries. *Suplementos* were issued to cover 1879–1899 and 1900–1908, as well as 571 more entries in *Adiciones a la Biblioteca Boliviana de G. Rene Moreno, 1602–1879* (Santiago: Barcelona, 1899). The whole work is updated by:

COSTA DE LA TORRE, Arturo. *Catálogo de la bibliografía boliviana: libros y folletos, 1900–1963.* 2 vols. La Paz: Universidad Mayor de San Andres, 1966–1973. Contains a further 15,000 entries.

Brazil

The bibliography of Brazil is immense. Useful introductions are:

SODRE, Nelson Werneck. *O que se deve ler para conhecer o Brasil.* 3rd ed. Rio de Janeiro: Letras e Artes, 1964. 46 chapters cover the history and culture of Brazil, each with a bibliography.

CONNIFF, M. L. and F. G. STURM. *Brazilian Studies: A Guide to the Humanities Literature.* Albuquerque, NM: University of New Mexico, Latin American Institute, 1986?

HARMON, Ronald M. and Bobby J. CHAMBERLAIN. *Brazil: A Working Bibliography in Literature, Linguistics, Humanities and the Social Sciences.* Tempe, AZ: Arizona State University Press, 1975.

MORAES, Rubens Borba de and W. BERRIEN. *Manual bibliográfico de estudos brasileiros.* Rio de Janeiro: Souza, 1949. 6,000 annotated entries covering the humanities and social sciences.

Two invaluable older works are the *Diccionario bibliographico brazileiro* of SACRAMENTO BLAKE (see p. 143) and:

SILVA, Innocencio F. da. *Diccionario bibliographico portuguez.* 22 vols. Lisbon: Imprensa Nacional, 1858–1923. Contains annotated entries for some 100,000 Portuguese and Brazilian publications. A *Guia bibliográfica* by Ernest SOARES was published in 1972.

Two valuable local bibliographies, specific to Rio de Janeiro and Rio Grande do Sul respectively, are:

BERGER, Paulo. *Bibliografía do Rio de Janeiro de viajantes e autores estrangeiros, 1531–1900.* Rio de Janeiro: Livraria São José, 1964.

BARRETO, Abeillard. *Bibliografía sul-riograndense: a contribuição portuguesa e estrangeira para o conhecimento e a integração do Rio Grande do Sul.* 2 vols. Rio de Janeiro: Conselho Federal de Cultura, 1973-1976.

Chile

Bibliografía de Chile. Havana: Orbe, 1977. Compiled for Cuban researchers by the Biblioteca 'Jose A. Echeverría' of the Casa de las Américas in Havana.

Commonwealth Caribbean

Some references to individual countries may be found in the general Caribbean bibliographies listed above and in the national bibliographies in the preceding section. The following country-specific bibliographies are also useful:

GRELL, V. J. and L. G. WHITE. *Montserrat: A Bibliography.* Plymouth: Montserrat Public Library, 1977.

A Selective List of Books, Pamphlets and Articles on St. Lucia and by St. Lucians Covering the Period 1844 to Date. Castries: St. Lucia Central Library, 1971.

STEELE, B. A. *Grenada Bibliography.* St. George's: University of the West Indies, Extra-Mural Department, 1983.

HALLETT, A. C. Hollis. *Bermuda in Print: A Guide to the Printed Literature on Bermuda.* Hamilton: The Island Press, 1985.

SHILLINGFORD, J. D. and L. SHILLINGFORD. *A Bibliography of the Literature on Dominica, WI.* Ithaca, NY: Cornell University, 1972.

Costa Rica

DOBLES SEGREDA, L. *Indice bibliográfico de Costa Rica.* 10 vols. San José: Lehmann, 1927–1936. A heavily annotated booksellers' list, arranged by broad subject area.

Cuba

Cuban book-production is covered by the impressive, multi-volume *Bibliografía cubana* by C. M. TRELLES Y GOVÍN: the volume on the seventeenth and eighteenth centuries contains some 2,000 entries, extensively annotated (2nd ed.; Havana: Imprenta del Ejército,

1927), some 25,000 items are cited for the nineteenth century (8 vols.; Matanzas: Quirós y Estrada, 1911–1915) and for the early twentieth century there are 8,500 entries (2 vols.; Matanzas: Quirós y Estrada, 1916–1917). The whole set was reprinted by Kraus in Nendeln, Liechtenstein in 1965.

For more recent times, a good bibliography is:

CHILCOTE, Ronald H. *Cuba, 1953–1978: A Bibliographic Guide to the Literature*. White Plains, NY: Kraus International, 1984.

Dominican Republic—See below under Haiti.

El Salvador

KRUSÉ, David Samuel and Richard SWEDBERG. *El Salvador Bibliography and Research Guide*. Cambridge, MA: Central America Information Office, 1982. Focuses on social science publications of the recent past.

Falklands/Malvinas

The 1982 war led to the publication of two useful bibliographies:

LARSON, Everett E. *A Selective Listing of Monographs and Government Documents on the Falklands/Malvinas Islands in the Library of Congress*. Hispanic Focus, no. 1. Washington, DC: Library of Congress, 1982.

MUNDO LO, Sara de. *The Falklands/Malvinas Islands: A Bibliography of Books, 1619–1982*. Urbana, IL: Albatros, 1983.

Guatemala

Modern Guatemalan publications are listed in a series that commences with early printed materials, and is thus listed in the next section. There is also a listing of the output of the country's major publisher:

Catálogo general de libros, folletos y revistas editados en la Tipografía Nacional de Guatemala desde 1892 hasta 1943. Guatemala: Tipografía Nacional, 1944. Supplements cover 1944–1953 and 1954–1962.

The Guianas

Material on French Guiana from the sixteenth century and the other Guianas and bordering territories from the nineteenth century is included in:

FAUQUENOY, Marguerite. *Bibliographie sur les Guyanes et les territoires avoisinants.* Paris: Office de la Recherche Scientifique et Technique d'Outre-Mer, 1966.

Haiti

Haiti is strikingly well covered by retrospective bibliographies. Works published in or about Haiti up to 1949 (including material on Hispaniola before 1804) are covered in just over 1,000 pages in:

BISSAINTHE, Max. *Dictionnaire de bibliographie haïtienne.* Washington, DC: Scarecrow Press, 1951. There is also a supplement covering 1950–1970, published in 1973, and further updates are published irregularly in the journal *Conjonction: Revue Franco-Haïtienne* (Port-au-Prince: Institut Français d'Haïti, 1966—).

Other bibliographies include:

LAGUERRE, Michel S. *The Complete Haitiana: A Bibliographic Guide to the Scholarly Literature, 1900–1980.* 2 vols. White Plains, NY: Kraus International, 1982. Imaginative literature is excluded.

PAGÁN PERDOMO, D. *Bibliografía general de la isla de Santo Domingo: contribución a su estudio.* 2 vols. San Pedro de Macoris: Universidad Central del Este, 1979.

LAWLESS, Robert. *Bibliography on Haiti: English and Creole Items.* Gainesville, FL: University of Florida, Center for Latin American Studies, 1985.

BALLANTYNE, Lygia M. *Haitian Publications: An Acquisition Guide and Bibliography.* SALALM Bibliography and Reference Series, 6. Madison, WI: SALALM, 1980.

Honduras

DANBY, C. and Richard SWEDBERG. *Honduras: Bibliography and Research Guide.* Cambridge, MA: Central America Information Office, 1984. Useful for comparatively recent publications.

GARCÍA, Miguel Angel. *Bibliografía hondureña.* 3 vols. Tegucigalpa: Banco Central de Honduras, 1971–1973. Covers publications from 1620–1971; a two-part supplement covers 1971–1972.

Martinique

Martinique: A Selected List of References. Washington, DC: Library of Congress Reference Department, 1942.

JARDEL, Jean-Pierre et al. *Bibliographie de la Martinique.* Fort-de-France: Centre d'Etudes Regionales Antilles-Guyane, 1969.

Mexico

A useful catalogue produced by a bookseller is:

Catálogo de libros mexicanos o que tratan de America... Bibliografía americana, 5. Mexico City: Porrúa, 1949.

The publishing activity of the country's major scholarly publisher is catalogued in:

LICEA DE ARENAS, Judith. *Repertorio de la producción bibliográfica de la Universidad Nacional Autónoma de México.* 2 vols. Mexico City: UNAM, 1983–1984.

Nicaragua

Materials published in or about Nicaragua, together with works by Nicaraguans published elsewhere, are comprehensively listed in:

Nicaraguan National Bibliography, 1800–1978. 3 vols. Redlands, CA: Latin American Bibliographic Foundation, and Managua: Biblioteca Nacional Ruben Darío, 1986–1987. The third volume lists serial publications and contains indexes and corrections.

More recent material is covered by:

Nicaragua revolucionaria: bibliografía, 1979–1984. Managua: Instituto de Investigaciones Económicas y Sociales, 1984.

Paraguay

There are two major bibliographies:

JONES, David Lewis. *Paraguay: A Bibliography.* New York: Garland, 1979.

FERNÁNDEZ CABALLERO, Carlos F. S. *The Paraguayan Bibliography: A Retrospective and Enumerative Bibliography of Printed Works of Paraguayan Authors.* 3 vols. Asunción: Paraguay Arandu Books, 1970–1983. Covers materials published from 1724 to 1974, and includes works about Paraguay by non-Paraguayans. Volume 2 appeared as SALALM Bibliography and Reference Series, 3 (Amherst, MA: SALALM, 1975).

Puerto Rico

PEDREIRA, Antonio Salvador. *Bibliografía puertorriqueña, 1493–1930.* Madrid: Hernando, 1932; reprinted, New York: Burt Franklin, 1974.

VIVO, Paquita. *The Puerto Ricans: An Annotated Bibliography.* New York: Bowker, 1973.

CARDONA, Luis A. *An Annotated Bibliography on Puerto Rican Materials and Other Sundry Matters.* Bethesda, MD: Carreta Press, 1983.

Surinam

The bibliography of Surinam is thoroughly covered up to 1980 in two works by the same author, both emanating from the Royal Dutch Institute of Linguistics and Anthropology:

NAGELKERKE, Gerard A. *Literature Survey of Surinam until 1940: Present Literature in the Library of the Royal Institute for Linguistics and Anthropology in Leyden.* Leyden: Royal Institute, 1972.

NAGELKERKE, Gerard A. *Suriname: A Bibliography, 1940–1980.* The Hague: Royal Institute, Department of Caribbean Studies, 1980.

Uruguay

ARREDONDO, Horacio. *Bibliografía uruguaya: contribución.* Montevideo: El Siglo Ilustrado, 1929. Contains some 1,000 entries, extensively annotated, for books published in or about Uruguay.

Venezuela

VILLASANA, Angel Raul. *Ensayo de un repertorio bibliográfico venezolano*. 6 vols. Caracas: Banco Central de Venezuela, 1969–1979. Lists by author some 36,000 works published from 1808 to 1950 on literature, history, and general culture.

Bibliographies of Early Publications

The printing press came to Latin America early in the sixteenth century: books were being printed in Mexico from the 1530s and in Lima from the 1580s. The spread of the press was slow, however; by the end of the eighteenth century it had reached only Cuba, Colombia, Guatemala, Chile, Ecuador, Santo Domingo, Trinidad and the Río de la Plata. But by the mid-nineteenth century, with the consolidation of independence from Spain and Portugal, virtually all the Latin American nations had a printing and publishing industry.

This section deals with the special bibliographies that exist to identify and describe the early publications of the Latin American nations. (Catalogues of libraries with special collections of early material are included in the chapter on PUBLISHED LIBRARY CATALOGUES, p. 46). Very early printed works need particularly detailed descriptions: there may be few copies if them in existence, and printing techniques of the time led to considerable variation between copies of the same edition. Many of the bibliographies listed below have copious illustrations, including facsimiles of pages from the books described. Less detail is needed in descriptions of nineteenth century imprints, many of which are included in the retrospective bibliographies listed above.

Argentina

The first press in Buenos Aires, the Imprenta de los Ninos Expósitos, is documented in:

GUTIÉRREZ, Juan María. *Bibliografía de la primer imprenta de Buenos Aires desde su fundación hasta el año de 1810 inclusive*. Buenos Aires: Imprenta de Mayo, 1866.

See also Río de la Plata below.

Brazil

Printing did not establish itself in Brazil until 1808. The following two bibliographies include early material about Brazil, or by Brazilians published elsewhere:

> *Bibliotheca Brasiliense: catálogo annotado dos livros sobre o Brasil ... pertencentes a José C. Rodrigues*. Pt. 1: 1492–1822. Rio de Janeiro, 1907.

> MORAES, Rubens Borba de. *Bibliographia Brasiliana: Rare Books about Brazil Published from 1504 to 1900, and Works by Brazilian Authors of the Colonial Period*. Rev. ed. 2 vols. Los Angeles, CA: UCLA Latin American Center, 1983.

Brazilian books and authors are included in the *Diccionario bibliographico portuguez* of Innocencio F. da SILVA (see above under Retrospective Bibliographies).

Chile

The great Chilean bibliographer José Toribio Medina was foremost in the study of early Latin American printing, in Chile as elsewhere:

> MEDINA, José Toribio. *Bibliotheca Hispano-Chilena, 1523–1817*. 3 vols. Santiago: Author, 1897–1899.

> MEDINA, José Toribio. *Bibliografía de la imprenta en Santiago de Chile desde sus orígenes hasta febrero de 1817*. Santiago: Fondo Histórico y Bibliográfico, 1961; reprinted with a supplement, Amsterdam: Israel, 1966.

In addition, 281 early titles are listed in chronological order in:

> *Impresos chilenos, 1776–1818*. 2 vols. Santiago: Biblioteca Nacional, 1963.

Colombia

Early Bogotá imprints are documented in:

> POSADA, Eduardo. *Bibliografía bogotana*. 2 vols. Bogotá: Imprenta Nacional, 1917–1925; reprinted, Nendeln: Kraus, 1976. Covers 1738–1831.

Costa Rica

LINES, Jorge A. *Libros y folletos publicados en Costa Rica durante los años 1830–1849*. San José: Universidad de Costa Rica, Facultad de Letras y Filosofía, 1944. Lists 103 items.

Cuba—See above under Retrospective Bibliographies.

Ecuador

STOLS, Alexandre A. M. *Historia de la imprenta en el Ecuador de 1755 a 1830*. Quito: Casa de la Cultura Ecuatoriana, 1956. Includes a listing of 264 publications.

MEDINA, José Toribio. *La imprenta en Quito, 1760–1818: notas bibliográficas*. Santiago: Elzeviriana, 1904; reprinted, Amsterdam: Israel, 1964. Detailed descriptions of 43 items.

Guatemala

Earlier periods are covered by:

MEDINA, José Toribio. *La imprenta en Guatemala, 1660–1821*. 2nd ed. 2 vols. Guatemala: J. de Pineda Ibarra, 1960.

O'RYAN, Juan Enrique. *Bibliografía guatemalteca de los siglos XVII y XVIII*. 2nd ed. Guatemala: J. de Pineda Ibarra, 1960.

Later printing is included in:

VALENZUELA, Gilberto. *Bibliografía guatemalteca y catálogo general de libros, folletos, periódicos, revistas etc.* 8 vols. Guatemala: J. de Pineda Ibarra, 1961–1964. Covers 1821–1960; volumes 4–8 (1861–1960) were compiled by G. Valenzuela Reyna.

All three works are partially updated by:

REYES MONROY, José L. *Bibliografía de la imprenta en Guatemala: adiciones de 1769 a 1900*. Guatemala: J. de Pineda Ibarra, 1969.

Haiti

Early works from Hispaniola are listed in the *Dictionnaire de bibliographie haïtienne* of Max BISSAINTHE (see above under Retrospective Bibliographies).

Mexico

Mexico City, site of the first printing press on the American continent, has naturally many bibliographies of its early printing. The classic listing is:

MEDINA, José Toribio. *La imprenta en México, 1539–1821.* 8 vols. Santiago: Author, 1908–1912; reprinted, Amsterdam: Israel, 1965. A well annotated catalogue of over 12,000 items. It has been supplemented by two works:

GONZALEZ DE COSSÍO, Francisco. *La imprenta en México, 1594–1820: cien adiciones a la obra de José Toribio Medina.* Mexico City: Robredo, 1947.

GONZALEZ DE COSSÍO, Francisco. *La imprenta en México: 510 adiciones a la obra de J. T. Medina.* Mexico City: UNAM, 1952.

Another major reference work, including locations in libraries for its 179 titles, is:

GARCÍA ICAZBALCETA, Joaquín. *Bibliografía mexicana del siglo XVI: catálogo razonado de libros impresos en Mexico de 1539 a 1600.* New ed., by Agustín Millares Carlo. Mexico City: Fondo de la Cultura Económica, 1954.

Eighteenth century printing is covered in great detail by:

LEÓN, Nicolás. *Bibliografía mexicana del siglo XVIII.* 6 vols. Mexico City: Díaz de León, 1902–1908. Comprehensive indexes to this work were compiled by Roberto VALLES (3 vols.; Mexico City: Vargas Rea, 1945–1946).

Paraguay

MEDINA, José Toribio. *Historia y bibliografía de la imprenta en el Paraguay, 1705–1727.* La Plata: Museo de La Plata, 1892.

See also Río de la Plata below.

Peru

Peru is another important country for early printing, and has attracted a large number of bibliographies. The most comprehensive is:

VARGAS UGARTE, Rubén. *Impresos peruanos.* 6 vols. Lima: San Marcos, 1953–1954, and Tipografía Peruana, 1956–1957. Covers the years 1584–1825.

Rather more specialised are:

MEDINA, José Toribio. *La imprenta en Lima, 1584–1824*. 4 vols. Santiago: Author, 1904–1907; reprinted, Amsterdam: Israel, 1965.

MEDINA, José Toribio. *La imprenta en Arequipa, en Cuzco, Trujillo y otros pueblos del Perú durante las campañas de la independencia, 1820-1825: notas bibliográficas*. Santiago: Elzeviriana, 1904; reprinted, Amsterdam: Israel, 1964.

Río de la Plata

FURLONG CÁRDIFF, G. *Historia y bibliografía de las primeras imprentas rioplatenses, 1700–1850: misiones del Paraguay, Argentina, Uruguay*. 4 vols. Buenos Aires: Guaranía, 1953–1959. Extensive bibliographical details, as well as biographical information on authors and printers.

MEDINA, José Toribio. *Historia y bibliografía de la imprenta en el antiguo virreinato del Río de la Plata*. La Plata: Museo de La Plata, 1982; reprinted, Amsterdam: Israel, 1965.

Uruguay

MEDINA, José Toribio. *Historia y bibliografía de la imprenta en Montevideo, 1807–1810*. La Plata: Museo de La Plata, 1892.

See also Río de la Plata above.

Venezuela

DRENIKOFF, Iván. *Impresos relativos a Venezuela desde el descubrimiento hasta 1821*. Caracas: Fundación para el Rescate del Acervo Documental Venezolano, 1978.

GRASES, Pedro. *Historia de la imprenta en Venezuela hasta el fin de la Primera República*. Caracas: Presidencia de la República, 1967. A selective listing of 118 titles.

MEDINA, José Toribio. *La imprenta en Caracas, 1808–1821: notas bibliográficas*. Santiago: Elzeviriana, 1904; reprinted, Amsterdam: Israel, 1964. Describes some 38 works from Caracas and other centres of printing.

AEW

Personal Bibliographies

The first obvious step in the investigation of personal bibliography is to search the catalogues of the libraries to which one has access. Works *by* an author ('primary sources') will naturally be found in the author catalogue, but in many UK libraries, even when there is a separate subject catalogue, material held by the library *about* an author (critical studies, biographies, bibliographies, festschriften and so on—'secondary sources') will also frequently be found in the author catalogue, alongside the author's works. The introduction of automation in more and more libraries is helping to rectify this anomaly.

Primary Sources

National bibliographies and catalogues of books in print, such as *Libros en venta* and *Libros argentinos ISBN*, are handy reference sources for an author's published works, although superseded volumes will be needed for older publications out-of-print. The grandfather of Hispanic bibliography is:

> PALAU Y DULCET, Antonio. *Manual del librero hispano-americano.* 2nd ed. 28 vols. Barcelona: Palau, 1948–1977. With *Indice alfabético de títulos-materias...* by Agustin PALAU CLAVERAS. 7 vols. Barcelona: Palau, 1981–1987. Despite the title, the coverage of Spanish America is uneven. Should nevertheless be borne in mind for authors publishing up to the mid-twentieth century, especially as it supplies comprehensive bibliographical details.

Rather older is the fundamental work of Portuguese bibliography:

> SILVA, Innocencio Francisco da. *Diccionario bibliographico portuguez.* 22 vols. Lisbon: Imprensa Nacional, 1858–1923. Often referred to as 'Innocencio'. This has been supplemented by:

> FONSECA, M. A. de. *Aditamentos ao Dicionário bibliográfico português...* Coimbra: Universidade, 1927.

For Brazilian materials, there is a further supplement:

CARMO, C. Assis do. 'Indice brasileiro ao Dicionário biblio-gráfico português...' *Revista do Livro* 9 and 10 (March and June 1958), pp. 235–251 and 231–248.

A writer's earlier works are frequently listed in his subsequent publications, opposite the title-page, on the back cover or elsewhere; such obvious sources should not be overlooked. In the literary field, bibliographies of specific genres (Argentine poetry, the Chilean novel and so forth) are likely to provide adequate primary bibliographies for individual authors. For writers publishing up to the 1930s, the series of Tentative Bibliographies for individual Latin American countries published by Harvard University Press during that decade provide useful listings of original works with full bibliographical data.

Various published indexes provide valuable aids to tracing literary works sufficiently short to have been published in journals or anthologies. Herbert H. Hoffman specialises in this service, but others are also active:

HOFFMAN, Herbert H. *Cuento Mexicano Index.* Newport Beach, CA: Headway Publications, 1978.

HOFFMAN, Herbert H. *Hoffman's Index to Poetry: European and Latin American Poetry in Anthologies.* Metuchen, NJ: Scarecrow Press, 1985.

HOFFMAN, Herbert H. *Latin American Play Index.* 2 vols. Metuchen, NJ: Scarecrow Press, 1983–1984. Covers 1920–1980.

LEAL, Luis. *Bibliografía del cuento mexicano.* Mexico City: Andrea, 1958.

LARRÁZABAL HENRÍQUEZ, Osvaldo et al. *Bibliografía del cuento venezolano.* Caracas: Universidad Central de Venezuela, 1975.

Bibliographies of Bibliographies

If primary or secondary materials for the study of an individual author do not come immediately to hand, they will have to be tracked down by way of a published bibliography on the person in question. This, in turn, may need to be traced through biblio-graphies of bibliographies. The latter sources may also be useful in producing references to bibliographies on specific subjects, periods, movements or literary genres which might in turn lead the researcher to material relevant to the author being studied. Of course, bibliographies of bibliographies may themselves need to be traced.

Especially recommendable in this regard are the following reference guides, devoted exclusively to Hispanic languages and literatures:

> BLEZNICK, Donald W. *A Sourcebook for Hispanic Literature and Language*. Philadelphia, PA: Temple University Press, 1974.

> WOODBRIDGE, Hensley C. *Guide to Reference Works for the Study of the Spanish Language and Literature, and Spanish American Literature*. New York: Modern Language Association of America, 1987.

These two works serve, as well as reference guides, as bibliographies of bibliographies in their own right; that is to say, they give details of bibliographies directly related to individual authors, which in their turn list the works of, and the secondary materials concerning, the author being studied.

There are many specialist bibliographies of bibliographies in the Latin American field, the flagship of the genre being:

> GROPP, Arthur E. *A Bibliography of Latin American Bibliographies*. Metuchen, NJ: Scarecrow Press, 1968. Gropp also published a *Supplement* (1971). References to bibliographies in journals are reserved for the companion work:

> GROPP, Arthur E. *A Bibliography of Latin American Bibliographies Published in Periodicals*. 2 vols. Metuchen, NJ: Scarecrow Press, 1976.

Scarecrow Press has published further supplements to this work by Daniel Raposo CORDEIRO, Haydée PIEDRACUEVA and Lionel V. LOROÑA; for the full sequence see GENERAL BIBLIOGRAPHIES, p. 88. Annual updates are published by SALALM as part of its Bibliography and Reference Series.

Bibliographies of literary bibliography include:

> BRYANT, Shasta M. *A Selective Bibliography of Bibliographies of Hispanic American Literature*. 2nd ed. Austin, TX: University of Texas Press, 1976. The 662 entries include works published in journals as well as monographic bibliographies.

ZUBATSKY, David. *Latin American Literary Authors: An Annotated Guide to Bibliographies*. Metuchen, NJ: Scarecrow Press, 1986. 'Covers bibliographies found in periodicals, books, dissertations and festschrift volumes.'

BECCO, Horacio Jorge. *Bibliografía de bibliografías literarias argentinas*. Washington, DC: Organization of American States, 1972.

BECCO, Horacio Jorge. *Fuentes para el estudio de la literatura venezolana*. 2 vols. Caracas: Centauro, 1978.

National bibliographies of bibliographies can also be useful as a source of personal bibliography; some of the major examples are listed in the chapter NATIONAL BIBLIOGRAPHIES (pp. 118–119).

Bio-Bibliographical References

Encyclopaedias and biographical dictionaries can be valuable sources for bio-bibliography both for the casual user and the researcher, especially when the articles include lists of references sources or suggestions for further reading. Particularly impressive in this respect is the Spanish *Enciclopedia universal ilustrada europeoamericana* ('Espasa'), with its extensive Latin American coverage and its wealth of bibliographical reference. The chapters on ENCYCLOPAEDIAS (p. 155) and BIOGRAPHIES (p. 267) discuss more works of both types that include bibliographical references. Some examples useful for literary research are:

UDAONDO, Enrique. *Diccionario biográfico colonial argentino*. Buenos Aires: Huarpes, 1945. Includes both historical and literary figures.

SACRAMENTO BLAKE, Augusto Victorino Alves. *Diccionario bibliographico brazileiro*. 7 vols. Rio de Janeiro: Typographia Nacional, 1883–1902; reprinted, Nendeln: Kraus, 1969. Arranged alphabetically by Christian name; indexes have been published by Jango FISCHER (Rio de Janeiro: Imprensa Nacional, 1937) and Octavio TORRES (Salvador: Fundação Gonzalo Moniz, 1961).

BEHAR, Ely. *Vultos do Brasil: dicionário bio-bibliográfico brasileiro*. São Paulo: Livraria Exposição do Livro, 1967.

Rojas, Luis Emilio. *Biografía cultural de Chile*. Santiago: Nascimento, 1974)

Further references to Latin American bio-bibliographies, biographical dictionaries, dictionaries of pseudonyms and other relevant works may be found in the works of Robert B. SLOCUM and Sara de MUNDO LO (see p. 269). A rather more specialised publication is:

HILTON, Sylvia-Lyn and Amancio LABANDEIRA FERNÁNDEZ. *Bibliografía hispanoamericana y filipina: manual de repertorios bibliográficos para la investigación de la historia y la literatura hispanoamericanas y filipinas*. Madrid: Fundación Universitaria Española, 1983.

Literary Bio-Bibliography

Histories of literature are obvious sources both of primary author bibliography (if only of the titles and dates of their published works) and of biography and critical assessment; a good index is a *sine qua non* for a work's usefulness as a reference tool, together with the presence of bibliographic surveys or critical references. An outstanding example of such a history of Hispanic literature is:

DÍAZ-ECHARRI, Emiliano and Jose María ROCA FRANQUESA. *Historia general de la literatura española e hispanoamericana*. 2nd ed. Madrid: Aguilar, 1966. Provides comprehensive coverage of Spanish American literature, with copious references to primary and secondary sources.

Apart from this work, Spanish America is not well served by histories of literature. The most detailed is:

ANDERSON-IMBERT, Enrique. *Spanish-American Literature: A History*. Detroit, MI: Wayne State University, 1969. A translation of the fourth Spanish language edition (Mexico City: Fondo de Cultura Economica, 1962–1964). Gives no critical references, but the index supplies the nationality and dates of some 2,700 authors referred to in the text.

For Brazilian literature, the following literary histories supply good working bibliographies of critical material on authors, and have excellent author indexes:

Moisés, Massaud. *História da literatura brasileira*. São Paulo: Cultrix and Universidade de São Paulo, 1983—. Three volumes so far published.

Hulet, Claude L. *Brazilian Literature*. 3 vols. Washington, DC: Georgetown University Press, 1974–1975.

Literary Dictionaries

Dictionaries of literature can provide a useful introduction to author bibliography, and have the advantage over literary histories that their alphabetical arrangement makes for handier reference. They are especially worthwhile when the entries are accompanied by good bibliographies.

Prototypes of the genre were the volumes of the series Diccionario de la literatura latinoamericana published in Washington, DC, by the Pan American Union between 1958 and 1963. The intention was to cover the whole of Latin America, but only six works were published: *Bolivia* (1958), *Chile* (1958), *Colombia* (1959), *Argentina* (2 vols., 1960–1961), *Ecuador* (1962) and *América Central* (2 vols., 1963). Conceived as dictionaries of literary history and criticism, they nevertheless supplement the critical assessment in each article with biographical details and respectable lists of primary and secondary bibliographical sources.

Further rich sources of biographical-critical information are:

Ward, Philip. *The Oxford Companion to Spanish Literature*. Oxford: Clarendon Press, 1978. Contains many Spanish American entries, with references to collected editions and criticism for major authors.

Becco, Horacio Jorge. *Diccionario de literatura hispanoamericana: autores*. Buenos Aires: Huemul, 1984. Does not list secondary sources.

Minchero Vilasaró, Angel. *Diccionario universal de escritores*. Volume 2: Argentina, Bolivia, Colombia, Costa Rica, Cuba, Chile, República Dominicana. San Sebastián: EDIDHE, 1957. Excellent for biography and primary sources; volume 1 covers the US; no further volumes have yet appeared.

For individual countries, the following dictionaries of literature are also to be recommended:

ORGAMBIDE, Pedro and Roberto YAHNI. *Enciclopedia de la literatura argentina*. Buenos Aires: Sudamericana, 1970.

GUZMÁN, Augusto. *Biografías de la literatura boliviana, 1520–1925*. Cochabamba: Amigos del Libro, 1982. Continued to 1950 by the same author's *Biografías de la nueva literatura boliviana* (Cochabamba: Amigos del Libro, 1982).

COELHO, Jacinto de Prado. *Dicionário das literaturas portuguesa, galega e brasileira*. 2 vols. Porto: Figueirinhas, 1968–1969. Extensive coverage of Brazil, with emphasis on literary history.

MENEZES, Raimundo de. *Dicionário literario brasileiro ilustrado*. 5 vols. São Paulo: Saraiva, 1969. Substantial biographies followed by comprehensive primary bibliographies.

SZMULEWICZ, Efraín. *Diccionario de la literatura chilena*. Santiago: Lautaro, 1977.

Diccionario de la literatura cubana. 2 vols. Havana: Letras Cubanas, 1980-1984. Lengthy biographies and comprehensive bibliographies.

MARATOS, Daniel C. and Marnesba D. HILL. *Cuban Exile Writers: A Bio-Bibliographic Handbook*. Metuchen, NJ: Scarecrow Press, 1986.

ALBIZUREZ PALMA, Francisco. *Diccionario de autores guatemaltecos*. Guatemala: Tipografía Nacional, 1984.

GONZÁLEZ, José. *Diccionario de autores hondureños*. Tegucigalpa: Editores Unidos, 1987.

OCAMPO DE GÓMEZ, Aurora M. and Ernesto PRADO VELÁZQUEZ. *Diccionario de escritores mexicanos*. Mexico City: UNAM, 1967. Lists 542 writers (including philosophers and historians), with biography, criticism, and primary and secondary bibliographies.

ARRIOLA GRANDE, Maurilio. *Diccionario literario del Perú: nomenclatura por autores*. 2 vols. Lima: Universo, 1983.

Diccionario de la literatura uruguaya. Edited by A. Oreggione and W. Penco. Montevideo: Arca/Credisol, 1987.

Diccionario general de la literatura venezolana (autores). Edited by L. Cardozo and J. Pinto. Mérida: Universidad de los Andes, 1974.

Retrospective Literary Bibliographies

While the biographical and critical information supplied by dictionaries of literature are valuable introductory sources, the researcher
will need recourse to specialist literary bibliographies for the more
obscure references. There is, of course, no shortage of individual
bibliographies devoted to such major writers as Borges, Neruda,
García Márquez, Rubén Darío or Carpentier; indeed three substantial bibliographies on the latter have already been published in the
1980s. For figures who have not attracted this level of treatment,
working bibliographies of primary and secondary materials will
frequently be found in biographies and critical studies of the authors
in question; beyond this, the major sources will be general bibliographies of Latin American literature.

An outstanding early contribution to the documentation of
secondary sources for the study of Spanish American authors, and
unique in its approach, is:

GRISMER, Raymond L. *Indice de doce mil autores hispanoamericanos:
una guía a la literatura de la América Española.* New York: H. W.
Wilson, 1939. A combined index to 130 bibliographies,
anthologies and critical works on 12,000 authors writing before
1939, producing cryptic references consisting of abbreviated
titles and page numbers. Reprinted as *A Reference Guide to
12,000 Spanish American Authors* (Detroit, MI: Blaine Ethridge,
1971).

Other general bibliographies of Latin American literature offer
narrower scope but more orthodox presentation; among the best are:

FLORES, Angel. *Bibliografía de autores hispanoamericanos: A
Bibliography of Spanish-American Writers, 1609–1974.* New York:
Gordian Press, 1975. Contains primary and secondary mater-
ial on almost 200 authors.

RELA, Walter. *Guía bibliográfica de la literatura hispanoamericana
desde el siglo XIX hasta 1970.* Buenos Aires: Casa Pardo, 1971.
Contains much useful material, but the indexes are unhelpful.
They are improved in its supplement:

RELA, Walter. *Spanish American Literature: A Selected Biblio-
graphy/Literatura hispanoamericana: bibliografía selecta, 1970–1980.*
East Lansing, MI: Michigan State University, 1982.

Bibliographical sources tend to categorise writers in different ways. For those specialising in specific genres or types, there are:

OCAMPO DE GÓMEZ, Aurora M. *Novelistas iberoamericanos: obras y bibliografía crítica.* 6 fasc. Mexico City: UNAM, 1971–1980. Exhaustive primary bibliographies and a mass of secondary sources.

FORSTER, Merlin H. *Historia de la poesía hispanoamericana.* Clear Creek, IN: American Hispanist, 1981. The excellent bibliography (pp. 248–324) gives primary and secondary sources for 56 poets.

FOSTER, David William. *The 20th Century Spanish-American Novel: A Bibliographic Guide.* Metuchen, NJ: Scarecrow Press, 1975. Gives critical references for 56 authors.

LYDAY, Leon F. and George W. WOODYARD. *A Bibliography of Latin American Theater Criticism, 1940–1974.* Austin, TX: University of Texas Press, 1976.

JACKSON, Richard L. *The Afro-Spanish American Author: An Annotated Bibliography of Criticism.* New York: Garland, 1980.

PORTER, Dorothy B. *Afro-Braziliana: A Working Bibliography.* Boston, MA: G. K. Hall, 1978.

Women writers are well covered by:

MARTING, Diane E. *Women Writers of Spanish America: An Annotated Bio-Bibliographical Guide.* Westport, CT: Greenwood Press, 1987.

KNASTER, Meri. *Women in Spanish America: An Annotated Bibliography from Pre-Conquest to Contemporary Times.* Boston, MA: G. K. Hall, 1977. Contains references on a highly selective list of authors.

The following offer the best selection of references on writers from individual countries:

FOSTER, David William. *Argentine Literature: A Research Guide.* 2nd ed., rev. New York: Garland, 1982.

CARPEAUX, Otto Maria. *Pequena bibliografia crítica da literatura brasileira.* 3rd ed. Rio de Janeiro: Letras e Artes, 1964. Outstanding bibliographies on almost 200 authors.

TOPETE, José Manuel. *A Working Bibliography of Brazilian Literature*. Gainesville, FL: University of Florida Press, 1957.

FOSTER, David William. *Chilean Literature: A Working Bibliography of Secondary Sources*. Boston, MA: G. K. Hall, 1978.

PORRÁS COLLANTES, Ernesto. *Bibliografía de la novela en Colombia*. Bogotá: Instituto Caro y Cuervo, 1976. 2326 novels covered.

FOSTER, David William. *Cuban Literature: A Research Guide*. New York: Garland, 1985.

FOSTER, David William. *Mexican Literature: A Bibliography of Secondary Sources*. Metuchen, NJ: Scarecrow Press, 1981.

FOSTER, David William. *Peruvian Literature: A Bibliography of Secondary Sources*. Westport, CT: Greenwood Press, 1981.

FOSTER, David William. *Puerto Rican Literature: A Bibliography of Secondary Sources*. Westport, CT: Greenwood Press, 1982.

For Chicano writers, there is no lack of coverage:

MARTINEZ, Julio A. and Francisco A. LOMELI. *Chicano Literature: A Reference Guide*. Westport, CT: Greenwood Press, 1985.

MARTINEZ, Julio A. *Chicano Scholars and Writers: A Bio-Bibliographical Dictionary*. Metuchen, NJ: Scarecrow Press, 1979.

EGER, Ernestina. *A Bibliography of Criticism of Contemporary Chicano Literature*. Berkeley, CA: University of California Press, 1982. Covers book, articles and dissertations.

TRUJILLO, Roberto G. and Andrés RODRÍGUEZ. *Literatura chicana: Creative and Critical Writings Through 1984*. Oakland, CA: Floricanto Press, 1985. Includes dissertations, videos and recordings.

Current Bibliographical Output

A number of serial bibliographies enable the student to keep up with current output on Latin American authors. Foremost among them is the *Handbook of Latin American Studies* (1935—; full citation on p. 90), currently published by the University of Texas at Austin. The literature section (found in the biennial 'Humanities' volume) provides a selective bibliography, with brief descriptive paragraphs, of new editions and critical works published during the two-year period covered, and is thus an important current source of new material on individual authors. The indexing is extensive.

For articles in journals, the *Hispanic American Periodicals Index* (HAPI) provides an annual listing by author and subject of articles and reviews culled from more than 200 periodicals, including most of the major literary journals, which tend not to be indexed elsewhere. It covers materials from 1970 onwards, and is published by the Latin American Center at the University of California, Los Angeles.

The *Humanities Index* (New York: H. W. Wilson, 1974—) indexes articles in English-language journals by author and subject, and is worth bearing in mind for Latin American literature references, as is the same publisher's *Essay and General Literature Index* (1900—), which indexes collections of essays. The UK counterpart of the former, the *British Humanities Index* (London: Library Association, 1962—) is not strong on Hispanic coverage.

The annual *Year's Work in Modern Language Studies* (Cambridge: Modern Humanities Research Association, 1931—) provides an excellent review of the previous year's crop of new critical editions, studies and articles on European languages and literatures. The dense narrative format can be irritating for quick reference, even with the aid of the author and subject indexes, but it allows its reviewers scope for subjective evaluations. The regular article on Latin American literature began in 1964, and deals with authors on a country-by-country basis; the section, 'Brazilian Literature' is occasionally postponed. The broadest coverage of any annual bibliography in the field is provided by the annual *MLA International Bibliography* (New York: Modern Language Association of America, 1922—), an unannotated listing of the previous year's output of critical materials on European languages and literatures, including dissertations and articles from some 1,500 journals. In the section on Latin American literature, coverage of individual writers is by chronological period within countries. There is a natural bias towards US sources.

The *Inter-American Review of Bibliography/Revista Interamericana de Bibliografía* (Washington, DC: Organization of American States, 1951—) includes quarterly classified lists of recent articles and dissertations in the Latin American field. The *Revista Hispánica Moderna* (New York: Columbia University, 1934—) used to provide a similar service with its 'Bibliografía Hispanoamericana/Hispánica' — perhaps the fullest classified bibliography of its kind—but discontinued it in 1969.

Back runs of all the above can naturally be used as sources of retrospective bibliography. The *Humanities Index* was preceded by (in succession) the *Social Sciences and Humanities Index*, the *International Index to Periodicals* and the *Readers' Guide to Periodical Literature*, dating back to 1905, while HAPI continues and improves upon the work of the Columbus Memorial Library's *Index to Latin American Periodicals: Humanities and Social Sciences* and *Index to Latin American Periodical Literature*, which together go back to 1929.

Citation Indexes

> *Arts and Humanities Citation Index.* 1976——. Philadelphia, PA: Institute for Scientific Information, 1979——.

This work is published in three main parts (the citation index plus separate indexes to subjects and sources), and collects references to authors and works found in text, footnotes or bibliography of the 1,300 or so journals indexed. This enables the student to identify a whole network of references of potential relevance, without having to wade through the possibly less relevant articles in which they are cited. For example, the 'Borges' entry in the subject index will refer the reader to a host of sub-topics and authors which, when traced in the source index, may yield additional citations of related interest. It thus provides a far wider range of reference than would be possible in a standard author bibliography. An annual hardback edition cumulates and adds to the softbound January-April and May-August issues.

Similer citation indexes exist for the sciences and the social sciences (see SUBJECT BIBLIOGRAPHIES, pp. 115, 117).

Pseudonyms

One of the most comprehensive sources of references to Spanish-American pseudonyms is Raymond L. GRISMER's *Indice de doce mil autores hispanoamericanos*, mentioned above under Retrospective Literary Bibliography. No complete modern index to Latin American pseudonyms exists. For authors before 1925, there is always the classic:

> MEDINA, José Toribio. *Diccionario de anónimos y seudónimos hispanoamericanos.* Buenos Aires: Universidad Nacional, 1925. This should be supplemented by Ricardo VICTORICA's two volumes of corrections and additions, *Errores y omisiones del*

Diccionario... (1928) and *Nueva epanortosis al Diccionario...* (1929). All three works were reprinted in Detroit, Michigan, by Blaine Ethridge in 1973.

For Brazil, there is:

BARROS PAIVA, Tancredo de. *Achegas a um diccionário de pseudonymos, iniciaes, abreviaturas e obras anonymas* ... Rio de Janeiro: Leite, 1929. Includes bio-bibliographical notes.

For more recent Spanish American authors writing pseudonymously, citations to dictionaries of pseudonyms for individual countries will be found in *Obras de referencia de América Latina* by Abel Rodolfo GEOGHEGAN (see p. 88) and the works of ZUBATSKY and WOODBRIDGE, mentioned above under Bibliographies of Bibliographies.

JW

Other Printed Sources

Encyclopaedias

General Encyclopaedias

While any good general encyclopaedia should serve as a quick reference source for basic facts about Latin America (as about anywhere else), the most comprehensive encyclopaedia specifically intended for Spanish and South American users is the *Enciclopedia universal ilustrada europeo-americana*. Despite the fact that it is somewhat out-of-date, 'EUI' or 'Espasa', as it is generally known, is a mine of information on anything from statistics of the climate of Guayaquil to the early twentieth-century uniforms of the Argentine army, illustrated in full colour plates. Bibliographies, maps and illustrations are excellent for their time. The full details are:

> *Enciclopedia universal ilustrada europeo-americana*. 70 vols in 71. Barcelona: Espasa-Calpe, 1907–1930. Continued by a ten-volume *Apéndice* (1930–1933) and regular *Suplementos*, at first annual and subsequently biennial, arranged under broad subject headings with individual indexes. A cumulated index to the 1934–1980 supplements appeared in 1983. Unfortunately, the supplements cannot remedy the progressive out-dating of the main text.

The Portuguese/Brazilian equivalent is rather less impressive, particularly from a bibliographic viewpoint, although it is also very well illustrated:

> *Grande enciclopédia portuguesa e brasileira*. 40 vols. Lisbon: Editorial Enciclopédia, 1935–1960. Volumes 37–40 contain an updating *Apéndice*, and the work is supplemented by a ten-volume *Actualização* (1981–1987). The main work deals mainly with Portuguese and common Luso-Brazilian topics; a four-volume *Parte complementaria: Brasil* started publication in 1967 but was discontinued after volume 2. According to the publishers, all the material intended for this part in fact appeared in the *Actualização*.

Also useful, particularly for information on the country of publication, are the various general encyclopaedias from Latin America itself. Notable among these are:

> *Diccionario enciclopédico UTEHA.* 2nd ed. 10 vols. Mexico City: Unión Tipográfica Editorial Hispanoamericana (UTEHA), 1964–1968. Supplemented by a two-volume *Apéndice* (1967).

> *Enciclopédia Barsa.* 16 vols. Rio de Janeiro: Encyclopaedia Britannica do Brasil, 1965. Also published in a Spanish edition by the Encyclopaedia Britannica's Buenos Aires subsidiary.

> *Gran Omeba: diccionario enciclopédico ilustrado.* 12 vols. Buenos Aires: Omeba, 1965–1967.

> *Grande enciclopédia Delta Larousse.* 12 vols. Rio de Janeiro: Delta, 1970. Contains what is probably the widest Brazilian coverage of all modern encyclopaedias.

Encyclopaedias of Latin America

An important older work of considerable size that will still often be found useful, is:

> *Diccionario enciclopédico hispanoamericano de literatura, ciencias, artes.* 30 vols. New York: Jackson, and Barcelona: Montaner y Simón, 1928. Volumes 1-23 comprise the original encyclopaedia as published in 1898, with a two-volume appendix, three supplementary volumes, and two more covering 'estos últimos años'—basically an updating to 1926. In spite of its title, this is essentially a general encyclopaedia, compiled from a Hispanic viewpoint.

Editorial Futuro of Buenos Aires produced a *Diccionario enciclopédico de las Americas* in 1947; Presses Universitaires de France published an *Encyclopédie de l'Amérique Latine* in 1954, and the Sociedad Latinoamericana de Japón has produced five editions of its Latin American encyclopaedia (in Japanese) since 1939, the latest in 1968. There is now in English:

> DELPAR, Helen. *Encyclopedia of Latin America.* New York: McGraw-Hill, 1974. Includes articles by over 100 contributors, but excludes the Commonwealth Caribbean and concentrates on the post-Independence period.

A much newer addition to the field is:

The Cambridge Encyclopedia of Latin America and the Caribbean. Edited by Simon Collier, Harold Blakemore and Thomas E. Skidmore. Cambridge: Cambridge University Press, 1985. Extensively illustrated, and arranged by topic rather than alphabetically.

Limiting itself largely but not entirely to history is:

MARTIN, Michael Rheta and Gabriel H. LOVETT. *Encyclopedia of Latin American History.* New ed., revised by L. Robert Hughes. Indianapolis, IN: Bobbs-Merrill, 1968. Despite its title, has articles on men of letters like Neruda and Borges, but not for such political figures as Frondizi or Kubitschek.

National Encyclopaedias

More specialised and therefore generally more detailed are the various encyclopaedias devoted to individual countries. As well as the incomplete second part of the *Grande enciclopédia portuguesa e brasileira* (see above), the following works are useful:

SANTILLÁN, Diego A. de. *Gran enciclopedia argentina.* 8 vols. Buenos Aires: Ediar, 1956–1963. With *Apéndice* (1964).

Enciclopedia de Cuba. 14 vols. Madrid: Enciclopedia y Clásicos Cubanos, 1973–1977. Organised by major subject: 'Historia', 'Poesía', 'Prosa' and so forth.

TAURO, Alberto. *Diccionario enciclopédico del Perú.* 3 vols. Lima: Mejía Baca, 1966–1967. With *Apéndice* (1975).

Diccionario Porrúa: historia, biografía y geografía de México. 5th ed. 3 vols. Mexico City: Porrúa, 1986.

Enciclopedia de México. Edited by José Rogelio Alvarez. 14 vols. Mexico City: Secretaría de Educación Pública, 1987–1988. An expanded reissue of the work originally published 1966–1977.

Encyclopedie van de Nederlandse Antillen. Edited by H. Hoetink. Amsterdam: Elsevier, 1969.

Encyclopedie van Nederlandsch West-Indië. Edited by H. D. Benjamin and J. F. Snelleman. 'sGravenhage: Nijhoff, 1914–1917; repr. 1981.

Encyclopedie van Suriname. Edited by C. F. A. Bruijning and J.
Voorhoeve. Amsterdam: Elsevier, 1977.

Encyclopaedias and Dictionaries of National History

Rather more limited in their compass are the Scarecrow Press series
of Latin American Historical Dictionaries, edited originally by
Alvar Curtis Wilgus, and currently by Laurence Hallewell. The
following volumes (of variable quality and coverage) have so far
been published:

Argentina, by Ione S. WRIGHT and Lisa M. NEKHOM (1977).
Bolivia, by Dwight B. HEATH (1972).
Brazil, by Robert M. LEVINE (1979).
The British Caribbean, by William R. LUX (1975).
Chile, edited by Salvatore BIZZARRO (2nd ed., 1988).
Colombia, by Robert H. DAVIS (1977).
Costa Rica, by Theodore S. CREEDMAN (1977).
Cuba, by Jaime SUCHLICKI (1988).
Ecuador, by Albert W. BORK and G. MAIER (1973).
El Salvador, edited by Philip R. FLEMION (1972).
French and Netherlands Antilles, by Albert GASTMANN (1978).
Guatemala, edited by Richard E. MOORE (Rev. ed., 1973).
Haiti, by Roland I. PERUSSE (1977).
Honduras, by Harvey K. MEYER (1976).
Mexico, by Donald C. BRIGGS and Marvin ALISKY (1981).
Nicaragua, edited by Harvey K. MEYER (1972).
Panama, edited by Basil C. and Anne K. HEDRICK (1970).
Paraguay, by Charles J. KOLINSKI (1973).
Peru, by Marvin ALISKY (1979).
Puerto Rico and the U.S. Virgin Islands, by Kenneth R. FARR
(1973).
Uruguay, by Jean L. WILLIS (1974).
Venezuela, edited by Donna K. and G. A. RUDOLPH (1971).

The series is scheduled to be completed shortly with a volume on the
Dominican Republic; it is hoped subsequently to publish revised
editions of some of the earlier volumes.

To these may be added:

Diccionario histórico argentino. Edited by Ricardo Piccirilli,
Francisco L. Romay and Leoncio Gianello. 6 vols. Buenos
Aires: Ediciones Históricas Argentinas, 1953–1955.

Dicionário de história do Brasil, moral e civismo. Edited by Brasil Bandecchi et al. 4th ed. São Paulo: Melhoramentos, 1976.

Dicionário histórico-biográfico brasileiro, 1930–1983. Edited by Israel Beloch and Alzira Alves de Abreu. 4 vols. Rio de Janeiro: Forense, 1984. Prepared by the Centro de Pesquisa e Documentação de História Contemporânea do Brasil of the Fundação Getúlio Vargas.

FUENTES, Jordi et al. *Diccionario histórico de Chile.* 8th ed. Santiago: Zig-Zag, 1984.

FUENTES, Jordi and L. CORTES. *Diccionario político de Chile, 1810–1966.* Santiago: Orbe, 1967.

Diccionario histórico y biográfico del Perú, siglos XV–XX. Edited by Carlos Milla Batres. 9 vols. Lima: Milla Batres, 1986.

Location and Use

A general, but not invariable, practice in library catalogues is to list encyclopaedias by their titles. There is also the possibility of entry under the name of the publisher, if he has commissioned the work: you may find the *Dicionário de história do Brasil,* for example, in some library catalogues under 'Melhoramentos' or 'Edições Melhoramentos'. If the listing is by title, much fruitless searching can be avoided by remembering that the word 'encyclopaedia' becomes 'encyclopedia' in North American usage and *enciclopedia* in Latin America, and that *diccionario* in Spanish loses a 'c' to become *dicionário* in Brazilian (but not Iberian) Portuguese.

A frequently overlooked advantage of many large encyclopaedias is the existence of the index volume (or volumes). Despite the normally alphabetical arrangement of topics, a first approach should always be made through the index, when there is one; in addition to referring to the main article on your subject, the index will frequently give references to other sections where the topic is treated, and save much cross-referring later.

BMH

Handbooks, Guides and Directories

The most comprehensive and discursive type of general reference source is the encyclopaedia, which is treated in the previous chapter. With their smaller size and more rapid publication schedule, handbooks, guides and directories can supplement and bring up to date the information found in the major encyclopaedias, or provide rapid access to it in a briefer and sometimes tabulated format. It is also notable that while most encyclopaedias arrange their material in alphabetical order, the works discussed here usually adopt a more systematic presentation.

Although there is no hard and fast division, handbooks and guides tend to contain brief, factual accounts of general topics, while directories exist to give current information on the status and whereabouts of individuals, institutions, organisations and business enterprises. All these reference forms generally undergo regular and thorough revision, thus providing more current information than would be possible in an encyclopaedia. The content of handbooks, guides and directories frequently overlaps, there being unfortunately no generally accepted terminology. They are treated below in two sections: the first covers compendia of general information, and the second lists some of the works which provide locations for persons and institutions.

Handbooks and Guides

International yearbooks, as well as similar works revised less frequently, provide current information on the individual states of the world and on international and regional organisation. Pre-eminent among them are *The Statesman's Year-Book* (London: Macmillan, 1864—), *The Europa Year Book* (London: Europa Publications, 1926—) and *The International Year Book and Statesman's Who's Who* (London: Skinner, 1953—). Although primary political, they also include much economic, historical and cultural information. Specifically for Latin America are two works which recently started publication:

South America, Central America and the Caribbean 1988. 2nd ed. London: Europa Publications, 1987. Every nation is given a full political and economic directory and statistical survey, and there are brief essays (mainly by British Latin Americanists) on the history and economy of each of the major countries. Also includes details of relevant international organisations, and background essays on general political and economic aspects of the region.

Nuestro mundo '85/'86. Madrid: Agencia Efe/Espasa-Calpe, 1985. Compiled from the OMNIDATA database of the Efe International News Agency, this compilation includes data from all the Hispanic nations of Europe and the Americas, together with the US, Israel and the Philippines. The section on each country begins with a message from the head of state, followed by geographical and historical surveys, political and economic data, material on communications, culture, sport and tourism, and a brief biographical listing of current 'personalidades'.

Both these works are mines of information, and it is to be hoped that they will be updated regularly. The nearest equivalent just for the Caribbean is *The West Indies and Caribbean Yearbook* (London: Skinner, 1926—), which emphasises commercial information.

Individual Countries

The American University in Washington, DC, has produced a series of 'Area Handbooks' for the United States Army, published by the Government Printing Office. These are remarkably comprehensive surveys of each of the countries of the world, revised at irregular intervals of about ten years. The earlier volumes, in green or brown covers, are entitled *Area Handbook for Chile* (or wherever), but the more recent editions, in white covers, are called *Chile* (etc.): *A Country Study.* They provide a wealth of information on history, social conditions, the media, government, geography, the armed forces—everything, in fact, that US forces posted there would need to know—and are conveniently arranged and indexed.

The Scarecrow Press series of Latin American Historical Dictionaries (see p. 158) may also be useful, though the volumes are uneven in quality, range and depth of coverage.

Individual Subjects

Space precludes a comprehensive listing of the many subject-specific handbooks of international or worldwide coverage. Two examples will suffice to illustrate the nature and range of this type of source:

> *Political Parties of the Americas.* Edited by Robert J. Alexander. 3 vols. Westport, CT: Greenwood Press, 1982. Includes for each country a useful survey of its recent history.

> KEEGAN, John. *World Armies.* 2nd ed. Detroit, MI: Gale Research, 1983. Arranged alphabetically by country, giving the status, strength and organisation of each of the armed forces.

Travel Guides

Many travel guides contain much general, historical and statistical data as well as basic tourist information: an example is the annual, and indispensable, *South American Handbook* (Bath: Trade and Travel, 1924—), with its lists of travel agents, hotels, embassies (of all major English-speaking countries) and miscellaneous 'useful addresses'. Travel guides are discussed in more detail in the Travel section of the chapter, CONTACTS WITH LATIN AMERICA (p. 340).

Guides for Students

A few years ago the Council on International Educational Exchange produced a *Student Guide to Latin America* (New York: Dutton, 1977). This has now been superseded by the Council's more general handbook:

> *Work, Study and Travel Abroad, 1988–1989.* 9th ed. New York: St. Martin's Press, 1988.

Directories

Perhaps no category of reference material is more ill-provided in academic library collections on Latin America than directories. This is perfectly understandable: since the main use of a directory is to supply current addresses (or other information) for an organisation or individual, it is almost pointless for a library to buy any it cannot afford to replace when new editions are issued, which may be every twelve months or less. Not all directories maintain this currency, however, as will be seen from the listings below. Knowing where one might profitably look for a particular address comes only with practice, and this is another field where assistance from qualified library staff is invaluable. Many libraries have, in desperation, built up their own card files of Latin American addresses.

For many purposes, of course, general international directories will provide adequate information on Latin America, and obviate the need to consult special works on the region. And even in some of the largest Latin American collections only the most general directory material is to be found; it is to this material that the following notes are largely confined.

Bibliographies

The biennial *Directory of Directories* (4th ed.; 2 vols., Detroit, MI: Gale Research, 1987) identifies a large number of Latin American directories and North American directories covering Latin America. They appear in the index under 'South America', 'Central America', 'West Indies' and the names of individual countries. The equivalent UK publication is *Current British Directories* (11th ed.; Beckenham, Kent: CBD Research, 1988).

General Directories

Still occasionally useful despite its age (though its lack of a name index makes consultation wearisome) is:

SABLE, Martin H. *Master Directory for Latin America*. Los Angeles, CA: UCLA Latin American Center, 1965.

Slightly more up to date is the brief:

Glossary of Institutions Concerned with Latin America. Toronto: Canadian Association of Latin Americanists, 1974.

And for national-level organisations, there is the recent:

Directorio latinoamericano: socio-económico, político, académico. 4 vols. Quito: Ediciones de Información Económica Latinoamericana, 1985.

Academic Directories

Possibly the most useful general reference work in this sphere is the annual *World of Learning* (London: Europa Publications, 1947—). Within the basic alphabetical arrangement by country, this lists academies, learned societies, major libraries, universities and institutes for general and special research, all with their addresses and the names of their directors.

Latin American studies, including courses, research centres, associations, government agencies, grants and libraries are covered (with some omissions) in:

> BRAY, David B. and Richard E. GREENLEAF. *Directory of Latin American Studies in the United States*. New Orleans, LA: Tulane University, Roger Thayer Stone Center for Latin American Studies, 1986.

> *Guía de instituciones que cultivan la historia de América*. Mexico City: Pan-American Institute for Geography and History, 1971.

> SABLE, Martin H. *The Latin American Studies Directory*. Detroit, MI: Blaine Ethridge, 1981.

Latin American studies in Europe, East and West, are listed in:

> MESA-LAGO, Carmelo. *Latin American Studies in Europe*. Latin American Monograph and Document Series, 1. New York: Tinker Foundation, 1979.

There is also a special guide to Washington, DC, published by the Woodrow Wilson International Center for Scholars:

> GROW, Michael. *Scholar's Guide to Washington, DC, for Latin American and Caribbean Studies*. Washington, DC: Smithsonian Institution Press, 1979.

For Central America (including foreign Meso-Americanists), there is:

> *Mesoamérica: directorio y bibliografía, 1950–1980*. Edited by Alfredo Méndez Domínguez. Guatemala City: Universidad del Valle de Guatemala, 1982.

Hispanic Latin Americanists are listed in:

> DEAL, Carl W. and Susan K. FLYNN. *Directory of Hispanic Latin Americanists*. Urbana, IL: Consortium of Latin American Studies Programs, 1981.

The basic list of Latin Americanist scholars in the United States is prepared in the Hispanic Division of the Library of Congress:

> *National Directory of Latin Americanists*. 3rd ed. Compiled by Inge Maria Harman. Washington, DC: Library of Congress, 1985.

The corresponding guide for Europe is produced by the Centro de Estudios y Documentación Latinamericanos (CEDLA) of Amsterdam University; it is briefer, but updated more frequently than its US counterpart:

Latinoamericanistas en Europa, 1985: registro bío-bibliográfico. 4th ed. Compiled by Peter Mason. Amsterdam: CEDLA, 1986.

Canadian Latin Americanists are listed by discipline in:

Directory of Canadian Scholars and Universities Interested in Latin American Studies. 3rd ed. Compiled by Walter C. Soderlund. Ottawa: Canadian Association of Latin American Studies, 1979.

Further guides to academics and researchers are listed in the chapter, UNIVERSITIES AND RESEARCH CENTRES (p. 314).

Business Directories

Market Guide, Latin America. New York: Dun and Bradstreet International, 1981—. Semi-annual, appearing in January and July.

Official International Business Directory of the Spanish Speaking World. Norwalk, CT: Aurora International, 1982/1983—. Published annually in October.

Foundations

STROMBERG, Ann. *Philanthropic Foundations in Latin America.* New York: Russell Sage Foundation, 1968.

Publishing and the Book Trade

La empresa del libro en América Latina. 2nd ed. Buenos Aires: Bowker, 1974.

Science and Technology

HILTON, Ronald. *The Scientific Institutions of Latin America, with Special Reference to Their Organization and Information Facilities.* Stanford, CA: California Institute of International Studies, 1970.

Science and Technology in Latin America. Edited by Christopher Roper and Jorge Silva. London: Latin American Newsletters, Longman, 1983.

Social Sciences

Directorio de centros latinoamericanos de investigaciones en ciencias sociales. 2 vols. Buenos Aires: Consejo Latinoamericano de Ciencias Sociales, 1968.

Directory of Development Research and Training Institutes in Latin America. 2 vols. Paris: Organisation for Economic Cooperation and Development, Development Centre, 1974.

Tourism

Directorio turístico/Tourism Directory. Washington, DC: Organization of American States, International Trade and Tourism Division, 1984—. Annual, appearing in January; lists mainly official agencies promoting tourism.

Telephone Directories

In Latin America as elsewhere, telephone directories are almost always the quickest and simplest means of finding any current address. Unfortunately, few libraries subscribe to those of any but the three or four largest Latin American cities, and many do not even offer these. The problem is particularly acute in the UK, and it is worth mentioning two libraries within walking distance of each other in the City of London which both have extensive range of Latin American telephone directories: these are the City Business Library in Basinghall Street and the Statistics and Market Intelligence Library of the Department of Trade and Industry on Ludgate Hill. In London's West End, Westminster Central Reference Library (St. Martin's Street, Charing Cross) has telephone directories of most of the region's major cities.

Even telephone directories, however, are not always up-to-date. Where the telephone service is run by the State, budgetary cut-backs may result in no directories' being issued for two or three years. An outdated copy is not always the library's fault.

LH

Language Dictionaries

Lexicography has advanced considerably in the last ten years, particularly in the production of bilingual dictionaries. Not only have standards improved—and in the Hispanic field they needed to—but the number of available dictionaries has also greatly increased. What follows, therefore, is a list of recommended dictionaries, with some indication of their strengths and weaknesses, and the particular tasks to which they are best suited.

Citation

Concern for consistency in citation may seem unnecessarily pedantic in the face of the library user's habit of going straight to the reference section to consult a foreign language dictionary. Furthermore, as such works are conveniently grouped together, dissatisfaction with one dictionary frequently leads the user to pick up the next one on the shelf without bothering to refer to the library's catalogue. Searching the catalogue for a particular dictionary can, in fact, be frustrating: many dictionaries are readily identified by a familiar or long-established name, which may bear no relation to the work's current manifestation. It may be that of the original compiler (often long dead), or of the original or current publisher; the exact title is frequently unknown. Faced with the habits of library users and the varying conventions of library catalogues, we have opted here to cite first the name of the compiler only if there is no more than one; in all other cases, even when primary responsibility is indicated, the title is given first.

Spanish Dictionaries

Spanish–English Bilingual Dictionaries

Cassell's Spanish–English, English–Spanish Dictionary. Edited by Anthony Gooch, Angel García de Paredes. London: Cassell, and New York: Macmillan, 1978. A revision of the 1959 edition, which was notoriously unreliable. Care is taken in the new edition to distinguish between translations, and grammatical information has been added. Necessary space is devoted to frequent words, and lexical trivia have been eliminated. Country labels are assigned to Spanish-American terms.

Collins Spanish–English, English–Spanish Dictionary/Collins diccionario español–inglés, inglés–español. By Colin Smith, Manuel Bermejo Marcos and Eugenio Chang-Rodríguez. 2nd ed. London: Collins, and Barcelona: Grijalbo, 1988. The first edition of this work (1971) marked an enormous advance in bilingual English–Spanish lexicography, consigning to oblivion a host of its immediate predecessors. The new edition retains the basic features of the first. By omitting archaic lexical clutter, Smith concentrates on the vocabulary of the 'average educated speaker', and high-frequency words (*dar, llevar*; 'go', 'for') are fully covered. It also enhances the treatment of familiar and slang expressions with indications of register in both languages. The already detailed coverage of Spanish American vocabulary, which receives regional and country labels, has been extended. Distinctions in sense are clear, and there is no shortage of examples. Still probably the best dictionary of its size for translation purposes.

Gran diccionario Larousse: español–inglés/English–Spanish. Edited by Ramón García-Pelayo y Gross et al. Mexico City: Larousse, 1983. An excellent work, first published as *Diccionario moderno español–inglés/English–Spanish* (1976), and the only real rival to the Collins. Useful for familiar language. Contains more entries than the Collins, with extensive coverage of specialised vocabularies. Choice between translations is clear, with good indications of usage. Spanish American usage, however, is not distinguished by country or region.

Larousse moderno español–inglés/English–Spanish. Edited by Ramón García-Pelayo y Gross et al. Paris: Larousse, 1986. A useful abridgement of the above work, with around the same number of words but shorter definitions and fewer examples. Stronger on Peninsular than American Spanish, and uses 'Amer.' rather than country labels.

RAVENTOS, Margaret H. *The Teach Yourself Books Spanish Dictionary.* London: English Universities Press, 1963. Reliable learner's dictionary with clear distinction between translations.

Concentrates on modern vocabulary, but gives no indication of Spanish American usage.

Simon and Schuster's International Dictionary: English–Spanish, Spanish–English. Edited by Tana de Gámez. New York: Simon and Schuster, 1973. Large desktop work, which includes much technical vocabulary. Frequently used words and expressions of are well covered and illustrated. Spanish American usage is indicated by regional and country labels.

WILLIAMS, Edwin B. *The Williams Spanish and English Dictionary.* Expanded ed. New York: Scribners, 1978. When it was first published, this work was welcomed for its inclusion of modern expressions, though it tends to give explanations rather than equivalents. The superabundance of headwords limits space for examples and for detailed coverage of frequent words. Spanish American usage is indicated, but with no country or regional labels.

Spanish Monolingual Dictionaries

On many occasions, no bilingual dictionary will give a satisfactory answer to the enquirer's question; it will then be necessary to consult a monolingual Spanish dictionary. These are the most useful:

Diccionario de la lengua castellana, en que se explica el sentido de las voces, su naturaleza y calidad ... compuesto por la Real Academia Española. 3 vols. Madrid: Francisco del Hierro, 1726. This first edition of the Academy dictionary is still the most useful for Golden Age Spanish, including idioms and proverbs. A facsimile has been published under the title *Diccionario de autoridades* (Madrid: Gredos, 1963).

Diccionario de la lengua española. 20th ed. 2 vols. Madrid: Real Academia Española, 1984. The latest fruit of the 1726 enterprise, and the dictionary on which many other monolingual Spanish dictionaries draw for their definitions. In spite of efforts at currency, it is still prescriptive and conservative. It remains, however, a lexical resource of enormous value. Spanish American usage is indicated by country and regional labels.

Diccionario general ilustrado de la lengua española. Barcelona: Bibliograf, 1987. A new version based on successive editions of the Vox dictionary (1945, 1953, 1973). Represents a major

attempt to produce a descriptive dictionary of the modern
language, including taboo and marginal expressions, while not
neglecting specialised vocabularies. Indicates Spanish American usage by country labels.

MOLINER, María. *Diccionario del uso del español.* 2 vols. Madrid:
Gredos, 1966. An indispensable work of reference, providing
both definitions and grammatical information. Moliner also
includes synonyms, antonyms, and semantically related words,
and the dictionary is especially useful for idioms and examples
of phraseology.

Spanish American Dictionaries

There are many dictionaries treating the usage and vocabulary of
specific Spanish American countries; for these the reader is referred
to:

FABBRI, Maurizio. *A Bibliography of Hispanic Dictionaries.* Imola:
Galeati, 1979.

No single dictionary of Spanish American usage can be recommended wholeheartedly, but the following are worth consulting:

Americanismos: diccionario ilustrado Sopena. Barcelona: Sopena,
1982.

BOYD-BOWMAN, Peter. *Léxico hispanoamericano del siglo XVI.* 16
microfiches with booklet. Madison, WI: Hispanic Seminary of
Medieval Studies, 1987. A compilation of citations from
documents rather than a dictionary of definitions. This is a
much-expanded version of the original book (London: Tam-
esis, 1971). Microfiche lexicons have also been produced for
the seventeenth, eighteenth and nineteenth centuries.

SANTAMARÍA, Francisco J. *Diccionario general de americanismos.* 3
vols. Mexico City: Robredo, 1942.

Other works, all entitled *Diccionario de americanismos,* have been
published by Augusto MALARET (3rd ed.; Buenos Aires: Emece,
1946), Marcos Augusto MORÍNIGO (Buenos Aires: Muchnik, 1966)
and Alfredo N. NEVES (Buenos Aires: Sopena Argentina, 1975).

Portuguese Dictionaries

It is important when using older dictionaries of Portuguese (or in using modern dictionaries when reading older texts) to remember that the original etymological spelling of the language was only gradually replaced by phonetic spelling over the period 1910–1940. Since the intergovernmental agreement of the latter year spelling in all parts of the Luso-Brazilian world has been practically uniform, except for the retention in metropolitan Portugal of etymological (but silent) c's or p's before certain other consonants; examples are *acção, tecto* and *adoptar* (Brazilian *ação, teto, adotar*). Minor variations in the use of accents and other diacritics have continued since 1940, but these hardly affect the foreign reader's consultation of dictionaries.

Portuguese–English Bilingual Dictionaries

Recent advances here have not matched those in the Spanish–English field. There does not yet exist a thoroughly recommendable bilingual Portuguese–English or English–Portuguese dictionary, and the following represents only a selection of the best available.

FERREIRA, Júlio Albino. *Dicionário inglês–português/Dicionário português–inglês*. New ed., edited by Armando de Morais. 2 vols. Porto: Domingos Barreira, 1951–1954. Useful and generally competent, although more space could have been devoted to the more frequently used words. European usage tends to predominate over Brazilian.

The New Appleton Dictionary of the English and Portuguese Languages/Novo dicionário Appleton das línguas inglesa e portuguesa. Edited by Antonio Houaiss and Catherine B. Avery. New York: Appleton-Century-Crofts, 1964. A dictionary of Brazilian Portuguese; good on technical vocabulary and idiomatic expressions. Unfortunately, there is no adequate distinction between different senses of the same word, and the usage of the more frequent words lacks exemplification.

Novo Michaelis dicionário ilustrado. Edited by Fritz Pietzschke. 2 vols. São Paulo: Melhoramentos, and Wiesbaden: Brockhaus, 1958-1961. Draws mainly on the 8th edition of the *Novo dicionário Michaelis* (1932). Competent, with adequate distinction between translations, although somewhat lacking in

examples. Good on idioms. Some copies are lettered on the
spine *Brockhaus Picture Dictionary.*

OLIVEIRA, Maria Manuela Teixeira de. *Dicionário moderno
português–inglês.* Edited by Colin M. Bowker et al. Porto: Porto
Editora, 1966. Portuguese–English only. Fairly comprehensive
coverage of European Portuguese, good on idioms and set
expressions, and useful for translation purposes.

TAYLOR, James L. *A Portuguese–English Dictionary.* 2nd ed.
London: Harrap, 1963. Also Portuguese–English only, and
probably the best available source for translation work. It is
good on idioms and technical terms and for Brazilian flora and
fauna, and there are useful notes on misleading cognates. A
slightly revised edition was published in 1970 by Stanford
University Press.

Dicionário inglês–português. By Leonel and Lino Vallandro. 3rd
ed. Porto Alegre: Globo, 1976. English–Portuguese only. Fails
to distinguish adequately between different senses of the same
word, and there is a tendency towards excessive lexical clutter.
Nonetheless, useful for translating expressions and set phrases.

Portuguese Monolingual Dictionaries

Given the variable quality of the available bilingual dictionaries,
consultation of monolingual Portuguese dictionaries may frequently
be necessary. The following are recommendable:

AULETE, Caldas. *Dicionário contemporâneo da língua portuguesa.*
3rd Brazilian ed. 5 vols. Rio de Janeiro: Delta, 1974. Derives
ultimately from an 1881 original, but has been much updated.

Novo dicionário da língua portuguesa. Edited by Aurélio Buarque
de Holanda Ferreira. 2nd ed. Rio de Janeiro: Nova Fronteira,
1986. Cover-title: *Novo dicionário Aurélio da língua portuguesa.*
Comprehensive, up-to-date and oriented towards Brazilian
usage. Includes citations from a variety of sources.

Pequeno dicionário brasileiro da língua portuguesa. 11th ed. Rio de
Janeiro: Civilização Brasileira, 1964.

SILVA, António de Morais. *Grande dicionário da língua portuguesa.*
10th ed. 12 vols. Lisbon: Confluência, 1949–1959. Another

long-established dictionary, whose origin can be traced to 1789. Includes citations from written sources.

GW

Maps and Atlases

Current Mapping

The bibliography of the mapping of Latin American countries, like the mapping itself, is uneven both in coverage and in quality. The one current listing devoted specifically to the area is the 'Cartography' section in the biennial Social Sciences volume of the *Handbook of Latin American Studies* (Austin, TX: University of Texas Press). Beyond this, there are only the worldwide mapping lists. One of the most useful of these is the *Geo-Katalog*, issued in two parts by Geo-Center, Internationales Landkartenhaus, Stuttgart. Part I, which appears annually, lists small scale maps, town plans, tourist maps and guides. Part II appears every four to five years and is published in sections in loose-leaf format. It covers, in great detail, all current topographic and thematic maps available for the American continent (and elsewhere), arranged according to a geographical classification. The *Geo-Katalog* is supplemented by *Geo-Kartenbrief*, which appears three to four times a year, listing all new maps, atlases and works of geographical interest.

The most up-to-date guide to current maps is:

> PARRY, R. B. and C. R. PERKINS. *World Mapping Today.* London: Butterworth, 1987. A country-by-country guide to the best available maps, with introductory chapters on mapping in general. Arranged by continent. There are geographical and publishers indexes, and index maps indicating the coverage of specific countries and regions.

There is also a useful annual publication:

> *Bibliographic Guide to Maps and Atlases.* Boston, MA: G. K. Hall, 1980—. Lists selected publications catalogued by the Library of Congress and New York Public Library. Follows a dictionary arrangement, with maps and atlases entered under name, title, subject and geographic area.

A recent general atlas of Latin America is:

Atlas Latinskoi Ameriki. Moscow: Akademia Nauk, 1968.

Retrospective Bibliography

Unfortunately, there is no single bibliography of Latin American maps drawn or published before 1900. As long ago as the 1940s a project was undertaken by the Spanish Ministry of Foreign Affairs to publish a collection of facsimiles of the important older maps covering South America. Its only tangible result was:

GUILLÉN Y TATO, Julio Fernando. *Monumenta Chartographica Indiana.* Volume 1: Regiones del Plata y Magellánica. Madrid: Sección de Relaciones Culturales, Ministerio de Asuntos Exteriores, 1942.

A significant collection of facsimile maps was also assembled in:

Cartografía y relaciones históricas de Ultramar. Madrid: Servicio Geográfico del Ejército, 1949——. A selection of facsimiles of the maps in the archives of the Servicio Histórico Militar and the Servicio Geográfico del Ejército in Spain. Five volumes have so far been published, each with an accompanying atlas: 1. América; 2. Estados Unidos y Canadá; 3. Méjico; 4. América Central; 5. Colombia, Panamá, Venezuela.

Another important collection of facsimiles is:

ALBA, Duque de. *Mapas españoles de América, siglos XV-XVII.* Madrid: Maestre, 1951.

For earlier mapping in general the most informative catalogue is:

A Catalogue of Maps of Hispanic America, Including Maps in Scientific Periodicals ... and Sheet and Atlas Maps ... 4 vols. New York: American Geographic Society, 1930–1932.

More recent, and including a useful introduction to the subject, is:

MONTEIRO, Palmyra V. M. *A Catalogue of Latin American Flat Maps, 1926–1964.* 2 vols. Austin, TX: University of Texas, Institute of Latin American Studies, 1967–1969.

Another account, covering a similar period, is:

Annotated Index of Aerial Photographic Coverage and Mapping of Topography and Natural Resources Undertaken in the Latin American

Member Countries of the Organization of American States. Washington, DC: Pan American Union, 1964–1965.

This comprises collections of index sheets for nineteen countries, each with accompanying text discussing the aerial photography, topographic mapping, geology, soil, land capability, vegetation and land use surveys undertaken. It is being updated by a series of Research Guides for individual countries, sponsored by the Pan-American Institute of Geography and History (PAIGH) but prepared and published in the country concerned. Volumes have appeared to date for Argentina (1983), Chile (1978), Colombia (1975), Costa Rica (1977), Ecuador (1982), El Salvador (1977), Guatemala (1978), Honduras (2nd ed., 1987), Mexico (1980), Nicaragua (1977), Panama (2nd ed., 1987) and Peru (1979).

The dispute between Argentina and Chile over the Beagle Channel gave rise to much geographical interest in the area, and the memorials prepared by each government for submission to the International Court of Arbitration contain large selections of facsimile maps from the seventeenth to the twentieth centuries.

Descriptions and evaluations of particular older maps may be found in general works on the history of cartography and exploration, and in the specialist journals *Imago Mundi* (Berlin, 1935—) and *The Map Collector* (Tring, 1977—).

Individual Countries and Country-Groups

Listed below for each country or area are (1) bibliographies and (2) important atlases, insofar as they are available.

Argentina

1. SELVA, M. *Catálogo de la Mapoteca.* Buenos Aires: Biblioteca Nacional, 1941–1949. Parts 1 and 2 cover atlases and maps of Argentina.

   TURCO GRECO, Carlos A. *Catálogo cartográfico de la República Argentina.* Buenos Aires: EUDEBA for the Consejo Nacional de Investigaciones Científicas y Técnicas, 1967.

2. *Atlas total de la República Argentina.* Buenos Aires: Centro Editor de America Latina, 1981—. 6 volumes issued to date, including political, physical and economic maps.

RANDLE, P. H. *Atlas del desarrollo territorial de la Argentina.* Buenos Aires: Oikos, 1981. An historical atlas with text and statistics.

Bolivia

2. *Atlas de Bolivia.* Barcelona: Geomundo, 1985.

CONDARCO MORALES, Ramiro. *Atlas histórico de Bolivia.* La Paz: San José, 1985.

Brazil

1. ADONAIS, Isa. *Mapas e planos manuscritos relativos ao Brasil colonial conservados no Ministerio das Relações Exteriores, 1500–1822.* 2 vols. Rio de Janeiro: Ministerio das Relações Exteriores, 1960.

Mapas e outros materiais cartográficos na Biblioteca Central do IBGE. 2 vols. Rio de Janeiro: Instituto Brasileiro de Geografia e Estatística, 1983–1984.

These may be supplemented by the irregularly-published *Bibliografia cartográfica (do Brasil)* from the Mapoteca of the Ministério das Relações Exteriores and by works covering specific regions, such as:

Bibliografia cartográfica do Nordeste. Recife: Superintendência do Desenvolvimento do Nordeste, 1965.

ADONAIS, Isa. *A cartografia da região amazônica, 1500–1961.* 2 vols. Rio de Janeiro: Conselho Nacional de Pesquisas, 1963.

Further sources may be traced in:

GORDINI, Marília Júnia de Almeida. 'Fontes de informação cartográfica no Brasil.' *Revista da Escola de Biblioteconomia da Universidade Federal de Minas Gerais* 6:1 (March 1977), pp. 45–66.

2. *Atlas nacional do Brasil.* Rio de Janeiro: Conselho Nacional de Geografia, 1966.

Brasil: carta internacional do mundo ao milionésimo... Commemorative ed. Rio de Janeiro: Instituto Brasileiro de Geografia, Depto. de Cartografia, 1972. The cover title is *Carta do Brasil ao milionésimo.*

THÉRY, Hervé. *Brésil, un atlas chorématique/Brazil, a Chorematical Atlas.* Paris: Fayard/Reclus, 1986.

Central America

1. KAPP, Kit S. *Central America: Early Maps up to 1860.* North Bend, OH: Author, 1974.

   PALMERLEE, Albert E. *Maps of Costa Rica: An Annotated Carto-Bibliography.* Lawrence, KA: University of Kansas Libraries, 1978.

   CALDERÓN QUIJANO, José Antonio. *Cartografía de Belice y Yucatán.* Seville: Escuela de Estudios Hispano-Americanos, 1978.

2. *Atlas de El Salvador.* 3rd ed. San Salvador: Instituto Geográfico Nacional, 1979.

   Atlas nacional de Guatemala. Guatemala: Instituto Geográfico Nacional, 1972.

Chile

1. MEDINA, José Toribio. *Ensayo acerca de una mapoteca chilena.* Santiago: Ercilla, 1889; reprinted, 1952.

   Cartografía hispano colonial de Chile. Santiago: Instituto Geográfico Militar, 1952. Facsimiles.

2. *Atlas de la República de Chile.* 2nd ed. Santiago: Instituto Geográfico Militar, 1983.

Colombia

1. CORTÉS, Vicenta. *Catálogo de mapas de Colombia.* Madrid: Cultura Hispanica, 1967.

   KAPP, Kit S. *The Early Maps of Colombia up to 1850.* London: Map Collectors' Circle, 1971.

2. *Atlas de Colombia.* Edited by Eduardo Acevedo Latorre. 3rd ed. Bogotá: Instituto Geográfico Agustín Codazzi, 1977.

   Atlas de cartografía histórica de Colombia. Bogotá: Instituto Geográfico Agustín Codazzi, 1985.

Commonwealth Caribbean

The early maps of many Commonwealth territories have been listed by the Map Collectors' Circle in London. Issues include:

1. Tooley, R. V. *The Printed Maps of Antigua, 1689–1899*. Map Collectors' Series, 55. London: Map Collectors' Circle, 1969.

   Campbell, Tony. *The Printed Maps of Barbados*. Map Collectors' Series, 21. London: Map Collectors' Circle, 1965.

   Palmer, Margaret. *The Mapping of Bermuda*. Map Collectors' Series, 19. 3rd ed. London: Holland Press Cartographica, 1983.

   Tooley, R. V. *Printed Maps of Dominica and Grenada*. Map Collectors' Series, 62. London: Map Collectors' Circle, 1970.

   Kapp, Kit S. *The Printed Maps of Jamaica up to 1825*. Map Collectors' Series, 42. London: Map Collectors' Circle, 1968.

   Tooley, R. V. *Printed Maps of St. Kitts, St. Lucia and St. Vincent*. Map Collectors' Series, 8. London: Map Collectors' Circle, 1972.

   Some Early Printed Maps of Trinidad and Tobago. Map Collectors' Series, 10. London: Map Collectors' Circle, 1964.

Most Commonwealth countries (and some other developing countries) are covered by:

   A Catalogue of Maps Published by the Directorate of Overseas (Geodetic and Topographical) Surveys. Tolworth, Surrey: Directorate of Overseas Surveys, 1960.

This is updated by Part IV of:

   Technical Cooperation: A Monthly Bibliography. London: Overseas Development Administration Library, 1964—.

The Overseas Survey Directorate, Ordnance Survey, has made available from October 1986 their *List of OSD Mapping Available for Open Sale*, which cites current available maps of Barbados, Bermuda, Belize, the British Virgin Islands, the Cayman Islands, Dominica, Grenada, the Grenadines, Guyana, Jamaica, Montserrat, Nevis, St. Christopher, St. Lucia, St. Vincent, Trinidad, Tobago, and the Turks and Caicos Islands. The list is scheduled for publication three times a year.

Cuba

1. FIGAROLA CANEDA, Domingo. *Cartografía cubana del British Museum: catálogo cronológico de los siglos XVI al XIX*. 2nd ed. Havana: Imprensa Nacional, 1910.

   GRIFFIN, A. P. C. *List of Books Relating to Cuba. With a Bibliography of Maps, by P. L. Phillips*. Washington, DC: Library of Congress, 1898.

2. *Atlas nacional de Cuba en el 10º aniversario de la Revolucion*. Havana: Academia de Ciencias de Cuba, Instituto de Geografía, 1970.

   Atlas de Cuba. Havana: Instituto Cubano de Geodesía y Cartografía, 1978.

Dominican Republic

1. SANTIAGO, P. J. and E. RODRÍGUEZ DEMORIZI. *Mapas y planos de Santo Domingo*. Santo Domingo: Taller, 1979.

   GONZÁLEZ, Julio. *Archivo General de Indias. Catálogo de mapas y planos de Santo Domingo*. Madrid: Dirección General de Archivos y Bibliotecas, 1973.

Ecuador

1. LARREA, Carlos M. *Cartografía ecuatoriana de los siglos XVI, XVII y XVIII*. Quito: Corporación de Estudios y Publicaciones, 1977.

French Caribbean

2. *Atlas des départements français d'Outre-Mer*. Paris: Centre d'Etudes de la Géographie Tropicale du CNRS, Office de la Recherche Scientifique et Technique d'Outre-Mer, 1977—. Parts 1–3 cover Martinique, Guadeloupe and French Guiana.

Haiti

2. *Atlas d'Haïti*. Talence, France: Centre d'Etudes de la Géographie Tropicale du CNRS, Université de Bordeaux, 1985.

Mexico

1. HAGEN, Carlos B. 'The New Mapping of Mexico.' *Western Association of Map Librarians Information Bulletin* 10:2 (March 1979), pp. 108-116.

JÁUREGUI O., Ernesto. *Mapas y planos contemporáneos de México.* Mexico City: UNAM, Instituto de Investigaciones Sociales, 1968.

TAMAYO, Jorge L. and R. ALCORTA GUERRERO. *Catálogo de la exposición de cartografía mexicana.* Mexico City: Pan-American Institute of Geography and History, 1941.

TORRES LANZAS, Pedro. *Relación descriptiva de los mapas, planos & [sic] de México y Florida existentes en el Archivo General de Indias.* 2 vols. Seville: Mercantil, 1900.

2. FLORESCANO, Enrique. *Atlas histórico de México.* Mexico City: Siglo XXI, 1983.

Nuevo Atlas Porrúa de la República Mexicana. 7th ed. Mexico City: Porrúa, 1986.

Panama

1. RHOADS, James Berton. *Cartographic Records of the Panama Canal.* Washington, DC: National Archives, 1956.

Subject Catalog of the Special Panama Collection of the Canal Zone Library-Museum, Balboa Heights. Boston, MA: G. K. Hall, 1964.

KAPP, Kit S. *The Early Maps of Panama up to 1865.* London: Map Collectors' Circle, 1971.

BERNSON, Alexander. 'Panama: A Bibliography of Twentieth Century General Maps and Atlases of the Republic of Panama in the Library of Congress.' *SLA Geography and Map Division Bulletin* 75 (March 1969), pp. 21–25.

2. *Atlas nacional de Panamá.* 2nd ed. Panama City: Comisión del Atlas, 1975.

Peru

1. TEMPLE, Ella Dunbar. 'La cartografía peruana actual, con particular referencia a los últimos planos de desarrollo nacional.' *Boletín de la Sociedad Geográfica de Lima* 83 (1964), pp. 13–60.

2. *Atlas histórico, geográfico y de paisajes peruanos.* Lima: Instituto Nacional de Planeación, 1970.

Puerto Rico

1. Pico, Rafael. *Cartography in Puerto Rico.* San Juan, PR: Government Development Bank, 1964.

Arranz Recio, María José and Maria Angeles Ortega Benayas. *Planos y mapas de Puerto Rico.* Archivo Histórico Nacional, Seccion de Ultramar, 6. Madrid: Ministerio de Cultura, 1987.

Morales Padrón, Francisco et al. 'Cartografía sobre Puerto Rico en París, Londres y Madrid.' *Anuario de Estudios Americanos* 18 (1961), pp. 615–649.

Surinam

1. Koeman, Cornelis. *Bibliography of Printed Maps of Suriname, 1671–1971.* Amsterdam: Theatrum Orbis Terrarum, 1973.

Koeman, Cornelis. *Links with the Past: History of Cartography of Suriname, 1500–1971.* Amsterdam: Theatrum Orbis Terrarum, 1973.

Venezuela

1. González, Julio. *Archivo General de Indias. Catálogo de mapas y planos de Venezuela.* Madrid: Dirección General de Archivos y Bibliotecas, 1968.

Morales Padrón, Francisco and J. Llavador Mira. *Mapas, planos y dibujos sobre Venezuela existentes en el Archivo General de Indias.* Series 1 and 2. Seville: Escuela de Estudios Hispano-Americanos, 1958–1965.

2. *Atlas de Venezuela.* 2nd ed. Caracas: Dirección de Cartografía Nacional, 1979.

González Oropeza, Hermann. *Atlas de historia cartográfica de Venezuela.* Caracas: Papi, 1983. Facsimiles of maps produced from 1490 to the mid-nineteenth century.

Major Map Collections

There is a published guide to map collections prepared for the International Federation of Library Associations and Institutions. This is:

WOLTER, John A. et al. *World Directory of Map Collections.* 2nd ed. Munich: K. G. Saur for IFLA, 1986.

In the United Kingdom there are several important general map collections that have good coverage of the region. In the London area, the British Library, the Public Record Office, and the National Maritime Museum at Greenwich have notable collections, and each has a published catalogue:

Manuscript Maps, Charts and Plans and Topographical Drawings in the British Museum. 3 vols. London: British Museum, 1844–1861.

Catalogue of Printed Maps, Charts and Plans. 15 vols. London: British Museum, Map Library, 1967. There is also a supplement (1978) covering 1965–1974 accessions.

Maps and Plans in the Public Record Office. Volume 2: America and the West Indies. London: Public Record Office, 1974.

National Maritime Museum: Catalogue of the Library. Volume 3: Atlases and Cartography. 2 parts. London: Her Majesty's Stationery Office, 1971.

Outside London there are three copyright deposit libraries, all aiming at worldwide map coverage. These are Cambridge University Library, the National Library of Scotland in Edinburgh and the Bodleian Library in Oxford. The latter issues a monthly list of selected map accessions.

In the United States, the most important map collection is that of the Geography and Map Division of the Library of Congress in Washington, DC. The card catalogue has been published as:

The Bibliography of Cartography. 5 vols. Boston, MA: G. K. Hall, 1973. There is also a *First Supplement* in 2 volumes (1980).

The Caribbean collections are also catalogued in:

SELLERS, John R. and Patricia MOLEN VAN EE. *Maps and Charts of North America and the West Indies: A Guide to the Collections in the*

Library of Congress. Washington, DC: Government Printing Office, 1981. Maps of the Caribbean are listed on pp. 367–456.

Other major US map collections are held by the American Geographical Society in Madison, Wisconsin, and by the New York Public Library.

Remote Sensing Imagery Resources

The two main earth resource satellite systems to include coverage of Latin America are the US Landsat series and the French SPOT satellite. Both offer imagery in a range of photographic products or on computer-compatible tapes (CCTs). Information about the imagery available and free search services may be obtained from both EOSAT (Earth Observation Satellite Company) for Landsat and from SPOT Image:

> EOSAT, EROS Data Center
> Sioux Falls SD 57198
> USA

> SPOT Image
> 16 bis, Avenue Edouard Berlin
> F 31030 Toulouse Cedex
> France

In the UK, the British Library Map Library holds the Landsat MicroCatalog of all available Landsat data together with imagery on 16mm microfilm or (from 1986) on microfiche. For online search facilities to the SPOT data catalogue, contact either the Nigel Press Association (Edenbridge, Kent) or the National Remote Sensing Centre (Royal Aircraft Establishment, Farnborough, Hants.).

JDE/BDF

Newspapers and News Magazines

Newspapers are unique and invaluable sources of information and opinion. They are also expensive, bulky and fragile, and libraries are often reluctant to acquire or keep them. A convenient and often unavoidable substitute, for recent decades at least, is the weekly, fortnightly or monthly news magazine. Most countries of the world, and practically all those in the Americas, now have at least one local imitator of the *Time*/*Newsweek* formula.

The content of newspapers and news magazines is necessarily selective. Selection will be determined primarily by the characteristics, interests and prejudices of the paper's target readership, but will clearly also be influenced by the proprietor's own views and attitudes, those of his advertisers and—most importantly in a Latin American context—by governmental and other external pressures, overt and covert. The researcher must endeavour to find out how these various factors apply in each individual case, and be aware of any sudden changes in them—such as those affecting the Mexican paper *Excelsior* in the 1970s or more recently *Ercilla* in Chile. In short, beware of interpreting a paper's current contents solely on a basis of its past policies.

Sources of Information on the Media

An excellent first step to understanding the nature of each country's media, with details concerning individual newspapers, is:

KURIAN, George Thomas. *World Press Encyclopedia.* 2 vols. New York: Facts on File, and London: Mansell, 1982. Not a directory of newspapers, but a guide, arranged alphabetically by country, to the nature and status of the press and other new media, their relations with the government, censorship, the education of journalists and other related topics.

There are also sections on the press in the US Army's *Area Handbook* series, which are currently entitled *Brazil* (etc.): *A Country Study*. For more information see HANDBOOKS, GUIDES AND DIRECTORIES, p. 161.

A bibliography of works about the press is:

GARDNER, Mary A. *The Press of Latin America: A Tentative and Selective Bibliography in Spanish and Portuguese.* Austin, TX: University of Texas Press, 1973.

Unfortunately, not even KURIAN is up-to-date enough: his chapter on Argentina, for instance, was prepared around 1980. For more prosaic information, such as current addresses, reference may be made to the current year's issue of *Benn's Press Directory* (international volume), or *Willing's Press Guide*, or (since neither is wholly comprehensive) a telephone directory of the town of publication.

For tracing older titles, there is:

A Chronological Listing of Leading Latin American Newspapers: A Tentative Selection of Newspapers Considered of Value for Historical Research... Compiled by John L. Hardesty. Washington, DC: Library of Congress, 1965. Published for the Conference on Latin American History and the Hispanic Foundation.

Supplementing this for the Gran Colombia countries is:

GUTIÉRREZ WITT, Laura. 'Newspaper Titles from Colombia, Ecuador and Venezuela Unavailable in US Libraries: A Survey.' In *Final Report and Working Papers* of SALALM XVIII, 1973. Amherst, MA: SALALM, 1975, pp. 433–456.

Leading Current Latin American and West Indian Newspapers

It is obviously impossible to list all the available Latin American newspapers here: what follows is a personal, and probably idiosyncratic, selection, with occasional notes on political stance, history or circulation figures.

Argentina, Buenos Aires: *La Nación*—quality paper, with 235,000 circulation; *La Prensa*—quality, 115,000; *Clarín*—tabloid, 530,000; *Buenos Aires Herald*—English language, outstanding for its independence during the regime of the generals.

Barbados, Bridgetown: *Advocate-News*.

Brazil, Belo Horizonte: *Estado de Minas*.
Brasília: *Correio Brasiliense*.

Porto Alegre: *Correio do Povo*.

Recife: *Diário de Pernambuco*; *Jornal do Commêrcio*—the oldest in South America.

Rio de Janeiro: *Jornal do Brasil*—quality paper, founded 1890; *O Globo*—important mass-circulation paper, with a circulation of 200,000 copies on weekdays and 425,000 on Sundays, owned by the largest TV network outside North America; *Latin American Daily Post*—Anglo-American English language paper, containing the formerly separate *Brazil Herald* as a four-page insert; *Jornal do Commêrcio*—founded 1827, but has lost its former preeminence.

São Paulo: *Estado de São Paulo*—respected, independent, the traditional voice of the coffee industry, Latin America's outstanding quality newspaper, and one of the world's bulkiest, with a national circulation of 185,000; *Folha de São Paulo* (formerly *Folha da Manhã*)—mass paper, challenging *O Globo* with aggressive promotion, even outside Brazil; *Gazeta Mercantil*—important business paper.

Chile, Santiago: *El Mercurio*—in its Valparaiso edition, the second oldest paper in South America, and the respected quality voice of Edwards banking interests; *La Epoca*—opposition tabloid founded in 1987 by the publisher of *Hoy* news magazine as a calculated challenge to the Pinochet regime; *La Nación*—government-owned since 1927; *La Tercera* (originally *Tercera de la Hora*)—the most important mass-circulation tabloid not owned by the Edwards family.

Colombia, Bogotá: *El Tiempo*—liberal; *El Espectador*—founded 1887.
Medellín: *El Colombiano*—conservative.

Costa Rica, San José: *La Nación*—quality tabloid.

Cuba, Havana: *Granma*—the official Party organ, also published in a weekly English-language edition. The title is that of the boat—named for the owner's grandmother—that Castro returned to Cuba in to begin his military takeover.

Dominican Republic, Santo Domingo: *El Caribe*.

Ecuador, Guayaquil: *El Telégrafo*—Ecuador's oldest paper.
Quito: *El Comercio*; *El Universo*.

Guatemala, Guatemala City: *El Imparcial*.

Guyana, Georgetown: *Guyana Chronicle* (and separate *Sunday Chronicle*).

Jamaica, Kingston: *Daily* (and *Sunday*) *Gleaner*—founded 1834; pro-JLP.

Mexico, Mexico City: *Excelsior*—liberal prior to the 1976 government takeover; *Novedades*—elite; *El Heraldo de México*—'yuppie'; *Nacional*—organ of the PRI; *Uno Más Uno*—opposition paper started by the journalists who left *Excelsior* in disgust in 1976; *Jornada*—more recently founded paper with similar antecedents to the preceding.

Nicaragua, Managua: *Barricada*—the Sandinista Front paper.

Panama, Panama City: *Star and Herald*—veteran English-language but Panama-owned paper; *Estrella de Panamá*—leading daily, which began in the 1850s as a Spanish-language column in the *Star* (now its sister-paper); *La Prensa*—opposition paper founded in 1979 when government pressure muted criticism in *Estrella*.

Peru, Lima: *La Prensa*—outstanding paper with moderate conservative stance and a circulation of about 100,000; *El Comercio*—founded in 1839, now with a circulation of around 90,000.

Trinidad, Port of Spain: *Guardian* (formerly *Trinidad Guardian*)—during the 1960s and 1970s the island's only daily, and in a running fight with the PNM government; *Sunday Guardian*—its sister-paper.

Venezuela, Caracas: *El Nacional*—liberal, with a circulation of around 140,000; *El Universal*—conservative, businessman's paper (around 130,000); *Ultimas Noticias*—popular (around 230,000): *Diario de Caracas*—independent, outspoken, elite tabloid, founded in 1979 (about 40,000).

European and North American Newspapers

European and North American newspapers are received more promptly and available in many more libraries than are those from Latin America. But only a few are notable for their coverage of the region; examples are *Le Monde* (Paris), the *New York Times* and the *Neue Zürcher Zeitung*. *The Miami Herald* has a sizable Caribbean readership, particularly in Panama; its Spanish language edition, *El Miami Herald*, has excellent Latin American coverage. Coverage by

UK newspapers is less good, though *The Times* and the *Financial Times* will be found useful, as will (in matters affecting ecology and human and Amerindian rights) *The Guardian*. The *International Herald Tribune* has a Latin American edition, and there is also the *Times of the Americas*, published in Washington from 1956; this has a newspaper format, but appears only fortnightly.

Newspaper Collections in Libraries

Few libraries provide very up-to-date service with newspapers, as most have sea mail subscriptions or purchase quarterly microform copy. For the most recent issues, it may be worthwhile asking at embassies or consulates, which will almost certainly receive their countries' major newspapers by air. On the other hand, many libraries that take hard copy papers do not care to face the costs of binding, microfilming or otherwise preserving them, and discard back files every six to twelve months or so. It is essential to enquire before visiting.

Newspaper Collections in the UK

The best collections of Latin American newspapers in the British Isles are those at the British Library's Newspaper Library (at Colindale in North London). Other important collections can be found in the libraries of the Universities of Essex and Glasgow.

Colindale's last general catalogue appeared in 1975. There is no current union list of newspapers of Latin American interest held by British libraries, and the records of the *British Union Catalogue of Latin Americana* (see UNION CATALOGUES AND UNION LISTS, pp. 63-64) are almost certainly incomplete. More than a decade ago the Social Sciences Research Council produced:

WEBBER, Rosemary. *World List of National Newspapers: A Union List of National Newspapers in Libraries in the British Isles*. London: Butterworths, 1976. A supplement to 1984 was published in the *British Library Newspaper Library Newsletter*, Supplement no. 1.

Unfortunately, this excludes the holdings of the British Library; it also interprets 'national' narrowly and rather quixotically, excluding even *O Estado de São Paulo* as provincial. It also has many other omissions: *Excelsior*, *El Heraldo de México* and *Nacional* (all held by English libraries) are examples with respect to Mexico alone.

Newspaper Collections in North America

Nearly 6,000 titles (including many long ago defunct), held by 72 US libraries, are listed in:

> CHARNO, Steven M. *Latin American Newspapers in United States Libraries: A Union List.* Austin, TX: University of Texas Press, 1968. Though now very out of date, this still represents the only source of information on many of the titles listed.

More recent titles are included in *New Serial Titles, 1950–1970* with its monthly supplements cumulated quarterly, annually and five-yearly (see PERIODICALS, p. 214). The Library of Congress publishes its own list:

> *Newspapers Received Currently at the Library of Congress.* 9th ed. Edited by Frank J. Carroll and John Plugg, Jr. Washington, DC: Library of Congress, 1984.

A guide to what is available in California (in 15 libraries) is:

> ROBINSON, Barbara J. *Latin American Newspapers in California Libraries: Southern California.* Los Angeles, CA: Southern California Consortium on International Studies, Latin American Committee, and UCLA Latin American Center, 1978.

and there are other specialised lists from individual libraries.

Newspapers in Microform

The Center for Research Libraries (CRL) in Chicago has built up a large microfilm archive of Latin American and other foreign newspapers, begun as the Foreign Newspapers Microfilm Project of the (American) Association of Research Libraries. The CRL loans or sells copies of its holdings, but only to member libraries. If the demand in your local institution justifies it, you may want to persuade your library to join the scheme. Further developments in the field are chronicled in the 'Annual Report on Microfilming Projects' (formerly the 'Microfilming Projects Newsletter'), produced annually by the Seminar on the Acquisition of Latin American Library Materials (SALALM), and disseminated to conference attendees at their annual meetings.

The Library of Congress issues an annual *Newspapers in Microform* in respect of its own holdings. This supplements its own catalogue *Newspapers in Microform: Foreign Countries, 1948–1983* (1984).

Many Brazilian microforms derive from a project of the Biblioteca Nacional in Rio de Janeiro to make all Brazilian newspapers and other periodicals available on microfilm or microfiche. A catalogue, first issued in 1981, was recently updated as:

> *Periódicos brasileiros em microforma: catálogo coletivo, 1984.* Coleção Rodolfo Garcia, 18. Rio de Janeiro: Biblioteca Nacional, 1985. Lists nearly 2,700 titles from 23 states.

Copies of the microfilms are available from the Plano Nacional de Microfilmagem de Periódicos Brasileiros, Avenida Rio Branco 219, 20.042 Rio de Janeiro RJ. Achievements include complete runs of *O Estado de São Paulo* (formerly, *A Província de São Paulo*) from 1875, and Rio's *Jornal do Commêrcio* from 1827.

Inter-Library Loan

It is generally not feasible to borrow newspapers in hard copy through inter-library loan, but it may be worth trying for photocopies of articles, if you have precise enough details. Issue and page number are seldom sufficient: most Latin American dailies are North American in style and size, with many sections (numbered, lettered or designated by title), each with its own pagination. Ideally, you should also cite column number too—and watch out for papers issued in more than one edition (*El Mercurio*, for instance, has separate editions for Santiago and Valparaíso), or the same title used in more than one country (*La Prensa* in Argentina, Panama, Peru and intermittently in Nicaragua) or city (the *Jornal do Commêrcio* of Rio is unconnected with the *Jornal do Commêrcio* of Recife). Photocopying individual newspaper articles frequently causes too many problems (see INTER-LIBRARY LENDING, p. 76), and you may well find it more convenient to try to borrow a microform copy.

Latin American News Magazines

As with the list of newspapers above, this is a personal selection of the leading news magazines published in the region.

Argentina: *Review of the River Plate*—fortnightly, business news with straight text, in English; *Visión*—also fortnightly, more general, illustrated but still business-oriented.

Brazil: *Veja*—Latin America's best-run weekly, with a New York office and a large staff of foreign correspondents, indexed annually

in hard copy and microform (circulation 850,000); *Afinal*—
Brazil's newest *Time*-format weekly, begun 1984; *Visão*—Brazilian
stablemate of the Argentine/Mexican *Visión*, fortnightly; *Exame*
—fortnightly, main magazine for financial and business news;
Manchete—picture weekly modelled on *Life*, with good, serious
articles, though libraries seem reluctant to stock it because of the
'cheesecake' element, which can attract mutilators; *Isto E*,
Senhor—a 1988 merger between two famous news magazines: *Isto
E*, famous for its outspokenness during the later years of military
rule, and *Senhor*, modelled on *The Economist*, whence came much
of its international copy.

Chile: *Ercilla*—weekly, which changed policy dramatically when it
was acquired by a financial group sympathetic to Pinochet;
Hoy—opposition weekly, founded in 1977 by Emilio Filippi when
he was ousted from *Ercilla*; *Mensaje*—a Jesuit monthly inclining to
the Christian Democrats, shut down by the government even
more often than *Hoy*; *Qué Pasa*—weekly, favouring democratic
capitalism.

Colombia: *Vea*—weekly; *Semana*—monthly (!).

Mexico: *Proceso*—denunciatory of the government; *Razones*—run by
former staff of *Proceso* antagonized by the latter's alleged lack of
objectivity; *Siempre*—leftist; *Visión*—fortnightly, same stable as its
Argentine namesake; *Tiempo*—pro-government weekly, which for
copyright reasons circulates in the US as *Hispanoamericano*.

Panama: *Analisis*; *Diálogo Social*.

Peru: *Oiga*—weekly; *Caretas*—fortnightly.

Venezuela: *Bohemia*—weekly (circulation 86,000); *Auténtico*—
(20,000); *Resumen*—(5,000).

Although it is now fifteen years old, a work that may still be useful
as a holdings list to news magazines in British and Irish libraries is
the Committee on Latin America's *Latin America History with Politics:
A Serials List* (see INTER-LIBRARY LENDING, p. 73).

Newsletters

There is a considerable—and increasing—supply of weekly, fortnightly and monthly digests of news from or concerning Latin
America. These derive most of their information from internal and

external press reports and from news agencies, but may also have their own independent sources. They are deliberately brief and sometimes strongly opinionated. They vary in price from free propaganda handouts to expensive investors' guides which few libraries can afford.

The dean of them all is the liberal and quite personal *Hanson's Latin American Letter* (Washington, DC, 1945—), a four-page weekly. The best known, however, are the publications of Latin American Newsletters Ltd., a London-based firm now in Argentine ownership. The original *Latin America* of April 1967 has undergone a number of changes. Currently it appears as the twelve-page *Latin America Weekly Report* (November 1979—), which summarises matters treated in more detail in the five regional, monthly reports: *Andean Group Report, Brazil Report, Caribbean Report, Mexico and Central America Report* and *Southern Cone Report*. Their *Informe Latinoamericano* (1982—) is the *Weekly Report* in Spanish. There is a fortnightly *Commodities Report*, and the monthly *Economic Report* recently resumed publication. Topics needing treatment at length receive it in *Latin America Special Reports* (available in Spanish as the *Informes Especiales*), published six times a year. Remember when looking for any of this publisher's newsletters that some libraries and catalogues treat 'Latin America' (or 'Latin American'—the publisher is not consistent) as part of the title, while others do not.

Similar in appearance and coverage to the Latin American Newsletters series is the *Latin American Monitor* (London, 1984—) with its five separate monthly sections on *Mexico and Brazil, Central America*, the *Andean Group*, the *Southern Cone* and the *Caribbean*.

Another London-based newsletter (though originally published in Bogotá) is Christopher Story's *Latin American Times* (1979—). This four-page monthly is independent and strongly opinionated: it is economically orthodox, politically rightist.

The almost bewildering variety of Washington-based newsletters includes the fortnightly looseleaf *Washington Letter on Latin America* (1981—) on Washington events affecting the region, especially in business; it is published in association with Latin American Newsletters. Other bimonthly looseleaf reports are the *Latin American Index* (1973—), emphasising news affecting trade, and the *Latin American Update/Update Latin America* (1975—) analysing US foreign policy. The Council on Hemispheric Affairs (COHA) issues the fortnightly eight-page *Washington Report on the Hemisphere* (alias *COHA's Washington Report*): liberal, with a regular 'Washington Watch' section on local events, decisions and reactions concerning

Latin America, and not to be confused with the *Hemisphere Hot Line
Report*. From the Washington suburb of Arlington, Virginia, comes
the *Latin American Report*, formerly *Translations on Latin America* (150
issues a year, 1967—).

Other US newsletters on the region as a whole are *Latin American
Market Report* (Coral Gables, FL, 1981—), *Business Latin America:
Weekly Report to Managers of Latin American Operations* (New York:
Business International Corporation, 1966—), useful for its commer-
cial and financial statistics; *Noticias: Weekly Digest of Hemisphere
Reports* (New York: National Trade Council, 1945—), a digest of
articles from Latin American sources; the fortnightly *Wagner Latin
American Newsletter* (Cottonwood, MA, 1977—) of 'current news
from Spanish language sources'; and the *Latin American Monthly
Economic Report* (Philadelphia, PA, 1986—). The North American
Congress on Latin America's monthly newsletter, *Latin America and
Empire Report* (New York, 1971–1977) has now become the bimonthly *NACLA Report on the Americas* (1977—), but frequency and
format changes make this less of a newsletter than it was. It focuses
on 'the political economy of the Americas' in terms of imperialism
and dependency. In addition, Latin American Information Sources
of New York produce the fortnightly *Lagniappe Letter*—the word
(they say) is Quechua for 'something extra'—and the *Lagniappe
Quarterly Report* of 'economic, political, financial and policy information'.

General newsletters from the region itself include *Noticias Aliadas*,
available in English as *Latinamerica Press* (Lima, 1969—), an
eight-page weekly focusing on human rights and other sociopolitical
issues of concern to the liberal wing of the Catholic Church; and
Semana Latinoamericana (Mexico City: Agencia Latinoamericana de
Servicios Especiales de Información, 1986—).

Among the geographically specialised newsletters are:

Brazil: *Brazil Watch* by Stephen Foster (Washington, DC: Orbis,
1828 L St NW, suite 660)—for economic, political and business
events; *Infobrazil* (Washington, DC: Center of Brazilian Studies,
Johns Hopkins University).

Central America: *Central America Report* (Guatemala City, 1974—)
—a weekly digest of information from chambers of commerce,
banks, government press releases and newspapers.

Chile: *Chilean Digest* (Kamloops, BC, 1980—).

Commonwealth Caribbean: *Caribbean Contact* (Kingston: Caribbean Conference of Churches, 1973—)—monthly, stressing human rights issues.

Mexico: *Mexico Letter* (McLean, VA, 1980—); *Mexico Report* (El Paso, TX).

Peru: *Andean Report*, formerly *Peruvian Times* (Lima, 1975—) —monthly, including brief notes from Bolivia, Chile, Colombia, Ecuador and Venezuela.

A now somewhat outdated listing of newsletters, news digests, news bulletins and other news sources and agencies is in:

Vivo, Paquita. *Latin America: A Selected List of Sources.* Washington, DC: Latin American Service, 1972.

More current, but limited to the US and Canada, is:

The Oxbridge Directory of Newsletters, 1987. 5th ed. Edited by Margie Domenech. New York: Oxbridge Communications, 1987.

News Digests

Information Latine of Paris and *Agencia Efe* of Madrid are daily. *Facts on File* (1944—) and *Deadline Data on World Affairs* (on cards or online, 1956—) are American weekly digests with worldwide coverage.

Keesing's Contemporary Archives, renamed in 1987 *Keesing's Record of World Events*, is Dutch in origin, but its UK edition (London, 1931—) is the most widely purchased digest in British libraries. It is now a looseleaf monthly, with permanent annual volumes. The indexes (of personal names and of countries subdivided by subjects) are continuously updated through the year, but its scope is rather limited by its insistence on describing such formal legal events as governmental changes and international agreements in almost textual detail. Information does not always appear promptly: the January 1987 issue, for example, reported results from the Brazilian elections of November 1986, and from the British Virgin Islands election of September 1986.

Cuba produces the bimonthly *Prensa Latina* (published in Mexico City), and the Instituto para la Integración de América Latin (a Buenos Aires dependency of the Inter-American Development Bank) notes economic news in its monthly *Archivo de Prensa*.

Clippings

Few libraries can afford the staff to maintain a subject-arranged
collection of newspaper clippings. Two in the UK that have
managed this continuously since the 1920s are the Economic
Department of Lloyds Bank International (formerly the Bank of
London and South America), and the Royal Institute of International Affairs (Chatham House) library, both in London. A very
detailed 'Presse Archiv' (three-quarters of it from Latin American
sources) has been maintained since the late 1960s by the Institut für
Iberoamerika-Kunde of Hamburg.

Information Services on Latin America of Oakland, California
has since 1970 published *ISLA*, a monthly packet service of
reproductions of clippings from nine leading US and international
newspapers (including the *Guardian/Le Monde* weekly international
edition), with a six-monthly index. The service is also available on
microfilm, or in regional packets covering smaller areas. ISLA's
parent company, DataCenter, also publishes *Central America Monitor*,
which appears 20 times each year and reproduces articles on the
region from 125 (mainly US) publications.

During the 1960s and 1970s a collection of cuttings from Latin
American newspapers on a wide range of religious and sociopolitical topics was gathered by the Centro Intercultural de
Documentación of Cuernavaca, Mexico (CIDOC). This was reproduced in both hard copy and microform, and many libraries
have complete sets.

A press cutting service on Brazil, tailored to individual subscribers' needs, is available from LuxJornal (Rua Frei Caneca 165,
20.211 Rio de Janeiro, RJ), and a similar service covering Central
America can be had from Inforpress Centroamericana (9a Calle
'A' 3-56, Zona 1, 01001 Guatemala City). An increasing number of
news sources are also available in machine-readable form; see the
chapter on DATABASES (p. 229).

Indexes

Few of the news sources mentioned above are indexed: *Veja* is an
exception already cited, and the National Library of Jamaica
(formerly the West India Reference Library of the Institute of
Jamaica) maintains an index to the *Daily Gleaner*. There are
published indexes to a few years of the Caracas newspapers *El
Nacional* and *El Universal*; and sporadic attempts have been made to

index some Uruguayan and nineteenth century Mexican newspapers.

Fortunately, it is usually easy to research a newspaper once the day of an event is known, and this information can often be found through *Keesing's Record of World Events* (see above) or the index to a major European or North American newspaper. The *New York Times* publishes a current index, twice monthly since 1907, with quarterly and annual cumulations, and has retrospectively indexed earlier volumes back to September 1851. There is also a separate *Obituaries Index* in two volumes (1858–1968 and 1969–1978). The similar official index to the London *Times* began in 1906; since 1973 it has also covered the weekly educational and literary supplements and the *Sunday Times*. An earlier period is covered by *Palmer's Index to the 'Times' Newspaper, 1790–1941*. There is also a specialised index of particular interest to Brazilianists:

> GRAHAM, Richard and Virginia VALIELA. *Brazil in the London 'Times', 1850–1905: A Guide*. SALALM Bibliography and Reference Series, 1. Washington, DC: SALALM, 1969.

Annual (and Part-Annual) Surveys

The Instituto de Cooperación Iberoamericana in Madrid, formerly the Instituto de Cultura Hispánica, has issued a series of partly overlapping annual surveys of events in Latin America since 1963: *Anuario iberoamericano* (1962–1969), *Síntesis informativa iberoamericana* (1971–1975) and the current *Documentación iberoamericana* (1963—). Since 1982 Holmes and Meier of New York have been publishing an annual country-by-country survey, *Latin America and Caribbean Contemporary Record*. Facts on File issued the annual *Latin America* compilation for the years 1972–1978. There are also supplements to one or two Latin American encyclopaedias issued as 'books of the year': an example is the 'Anuário' of the Brazilian *Enciclopédia Barsa*.

Much briefer surveys appear as 'News from the Hispanic World' in *Hispania*, published quarterly by the American Association of Teachers of Spanish and Portuguese (Stanford, CA, 1918—), and as 'Chronik' in Verlag Klaus Dieter Vervuert's thrice-yearly *Ibero-amerika* (Frankfurt, 1977—).

Broadcasting

The British Broadcasting Corporation Monitoring Service provides information on foreign broadcasting in two publications: the daily

Monitoring Report and the six-times weekly *Summary of World Broadcasts*, of which part 5 covers Latin America. The US equivalent is the *Daily Report: Latin America* of the Foreign Broadcast Information Service. This has been indexed since 1978 by News Bank, Inc. as *Index, FBIS Daily Report: Latin America*, originally quarterly, but monthly since 1983, with annual cumulations.

LH

Official Publications

Official publications (or government documents, as they are usually called in the United States) originate at every level of government —municipal, provincial, national and international. For dependent territories such as Puerto Rico there will also be relevant publications of the metropolitan authorities.

Government publications can be important in almost every field of study, from pure science to literature—and this is particularly true in smaller countries which may lack a significant commercial book industry. In the case of the West Indies, there is a useful introduction to the range and nature of government publishing:

> HALLEWELL, Laurence. 'West Indian Official Publishing and UK Official Publishing on the West Indies: Before Independence and After.' In *Twenty Years of Latin American Librarianship: Final Report and Working Papers* of SALALM XXI, 1976. Amherst, MA: SALALM, 1978, pp. 201–221.

Citation

Official publishing presents its own special difficulties, both in discovering what has been published and in locating a known item in a library catalogue. Authorship is sometimes attributed to a named individual, but this is exceptional and is ignored in some library catalogues. Most libraries enter government publications under the name of the country or other political unit, with the name of the department immediately responsible as a subheading: thus, 'Trinidad and Tobago. Central Statistical Office'. Some libraries, however, use other systems, such as 'Political unit—Date—Department' or 'Political unit—Ministry—Department—Title'. Sometimes, if the name of the issuing body can stand on its own, titles are entered directly under it, as in the case of the Instituto Brasileiro de Geografia e Estatística. The advent of the new *Anglo-American Cataloguing Rules* (AACR2) in 1978 has led to much simplification in the entry of government publications: now the great majority of them are entered directly under title.

Periodicals (serials) are also usually entered under title, although in many older library catalogues they may be found entered under the name of the issuing body in the same way as monographs. They are sometimes found in the library's main catalogue, and sometimes relegated to a separate catalogue; practice varies from library to library.

Even the form of name used in the headings may vary. Some libraries use 'Great Britain' and others 'United Kingdom'; the British Library's *General Catalogue of Printed Books* uses 'England'. Many English libraries, and some American ones, have 'Argentine Republic' rather than 'Argentina'. In some instances older forms of spelling may have survived—'Hayti', 'Parahyba' and so on. This is becoming less common, however, as the use of databases and shared cataloguing brings about greater conformity.

Government bodies frequently change their names, and these changes are of course reflected in the library catalogue. Materials appearing at lengthy intervals, such as five-year plans, are especially likely to change issuing bodies between one publication and the next. Library catalogues vary considerably in the amount of detailed cross-referencing they make between successive organizational names; the United States *National Union Catalog* (see UNION CATA-LOGUES AND UNION LISTS, pp. 62–63) is particularly helpful in this respect. Acronyms of government bodies can also be troublesome; see ACRONYMS AND ABBREVIATIONS (p. 357).

General Bibliographies

The researcher will often lack sufficient details to track down an item in a library catalogue. When this happens, or when there is a need to know what government publications exist on a certain topic, there are a number of guides that may be consulted. The most recent comprehensive guide is:

PALIC, Vladimir M. *Government Publications: A Guide to Biblio-graphical Tools*. Oxford: Pergamon Press, 1976. Pp. 214–238 are devoted to Central and South America.

Older but still useful publications include:

CHILDS, James Bennett. *Government Publications (Documents)*. Washington, DC: Library of Congress, 1974.

GROPP, Arthur E. *A Bibliography of Latin American Biblio-graphies.* Metuchen, NJ: Scarecrow Press, 1968. Also its supplements, cited in full on pp. 88–89.

PERAZA SARAUSA, Fermín. *Bibliografías sobre publicaciones oficiales de la America Latina.* Gainesville, FL: Author, 1964.

UK Government Publications

British official publishing on Latin America can be traced in the daily, monthly and annual catalogues of Her Majesty's Stationery Office (HMSO). HMSO material relating to Trinidad and Tobago has been listed in:

McDOWELL, Wilhelmina. 'Official Publications on Trinidad and Tobago, 1797–1962.' Unpublished fellowship thesis. London: Library Association, 1971.

Since 1979 an increasingly large number of titles has been published directly by the government department concerned rather than by HMSO; these items are best traced in the *Catalogue of British Official Publications Not Published by HMSO* (Cambridge: Chadwyck-Healey, 1981—; a keyword index is also available on microfiche). For older material the official published indexes to Parliamentary Papers can be particularly rewarding. Some British government publications can also be traced through the *British National Bibliography*.

US Government Publications

Over the years the United States government has published a great deal of material relating to Latin America. Most of this can be traced in the *Monthly Catalog of US Government Publications* (Washington, DC: Government Printing Office, 1895—), and in the cumulative title and subject indexes (covering 1789–1976 and 1900–1971 respectively) published commercially to supplement it. The Congressional Information Service's *CIS US Serial Set Index, 1789–1969* and the subsequent *CIS Index* are also valuable tools for tracing the relevant Congressional publications of the period. For a general introduction to this vast area see:

APPERSON, Frances and Sally CRAVENS. 'US Government Publications on Latin America.' In *Final Report and Working Papers* of SALALM XIX, 1974. Amherst, MA: SALALM, 1976, vol. 2, pp. 401–415.

Latin American Government Publications

No Latin American government currently issues catalogues of its
publications as comprehensive as those of HMSO or the US
Government Printing Office, but many individual departments issue
lists of their own publications. The standard guide, now somewhat
outdated, is:

> CHILDS, J. B. *A Guide to the Official Publications of the Other
> American Republics.* 19 parts. Washington, DC: Library of
> Congress, 1945–1949; reprinted in 2 volumes, New York:
> Johnson, 1964.

The nineteen parts of this work cover Latin America country by
country, with the exception of Mexico (for which see KER below,
under Individual Countries).

The working papers of the annual Seminar on the Acquisition of
Latin American Library Materials (SALALM) should also be
consulted, especially those of seminars IX, X and XI of 1964–1966,
where there are several listings of official publications. Full details
may be found under 'Government publications' in the *Index to the
SALALM Papers, 1956–1980*, edited by Barbara G. Valk (Madison,
WI: SALALM, 1984) and its *Supplement* covering 1981–1985 (1989).
SALALM VIII (1963) includes as Working Paper 11 the
bibliography by PERAZA SARAUSA cited above, subsequently revised
and reprinted by the author.

The various national bibliographies also cover official publishing
to some degree, and are particularly useful for provincial and local
government publications, which are omitted from most other
sources. Unfortunately in Latin America, as in other parts of the
world, national bibliographies are not always particularly current,
either in coverage or frequency: see NATIONAL BIBLIOGRAPHIES, p.
118. For Brazil, however, a further very useful source is the *Library
of Congress Accessions List: Brazil* (see p. 48), which includes state
and local government material as well as central government publications.

Many research institutes list official publications in their fields of
interest, and there are also bibliographies issued by international
organizations: the Unesco Bibliographic Handbook series is an example.

Organization manuals are useful, since the list of departments can
give an indication of the kinds of publications that might be
available, and because the exact name of the department is one of
the most important but elusive details needed to locate its

publications. The book by Vladimir PALIC cited above incorporates his previous work, *Government Organization Manuals: a Bibliography* (Washington, DC: Library of Congress, 1976), and thus includes the most comprehensive and recent list of this type of material. When no manuals are available, recent listings of the names of government departments may be found in such publications as national budgets and telephone directories.

Latin American Official Serials

Since a large number of government publications appear as serials, many can be traced through serial bibliographies (see PERIODICALS, pp. 211-215). Rather old now, but still useful, is:

> GREGORY, Winifred. *List of the Serial Publications of Foreign Governments, 1815–1931*. New York: Wilson, 1931; reprinted, New York: Kraus, 1966.

This includes locations in US libraries, but has been effectively superseded for many Central and South American countries by:

> MESA, Rosa Quintero. *Latin American Serial Documents: A Holdings List*. Ann Arbor, MI: University Microfilms for Florida University Libraries, 1968—. To be in 19 volumes, 12 of which have so far appeared; countries covered to date include Colombia, Brazil (both 1968), Cuba (1969), Mexico (1970), Argentina (1971), Bolivia, Chile, Ecuador, Paraguay (all 1972), Peru, Uruguay (both 1973) and Venezuela (1977). From volume 5 the series was issued by Bowker in New York.

There is also a useful publication covering Argentina:

> FERREIRA SOBRAL, Eduardo F. *Publicaciones periódicas argentinas, 1781–1969*. Buenos Aires: Ministerio de Agricultura y Ganadería, 1971.

Individual Countries

It is not possible to list here all the works on each Latin American country (a comprehensive list is given in PALIC), but the following will serve as examples of the kinds of materials available.

Brazil

LOMBARDI, Mary. *Brazilian Serial Documents: A Selected and Annotated Guide.* Bloomington, IN: Indiana University Press, 1974.

RICHARDSON, Ivan L. *Bibliografia brasileira de administração pública e assuntos correlatos.* Rio de Janeiro: Fundação Getúlio Vargas, 1964.

Colombia

PERAZA SARAUSA, Fermín and José Ignacio BOHÓRQUEZ C. *Publicaciones oficiales colombianas.* Biblioteca del bibliotecario, 69. Gainesville, FL: Author, 1964.

Mexico

KER, Annita M. *Mexican Government Publications: A Guide to the More Important Publications of the Government of Mexico, 1821–1936.* Washington, DC: Government Printing Office, 1940.

FERNÁNDEZ ESQUIVEL, Rosa M. *Las publicaciones oficiales de México: guía de publicaciones y seriadas, 1937–1967.* Mexico City: UNAM, Seminario de Investigaciones Bibliotecológicas, 1967.

Venezuela

MARTÍNEZ DE CARTAY, Beatriz. *Catálogo de publicaciones oficiales, 1840–1977.* Mérida: Imprenta Oficial, 1978.

Catálogo de publicaciones, 1959–1963. Caracas: Presidencia de la República, 1963.

British Virgin Islands

PENN, Verna A. *Government Reports: A Union Catalogue of Government Reports Held in the Public Library and Government Departments.* Tortola: Chief Minister's Office, 1975.

International Organisations

The publications of international organisations are extremely important in Latin American studies. One problem in dealing with them, however, is that of language: thus, it may not be immediately obvious that the CEPAL *Lista de siglas latinoamericanas* will be found in a library catalogue under 'United Nations. Economic Commission for Latin America' as *Latin American Initialisms and Acronyms*. Also, although publication in two or more languages is common, it not infrequently happens that the original language edition has a fuller text than the translation.

The difficulties of locating official publications in library catalogues discussed at the beginning of this chapter apply particularly to the output of international organisations. The chief problems (apart from the language) are the pervasiveness of acronyms and the extent to which the library's chosen headings reflect the hierarchy of subordinate bodies and departments. For example, the Economic Commission for Latin America may be entered under its own name, in English or Spanish, or as a subheading under the United Nations (as above).

Changes of name are particularly prevalent within the Organization of American States. It is notable that what is now its General Secretariat was until 1970 known as the Pan American Union, which many library catalogues treat as a totally separate body.

Also worth remembering is the fact that some libraries have given up the unequal struggle of cataloguing individually the huge quantities of material they receive from the various international organisations. Instead, they rely exclusively on published catalogues and indexes, which may be marked up to show the library's holdings, and include none of the publications in the library's own catalogues.

A guide to Inter-American Development Bank materials from 1960 to 1974 can be found in:

MESA, Rosa Quintero. 'The Publications of the Inter-American Development Bank.' In *Final Report and Working Papers* of SALALM XIX, 1974. Amherst, MA: SALALM, 1976, vol. 2, pp. 225–237.

Other, more general, guides to the publications of international organizations are:

DIMITROV, Theodore Delchev. *Documents of International Organizations: A Bibliographical Handbook*. London: International University Publications, 1973.

DIMITROV, Theodore Delchev. *World Bibliography of International Documentation*. 2 vols. Pleasantville, NY: UNIFO, 1981.

HAAS, Michael. *International Organizations: An Interdisciplinary Bibliography*. Stanford, CA: Hoover Institution, 1973.

HAJNAL, Peter I. *International Information: Documents, Publications and Information Systems of International Governmental Organizations*. Englewood, CO: Libraries Unlimited, 1988.

For serials, reference may also be made to the 'Index of Publications of International Organizations' in *Ulrich's International Periodicals Directory*, and the similarly-named index in its companion volume, *Irregular Serials and Annuals: An International Directory*, both published biennially by Bowker in New York. The two parts have from 1988 been combined into a single three-volume work.

United Nations

Since the foundation of the United Nations at the end of World War II, the basic tool for gaining access to the vast number of documents it produces has been the *United Nations Document Index*. This has changed name and format a number of times during its history, and since 1979 has been known officially as *UNDOC: Current Index*. A cumulated index covering the years 1950–1962 has been published:

> *United Nations Document Index: Cumulated Index, Volumes 1–13, 1950–1962*. 4 vols. New York: Kraus-Thomson, 1974.

Other very useful indexes to UN material are:

> *The Complete Reference Guide to United Nations Sales Publications, 1946–1978*. 2 vols. Pleasantville, NY: UNIFO, 1982.

> *Register of United Nations Serial Publications*. Geneva: Inter-Organization Board for Information Systems, 1982.

Since 1977 the Economic Commission for Latin America (CEPAL) has produced its own list, under the title *Cepalindex: resúmenes de documentos*.

Organization of American States

A regularly-issued but variously titled *Catalogue of Publications* has been issued by the Pan American Union and its successor-body, the OAS, since 1950. It currently appears annually. A select list of OAS publications also appears at the back of each quarter's *Inter-American Review of Bibliography/Revista Interamericana de Bibliografía*. For older material the following work is indispensable:

Official Records Series of the Organization of American States: Guide, Outline and Expanded Tables. Washington, DC: Pan-American Union, 1961.

Pan-American Health Organization

The Pan-American Health Organization has issued a *Catálogo de publicaciones de la OPS, 1975–1984.* (Washington, DC: PAHO, 1984).

Library Catalogues

Published library catalogues are themselves standard bibliographic sources for the study of official publications, especially those of the British Library (formerly the British Museum), the Bibliothèque Nationale in Paris and the Library of Congress (*National Union Catalog*). The subject catalogue of the British Library of Political and Economic Science at the London School of Economics is published as *A London Bibliography of the Social Sciences*. As a growing number of libraries make their catalogues available online or on microfiche these will become an increasingly important source. See PUBLISHED LIBRARY CATALOGUES (p. 46).

For special classes of official publications treated elsewhere, see CENSUSES (p. 276), LAW AND LEGISLATION (p. 282) and STATISTICS (p. 299).

JRP

Periodicals

A periodical can be defined as a serially issued publication, presented in consecutively numbered and/or dated parts and normally containing more than one article or piece of writing, that is intended to appear indefinitely at regularly stated intervals—generally more frequently than once a year. The term excludes other serials such as newspapers, which are treated under NEWSPAPERS. AND NEWS MAGAZINES (p. 185), and annually published reference books, which are discussed under HANDBOOKS, GUIDES AND DIRECTORIES (p. 160). Yearbooks, annual periodicals and less frequently published serials may be treated as periodicals by some libraries, but it is not common practice to do so. Similarly, while periodicals published by government agencies technically fall into the category dealt with in this chapter, they are in practice often handled separately by libraries, and are covered here in the chapter on OFFICIAL PUBLICATIONS (p. 199). Everything else—journals, bulletins, magazines, reviews, and all the other names under which periodicals flourish—is discussed below.

Catalogue Citation

Under current cataloguing rules periodicals should be cited exactly as the name appears on the title-page. An exception is made only when two or more publications bear the same name: in these instances, the titles are defined by the city of publication—or the sponsoring body, if the latter forms a part of the name; for example, '*Diálogos* (Río Piedras, Puerto Rico)' or '*Review* (Center for Inter-American Relations)'. Catalogue entries are arranged in strict alphabetical sequence, including in the filing order all words except initial articles.

Unfortunately, although much retrospective cataloguing is now taking place, older records still often reflect other rules. Thus in many library catalogues periodicals that should be listed by title may be found under their place of publication, or sponsoring body, or both. The British Library's *General Catalogue of Printed Books to*

1975, for instance, has a special heading 'Periodical Publications', under which it lists all titles by place (except for those issued by governments, institutions and societies) with cross references from the actual titles. Filing rules may also vary from one catalogue to another.

The increasingly widespread appearance of machine-readable catalogues has of course mitigated many of these difficulties. Information can be searched on a computer using keywords appearing in any order in the title, thereby eliminating the need to know which element is given first. Barring the availability of a machine-readable catalogue, it is advisable to obtain the assistance of a specialist librarian to help locate citations to elusive titles.

Name Changes

Periodicals have a disturbing tendency to change their names. These alterations usually reflect a change of coverage, fequency, format, sponsoring body or editorial policy; the amalgamation of two publications; or perhaps only the desire to be more concise, descriptive of content or fashionable. Again by the most modern cataloguing rules, when even a minor variation occurs the original publication technically ceases and a new one begins, thereby generating a new catalogue record. Cross references to and from the original or previous title should tie the various evolutions of the periodical together.

Numbering

Systems of numbering vary greatly. Some periodicals indicate continuity only by date, some only by the sequential numbering of issues, some by both. Many periodicals group issues together in numbered volumes, usually (but not always) on an annual basis. Each volume may be accompanied by its own sequence of issue numbers, or the issue numbers may continue year after year, independent of volume numbers. Similarly, pages may be renumbered in each issue or may continue consecutively throughout the volume. Some Latin American journals may add to or replace the volume number with a year-number (*año, ano*), and a few group volumes together into multiannual *tomos*.

Not infrequently a periodical that has undergone an internal change, or has revived from a period of dormancy, or has simply been published for so long that the numbers have become very large, will begin a new series or *época*, generally accompanied by a new sequence of *tomo*/year/volume/issue numbers. When a title change occurs, the numbering may begin anew or may continue the sequence begun under the previous title.

The financial and other difficulties that beset periodicals, and particularly Latin American ones, often cause irregularities in their publication schedule which may reflect in their numbering and dating systems. It is common, for instance, to find two, three, or even four numbers issued together to make up for publication delays. Periodicals that fall several years behind schedule may ignore the intervening time period and display a current date while continuing the regular numbering sequence. Others may be published out of sequence to create an impression of currency, and some periodicals have been known to omit a number altogether, or even to publish two issues bearing the same number or date. Sometimes, the first issue of a new periodical facing an uncertain future will be published as 'Volume 1, number 0', in the hope that the subscription response will be sufficiently strong to ensure subsequent publication on a regular basis.

Cessations

Given the notorious irregularity of Latin American periodicals it is generally difficult to determine whether a title has actually ceased publication or has simply fallen behind schedule. Occasionally, a cessation notice will be sent from the publisher or announced in the final issue of the journal, and this information will be added to the library's catalogue record. More commonly, however, a publisher will hope to find the means to continue, and the catalogue record will remain open indefinitely.

Two sources that regularly list cessations of periodicals are *Ulrich's International Periodicals Directory* (New York: Bowker, 1943—), issued annually with quarterly updates, and the *Hispanic American Periodicals Index* (HAPI; described below under Indexes). It should be noted that neither of these sources is complete, and that HAPI only notes the demise of journals it has been indexing. Moreover, the cessations that are listed in both sources appear only in the year that they come to the attention of the publishers; it may therefore be necessary to search through several volumes to locate the cessation date of a particular title. Cessations are also noted in the (irregular) 'New Periodicals' section of the quarterly *SALALM Newsletter*

(Madison, WI: SALALM, 1973—). For information about more obscure titles it is best to write direct to the publisher.

Identification

The most recent, comprehensive lists of Latin American periodicals in the social sciences and the humanities published worldwide are:

> *Catalogue collectif de périodiques sur l'Amérique Latine disponibles en France*. Paris: Centre National de la Recherche Scientifique, 1985. Cites approximately 1,400 periodicals and other serials, including for each the publisher, beginning date, frequency, language, International Standard Serial Number (ISSN), and locations in France where the item is held. Arranged by country, with title and publisher indexes. Includes the publications of international and Latin American regional organisations.

> Covington, Paula Hattox. *Indexed Journals: A Guide to Latin American Serials*. SALALM Bibliography and Reference Series, 8. Madison, WI: SALALM, 1983. Lists about 1,500 periodicals in the social sciences and the humanities by title, subject and country of publication. Includes sources where the journals are indexed or abstracted, but does not provide publishing information.

Older, but including scientific and technical periodicals published by Latin American academic institutions, is:

> Levi, Nadia. *Guía de publicaciones periódicas de universidades latinoamericanas*. Mexico City: UNAM, 1967. Updated by the author's 'New Serials in Latin American Universities since 1962' in *Final Report and Working Papers* of SALALM X, 1965 (Washington, DC: Pan American Union, 1968), vol. 2, pp. 297–316.

There are several smaller, more specialised book-length listings of periodical titles that are useful primarily because they include annotations. Although the amount of description varies, all of the following give at least some indication of content:

> Birkos, Alexander S. and Lewis A. Tambs. *Academic Writer's Guide to Periodicals, I: Latin American Studies*. Kent, OH: Kent State University Press, 1971. Limited to periodicals that regularly contain articles written in English, the guide is

designed to help the researcher find a publisher for his own research. Includes for each title full publishing information, a description of editorial scope and policy, and a list of sources where the item is indexed or abstracted.

Liste mondiale des périodiques spécialisés: Amérique Latine. Paris: Maison des Sciences de l'Homme, 1974. Includes 381 titles published throughout the world in the social sciences and the humanities. Gives complete publishing information and a brief description of contents.

ZIMMERMAN, Irene. *A Guide to Current Latin American Periodicals: Humanities and Social Sciences.* Gainesville, FL: Kallman Press, 1961. Contains lengthy, evaluative annotations describing 668 scholarly journals published in Latin America and the US. Although now quite dated, this is still the best source available for descriptive information about important, longstanding titles. Also includes discussions of the periodical publishing industry in the countries treated.

A highly selective but more recent descriptive listing is:

GRAHAM, Ann and Richard D. WOODS. 'Latin American Periodicals for Libraries.' *Serials Librarian* 3:1 (Fall 1978), pp. 77–88.

Annotated bibliographies of periodicals on specific topics are also available. Some examples include:

FOSTER, David William. 'An Annotated Registry of Scholarly Journals in Hispanic Studies.' *Inter-American Review of Bibliography* 28:2 (April–June 1978), pp. 131–137. Covers language and literature only.

HAMERLY, Michael T. 'Historical and Related Journals of Spanish South America: A Current and Retrospective Checklist.' *Handbook of Latin American Studies* 36 (1974), pp. 194–200.

Guide to Latin American Scientific and Technical Periodicals: An Annotated Listing. Washington, DC: Pan American Union, and Mexico City: Centro de Documentación Científica y Técnica, 1962.

TANODI, Aurelio. 'Latin American Archives Periodicals.' *Journal of Information Science* 3 (April 1981), pp. 90–100.

VALDÉS, Nelson P. 'A Bibliography of Cuban Periodicals Relating to Women.' *Cuban Studies/Estudios Cubanos* 12:2 (July 1982), pp. 73–80.

There are also sources that identify the periodical output of individual countries; for example:

Directorio de publicaciones mexicanas, 1981. Guanajuato: Departamento de Investigaciones Bibliotecológicas, 1982.

Handbuch der deutschen Lateinamerika-Forschung. Bonn: Deutscher Akademischer Austauschdienst, 1980. With *Supplement*, 1981. Appendix 3 lists Latin American periodicals published in West Germany, with their publishers' addresses.

Accessions List, Brazil: Cumulative List of Serials, 1975–1980. Rio de Janeiro: Library of Congress Office, Brazil, National Program for Acquisitions and Cataloging, 1982. Records all the Brazilian titles acquired by the LC office in Rio. Supplemented bimonthly with annual cumulations in a section of *Library of Congress Accessions List, Brazil.*

In addition, a few commercial vendors of Latin American periodicals now issue catalogues of publications currently available in their countries.

For other bibliographies of Latin American periodical titles see the section 'Periodicals' in Arthur E. GROPP's *A Bibliography of Latin American Bibliographies* (Metuchen, NJ: Scarecrow Press, 1968), its subsequent five-year cumulations through 1984 (also published by Scarecrow) and its annual supplements from 1984–1985, edited by Lionel V. LOROÑA and published by SALALM as part of its Bibliography and Reference Series (see pp. 88–89). Lists of new titles also appear regularly in the *SALALM Newsletter.* More sources are given below under Location.

Location

Published union lists of serials identify libraries where specific periodicals are held. For material available in Britain the best sources are the *British Union Catalogue of Periodicals* (BUCOP; London: Butterworths, 1955–1958, with supplements to 1974) and the somewhat outdated but more specific three-volume series Latin American Serials compiled by the Committee on Latin America between 1969 and 1977. For periodicals held by libraries in France, refer to the *Catalogue collectif des périodiques sur l'Amérique Latine disponibles en France*, cited above under Identification. Locations of titles held in North America can be found in the *Union List of Serials in the United States and Canada* (ULS; New York: H. W. Wilson, 1965), and in its continuation, *New Serial Titles, 1950–1970* (NST) with a *Subject Guide* (New York: Bowker, 1973–1975). This list is updated monthly with quarterly, annual and five-yearly cumulations. These and other union lists are discussed in more detail under INTER-LIBRARY LENDING (pp. 73–74).

The Online Computer Library Center (OCLC) database contains serials, as well as other library materials, and lists for each title the OCLC member libraries and affiliates in which it is held. OCLC libraries include most academic institutions in the US, as well as a growing number of libraries in Canada and Europe. Another, smaller online union list is the Research Libraries Information Network (RLIN) database, which records the holdings of its 78 member institutions in the US. For further details see DATABASES (p. 231).

Several Latin American countries have produced union lists of periodicals which, though they are out-of-date and may be general rather than confined to Latin American titles, can be of particular interest for the country of origin's own periodical output.

Argentine holdings can be found in:

Catálogo colectivo de publicaciones periódicas. 2nd ed. Buenos Aires: Consejo Nacional de Investigaciones Científicas y Técnicas, 1962. There is also a *Suplemento a la 2a edición* (1972).

For Costa Rican periodicals there is:

Catálogo colectivo de publicaciones periódicas existentes en Costa Rica. San José: Consejo Nacional de Investigaciones Científicas y Tecnológicas, 1976.

Holdings for the Dominican Republic (ten libraries) can be traced in:

Catálogo colectivo de publicaciones periódicas de la República Dominicana. Santo Domingo: Centro de Informacion Científica y Tecnológica, 1981.

For Mexico there is:

VELÁSQUEZ GALLARDO, Pablo and Ramón NADURILLE. *Catálogo colectivo de publicaciones periódicas existentes en las bibliotecas de la República Mexicana.* 2 vols. Mexico City: Instituto Nacional de Investigaciones Agrícolas, 1968. Covers 130 libraries.

The holdings of some 77 Uruguayan libraries are surveyed in:

Catálogo colectivo de publicaciones periódicas existentes en las bibliotecas universitarias del Uruguay: actualización 1969–1975. Montevideo: Universidad de la República, Escuela Universitaria de Bibliotecología y Ciencias Afines, 1977–1980.

Australian holdings are recorded in:

Union List of Latin American Serials in Six Australian Libraries. Bundoora: La Trobe University Library, 1976. Contains nearly 1200 official and unofficial serials held by La Trobe, the National Library of Australia and four other Australian libraries. Newspapers are excluded.

Other sources list the holdings of special collections in individual libraries or groups of libraries; for example:

BOLAND, Roy and Alan KENWOOD. *A Select Bibliography of Serials Relating to Hispanic Language, Literature and Civilization Held by Libraries in Australia and New Zealand.* Auckland: Auckland University Library, 1984.

Catálogo colectivo nacional de publicaciones periódicas en ciencias naturales, salud y agropecuarias. 2 vols. Bogotá: Instituto Colombiano para el Fomento de la Educación Superior, 1977. Lists the holdings of some 230 Colombian libraries.

MUNDO LO, Sara de and Beverly PHILLIPS. *Colombian Serial Publications in the University of Illinois Library at Urbana-Champaign.* SALALM Bibliography and Reference Series, 4. Austin, TX: SALALM, 1979.

VARONA, Esperanza B. de. *Cuban Exile Periodicals at the University of Miami Library: An Annotated Bibliography.* SALALM Bibliography and Reference Series, 19. Madison, WI: SALALM, 1987.

The published catalogues of individual libraries also sometimes include periodicals (see PUBLISHED LIBRARY CATALOGUES, p. 46), and many libraries issue lists of currently received titles.

Contents

Indexes, abstracts, bibliographies and other finding-aids furnish
access to individual articles appearing in periodicals. The best source
for identifying indexes and abstracts that regularly cover Latin
American periodical literature, as well as for identifying the sources
in which individual periodicals are analysed, is Paula COVINGTON's
Indexed Journals, cited above under Identification. This 1983 publication lists and describes more than a hundred indexing and
abstracting services in the social sciences and the humanities that
include one or more journals published in, or exclusively about,
Latin America. The sources are arranged by title and subject. A
paragraph at the end of each subject section evaluates the relative
coverage of the services cited, discusses relevant bibliographies and
refers the reader to other indexes and abstracts which do not include
Latin American materials but which may contain information on
Latin American topics. Further sections list journal titles and the
sources in which they are covered.

Indexes

The major general index for current Latin American periodicals is:

> *Hispanic American Periodicals Index* (HAPI). Edited by Barbara
> G. Valk. Los Angeles, CA: UCLA Latin American Center,
> 1977—. A subject and author index analysing approximately
> 250 scholarly journals in the social sciences and humanities
> published worldwide. Latin American coverage includes all of
> Central and South America, Mexico and the Caribbean area.
> Also indexed are leading journals treating Hispanics in the
> United States. Book reviews are included. A three-volume set
> encompassing the years 1970–1974 is succeeded by annual
> volumes covering journals published from 1975 to the present.

To locate articles published before 1970, refer to the indexes
prepared from 1929 to 1970 by the Columbus Memorial Library of
the Pan American Union in Washington. The full set includes:

> *Index to Latin American Periodical Literature, 1929–1960.* 8 vols.
> Boston, MA: G. K. Hall, 1962.

> *Index to Latin American Periodical Literature, 1961–1965.* 2 vols.
> Boston, MA: G. K. Hall, 1970.

Index to Latin American Periodical Literature, 1966–1970. 2 vols. Boston, MA: G. K. Hall, 1980.

Indice general de publicaciones periódicas latinoamericanas: humanidades y ciencias sociales/Index to Latin American Periodicals: Humanities and Social Sciences. Metuchen, NJ: Scarecrow Press, 1961–1970. Quarterly, with annual cumulations to 1969.

More specialised but also useful for recent information are:

CLASE: Citas latinoamericanas en sociologia y economia. Mexico City: Centro de Información Científica y Humanística (CICH), UNAM, 1976—. Quarterly. Indexes about 150 journals published in Latin America by keyword, author and sponsoring institution. Also prints the contents pages of all cited issues. Does not cumulate. In 1983 coverage was broadened to include the humanities, but journals on economics still predominate. Now available along with other UNAM indexes on CD-ROM.

CARINDEX. St. Augustine: University of the West Indies, 1977—. Semi-annual, produced by the Indexing Committee (English-Speaking Area) of the Association of Caribbean University and Research Libraries (ACURIL). Indexes by subject some 80 periodicals and newspapers in the social sciences and the humanities published in the English-speaking Caribbean. Includes book reviews. 23 major titles are indexed in full, the remainder selectively.

For articles on Mexican Americans refer to HAPI (see above) or to:

Chicano Periodicals Index (ChPI). *1967–1978,* Boston, MA: G. K. Hall, 1981; *1979–1981,* Boston, MA: G. K. Hall, 1983; *1982–1983—,* Berkeley, CA: University of California Chicano Studies Library Publications Unit, 1985—. Each volume updates the contents of periodicals indexed previously and adds new titles, which are indexed retrospectively. Later volumes also include articles about Mexican Americans appearing in non-Chicano scholarly journals and popular magazines. Indexing is by subject, author and title.

Other indexes, including those of individual periodicals, are listed in *A Bibliography of Latin American Bibliographies* and its supplements, cited above under Identification. For additional sources of book reviews appearing in periodicals see BOOK REVIEWS (p. 273).

Subject Bibliographies

Bibliographies of periodical articles on specific subjects are readily found in all the above-mentioned indexes and, of course, in the *Bibliography of Latin American Bibliographies*. Several general bibliographies of Latin American periodical articles are also published on a regular basis. Among these are:

> *Bibliographie latinoaméricaine d'articles* (formerly *Bibliographie d'articles de revues*). Paris: Institut des Hautes Etudes de l'Amérique Latine, 1975—. Semi-annual. Social sciences and humanities.

> *Dokumentationsdienst Lateinamerika/Documentación latinoamericana.* Hamburg: Institut für Iberoamerika-Kunde/Dokumentation-Leitstelle Lateinamerika, 1971—. Quarterly. Social sciences.

> *Indice de ciências sociais.* Rio de Janeiro: Instituto Universitário de Pesquisas do Rio de Janeiro (IUPERJ), 1979—. Semi-annual. Sociology, political science, anthropology. Despite its title, this is a bibliography rather than an index.

Central to any review of the periodical literature on Latin America is the *Handbook of Latin American Studies* (Boston, MA: Harvard University, 1935—). Prepared annually by the Hispanic Division of the Library of Congress, it is currently published by the University of Texas at Austin. Since 1964 the *Handbook* has covered the social sciences and the humanities in alternate years. Included are annotated citations to monographs, edited works and documents as well as to periodical articles selected from a broad range of international publications. Also of interest is the *Bulletin bibliographique Amérique Latine* (Paris: Recherches sur les Civilisations, 1982—) which includes, among other materials, articles appearing in about 70 periodicals published in France. Both of these sources should be consulted routinely to supplement the information obtained from periodical indexes and specialised subject bibliographies.

Current Contents

In addition to *CLASE* (mentioned above) there are two major sources that print the contents pages of current journals pertaining to Latin America. Of these, the older and more complete, but unfortunately the slower to appear, is:

Sumario actual de revistas. Madrid: Instituto de Cooperación Iberoamericana, 1973—. Irregular.

For the contents of the more recent issues of approximately 70 titles published worldwide, see:

Contents of Periodicals on Latin America. Miami, FL: University of Miami, Institute of Interamerican Studies, 1983—. Quarterly.

In addition, some periodicals, such as *Pensamiento Iberoamericano* and *Problemas del Desarrollo* regularly list the contents of other publications at the back of each issue.

Offprints and Photocopies

Periodical articles are sometimes distributed separately as 'offprints', and these can be found by means of the author catalogue. Other articles can be photocopied in the library, while photocopies of articles that are not available in one's own library are often obtainable through inter-library loan services (see INTER-LIBRARY LENDING, p. 71).

Purchase

Latin American periodicals are best purchased direct from the publisher or his subscription agent. Ordering information, including frequency of publication and annual subscription costs, usually appears on the inside front cover of each issue. If a recent copy of the periodical is not available for inspection, publishers' addresses can be found in many of the sources cited above under Identification and Contents as well as in *Ulrich's International Periodicals Directory* (New York: Bowker, 1943—).

If you wish to use a general subscription agent, one of the most reliable is Faxon, a company that deals exclusively in subscription services and has offices in the United States (The Faxon Company, 15 Southwest Park, Westwood, MA 02090), Canada (Faxon Canada Ltd., 3034 Palstan Road #308, Mississauga, Ontario L4Y 2Z6) and Europe (Faxon Europe, Postbus 197, 1000 AD Amsterdam, The Netherlands). Subscriptions to periodicals published in specific Latin American countries can often be obtained from bookdealers in those countries; a brief list can be found under BOOKSELLERS (pp. 82–83).

Whichever method of purchase is selected, it is wise to request an airmail subscription, despite the added cost. Airmail delivery will ensure reasonably prompt receipt of the material (sea mail can take three months or more) and will minimize the likelihood of lost or damaged issues, which may well be irreplaceable.

BGV

Theses and Dissertations

In her article 'Latin American Doctoral Dissertations of the 1960s' (*Latin American Research Review* 18:3 (1983), pp. 157–164) Nelly S. GONZALEZ notes that in the matter of North American dissertations on Latin America 'the production of a single decade [the 1960s] represented an increase of more than 150 percent over the number of dissertations submitted over the previous ninety years.' There is no reason to presume that this industry has slackened in the 1970s or 1980s; but at least in the last decade it has been easier to keep track of these unpublished works, as bibliographic control has been extended to cover them.

Terminology

The words 'thesis' and 'dissertation' are often used interchangeably, though officially they have opposite meanings on either side of the Atlantic. In the US a dissertation will be prepared at the doctoral level and a thesis at the Master's level; in the UK the meanings are reversed. US (Masters') theses and UK (Masters') dissertations are rarely listed in bibliographies; the main sources of reference limit themselves to doctoral work. In this article 'thesis' is used as a general term to include all scholastic exercises presented for a degree.

General Guides

The starting point for finding out about theses from a particular country is a work prepared for the International Federation of Library Associations and Institutions:

BORCHARDT, D. H. and J. D. THAWLEY. *Guide to the Availability of Theses*. IFLA Publications, 17. Munich: K. G. Saur, 1981. Explains, country by country, the method of thesis control: whether they are included in the national bibliography, as in Canada, or if a separate national listing is published, as in Belgium. It then lists all the universities, and gives details of the availability and bibliographic control of their theses.

A companion volume has also been issued, to cover materials not emanating from universities:

> ALLEN, G. G. and K. DEUBERT. *Guide to the Availability of Theses*. II: Non-University Institutions. IFLA Publications, 29. Munich: K. G. Saur, 1984.

Bibliographies

For the investigation of theses from a subject viewpoint, there is an international, annotated listing, covering materials issued up to 1983–1984. This is:

> REYNOLDS, Michael M. *Guide to Theses and Dissertations: An International Bibliography of Bibliographies*. Rev. ed. Phoenix, AZ: Oryx Press, 1985. Includes five pages of bibliographies of Latin America and Caribbean theses, including completed theses and those in progress.

The handiest bibliography specific to Latin Americanist theses in most of the English-speaking world is:

> HANSON, Carl A. *Dissertations on Iberian and Latin American History: An Interdisciplinary Bibliography of Dissertations Completed in the U.S., Great Britain, Canada and Ireland, 1889–1969*. Troy, NY: Whitston, 1975.

Given the comprehensiveness of the works by BORCHARDT and REYNOLDS, listed above, for retrospective bibliography, the remainder of this chapter will concentrate principally on how researchers can learn of the most recently completed theses (and thesis bibliographies) in the field of Latin American studies, with an emphasis on works produced in the UK and North America.

Bibliographies of Current Theses

The *Handbook of Latin American Studies* is published annually by the University of Texas Press, alternate volumes covering the humanities and the social sciences. The subject index to each volume includes the heading 'Dissertations and Theses', and its coverage of books and periodical articles make it a useful source for keeping track of theses that appear in these forms.

The Seminar on the Acquisition of Latin American Library Materials (SALALM) also has a heading 'Dissertations, Academic' in its annual *Bibliography of Latin American and Caribbean*

Bibliographies edited by Lionel V. Loroña (Madison, WI: SALALM. 1983—; previously included in the *Final Report and Working Papers* of the annual Seminar). The 1984–1985 edition alone lists nine thesis bibliographies, four of which appeared in periodicals.

The major listing of Latin American thesis bibliographies appearing in periodicals, however, is in the annual *Hispanic American Periodicals Index* (HAPI) (Los Angeles, CA: UCLA Latin American Center, 1977—). Again, the subject heading under which they appear is 'Dissertations, Academic'.

North American Dissertations

The principal retrospective index to theses from the US and Canada is:

> *Comprehensive Dissertation Index.* 37 vols. Ann Arbor, MI: Xerox University Microfilms, 1974. Lists North American material from 1861 to 1972, and is kept up to date with annual supplements.

Current North American dissertations appear very quickly in *Dissertation Abstracts International*, published monthly in Ann Arbor by University Microfilms International (UMI). Even with the indexes provided, however, it is a laborious process to find Latin American references in the information emanating from over 400 institutions in the United States and Canada. (Some European theses are also included.) For this reason, UMI itself publishes area listings taken from the main volumes:

> DEAL, Carl W. *Latin America and the Caribbean: A Dissertation Bibliography.* Ann Arbor, MI: UMI, 1977. This is supplemented by:

> WALTERS, Marian C. *Latin America and the Caribbean II: A Dissertation Bibliography.* Ann Arbor, MI: UMI, 1980.

> *Research on Latin America: A Catalog of Doctoral Dissertations.* Ann Arbor, MI: UMI, 1983—. An irregular series of pamphlets; issues have appeared so far covering 1972–1983, 1982–1984 and 1984–1986. Arrangement in all the volumes is by subject, subdivided by country.

Regular listings of relevant current materials from *Dissertation Abstracts International* also appear in two periodicals. These are:

Revista Interamericana de Bibliografía/Inter-American Review of Bibliography. Washington, DC: Organization of American States, 1951—. Quarterly. Beginning with 29:2 (1979) every issue has a section 'Tesis doctorales recientes/Recent doctoral dissertations', listing recently completed dissertations on Latin America and the Caribbean prepared in the US or Canada.

Hispania. Stanford, CA: American Association of Teachers of Spanish and Portuguese, 1917—. Now published in Los Angeles. Quarterly. Each year's May issue includes a list of dissertations completed and in progress in the fields of Hispanic and Luso-Brazilian languages and literatures.

A recent country-specific bibliography is:

SULLIVAN, William M. *Dissertations and Theses on Venezuelan Topics, 1900–1985.* Metuchen, NJ: Scarecrow Press, 1988.

United Kingdom Theses

The major retrospective listing of theses from the British Isles is provided by:

BILBOUL, Roger R. and F.L. KENT. *Retrospective Index to Theses of Great Britain and Ireland, 1716–1950.* 5 vols. Oxford: European Bibliographical Centre/Clio Press, 1976–1977. Volume 1 treats the social sciences and humanities, leaving volumes 2–5 to the sciences. There are author and subject indexes.

Current British theses are listed in the quarterly *Index to Theses Accepted for Higher Degrees by the Universities of Great Britain and Ireland.* 1950/1951—. London: Association of Special Libraries and Information Bureaux, 1953—. The arrangement is by subject, and material of Latin American interest is retrievable only by use of the index. Those theses which are microfilmed by the British Library Document Supply Centre are listed in the monthly *British Reports, Translations and Theses* (Boston Spa: BLDSC, 1981—). This is also arranged by subject.

For information on recently completed university theses in the area of Latin American research there are two sources, both irregular. The Institute of Latin American Studies of the University of London publishes *Research on Latin America in the Humanities and Social Sciences, Incorporating Theses Completed and in Progress.* The latest edition appeared in 1988, and further biennial issues are planned. Completed research in the Hispanic field in general is also recorded from time to time in the *Bulletin of Hispanic Studies* (Liverpool: Liverpool University Press, 1923—). The latest occasion was:

> JOHNSON, Margaret. 'Theses in Hispanic Studies Approved for Higher Degrees by British and Irish Universities, 1979–1982.' *Bulletin of Hispanic Studies* 61:2 (1984), pp. 233–261. An equivalent article covering 1983–1988 is due for publication in 1989.

Theses accepted for the Fellowship of the Library Association can be a useful source of information on the Latin American bibliographic and library scene. They are listed and abstracted in the monthly *CABLIS: Current Awareness Bulletin for Librarians and Information Scientists* (London: Library Association Library, 1975—), and are available for loan direct from the library.

Theses from Other Countries

Lists of theses from Latin American universities are hard to find. HAPI frequently identifies those that are listed in Latin American journals, and there is a recent bibliography of Mexican theses on the history of Mexico:

> *Segundo catálogo de teses sobre historia de México.* (Mexico City: Comité Mexicano de Ciencias Históricas, 1984). With *Adenda al Segundo catálogo...* (1985) and *II Adenda al Segundo catálogo...* (1987).

Availability

In the UK, researchers can obtain copies of most theses from the British Library Document Supply Centre via inter-library loan (see INTER-LIBRARY LENDING, p. 71). The Centre will purchase microfilm copies of North American theses on demand, and requests should be accompanied by the UMI number, as given in *Dissertation Abstracts International*. Most British theses are also to be found at the BLDSC, where they are deposited by the universities, and these are also available for loan on microfilm, subject to conditions imposed by the author. Those universities which deposit at Boston Spa are listed at the front of the *Index to Theses* cited above, together with any conditions as to their use. Theses from non-depositing universities are generally available at the appropriate university library.

SEJ

Non-Print Sources

Databases

In line with the evolution of information technology there has been, within the last few years, a dramatic increase in the availability of bibliographic, textual and statistical material in electronic form, accessible online or from disk or CD-ROM. Much published material is now printed using some form of electronic input, storage and processing: this book is an example. It is thus a comparatively easy step to make the information available, commercially or otherwise, from a database that is marketed via a 'host' organisation. (The host—UK usage—is known in the US as the database vendor or 'gateway' service). The host supplies the database; clients may then search the file online, either from a remote terminal using a datalink or telephone hook-up, or from an inhouse computer containing regularly updated versions of the database.

Such, at least, is the theory. For the Latin Americanist, however, the reality is less inspiring. Lacking the comprehensive 'core' databases that are already available in such fields as medicine and agriculture, the researcher in humanities and social sciences will probably have to search many files to obtain all the information available. It should also be remembered that at certain times the costs may be uneconomic, and that expensive time can be used fruitlessly if the researcher is not familiar with appropriate search language and commands. Searching different databases may require the use of several sets of command instructions—compatibility in this respect is still some way off, and may not even be desirable. For this reason, many institutions appoint a database specialist through whom searches must be made: the reduction of online charges seems to compensate for the specialist's salary. Frivolous searches are discouraged. For those unfamiliar with database searching, then, the best course is to enquire whether there is someone available in the library (or university) who is willing to initiate a student into its mysteries.

This chapter will discuss the principal bibliographic and textual databases available for use in social science and humanities research on Latin America, devoting special attention to the few files that focus solely on the region. Each database, as it is mentioned, will be followed by the name of the host or vendor; full details of these are listed in the appendix.

A regularly-revised reference work provides useful general information on databases and information systems. This is:

> *Encyclopedia of Information Systems and Services, 1989.* 9th ed. Edited by Amy Lucas. 2 vols. Detroit, MI: Gale Research, 1988. New editions appear every one to two years.

This can be supplemented by:

> *Directory of Online Databases.* New York: Cuadra/Elsevier, 1979——. Quarterly.

For those who need an introduction to the techniques of database searching, a recent manual is:

> GLOSSBRENNER, Alfred. *How to Look It Up Online.* New York: St. Martin's Press, 1987.

General Files

Existing online resources support the Latin American studies field reasonably well: powerful subject databases now cover all the major branches of the field, including history, literature, political science, sociology, economics and anthropology. Indeed, there are probably hundreds of accessible files that provide at least some treatment of the region; the problem is that most of the key databases are general sources that do not specialise in Latin America. To handle in-depth queries on the region the busy student or librarian may need to consult more than two dozen basic files, nearly all of which are computerised versions of familiar, published indexing and abstracting services. Of these, the most convenient multi-disciplinary coverage of Latin America is offered by Social SciSearch (DIALOG, BRS, Data-Star), based on the *Social Sciences Citation Index* (see p. 117); Arts and Humanities Search (BRS, DIALOG), based on the *Arts and Humanities Citation Index* (p. 151); the Humanities Index (Wilsonline) and the Social Sciences Index (Wilsonline), both from the journals of the same name (p. 150 and p. 117); and PAIS International (BRS, DIALOG, Data-Star), a combined version of the *PAIS Bulletin* and the *Foreign Language Index* (p. 116).

Helpful subject databases include Historical Abstracts (DIALOG), United States Political Science Documents (DIALOG), MLA Bibliography (DIALOG, Wilsonline—see p. 150), Economic Literature Index (DIALOG—the online counterpart of *Journal of Economic Literature* and *Index of Economic Articles*) and Sociological Abstracts (BRS, DIALOG, Data-Star).

All of the major subject databases cite journal articles, but some of them also treat books, dissertations and conference papers—all prime vehicles for the dissemination of new Latin Americanist research. Similarly, although the majority of US files concentrate on English language materials, there are European sources available to compensate for this bias. An example is SOLIS (STN International), produced by the Informationszentrum Sozialwissenschaften in Bonn. SOLIS indexes German writings on sociology, social history, labour economics, demography and social psychology, and lists more that 1,000 books, articles, reports and conference papers on Latin America.

The various subject files are complemented by a number of other vital online resources. Among the bibliographic services available in many libraries in North America and the UK are OCLC (Online Computer Library Center)—a vast bibliographic database containing more than fifteen million citations, made up from the holdings of most academic institutions in the US, including the Library of Congress, and some in Europe, and RLIN (Research Libraries Information Network), an online catalogue of the holdings of 78 US research libraries. In addition, increasing numbers of UK research libraries are making their own catalogues accessible online, many through the recently-established CURL (Consortium of University and Research Libraries) database. More details can be found in the chapter on PUBLISHED LIBRARY CATALOGUES (pp. 52–53).

Newspapers and newswires also constitute important online sources of information on Latin America. Among the leading US newspapers in terms of Latin American coverage are the *New York Times* (available on NEXIS), the *Washington Post* (DIALOG, NEXIS, PROFILE, VU/TEXT) and the *Miami Herald* (VU/TEXT). Access to these newspapers is also provided by some bibliographic files. Helpful full-text newswires include Associated Press (DIALOG, NEXIS, PROFILE, VU-TEXT and others), United Press International (DIALOG, NEXIS), Reuters (DIALOG, NEXIS), Agence-France Press (QUESTEL) and TASS (NEXIS, PROFILE). The Rome-based Inter Press Service, or IPS (NEXIS), is particularly helpful to the Latin Americanist in that it specialises in Third World news coverage. A related full-text source is the BBC Summary of World Broadcasts (NEXIS, Profile). Corresponding to the printed *Summary of World Broadcasts* produced by the British Broadcasting Corporation Monitoring Service (see pp. 197–198), this handy file offers daily translations of selected radio broadcasts from Latin America and the rest of the world. Retrospective coverage extends back to 1979 (NEXIS) or 1982 (Profile). Its research value is enhanced by the fact that the counterpart products of the US Foreign Broadcast Information Service (FBIS) are not available online.

Region-Specific Files

Very few online files are devoted exclusively to Latin American affairs, and those that do exist are numerical or textual databases; the region as a field of study still lacks the convenience of a good area studies file along the lines of Mideast File (DIALOG) or Middle East: Abstracts and Index (DIALOG). Moreover, because the Latin American regional files that are available are generally narrow in scope and coverage, they tend to be carried only by specialised vendors such as NEXIS, NewsNet and QUESTEL.

The only bibliographic file to be devoted exclusively to Latin American studies is Amérique Latine, a component of the multi-disciplinary FRANCIS database (QUESTEL). Updated once a year, Amérique Latine contains several thousand citations dating back to 1980, covering books, reports, theses, articles and conference papers produced in France and other French-speaking countries. Its value derives from its unmatched coverage of current French social sciences and humanities scholarship on Latin America. France is one of the leading European centres of research on the region, but very little of its scholarly production is cited by other commercial databases. Most of the works found in the file are written in French (85 per cent) and Spanish (13 per cent). Titles, descriptors (in French, English and Spanish) and abstracts offer ample targets for subject searches.

The largest and oldest region-specific database is Latin America Newsletters (NEXIS), which offers full-text access to a number of the respected serial publications of the London-based organisation, Latin America Newsletters, Ltd. (see p. 193). Included in the file are computerised versions of the *Latin America Weekly Report*, all five *Latin America Regional Reports* and *Latin America Commodities Report*. Students and researchers have long depended on these newsletters (parts of whose weekly files date back to 1967) for their informative and balanced reports of current political, military, economic and social developments throughout Latin America. Because the corresponding printed works lack any cumulative indexing, this database is a rather more convenient method of accessing the information than the hard copy, and a very welcome addition to the online menu.

Two relatively new specialised textual databases are Central America Update (DIALOG, Data-Star, NewsNet) and Latin American Debt Chronicle (DIALOG, Data-Star, NewsNet). Both of these files are produced by The Latin American Database, a nonprofit entity of the Latin American Institute at the University of New Mexico, Albuquerque. Database personnel monitor newswires, newspapers and radio broadcasts to produce twice-weekly summaries and analyses of contemporary Latin American affairs. As the names suggest, Central America Update follows economic, trade, political and human rights developments throughout Central America, while Latin American Debt Chronicle traces political, economic and financial aspects of the ongoing foreign debt crisis in Latin America. Both files extend back through 1986. On DIALOG and Data-Star they form part of the PTS Newsletters database.

A few other source databases also focus on Latin America. Monthly Latin America (WEFA Group) and Latin America Forecast (WEFA Group) contain thousands of monthly and annual time-series compilations of macroeconomic data. Current, historical and forecast figures for Argentina, Bolivia, Brazil, Chile, Colombia, Ecuador, Mexico, Peru, Uruguay and Venezuela are recorded.

Political Risks: South America (Data-Star, NewsNet) is a textual file that discusses and forecasts political, economic and social conditions in Argentina, Bolivia, Brazil, Chile, Colombia, Ecuador, Peru, Uruguay and Venezuela. The companion file, Political Risks: North and Central America (Data-Star, NewsNet), treats the Dominican Republic, Haiti, Jamaica, Mexico and the six republics of Central America (Costa Rica, El Salvador, Guatemala, Honduras, Nicaragua and Panama). Providing analytical narratives along with background statistics, these files represent online versions of printed business risk assessments produced by Frost and Sullivan, Inc. Online updates are made on an annual basis.

This survey would not be complete without a mention of some of the relevant files that exist outside the standard commercial database system. Several libraries in the US and Mexico have cooperated to develop the BorderLine bibliographic database of books and other materials on the United States-Mexico border region. This file is loaded on the ORION library information system of the University of California, Los Angeles. Online access is available to outside users on a fee basis; the staff can also generate offline printouts on specific topics. A printed bibliography of some 9,000 entries, reflecting the contents of the file through June 1986, has recently been prepared by Barbara G. VALK (*BorderLine*. Los Angeles, CA: UCLA Latin American Center, 1988).

During the last decade or so many universities, research centres and government agencies in Latin America have also created useful bibliographic and numeric databases. Some examples are the Centro de Informacion Científica y Humanística files of UNAM (Mexico City), the Latin American Population Documentation System files of the Centro Latinoamericano de Demografía (Santiago de Chile) and the Information and Documentation Service files of the Unesco Regional Center for Higher Education in Latin America and the Caribbean (Caracas). Of course, gaining direct access to a foreign database may be a rather difficult undertaking. The Universidad Nacional Autonoma de Mexico has recently offered six of its bibliographical databases (BIBLAT, CLASE, DESA, INFOBILA, MEXINV and PERIODICA) for purchase on CD-ROM under the general name of Latin American Bibliography.

Futures

It will be plain from the foregoing that there is still much to be achieved in the matter of adequate coverage of Latin American materials in commercial databases. Perhaps the major lacuna, with regard to US databases, is their weakness in Spanish and Portuguese language materials—articles in Latin American journals and works produced by Latin American publishers. The UCLA Latin American Center has attempted repeatedly to help alleviate this problem by making the *Hispanic American Periodicals Index* (HAPI; see p. 216) available in database format, either on tape or on CD-ROM, but thus far their efforts have been thwarted by a combination of unfavourable market projections and prohibitive start-up fees. There seems to be little chance of the other basic bibliographic tool for Latin Americanists, the *Handbook of Latin American Studies* (see p. 90), becoming available as a commercial database in the foreseeable future, as the book is not maintained in machine-readable form. Fortunately, HLAS is well indexed and widely available in its hard-copy format.

The other principal defect in database coverage is the difficulty, already referred to, of access from the US and Europe to many databases generated inside Latin America. Here, it seems, matters are likely to improve. The development during 1987/1988 of BITNET gateways in Miami and Los Angeles and nodes within Latin America may well open up the possibility of the transfer and updating of databases with greater facility. Europe still has to consider how it can best participate in the grand exchange of information: direct computer to mainframe links between South America and Europe still have to travel via the United States. It has recently been proposed that the European documentation centres concerned with Latin America region should aim to establish better lines of communication by the appropriate year 1992.

Caveats

The researcher should always remember that however good the channels of communication, they can never improve on the original quality of the information offered by the hosts or database vendors. Much of the database material referred to above is of the 'textline' variety, where the user is electronically scanning newspapers and periodicals; in this case, access to the items of information required can only be as good as the system's indexing facilities. Analyses prepared specifically for online access depend for their accuracy on the acuteness of the analyst and the quality of the information on which they are based. All the user can do is to attempt to choose the service that has the best analysts, and hope that it is carried by a host or gateway service that uses familiar search software. And remember, too, that current technology does not as yet permit the complete amateur to make searches economically: in extreme cases it may cost hundreds of pounds or dollars to access an issue of a newspaper that sells for a few pence. Expert help should always be sought before attempting a first-time search; when proficiency in database use is finally attained, it will be found to be well worth the efforts involved.

HC/PG

Appendix

Some Major Database Vendors and Gateway Services

BRS
BRS Information Technologies
1200 Route 7
Latham, NY 12110

Telephone: (800) 468–0908 or (518) 783–1161

Some 140 bibliographic and non-bibliographic files.

DATA-STAR
D-S Marketing
Plaza Suite
114 Jermyn Street
London SW1Y 6HJ
England

Telephone: 01–930 5503 or (800) 221–7754

DIALOG
Dialog Information Services
3460 Hillview Avenue
Palo Alto, CA 94304

Telephone: (800) 334–2564 or (415) 858–3785

Some 300 bibliographic and non-bibliographic files.

EASYNET
Telebase Systems
763 West Lancaster Avenue
Bryn Mawr, PA 19010

Telephone: (800) 841–9553 or (215) 296–2000

Gateway access to BRS, DIALOG, NewsNet, QUESTEL, Wilsonline, VU/TEXT and other major domestic and foreign vendors.

NEXIS
Mead Data Central
9393 Springboro Pike
PO Box 933
Dayton, OH 45401

Telephone: (800) 227–4908 or (513) 865–6800

Full-text access to more than 150 newspapers, magazines, newswires and newsletters.

NEWSNET
NewNet, Inc.
945 Haverford Road
Bryn Mawr, PA 19010

Telephone: (800) 345–1301 or (215) 527–8030

Full-text access to some 330 newsletters and newswires.

PROFILE
Profile Information
79 Staines Road West
Sunbury-on-Thames TW16 7AH
England

Telephone: 0932 761444

Full-text access to more than 40 newsletters, newswires and newspapers.

QUESTEL
Questel, Inc.
5201 Leesburg Pike, Suite 603
Falls Church, VA 22041

Telephone: (800) 424–9600

Questel, Inc.
83-85 Boulevard Vincent Auriol
75013 Paris
France

Telephone: 45 82 64 64

Some 50 bibliographic and non-bibliographic files.

STN INTERNATIONAL
Chemical Abstracts Service
2540 Olentangy River Road
PO Box 3012
Columbus, OH 43210

Telephone: (800) 848–6533 or (614) 421–3600

More than 50 bibliographic and non-bibliographic files.

VU/TEXT
VU/TEXT Information Services
325 Chestnut Street
1300 Mall Building
Philadelphia, PA 19106

Telephone: (800) 323–2940 or (215) 574–4400

Full-text access to more than 60 newspapers, magazines and newswires.

WEFA
WEFA Group
150 Monument Road
Bala Cynwyd, PA 19004

Telephone: (215) 667–6000

WILSONLINE
H. W. Wilson Company
950 University Avenue
Bronx, NY 10452

Telephone: (800) 367–6770 or (212) 588–8400

Online versions of more than 20 printed indexes.

Microforms

Although the use of microphotography dates back to 1839, its exploitation as a low-cost, compact medium for document storage and dissemination was not seriously considered until the 1930s, and its widespread acceptance in academic and research libraries is a still more recent innovation. Researchers might not, therefore, be fully aware of the range and uses of microformats that they are likely to encounter in the course of their research.

Formats

Microfilm was for many years the principal format: positive or negative continuous roll film, usually 35mm or 16mm, stored on reels or housed in plastic cartridges or cassettes. This medium is the one most commonly used for reproducing long runs of serial publications such as newspapers or government documents. Cassette storage of film is to be preferred, as it provides for greater speed and simplicity of loading, in addition to giving the films increased protection from damage. Many libraries, however, still have most of their films on reels. The words 'microfilm' and 'film' are frequently used to cover both microfilm proper and microfiche.

Microfiche or 'fiche' has increased greatly in popularity in recent years. It consists of microfilm in flat format, ranging from 3″ × 5″ to 5″ × 8″ in size, and is available in a variety of reduction ratios, the highest (i.e., smallest) of which is described as 'ultrafiche'. Each fiche usually has an eye-legible heading to make selection simpler. Microfiche can be stored in various ways: file boxes, envelope folders and revolving envelope carousels are all common. Fiche is generally more convenient to use than reel– or cassette–mounted continuous film, as it enables the reader to locate individual items or pages more easily, and to move back and forth from one page to another.

Other flat formats include *aperture cards* (once known as 'peek-a-boo cards')—frames or strips of film mounted over openings in cards, often punched for machine filing; and *micro-opaques*—greatly reduced facsimiles in the form of print on paper or card ('microprint' or 'microcards'). This is a very economical method of reproduction, but the end product, though more durable, produces a less satisfactory image quality than conventional transparent film.

Bibliography

Microforms provide far better access than was previously available to all categories of Latin American research materials. The development of arrangements for their bibliographic control, however, is still far from satisfactory. Most institutions carry out microfilming programmes of their own as well as acquiring commercially produced works. Unfortunately, not all libraries issue guides to their microform collections, and some do not even include microforms in their main catalogues. The researcher may therefore need to engage in some detective work in order to ascertain what material exists in his or her subject field.

An out-of-date but still occasionally useful introductory guide to some of the resources available is:

> SABLE, Martin H. *A Guide to Nonprint Materials for Latin American Studies*. Detroit, MI: Blaine Ethridge, 1979. Includes subject, title and format indexes, together with an annotated directory of private and commercial institutions involved in microfilming Latin Americana.

The Seminar on the Acquisition of Latin American Library Materials (SALALM) has long been the organisation most concerned with the dissemination of information on microfilming projects specifically concerned with Latin America. The coverage began with:

> DIAZ, Albert J. 'Selected List of Microreproduced Material Relating to Latin America'. In *Final Report and Working Papers* of SALALM IX, 1964. Washington, DC: Pan American Union, 1965, vol. 1, pp. 161–172.

This has been supplemented by SALALM's 'Microfilming Projects Newsletter', published regularly from 1970 through 1982 as part of the organisation's annual *Papers*, and subsequently issued as a preprint with conference registration material. The newsletter lists recently completed and ongoing projects in microfilming monographs, serials, newspapers, pamphlets and archive collections of

Latin American interest, giving full details of the responsible institution. It has been indexed in:

> HODGMAN, Suzanne. 'Microfilming Projects Newsletter: Index'. In *Library Resources on Latin America: New Perspectives for the 1980s: Final Report and Working Papers* of SALALM XXV, 1980. Madison, WI: SALALM, 1981, pp. 123–162.

Some publishers have made a practice of issuing book, pamphlet, archive or documentary collections in major microform sets, usually accompanied by a hard-copy guide and index. A valuable guide and introduction to these is:

> *Microform Research Collections: A Guide.* Edited by Suzanne Cates Dodson. 2nd ed. Westport, CT: Meckler, 1984. Arranged by subject, with an index of authors, editors and titles. Each entry reviews the scope and content of the collection, lists its publisher, format, availability and price, and identifies any accompanying bibliographies and indexes.

More general guides are:

> *Guide to Microforms in Print.* (Incorporating *International Microforms in Print*). Westport, CT: Meckler, 1961—. Annual. Includes books, journals, newspapers, government publications and archival materials, entered in alphabetical sequence under author and title. Each entry includes information on format, publisher, date and price. There is a companion volume:

> *Subject Guide to Microforms in Print.* Westport, CT: Meckler, 1975—. Arranged by alphabetical subject headings.

For more detailed information on current projects of Latin American interest, important sources are the publicity leaflets and catalogues issued by individual publishers. They can be traced through:

> *Microform Market Place: An International Directory of Micropublishing.* Westport, CT: Meckler, 1974—. Biennial. Lists both commercial and non-commercial organisations, with information on the formats offered by each, their subject interests and publication programmes. Contains a bibliography, together with subject and geographic indexes.

Publicity material can also be consulted in:

Micropublishers' Trade List Annual. Alexandria, VA: Chadwyck-Healey, 1978—. Presents on microfiche, in loose-leaf
format, the catalogues and brochures of micropublishers
throughout the world.

Bibliographies also exist for microform publications of specific types
of material (newspapers and dissertations, for instance), and several
library catalogues have now been issued on COM (computer output
microform) to give them a wider availability. More information on
these types of materials may be found in the relevant chapters of this
book (NEWSPAPERS AND NEWS MAGAZINES, p. 185, THESES AND
DISSERTATIONS, p. 221, and PUBLISHED LIBRARY CATALOGUES, p.
46).

Microforming Projects

Important primary research materials, such as newspapers and press
cuttings, government documents (ministerial reports, statistical
serials and census returns, for example) and ephemera (for instance,
broadsides, political pamphlets and posters—all of prime importance
in the field of Latin American political and social studies), have
always been difficult for libraries to acquire consistently. Moreover,
once acquired, they are notoriously prone to rapid deterioration.
Microfilming initiatives, and cooperative projects in particular,
enable complete runs or collections of homogeneous material to be
assembled, reproduced and widely disseminated, thus achieving the
librarian's triple aim of completeness, preservation and general
availability. A leader in cooperative filming initiatives in the field of
Latin American studies is the Latin American Microform Project
(LAMP). Founded in 1975 as a project of the Center for Research
Libraries (CRL) in Chicago, Illinois, LAMP is composed of a
consortium of member libraries, which collaborate with scholars and
bibliographers in selecting and assembling suitable materials for
filming. In order to avoid duplication of effort, LAMP maintains
close contact with the microfilming activities of the Library of
Congress Preservation Program. Although most LAMP member
institutions are located in North America, filming is also carried out
in Europe and in Latin America itself. Microforms may be
borrowed from CRL by member libraries, or reproduced for
purchase by non-members.

In the last few years there has been a general increase in the use of
microform as a preservation medium. Faced with the inevitable and

rapid decay of some printed materials, notably post-1800 books, journals and newspapers, coupled with the high cost of conservation treatment, many libraries have turned to making a 'master' microform of deteriorating items and restricting the use of the original—in some cases even discarding it. Subject to considerations of copyright, they can then supply local users and other libraries with positive copies.

To find out what material has already been filmed in the UK, one should consult the Register of Preservation Microforms (RPM). This is a British Library online file operated through the LOCAS system, which is run by the British Library Bibliographic Services. This lists all the filming from the BL's conservation microfilming programme since its inception in 1976; it also includes records of the filming done since 1986 by the Library's Photographic Service to meet customer orders. In due course, earlier records will be incorporated, together with data on manuscripts, maps and other non-book materials.

A parallel file for the United States is available in an annual hard-copy format:

> *National Register of Microform Masters* (NRMM). Washington, DC: Library of Congress, 1965—. Like RPM, lists negative master films made for preservation purposes which can be used to generate positive film or hard copies. Since 1970, all items have been listed in a single alphabetical sequence; earlier editions were arranged by Library of Congress card number or *National Union Catalog* number.

NRMM is supplemented by:

> *National Preservation Report*. Washington, DC: Library of Congress, 1973—. Published three times a year, this bulletin reports on preservation microfilming activities of the Library of Congress and other North American and foreign institutions. Includes statements of intention to microfilm.

The Future

Although microforms still tend to be regarded as relative newcomers to the field of information provision, they have already been in part supplanted by newer technological developments. Direct online access to catalogues, bibliographies and texts is becoming an increasingly convenient and popular research method, as is access via CD-ROM (compact disc—read-only memory). Nevertheless, for regular and meticulous examination of specific documents, micro-formats seem set to be the norm for many years to come. The Universidad Nacional Autónoma de México, for example, now provides CD-ROM access to over 165,000 journal article records in six multidisciplinary databases as part of its Latin American Bibliography Project; for continued individual use, however, all the documents cited are made available to enquirers in microform.

MJ

Sound Recordings

Over the last few years there has been an astonishing improvement in the scope and depth of sound resources available in the UK for the study of Latin American culture. This should not indicate complacency, however, for it will soon become apparent that there is still an enormous amount even of basic work to be done in Europe, and that the bulk of the sources, particularly repositories of original recordings, are in the US. Nevertheless, scholars confined to the British Isles will still be able to make headway—although the fruits of their labour may consist of numerous citations and few auditions. This article is structured loosely, with first, general printed sources on musical and literary recordings, followed by information about collections found in institutions in the Americas and in Europe.

General Printed Sources

A general guide to the field can be found in:

> SABLE, Martin H. *A Guide to Non-Print Materials for Latin American Studies.* Detroit, MI: Blaine Ethridge, 1979.

Music plays a central role in the lives of Latin Americans, much of it connected with rituals having long and intriguing histories. It is therefore fitting that music is the concern of a large proportion of the sources discussed here: other types of recording follow. Many of the bibliographical works cited in the subject bibliography on Music (pp. 112–114) are applicable, including the 'Americas' volume of *Information on Music: A Handbook of Reference Sources in European Languages*, by Guy A. MARCO and others (1977), in which each Latin American area included is followed by a discography. The quarterly *RILM Abstracts* (Kassel, 1967—) also includes a discography section (09), as well as one on Latin America (36). Sound recordings are also treated in the *New Grove Dictionary of Music and Musicians* (1980) and in Gilbert CHASE's *Guide to the Music of Latin America* (1962), though the comprehensive discography of the latter volume refers to

many non-current recordings. The discographical information is
updated in:

BÉHAGUE, Gerard. 'Latin American Music: An Annotated
Bibliography of Recent Publications.' *Yearbook of Inter-American
Music Research* 11 (1975), pp. 190–218.

It is usually convenient to distinguish between the activities and
products of the commercial recording industry and the results of field
recordists and ethnomusicologists; the two operations are not,
however, necessarily exclusive, as is indicated in:

GRONOW, Pekka. 'Ethnic Recordings: An Introduction.' In
Ethnic Recordings in America: A Neglected Heritage. Washington,
DC: Folklife Center, Library of Congress, 1982, pp. 1–49. This
brief study of the history of the American recording industry's
activities in Latin America incorporates a checklist of 78 rpm
foreign language records (pp. 32–49), giving details of the
Latin American series of such major companies as RCA and
Columbia.

Gronow refers to the North American interest in Latin America as
'a puzzling mosaic that has been little studied'. Certainly the ground
work of compiling numerical catalogues of records issued has hardly
begun. This basic names-and-numbers research can be aided by
published commercial catalogues and national discographies; unfortunately, Latin America provides few of these facilities. To date only
Brazil has attempted the production of a national discography:

Discografia brasileira 78rpm, 1902–1964. 5 vols. Rio de Janeiro:
Funarte, 1982.

In 1978 the Venezuelan national library announced its intention to
include sound recordings in its national bibliography; this seems not
to have happened, however. The area of Latin America that has
attracted the most thorough discographical research to date continues to be Brazil, with its internationally acclaimed popular music:

EFEGE, Jota. *Figuras e coisas da musica popular brasileira.* 2 vols.
Rio de Janeiro: Mec/Funarte, 1979–1980. A compilation of
articles written between 1940 and 1978.

PERRONE, Charles A. 'An Annotated Interdisciplinary Bibliography and Discography of Brazilian Popular Music.' *Latin
American Music Review* 7 (1986), p.302–340. The discography
(pp. 334–340) concentrates on 'contemporary manifestations',

and the bibliography includes many items with complete discographies of individuals.

Mexico too, possibly on account of its proximity to the US, has attracted some discographical research:

MÉNDEZ GUTIÉRREZ, Leticia. 'El movimiento de música folklórica en México: apuntes para su estudio.' Thesis. Mexico City: Universidad Iberoamericana, 1980. Researches the folk music movement of 1962–1978 and includes a discography and an analysis of record production.

HICKERSON, Joseph C. 'Early Field Recordings of Ethnic Music.' In *Ethnic Recordings in America* (see above), pp. 67–84. Includes an appendix, 'Mexican-American folksong and music on field recordings in the Archive of Folk Song, Library of Congress'.

Returning to the more general discographical picture for ethnic or traditional music, the best guide to resources and an ideal starting point is:

COHEN, Norm and Paul F. WELLS. 'Recorded Ethnic Music: A Guide to Resources.' In *Ethnic Recordings in America* (see above), pp. 175–250. Includes a Hispanic section (pp. 190–196) listing collectors, recordings, companies and archives.

Other general guides to this area include:

OLSEN, Dale. 'Symbol and Function in South American Indian Music' and 'Folk Music of South America: A Musical Mosaic'. Both in *Music of Many Cultures: An Introduction*, edited by Elizabeth May. Berkeley, CA: University of California Press, 1980, pp. 363–385 and pp. 386–425.

Field recordings on cylinders were being made in South America as early as 1905. The activities of some of these earliest recordists are detailed in:

ARETZ, Isabel. 'Colecciones de cilindros y trabajos de musicología comparada realizados en Latinoamérica durante los primeros treinta años del siglo XX.' *Revista Venezolana de Folklore* 4 (December 1972), p. 54.

Periodicals useful for the study of traditional music include:

Journal for Ethnomusicology (previously *Ethnomusicology*). Ann Arbor, MI: Society for Ethnomusicology, 1953—. 3 issues per year. The 'Current Bibliography, Discography and Filmography' section is one of the most valuable sources on current research. Also contains substantial record reviews, as does its more geographically specific companion:

Latin American Music Review. Austin, TX: University of Texas Press, 1980—. Semi-annual.

Another 'coordinating resource' can be found in:

Latin American Masses and Minorities: Their Images and Realities: Papers of SALALM XXX, 1975. 2 vols. Madison, WI: SALALM, 1987. Included are an article and three bibliographies on Latin American ethnomusicology by the indefatigable John M. SCHECHTER (see below), and the bibliographically comprehensive article by Malena Kuss (see p. 113).

A forthcoming work of the latter author, referred to in her article, is potentially indispensable:

Kuss, Malena and Donald THOMPSON. *Directory of Music Research Libraries: South America, Central America, Mexico and the Caribbean.* Répertoire International des Sources Musicales, Series C, 7. Kassel: Bärenreiter, forthcoming 1989. Described as 'a census-catalog of music holdings in public and private Latin American and Caribbean libraries, archives, museums or any other type of repository, of manuscript, printed and recorded music'.

Important material on popular music from Latin America— bearing in mind the wide connotations of those terms in this context—has recently been appearing in *Popular Music* (Cambridge: University Press, 1981—); the May 1987 issue (6:2) was devoted exclusively to Latin America, with useful discographies.

On the subject of popular and traditional music, two publications which focus on the way North Americans perceive South American music via recordings are:

DURAN, Gustavo. *Recordings of Latin American Songs and Dances: An Annotated, Selective List of Popular and Folk-Popular Music.* 2nd ed. Revised by Gilbert Chase. Washington, DC: Pan-American Union, 1950.

ROBERTS, John Storm. *The Latin Tinge: The Impact of Latin American Music on the United States.* New York: Oxford University Press, 1979.

In comparison with other genres, art music fares rather feebly on record; this is perhaps not surprising in a musical culture which has remained relatively impervious to Western symphonic music, and where many musicians testify to acknowledging little or no difference between categories of music. Apart from Villa-Lobos, Chávez and Ginastera, Latin American composers are poorly represented on disc. The only overview of such recordings discovered is almost twenty years old:

'Latin American Long Playing Records Available in the United States.' *Inter-American Music Bulletin* 71 (May 1969), p.42–46.

Available recordings are listed in published catalogues such as the *Gramophone Classical Catalogue* (London: General Gramophone Publications, 1953—), *The New Schwann* (Boston, MA: ABC Schwann, 1983—) and the *Bielefelder Katalog Klassik* (Stuttgart: Vereinigte Motor-Verlag, 1960—).

Literature Recordings

The Archive of Hispanic Literature on Tape at the Library of Congress began collecting in 1943, and in 1987 consisted of nearly 600 recordings by Latin American, Caribbean, Iberian and Chicano authors. In recent years interviews have been videotaped, the first being Borges in 1977. A guide to this collection was published as:

AGUILERA, Francisco. *A Guide to the Archive of Hispanic Literature on Tape.* Edited by Georgette M. Dorn. Washington, DC: Government Printing Office, 1974. Also a *Supplement* (1977).

All this material is included and updated in:

WHITTINGTON, Jennifer. *Literary Recordings: A Checklist of the Archive of Recorded Poetry and Literature in the Library of Congress.* Rev. ed. Washington, DC: Library of Congress, 1981. Some of the material has been released on commercial LPs, and other recordings have been made available to non-profit institutions.

For Caribbean literature, including materials relating to the Spanish-speaking areas, there is a published listing:

> KEANE, Christiane. *Caribbean Literature: A Discography*. London: Atcal, 1984. Includes holdings relating to Caribbean literature in the National Sound Archive.

Institutions in the Americas

The most important Latin American music collections in North American libraries are to be found at the Library of Congress, New York Public Library, the Columbus Memorial Library of the Organization of American States (Washington DC), the Universities of Arizona (Tucson), Miami (Coral Gables) and Texas (Austin), and the Lilly and School of Music Libraries of Indiana University (Bloomington). The latter university has also produced an important published catalogue:

> *Music from Latin America Available at Indiana University: Scores, Tapes and Records*. 2nd ed., compiled by Juan Orrego Salas. Bloomington, IN: Latin American Music Center, 1971.

One of the finest collections of early recordings of traditional music on cylinder and disc exists in Indiana University's Archives of Traditional Music, whose holdings extend also to popular music. Details of the collection can be found in:

> *A Catalog of Phonorecordings of Music and Oral Data Held by the Archives of Traditional Music*. Boston, MA: G. K. Hall, 1975.

Readers should work from the index of geographical areas, culture groups and subjects to the catalogue itself, which consists of photographed index cards in accession and alphabetical order. More work on the holdings appears in the section on archive materials in:

> SMITH, Ronald. 'Latin American Ethnomusicology: A Discussion of Central America and North South America.' *Latin American Music Review* 3 (1982), pp. 1–16.

Another major repository of traditional music is the Archive of Folk Culture at the Library of Congress, which has a substantial collection of field recordings from many Latin American locations and is particularly strong in the music of the US–Mexico borderlands. Further information can be found in:

Inventory of the Bibliographic and Other Reference and Finding Aids.
Prepared by the Archive of Folk Culture. Washington, DC:
Library of Congress, 1984.

A few examples of music from the collection have been put onto disc
and cassette, and are available by mail order from the Library
(Washington, DC 20540).

Much pioneering work has been done by John M. Schechter at
the Belfer Audio Laboratory and Archive of Syracuse University, a
research institution completed in 1982 that contains exclusively
audio materials. The archive holds some quarter of a million sound
recordings on disc, including the Bell Collection of 45 rpm singles
from the Caribbean area. A microfilm catalogue of the collection is
underway; in the meantime, Schechter has in his own words 'barely
scratched the surface' of the Bell Collection with a 57-page
discography, available from the author upon request.

The holdings of several major audio archives are listed in the
Rigler and Deutsch Index (Associated Audio Archive, 1983), a COM
index of pre-LP commercial recordings held by the Rodgers and
Hammerstein Archives, the Syracuse University Audio Archives,
the Yale University Archive of Historical Sound Recordings, the
Recorded Sound Collections of the Library of Congress, and the
Stanford University Archives of Recorded Sound. The information
is sorted in various sequences, including performer and label and
matrix number. Most of the series of recordings referred to by
GRONOW (see above) will be found there, but regrettably in an
incomplete form; worse, the index (compiled by non-professional
labour) is replete with inaccuracies.

Details of the holdings of major collections in Albuquerque and
Pittsburgh are to be found, respectively, in:

SUBLETTE, Ned. *A Discography of Hispanic Music in the Fine Arts
Library, University of New Mexico.* Westport, CT: Greenwood
Press, 1978. An inventory of about 12,000 recordings covering
South and Central America and Mexico, with separate
sections for art music, flamenco and folk music.

LOTIS, Howard. *Latin American Music Materials Available at the
University of Pittsburgh and at the Carnegie Library, Pittsburgh.*
Pittsburgh, PA: Center for Latin American Studies, University of Pittsburgh, 1981. An annotated bibliography and
discography appears on pp. 56–109.

In South America itself there are now a number of organisations devoted to the preservation and documentation of sound recordings. The oldest is the Instituto Interamericano de Etnomusicología y Folklore (INIDEF) in Caracas, Venezuela. This is essentially a repository for field recordings, and reports appear in its own publication *Revista INIDEF* (1975—). In Buenos Aires the Fonoteca Nacional del Instituto de Musicología 'Carlos Vega' collects recorded music from Argentina and neighbouring countries. It produces LP discs of some of its collections. In Otavalo, Ecuador, the Instituto Otavaleño de Antropología has catalogues of recordings made in the Sierra and Oriente regions; in Bogotá the Instituto Colombiano de Antropología engages in musicological activities, and finally in Santiago, Chile, there is CENECA, The Centro de Indagación y Expresión Cultural y Artística, whose efforts appear to be concerned primarily with the dissemination of information through festivals and conferences.

Institutions in Europe

British libraries having appreciable collections of Latin American music include the British Library Reference Division, Westminster Central Music Library (160, Buckingham Palace Road) and the University of London Music Library (Senate House, Malet Street).

With regard to audio resources, however, Paris has traditionally been a better place than London to find recordings from Latin America: the huge record store FNEC in the shopping centre at Les Halles carries a large selection of imports. The current state of the holdings at the Phonothèque National, however, is not known; the only indication is a publication issued almost forty years ago:

> *Collection Phonothèque Nationale (Paris)*. Paris: Unesco, 1952. Prepared by the International Commission on Folk Arts and Folklore. Contains references to recordings from Chile, Bolivia, Argentina and Brazil.

In the UK the major sound archives are found in London: the British Broadcasting Corporation Sound Archives and the National Sound Archive of the British Library. The BBC Sound Archives are not usually accessible to the public, but have the beginnings of a published catalogue:

> STEWART, Madeau. *BBC Sound Archives: A Catalogue of the Folk and National Music Recordings*. London: British Broadcasting

Corporation, 1983. A guide to the Archive's recordings from all countries except Britain; best approached by checking the name of the desired country for a summary of the material on file and a list of the appropriate subject headings, and then following these up in the main subject sequence. Updates can be found in the microfiche *BBC Sound Archive Index*.

The National Sound Archive (23 Exhibition Road, London SW7 2AS) holds the largest publicly accessible collection of Latin American recordings outside the US. Many of the publications referred to in this article can be consulted in the Archive's own library or in other departments of the British Library. There is currently no published index to the NSA's holdings; users are advised to make arrangements to consult available substitutes (such as handlists and checklists compiled by the subject curators), and to seek assistance from senior staff in following up references to published sources.

Although the emphasis of this article has hitherto been predominantly musical, the National Sound Archive holds a variety of other types of material which may give some idea of the scope of sound recordings in existence. In the field of *environmental recordings* there are BBC sound effects, including the sound of a Brazilian village and the atmospheres of the Argentine pampas and a Venezuelan jungle. Almost all the commercially issued *wildlife recordings* are held, including many South American species; also more than 3,000 unpublished recordings, including duplicate copies of material in the BBC Natural History Sound Archives, donations from amateur recordists and professional biologists, and recordings made by NSA staff on 'Operation Raleigh' expeditions to Peru and Costa Rica. All of these recordings are indexed, and can be consulted on application to the British Library of Wildlife Sounds (BLOWS) curator. *Literary recordings* include commercial series such as the 'Voz Viva de México' series of modern writers (notably, Octavio Paz) produced by the Universidad Nacional Autónoma de México, and the Argentine 'AMB Discográfica' of documentary and theatrical material, including important recordings of Jose Luis Borges, Pablo Neruda and Gabriel García Márquez. NSA staff have made some recordings of contemporary writers, including Mario Vargas Llosa, Ariel Dorfman and Jose Ibarguengoitia, reading their own works. In addition, the Archive has a major collection of *political and documentary recordings*. These include speeches by Che Guevara (donated by the Cuban Embassy), and BBC archive material including speeches by Juan Perón and interviews with Salvador Allende and Anastasio Somoza, and sound coverage of the Falkland/Malvinas conflict.

CC

Visual Materials

The study of Latin America through visual media has increased immensely over the last few years, though critical attention has been focused principally on cinema and the photograph. This article will treat mainly these two media.

Photography

There are several different approaches that one can take to the study of Latin American photographs: first, as examples of a medium of expression that has been widely practised in the region since its inception 150 years ago; secondly, as documents or primary sources of information about a wide range of subjects, often providing information not available in written or printed sources; or thirdly, as research tools for social scientists wishing to make their own records of Latin American societies and cultures. For an extensive, annotated list of sources treating all aspects of Latin American photography, see:

> LEVINE, Robert E. *Windows on Latin America: Understanding Society Through Photographs.* Miami, FL: University of Miami, South Eastern Council on Latin American Studies, 1987.

Photographic History

Until recently, there has been little literature available on the history of Latin American photography. Now, a small number of photo-historians in Mexico, Colombia and other countries are researching and publishing authoritative works that reflect a Latin American perspective on the history of this influential medium. A few of the major works are:

> BILLITER, Erika. *Fotografía latinoamericana.* Madrid: El Viso, 1982. Translated from the catalogue of a major exhibition of Latin American photography (1860–1981) held at the Kunsthaus, Zurich. Contains full-page reproductions of many

photographs, biographies of the photographers and an informative introductory text.

Documentos gráficos para la historia de México. 2 vols. Mexico City: Sureste, 1985-1987. Essays on the history of Mexican photography, with illustrations and bibliography.

FERREZ, Gilberto and Weston J. NAEF. *Pioneer Photographers of Brazil, 1840–1920.* New York: Center for Inter-American Relations, 1976. Early history of photography in Brazil, including portfolios of fifteen photographers.

McELROY, Douglas Keith. *Early Peruvian Photography: A Critical Case Study.* Ann Arbor, MI: UMI Research Press, 1984. Development of photography in nineteenth century Peru and examination of the role of the photographer in society.

SERRANO, Eduardo. *Historia de la fotografía en Colombia.* Bogotá: Museo de Arte Gráfico, 1983. Authoritative history, 1840–1950, lavishly illustrated in black-and-white and in colour.

'Latin American Photography.' *Aperture* 109 (Winter 1987). Entire issue devoted to current trends in Latin American photography, with essays and book reviews by photographer and photo historians.

Photos as Documents

Pictures are essential documents for the study of Latin American history, particularly in matters concerning the non-literate masses, whose story was so rarely recorded in texts. For the period before 1840, pictorial sources may take the form of paintings, drawings or prints; since the invention of photography, photographs have usually been considered the most accurate and authentic visual documents.

There is a danger, however, in equating the photographic image with 'reality'. Photographers are invariably subjective in what they choose to record and how they choose to record it. Both the personal vision and the cultural conditioning of the photographer affect his or her work. Photos can, moreover, be manipulated in the darkroom or by computer, with results that can be nearly impossible to detect. Photos can be cropped or flopped when they are reproduced; they may be wrongly captioned, or published in a context or manner different from the original intent of the photographer.

It is essential, then, to obtain as much information as possible about the photograph itself—its subject, author, date and original purpose—before attempting any interpretation. Unfortunately, particularly in the case of historical photos, such information may be extremely difficult, if not impossible, to obtain. Using photos as documents may involve real detective work. Some useful techniques for identifying photos and a discussion of their importance as sources may be found in:

WEINSTEIN, Robert A. and Larry BOOTH. *Collection, Use and Care of Historical Photos*. Nashville, TN: American Association for State and Local History, 1977.

MRAZ, John. 'Particularidad y nostalgia.' *Nexos* 8 (July 1985), pp. 9–12.

Photography as a Research Tool

Very often, as well as using photos as primary sources of information, social scientists use photography as a research tool. Such applications of the medium may include the use of aerial views to study demography or topography; sequential photography to record and study processes such as craft production, agricultural methods, ceremonies or stages of social interaction; the use of photos as a stimulus for interviewing; or creating photographic inventories of material culture, such as of all the objects in a home. It is in this realm of visual anthropology that one should be acutely aware of the role of cultural bias and conditioning. One of the best sources for an in-depth discussion of data gathering methods and analysis of photographic records is:

COLLIER, John, Jr., and Malcolm COLLIER. *Visual Anthropology: Photography as a Research Method*. Albuquerque, NM: University of New Mexico Press, 1986.

Sources of Latin American Photographs

Within Latin America, many historic photographic collections remain in private hands—that is, with the photographers, subjects or collectors of the photos, or their descendants. Nevertheless, in most countries the national archive and national library house significant picture collections, including photographs. Other sources include museums and cultural centres, public and private institutes, universities and archives of newspapers and other publishers. The Fondo Audiovisual of the Banco Central del Ecuador in Quito, Ecuador, the Fototeca of the Instituto Nacional de Antropología e Historia in

Pachuca, Hidalgo, Mexico and the Departamento de Colecciones Fotográficas of the Biblioteca Nacional in Caracas are particularly noteworthy. The collections really need to be visited, as most institutions do not have sufficient staff to conduct research in response to outside requests.

There are also important sources of Latin American photographs outside Latin America, particularly in the United States; few British or European research institutions collect extensively in the field. Among the most significant sources in the US are the Library of Congress and the Anthropological Archives of the Smithsonian Institution, Washington, DC; the New York Public Library; the Latin American Library at Tulane University, New Orleans; the General Library of the University of New Mexico, Albuquerque; the Benson Latin American Collection of the University of Texas at Austin; the Peabody Museum, Harvard University; the California Museum of Photography at the University of California, Riverside; The Fowler Museum of Cultural History and the Library of the University of California, Los Angeles; and the Amon Carter Memorial Museum, Fort Worth. There are also, of course, numerous commercial and private collections of photos of Latin America taken by North American and other foreign photographers.

Listed below are some of the most useful sources for locating Latin American photographs:

DAVIDSON, Martha et al. *Picture Collections: Mexico*. Metuchen, NJ: Scarecrow Press, 1988. Guide to over 500 sources of photos, paintings, prints, drawings and other pictorial documents in Mexico. Indexed by subject, source and artist.

EAKINS, Rosemary. *Picture Sources: UK*. London: Macdonald, 1985. Guide to more than 1,000 public and private collections in the United Kingdom, indexed by collection and subject matter. Latin Americana can be found by referring to country headings in the subject index.

Répertoire des collections photographiques en France. 5th ed. Paris: Documentation Française, 1980. Guide to more than 1,000 photographic collections in France, indexed by subject (Latin American material may be found by country). Includes a directory of photo agencies and associations, and a bibliography of other guides to European collections.

WILGUS, A. Curtis. *Latin America: A Guide to Illustrations*. Metuchen, NJ: Scarecrow Press, 1981. Indexes of published illustrations on topics pertaining to Latin America. Picture credits in the publications may be used to locate original sources.

For information about contemporary photographers of Latin America a key source is the Consejo Mexicano de Fotografía in Mexico City (Tehuantepec 214, Colonia Roma, 06760 México DF). The Center for Creative Photography in Tucson, Arizona, can also provide information on contemporary Latin American photography.

Film

Latin American cinema has increased greatly in importance in recent years, a fact reflected in the growing academic interest it has engendered, particularly in the US. This section lists some of the general sources pertaining to the study of Latin American film production, and provides a guide to the availability of films from and about the region. While most of the titles given here emphasise feature length productions, some also deal with documentary films and shorts. Because Latin American cinema is a such an emerging field, it may be necessary occasionally to consult some of the international film reference sources in addition to the titles described below.

Handbooks and Guides

The titles listed here provide a broad overview of film history and activity in Latin America. A short general introduction to the topic, with a brief history and discussion of current research issues, can be found in:

MOSIER, John. 'Film.' In *Handbook of Latin American Popular Culture*. Edited by Harold E. Hinds Jr and Charles M. Tatum. Westport, CT: Greenwood, 1985, pp. 173–189. Includes a bibliography and a discussion of reference works.

Three works showing European interest in the subject are:

CHANAN, Michael. *Twenty-Five Years of Latin American Cinema*. London: British Film Institute/Channel Four, 1983. Seven essays by various hands on the preoccupations of modern Latin American film.

HENNEBELLE, Guy and Alfonso GUMUCIO-DAGRÓN. *Les cinémas de l'Amérique Latine.* Paris: Lherminier, 1981. Covers the film industries of twenty-six countries, including the US Chicano cinema. Contains extensive filmographies, though technical credits are often incomplete.

SCHUMANN, Peter B. *Handbuch des lateinamerikanischen Films.* Frankfurt: Vervuert, 1982. Less comprehensive than the preceding work, but provides a broad narrative on the film production of thirteen countries. Of special interest is the section of plot summaries for selected films produced from the 1960s though the 1980s. An abridged version (lacking the plot section) is now available in Spanish as *Historia del cine latinoamericano* (Buenos Aires: Legasa, 1987).

A more general, ongoing reference work is:

International Film Guide. Edited by Peter Cowie. Annual. London: Tantivy Press, 1964—. Covers film industries on a country-by-country basis, although not all the Latin American nations with film production are covered consistently from year to year. Further information on Latin America can be found in the (sometimes outdated) sections on film festivals, film schools, film archives and film magazines.

A more specialised introduction is:

WEST, Dennis. *Contemporary Brazilian Cinema.* Albuquerque, NM: Latin American Institute, University of New Mexico, 1985. A useful and concise introduction, with a bibliography including books, periodical articles and published screenplays.

Bibliographies

Two bibliographies covering the whole region are:

BURTON, Julianne. *The New Latin American Cinema: An Annotated Bibliography of Sources in English, Spanish and Portuguese.* New York: Smyrna Press, 1983. A very useful source, now expanded from the original 1976 edition to include US Hispanic cinema.

SCOTT, Robert. 'Bibliography of Latin American Cinema: Film Journal Articles in English.' *Jump Cut* 30 (March 1985), pp. 59–61. An unannotated bibliography arranged by region and countries.

There are also country-specific bibliographies, of which a good example is:

ALMOINA, Helena. *Bibliografía del cine mexicano*. Mexico City: UNAM, Filmoteca, 1985. Unannotated citations arranged by author or title in sections. Includes books and theses.

In addition to these, film is also covered by several important, more general bibliographical sources:

Handbook of Latin American Art/Manual de arte latinoamericano. Edited by Joyce Waddell Bailey. Santa Barbara, CA: ABC/ Clio Press, 1984—. The first volume of this work includes a subsection on film within the general geographic arrangement.

Internationale Filmbibliographie/Bibliographie internationale du cinéma/International Motion Picture Bibliography. Munich: Filmland Presse, 1979–1980—. Annual. Includes citations on Latin American film from mostly North American and European sources, arranged by subject and indexed by author and title. The coverage is restricted to books.

Since 1976 the *Handbook of Latin American Studies* (see p. 90) has carried an occasional bibliographic section on Latin American film. Owing to the paucity of published titles available for review, the section now appears alternately with one on folklore in the biennial 'Humanities' volume. Full regional bibliographies have so far appeared in volumess 38 (1976), 40 (1978) and 48 (1986), with special bibliographies on the revolutionary Cuban cinema in volume 39 (1977) and Brazilian cinema in volume 44 (1982).

Filmographies

No complete, comprehensive filmography exists for Latin America, though some information can be found in general sources, such as:

CYR, Helen W. *A Filmography of the Third World, 1976–1983: An Annotated List of 16mm Films*. Metuchen, NJ: Scarecrow Press, 1985. Arranged by region with a subarrangement by country, this source is designed to assist in the location of films available for sale or rental. Includes a list of distributors. An update for 1984–1989 is in preparation.

LIMBACHER, James L. *Feature Films: A Directory of Feature Films on 16mm and Videotape Available for Rental, Sale and Lease*. 8th ed. New York: Bowker, 1985. Includes films from Latin America, though national origins are not indicated: some may be identified from the 'Foreign Language Index', though titles are often cited only in English translation. Issued on a biennial basis, with quarterly supplements in the periodical *Sightlines*.

Magill's Survey of Cinema: Foreign Language Films. Edited by Frank N. Magill. 8 vols. Englewood Cliffs, NJ: Salem Press, 1985. Only 42 Latin American films are included (out of a total of 700). Volume 8 contains comprehensive indexes for titles, dates and names of persons involved.

Filmographies of varying quality also exist for some individual countries. Mexico is especially well covered, owing to the efforts of Emilio García Riera:

GARCÍA RIERA, Emilio. *Filmografía mexicana: medio y largo metrajes*. Mexico City: Cineteca Nacional, 1985—. Intended to provide a complete filmography of Mexican film production since the silent period, with technical credits and plot summaries. Arranged in chronological order and indexed by title, production company and names of those involved. The first volume covers 1906–1940.

GARCÍA RIERA, Emilio. *La guía del cine mexicano: de la pantalla grande a la televisión, 1919–1984*. Mexico City: Patria, 1984. Intended as a television viewing guide, this is a catalogue of some 1,500 Mexican films with critical plot synopses and incomplete technical credits, indexed by director and date.

GARCÍA RIERA, Emilio. *Historia documental del cine mexicano*. 9 vols. Mexico City: Era, 1969–1978. An important comprehensive history of Mexican sound films through 1966. The volumes cover chronological periods: each includes historical narrative, a thorough filmography and its own index.

Guía de Filmes. Rio de Janeiro: Embrafilme, 1967—. Annual. Gives incomplete coverage of Brazilian production for each year, together with general statistics on film attendance in Brazil. Retrospective indexes are being produced, with the intention of providing a complete Brazilian filmography from 1897.

MARTÍN, Jorge Abel. *Cine argentino*. Buenos Aires: Corregidor, 1976—. An annual publication, giving incomplete coverage of

Argentine production. Includes biographical data and obituaries.

WILLIAMS, Gayle A. 'A Latin American Filmography, 1977–1981.' In *The Central American Connection: Library Resources and Access: Papers* of SALALM XXVIII, 1983. Madison, WI: SALALM, 1985, pp. 177–215. Supplies technical credits for 226 feature films. Indexed by date and country.

Availability

Despite the increase in the number of printed monographs and articles appearing on the subject of Latin American film, it is still not easy to view the films themselves. Only a few feature length films (and fewer documentaries) become available for theatre exhibition in either the US or the UK. The *International Film Guide* and the works by CYR and LIMBACHER, listed above, include some information on distributors and availability for sale or rental.

In the US, the growing market for video cassette tapes has begun to cater to Spanish speakers; most of the films available are Spanish or Mexican, but some come from Argentina or elsewhere. The scope of the available material can represent the best of these cinemas, but is bound also to include low-budget comedies and action films. The growth of Hispanic communities across the US has encouraged the development of Spanish language television networks, which include Latin American films in their programming. In addition, many public and university libraries are beginning to add videotapes to their collections.

In the UK, the situation is worse: leaving aside some occasional adventurous late-night programming on Channel Four, virtually the only access to Latin American cinema is through local film societies or specialist cinemas and the National Film Theatre (NFT) in London. The British Film Institute (which runs the NFT) has a library holding the largest collection in Britain of literature on Latin American cinema, and also publishes the quarterly *British National Film and Video Catalogue*, cumulated annually, which records all films and videocassettes available for non-theatrical loan or sale in the UK.

Other Visual Sources

Art galleries and museums, outside as well as inside Latin America, are self-evidently important sources of visual materials for the study of the social and cultural history of the region. It would be impossible here to list all the relevant museums and galleries: most nations of Latin America have their own national ethnographic and artistic collections, as well as museums devoted to specific regions, events or personalities. Nor should it be forgotten that many artefacts and works of art from the region have, over the centuries, come to be in major collections in Europe and North America.

A useful guide to museums worldwide, including art museums, is:

> *The Directory of Museums.* Edited by Kenneth Hudson and Ann Nichols. 2nd ed. London: Macmillan, 1981. Brief descriptions of the collections of around 30,000 museums, arranged alphabetically by country and city. Each country has a short introductory paragraph characterising its museum collections. Includes a selected bibliography.

A more concise listing, with complete information about available audio-visual materials, is:

> *World Museum Publications: A Directory of Art and Cultural Museums, Their Publications and Audio-Visual Materials.* New York: Bowker, 1982.

For the United States and Canada only, there is the annual:

> *The Official Museum Directory.* New York: American Association of Museums, 1971——. Provides essential information concerning more than 6,000 museums of art, history and science.

A good introduction to art galleries can be found in:

> *Art Museums of the World.* Edited by Virginia Jackson et al. Westport, CT: Greenwood Press, 1987. A selective guide, with scholarly, signed descriptions of some 200 art collections.

See also the section on Art and Architecture in the chapter SUBJECT BIBLIOGRAPHIES (pp. 100–102).

MD/GAW

Specialised Information Sources

Biographies

The principal biographical sources for established historical and literary figures are of course the major encyclopaedias. Unfortunately, when it comes to locating biographical information on rather less well-known figures, matters are by no means clear-cut. Resources for collective biography generally fall into one of two classes: current sources dealing with prominent living personalities, typified by the annual British publication *Who's Who* (London: Black, 1849—), and retrospective sources which include only the famous dead, also typified by a UK publication: the *Dictionary of National Biography* (London: Smith, Elder, 1908–1909, with decennial updates from 1912 to date). The categories are not always mutually exclusive, but as so few publications bridge the gap it will be convenient here to treat the two classes separately.

Current Biography

There is currently no satisfactory and comprehensive listing of all prominent living Latin Americans, though one exists for the West Indies. This is the biennial *Personalities Caribbean: The International Guide to Who's Who in the West Indies, Bahamas and Bermuda* (Kingston: Personalities, 1962—). For the remainder of the region, the more prominent political or literary figures can frequently be found in such general sources as:

The International Who's Who. London: Europa Publications, 1935—. Annual.

Who's Who in the World. Wilmette, IL: Marquis Who's Who, 1971—. The current edition is the 8th (1987–1988). Biennial.

Another general work that is sometimes of use is the monthly *Current Biography* (New York: H. W. Wilson, 1940—), which cumulates annually into the *Current Biography Yearbook*. Each year includes details of around 150 currently prominent figures; biographies are indexed annually, and there is a *Cumulated Index, 1940–1970* (1973).

The most recent attempt at a current biographical compendium for Latin America was:

Who's Who in Latin America: A Biographical Dictionary of Notable Living Men and Women of Latin America. 3rd ed. Edited by Ronald Hilton. 7 vols. Stanford, CA: Stanford University Press, 1946–1951; republished in 2 vols., Detroit, MI: Blaine Ethridge, 1971. Good for its period, but wearisome to consult, as each country has its own alphabetical sequence.

A large number of the individual countries of the region publish their own 'who's whos' (*Quién es quién, Quem é quem*), but the resultant works are of varying comprehensiveness and regularity. Perhaps the best is the more-or-less triennial:

Diccionario biográfico de Chile. Santiago: Empresa Periodística Chilena, 1936—. The current edition is the 18th (1984–1986).

Other reasonably up-to-date examples are:

Quién es quién en Colombia. Bogotá: Themis, 1978.

Who's Who in Costa Rica, 1979–1980. San José: Lubeck, 1979.

Diccionario biográfico de México. 3 vols. Monterrey: Revesa, 1968–1974. Each volume has its own A–Z sequence.

Quién es quién en el Paraguay. 8th ed. Buenos Aires: Monte Domecq, 1980.

Quién es quién en el Uruguay. Montevideo: Central de Publicaciones, 1980.

and references to many more may be found in:

Farrell, Mary A. *Who's Whos: An International Guide to Sources of Current Biographical Information.* New York: New York Metropolitan Reference and Research Library Agency, 1979.

A warning should perhaps be given concerning the apparently comprehensive *Quién es quién en la América del Sur* (Buenos Aires: Publicaciones Referenciales Latinoamericanas, 1982); despite its optimistic title, the first edition (1982–1983) covers only the Argentine Republic, and it is doubtful if any further parts or editions have appeared.

Retrospective Biography

The principal international bibliography of retrospective biography
is:

SLOCUM, Robert B. *Biographical Dictionaries and Related Works*.
2nd ed. 2 vols. Detroit, MI: Gale Research, 1986.

For Latin America, a specialised work still frequently useful despite
its age, is:

TORO, Josefina del. *A Bibliography of the Collective Biography of
Spanish America*. Rio Piedras, PR: Universidad de Puerto Rico,
1938; reprinted, New York: Gordon Press, 1976.

But potentially the major biographical source for Latin America is a
microfiche collection, not yet complete:

Archivo biográfico de España, Portugal e Iberoamérica (ABEPI).
Edited by Victor Herrero Mediavilla and L. Rosa Aguado
Nayle. Munich: K. G. Saur, 1986—. Around 1500 fiches. A
collection of pre-twentieth century biographical descriptions
cumulated into one alphabetical sequence. Indexed by the
hard-copy *Índice biográfico de España, Portugal e Iberoamérica* (due
in 1989), an important reference work in itself, which will
hopefully be bought by many libraries not prepared to acquire
the whole microfiche set.

In hard copy, another indispensable finding-aid for Latin American
biography is still in course of publication:

MUNDO LO, Sara de. *Index to Spanish American Collective Biography*. 4 vols. Boston, MA: G. K. Hall, 1981–1985. A
well-annotated bibliography of biographical sources existing in
North American libraries, with locations; works containing
less than around 300 biographies are analysed, and the
'biographees' are indexed. The volumes cover: 1. The Andean
Countries; 2. Mexico; 3. Central America and the Caribbean;
and 4. The River Plate Countries. Further volumes are
promised, to cover general Spanish American sources and
(despite the work's overall title) Brazil.

A general retrospective listing of Latin American biography, quite
old now but still occasionally useful, can be found in:

AZPURÚA, Ramón. *Biografías de hombres notables de Hispanoamérica*. 4 vols. Caracas: Imprenta Nacional, 1877. This is

perhaps best consulted in the facsimile edition with corrections, indexes and portraits, prepared by a team of historians led by Blas Bruni Celli (Caracas: Mario González, 1982).

Other major works of collective biography are listed below by country.

Argentina

YABEN, Jacinto R. *Biografías argentinas y sudamericanas.* 5 vols. Buenos Aires: Metropolis, 1938–1940. Also includes notable historical figures from other parts of the region.

CUTOLO, Vicente Osvaldo. *Nuevo diccionario biográfico argentino, 1750–1930.* 7 vols. Buenos Aires: Elche, 1968–1985.

Brazil

The *Diccionario bibliographico* of SACRAMENTO BLAKE (see PERSONAL BIBLIOGRAPHIES, p. 143) is useful for pre-twentieth century biography. This and many other retrospective dictionaries for Brazil are listed in, and have a combined index by surname provided for them by:

GALANTE DE SOUSA, Jose. *Indice de biobibliografia brasileira.* Rio de Janeiro: Instituto Nacional do Livro, 1963.

Specialists in the modern history of Brazil should not overlook the *Dicionário histórico-biográfico brasileiro, 1930–1983,* detailed in the chapter on ENCYCLOPAEDIAS (p. 159).

Chile

FIGUEROA, Virgilio. *Diccionario histórico biográfico (y bibliográfico) de Chile, 1800–1931.* 5 vols. Santiago: Balcells, 1925–1931; reprinted in facsimile, Nendeln, Liechtenstein: Kraus Reprint, 1974.

The earlier period is covered by:

MEDINA, José Toribio. *Diccionario biográfico colonial de Chile.* Santiago: Elzeviriana, 1906. Corrections are listed in:

PRIETO DEL RIO, Luis Francisco. *Muestras de errores y defectos del 'Diccionario biográfico colonial de Chile' de José Toribio Medina.* Santiago: Imprensa Chile, 1907.

Colombia

OSPINA, Joaquin. *Diccionario biográfico y bibliográfico de Colombia.*
3 vols. Bogotá: Cronos, Aguila, 1927–1939.

Cuba

PERAZA SARAUSA, Fermín. *Diccionario biográfico cubano.* 14 vols.
Havana: Anuario Bibliográfico Cubano, 1951–1968. The
original scheme of this publication was adversely affected by
the Cuban revolution. Volumes 1–7 contain the first alphabetical sequence; volumes 8–11 the second, abandoned after the
letter I. Volumes 12–14 (Published in Gainesville, Florida)
present separate alphabetical sequences with indexes to the full
series.

Ecuador

DESTRUGE, Camilo. *Album biográfico ecuatoriano.* 2nd ed. 2 vols.
Guayaquil: Banco Central del Ecuador, 1984.

A new work combining current and retrospective biography is in
course of publication:

PÉREZ PIMENTEL, Rodolfo. *Diccionario biográfico del Ecuador.*
Guayaquil: Universidad de Guayaquil, 1987—. Five volumes
have appeared so far, each with its own alphabetical sequence.

Mexico

PERAL, Miguel Angel. *Diccionario biográfico mexicano.* 2 vols.
with *Apéndice.* Mexico City: Editorial P.A.C., 1944.

Peru

MENDIBURU, Manuel de. *Diccionario histórico-biográfico del Perú.*
2nd ed. 11 vols. Lima: Gil, 1931–1935. Supplemented by:

SAN CRISTOVAL, Evaristo. *Apéndice al Diccionario histórico-
biográfico del Perú.* 4 vols. Lima: Gil, 1935–1938.

The two works above are to be combined in a new third edition
(Lima: Editorial Arica, 1976—), but only one volume has appeared
to date, covering 'Abad-Amat'.

Uruguay

FERNÁNDEZ SALDAÑA, José Mario. *Diccionario uruguayo de biografías 1810–1940*. Montevideo: Amerindia, 1945.

Venezuela

Venezolanos eminentes. 1st series. Caracas: Fundación Eugenio Mendoza, 1983. Contains only twenty biographies; it is to be hoped that the Fundación will produce further series.

There are innumerable reference works covering Latin American notables by profession, by period or by region; these can be traced from the bibliographies mentioned above or in the chapters on GENERAL BIBLIOGRAPHIES (p. 87) and PERSONAL BIBLIOGRAPHIES (p. 140). Sources of information on academics and others involved in study and research on Latin America are listed in the section HANDBOOKS, GUIDES AND DIRECTORIES (pp. 164–165).

RAM

Book Reviews

This article discusses sources of evaluative and critical reviews of recent publications on and from Latin America. The much more numerous sources of simple listings of new works (many of which have brief annotations) are discussed above in the chapters on BIBLIOGRAPHIES (pp. 85–152).

Categorisation

Reviews (*reseñas*, *resenhas*) come in four broad types:

Current reviews for the general reader, written by professional journalists. They tend to be brief, but can run to some length if the book is considered particularly newsworthy. They appear in newspapers, particularly the Sunday 'literary' or 'cultural' supplements, and in general magazines—in Latin America as in the developed world. Since such media are concerned with the book as news, publication is prompt, usually within a week or so of the book's publication date. South American examples of this genre are the Sunday edition of *O Estado de São Paulo* and the news magazine *Visión*.

Articles in commercial book reviewing journals, often written by invited contributors. They are usually of moderate length and fairly current. The intended readership will vary with the specialisation (if any) of the journal, but will usually be more bookish or academic than that of the 'current review'. The outstanding UK example is the weekly *Times Literary Supplement*. Besides its regular reviewing (by no means restricted to English language works), this has a special Latin American issue once a year, reviewing books from and about the region. The US equivalent is the *New York Times Book Review*. Brazilian examples include the *DO (Leitura)* of São Paulo and the *Suplemento Literário* of Minas Gerais, both of which happen to be the separately published supplements to the official gazettes of their respective states, and (also from São Paulo) the monthly *Leia*.

Scholarly reviews written by academics and other specialists, which frequently do not appear until months, sometimes years, after the book's publication. Almost every academic, scientific or technical journal will include reviews of significant books in its field. The major US examples are the *Hispanic American Historical Review* (Duke University), and the *Inter-American Review of Bibliography/Revista Interamericana de Bibliografía* (Organization of American States). On the literary side, important titles are *Review* (Center for Inter-American Relations) and *World Literature Today* (University of Oklahoma). For the British Latin Americanist, major journals are the *Bulletin of Latin American Research* (Society for Latin American Studies), and *Journal of Latin American Studies* (Cambridge University).

Review articles, or scholarly reviews of several more-or-less new works on the same or closely related subjects, which often amount to a bibliographic essay on recent literature on the topic. These may appear in either learned or book-reviewing journals: one journal making a feature of review articles is the *Latin American Research Review* (University of New Mexico).

Location

Reviews appearing in a particular journal or newspaper can of course be traced from its index (if one exists). Since 1973 the (London) *Times Literary Supplement* has been included in the coverage of the official index to *The Times*. Similarly, reviews of the works by a particular author may be traced from a bibliography of him, if it is detailed enough. For more general searching, there are two types of guides: those that provide an abstract or summary of the review, and those that merely index it.

Review Abstracts

Covering all of Latin America and the Caribbean, but limited to works in English and Spanish, is:

> MATOS, Antonio. *Guía de las reseñas de libros de y sobre Hispanoamérica/A Guide to Reviews of Books From and About Hispanic America*. Detroit, MI: Blaine Ethridge, 1976–1985. Annual volumes, containing annotated citations, cover materials published from 1972 to 1982. The 1983 issue (2 vols.) was published in 1986 by Garland Publishing, New York. Two

earlier, unannotated volumes published in Rio Piedras (Puerto Rico) in 1965 and 1973, cover the periods 1960–1964 and 1965 respectively.

Unfortunately, nothing has been published for the years 1966–1971. The editor is himself hoping to produce limited editions of the 1984 and 1985 issues at the Catholic University of Puerto Rico, to appear in 1989.

Abstracts of reviews of works in English, including works translated into English, may be found in the *Book Review Digest* (New York: H. W. Wilson, 1905—), which appears monthly with quarterly cumulations and annual volumes. Only the more widely reviewed titles are included. Reviews of translations (of Latin American novels, for example) will of course appear in the year of publication of the translation, which may be a decade or more after the original.

Indexes to Reviews

The *Hispanic American Periodicals Index* (HAPI) indexes book reviews, but only those that appear in the periodicals it regularly analyses. General review indexes that may be useful include:

> *Internationale Bibliographie der Rezensionen wissenschaftliche Literatur.* Osnabrück: Dietrich, 1971—. Semi-annual; covers reviews from about 1968.

> *Index to Book Reviews in the Humanities.* Detroit, MI: Philip Thomson, 1960—. Annual.

> *Book Review Index.* Detroit, MI: Gale, 1965—. Bimonthly.

For older reviews, there are:

> *Combined Retrospective Index to Book Reviews in Humanities Journals, 1802–1974.* 10 vols. Woodbridge, CT: Research Publications, 1982–1984. This is complemented by:

> *Combined Retrospective Index to Book Reviews in Scholarly Journals, 1886–1974.* 15 vols. Arlington, VA: Carrollton Press, 1979–1982.

LH

Censuses

Origins

Spanish American official censuses go back as far as 1579; few early censuses were published, however, and those that still survive in manuscript form are not always to be found in the appropriate national archives. The 1579–1582 Mexican census, for example, has been acquired by the University of Texas, while the 1700 census of Lima is in the Biblioteca Nacional in Madrid; and the first reliable British colonial census—that of Port of Spain in 1835—is held by the Foreign and Commonwealth Office Library in London. A project to collect and collate all surviving materials from the colonial Latin American censuses was undertaken jointly by the universities of Oxford and Syracuse, under the direction of David Browning; unfortunately the results are not yet commercially available.

The first printed censuses from Latin America are those of Chile (1777), Honduras (1791) and Mexico (1793). There is a printed census for El Salvador dating from 1807, and one covering Greater Colombia (including data on Ecuador and Panama) from 1825. Most other countries' series also start in the nineteenth century—Argentina in 1869 and Brazil in 1872, for example. Some countries, however, did not conduct censuses until the twentieth century: the Dominican Republic had its first census in 1920, Haiti and Surinam had theirs as late as 1950.

It is worth remembering that a number of individual colonies, provinces and towns conducted their own local censuses before national censuses were undertaken, and many of these are available in printed form.

Frequency

Most countries take their national census decennially, usually in the last year (i.e. the 'zero' year) of each decade, although until World War II most British colonial administrations held them in the first year (year '1')—the same year as the UK domestic census. Wars, revolutions and other causes have interrupted the sequence from time to time: thus Brazil had no census of 1910 or 1930; Peru took none between 1876 and 1940; a cholera epidemic frustrated Jamaica's 1851 census; and economic stringency prevented several British colonies from holding their 1931 census.

The United Nations attempted, not wholly successfully, to get all countries in the region to hold a census in 1960. This persuaded several countries to join those with 'zero' year censuses.

Non-demographic censuses—i.e., censuses of agriculture, manufacturing, service trades and the like—are sometimes held as part of the main decennial census and sometimes completely separately. Practice varies from country to country, as does the frequency.

Publication

The publication of census results has become in recent years a major undertaking. Usually a provisional or summary volume appears first, between one and five years after the census was actually taken; this is followed in due course by the definitive tabulations, with one volume for the country as a whole, and others for detailed provincial or departmental figures. An example is the Brazilian census of 1970, which required more than 80 large volumes to report all the data collected.

Bibliography

The most comprehensive listing of demographic censuses is:

> *International Population Census Bibliography.* Census Bibliography no. 1: Latin America and the Caribbean. Austin, TX: Bureau of Business Research, 1965. With *Supplement* (1968). Produced by the Population Research Center at the University of Texas.

This has subsequently been supplemented and updated by:

> GOYER, Doreen S. *International Population Census Bibliography: Revision and Update, 1945–1977.* New York: Academic Press, 1980.

The same author has also produced a useful guide to demographic censuses of the Americas:

> GOYER, Doreen S. and Eliane DOMSCHKE. *The Handbook of National Population Censuses.* [Volume 1:] Latin America and

the Caribbean, North America and Oceania. Westport, CT: Greenwood Press, 1983.

Economic as well as population censuses are included in:

HARVEY, Joan M. *Statistics America: Sources for Social, Economic and Market Research; North, Central and South America.* 2nd ed. Beckenham, Kent: CBD Research, 1980.

The most recent work on the subject is published under the auspices of the SCONUL Advisory Committee on Latin American Materials. It includes both demographic and economic censuses, together with their locations in British libraries:

TRAVIS, Carole. *Guide to Latin American and West Indian Census Materials: a Bibliography and Union List.* London: British Library and the Institute of Latin American Studies, 1989. Two provisional sections of this work have been published separately:

WADE, Ann E. *Venezuela.* London: Institute of Latin American Studies, 1981.

TRAVIS, Carole. *Chile.* London: Institute of Latin American Studies, 1982.

The following source includes economic censuses, but lists only materials held by libraries in Paris:

Bibliographie des recensements démographiques et économiques des pays d'Amérique Latine existants à Paris. Paris: Centre de Documentation, Institut des Hautes Etudes de l'Amérique Latine, 1967.

Censuses of industry and services are also listed in the 'Americas' section of:

Bibliography of Industrial and Distributive Trade Statistics. 4th ed. New York: United Nations, Statistical Office, 1975.

A useful bibliographical periodical in the field of demography is:

Population Index. Princeton, NJ: Princeton University, Office of Population Research, 1969—. Bimonthly.

Earlier volumes of this have been collected as:

Population Index Bibliography: Cumulated, 1969–1981. 4 vols. Boston, MA: G.K. Hall, 1984.

It is worth remembering that many censuses can be traced through the lists and catalogues of the various national statistical offices. Some of these have produced their own lists of censuses. For example, Peru:

Bibliografía sobre censos y estadísticas realizados en el Perú. Lima: Ministerio de Trabajo, Biblioteca General, 1974.

For population censuses of the Commonwealth, there is:

KUCZYNSKI, Robert R. *Demographic Survey of the British Colonial Empire.* Volume 3: West Indian and American Territories. London: Oxford University Press, 1953.

Population data for Mexico is covered in essay form by:

COOK, Sherburne F. and Woodrow Wilson BORAH. 'Materials for the Demographic History of Mexico, 1500-1960.' In their *Essays in Population History, Mexico and the Caribbean*, vol. 1. Berkeley, CA: University of California Press, 1971.

Two important contributions to the methodology of census-taking have appeared in Argentina:

TORRADO, Susana. *Los censos de población y vivienda en la década de 1980 en America Latina.* CLACSO Investigación e información sociodemográficas, 2. Buenos Aires: Consejo Latinoamericano de Ciencias Sociales, 1981.

Los censos de población del 80: taller de análisis y evaluación. Estudios INDEC, 2. Buenos Aires: Instituto Nacional de Estadística y Censos, 1985.

Locating Censuses in Your Library

Census material is entered in many library catalogues under the name of the appropriate government department, usually as a subheading under the name of the country or other political unit. Unfortunately, the hierarchy of government departments, to say nothing of their frequent changes of name, can present complications. The Brazilian census of 1940, for example, was issued by the Comissão Censitário Nacional of the Serviço Nacional de Recenseamento of the Conselho Nacional de Estatística, itself a branch of the Instituto Brasileiro de Geografia e Estatística, and may have been recorded in different library catalogues under any one, or any combination, of these headings. Alterations in the administrative structure of a government entail frequent changes of name, which are then faithfully recorded in library catalogues, hopefully with some cross-referencing between them.

In the West Indies there is an additional complication, in that some censuses were undertaken by individual territories while others were cooperative projects. The 1946 West Indian census was published in Kingston by the Jamaican Central Bureau of Statistics; the 1960 census was divided into the *West Indian Population Census*, covering the westerly and northern territories, issued in Jamaica, and the *Eastern Caribbean Population Census*, covering Guiana, Trinidad and Tobago, Barbados and the Windward Islands, published in Trinidad; and the 1970 census appeared as the *Commonwealth Caribbean Census*, published under the auspices of the Census Research Programme of the University of the West Indies.

Some libraries simplify matters by entering censuses under 'Name of country—Census—Date' (for example, 'Mexico—Census—1960'), but this tends to apply only to population, rather than economic, censuses. The advent of the new set of *Anglo-American Cataloguing Rules* (AACR2) in 1978 brought a significant change of practice, in that most government publications, including censuses, are now entered by title rather than by issuing body. Whether this improves matters or complicates them still further is a matter of opinion.

Because of these difficulties, it is generally quicker and easier to use a library's subject catalogue rather than the author catalogue. If the library uses Library of Congress subject headings, all population censuses will be entered under 'Name of country—Census—Date', as cited in the previous paragraph. Economic censuses will be found under the relevant subject heading with the subhead 'Statistics': for example, 'Agriculture—Uruguay—Statistics', or 'Argentina—Industries—Statistics'. Library staff will be able to advise which is the correct heading to look under.

Censuses in Other Libraries

It is seldom practicable to obtain complete censuses through inter-library loan. The very bulk of the material, together with many libraries' quite justifiable reluctance to loan such basic reference sources, mean that it is usually easier and cheaper for the researcher to visit another library that possesses the required item than to try to have it sent for. Nor can libraries spare the staff time to undertake the extraction of data for researchers unable to make a personal visit.

Inter-governmental agreements to exchange government publications mean that many foreign censuses are available in the Official Publications Library of the British Library (Humanities and Social Sciences), or the equivalent section of the Library of Congress. Unfortunately, exchange schemes do not function perfectly, and there are many gaps in the British Library's holdings. Also, at least until the British Library moves to its new premises on the Euston Road (currently predicted for the late 1990s), much of the material has to be fetched from the Woolwich Depository, involving at least a day's delay. A significant proportion of the documents remain uncatalogued, and readers should check with Official Publications Library staff to determine whether or not a particular item is in stock.

Foreign censuses are also collected systematically by a number of other libraries in the UK, notably the British Library of Political and Economic Science (at the London School of Economics), the Foreign and Commonwealth Office Library, the Institute of Development Studies at the University of Sussex, and the Office of Population, Census and Surveys. Full details of library holdings in Britain of Latin American and Caribbean censuses can be found in the union list by Carole TRAVIS, cited above.

In the US, in addition to the Library of Congress, the Population Research Center of the University of Texas at Austin has major holdings of demographic census material; censuses held in other libraries may be traced through databases such as OCLC and RLIN.

Alternative Sources of Census Information

Although published censuses are necessarily selective in the data included, they still contain more detail than is necessary for many purposes. When a particular census is not available, or when not all the published data is required, a good substitute is often provided by *Anuarios estadísticos* and similar publications of the various countries. More information on these can be found in the chapter on STATISTICS (p. 299).

JRP

Law and Legislation

Conducting Research

Law and legislation constitute a separate, distinct body of literature with its own indices, bibliographies and reference works (see below), as well as library collections which are generally administered apart from other fields in the social sciences. For Latin America, additional complexities arise, given the different countries' legal systems. Most countries use codified civil law, which reduces the entire corpus of laws into one authoritative text. Most codification is based on the Napoleonic Code; exceptions are the laws of Cuba, Puerto Rico, Panama and Honduras. The Caribbean islands with British and Dutch colonial legacies tend, of course, to reflect the legal systems operating in the homeland. In undertaking an extensive research project which requires publications from different countries and time periods, it is generally necessary to utilise research strategies that accommodate the differences in legal systems and their literature. Wherever possible, the introductions to the major bibliographies and indices should be read carefully, noting how the literature is organised, and how it is issued. Useful information on the background to Latin American law can be found in:

CLAGETT, Helen L. *The Administration of Justice in Latin America.* New York: Oceana, 1952.

DE VRIES, Henry P. and José RODRÍGUEZ NOVAS. *The Law of the Americas: An Introduction to the Legal Systems of the Latin American Republics.* Dobbs Ferry, NY: Oceana, 1965.

MEDINA, Rubens and Cecilia MEDINA-QUIROGA. *Nomenclature and Hierarchy: Basic Latin American Legal Sources.* Washington, DC: Library of Congress, 1979. Contains a country-by-country definition of terms.

A basic introductory text is:

GOLBERT, Albert S. and Yenny N. GINGOLD. *Latin American Law and Institutions.* New York: Praeger, 1962. Emphasises the major changes in selected areas such as trade regulation and labour, contract, corporation and constitutional law.

Spanish and Portuguese legal terminology are well explained in dictionaries published in Mexico and Brazil respectively:

PINA, Rafael de. *Diccionario de derecho.* 14th ed. Mexico City: Porrúa, 1986.

MAGALHÃES, Humberto Piragibe. *Dicionário juridico.* 4th ed. 2 vols. Rio de Janeiro: Trabalhistas, 1984.

Texts of Legal Materials

The actual texts of decrees, laws, legislation, treaties and the like appear in a variety of publications, including official gazettes, serials, and individual volumes of a country's legal code. Official gazettes (*Gaceta Oficial, Boletín Oficial* or similar) are published by virtually all governments, and comprise a vital, current source of information on laws and legislation; unfortunately, they suffer the same drawbacks as newspapers, being both bulky and fragile, and are thus held by comparatively few libraries. Full details concerning the contents of these works, together with some US holdings, can be found in the bibliographies of government serial publications by Winifred GREGORY and Rosa Q. MESA described in the OFFICIAL PUBLIC-ATIONS chapter of this volume (p. 203).

On a selective basis, some legal texts are also available through a diverse group of publications prepared by the Organization of American States. These include treaties, conventions, legislation, constitutions and laws governing particular areas of activity. Consult the OAS *Catalog of Publications*, issued annually in Washington, DC. Some publishers in the US provide translations of foreign legal materials: particularly useful is the annual *Martindale-Hubbell Law Directory* (New York, 1937—), with its 'Law Digests, Uniform Acts, A.B.A. Section, Digests of Laws of Foreign Countries'. Drawn from the current civil and other codes, as well as decrees, the laws for each country appear by topic. For the complete text, however, one must still refer to the full code or decree, as separately published.

Citation

Several different rules exist for the citation format of legal materials in card catalogues and online systems. Since the early 1980s, most libraries have adopted the *Anglo-American Cataloguing Rules* (AACR2), which unfortunately have some important differences from earlier rules—rules still in force in many catalogues. Previously laws, contracts and codes simply appeared under the name of the country concerned followed by 'Laws, statutes, etc.' Now, however, the format of the information is by country, followed directly by the *title* of the work (law, code, statute or whatever): thus 'Peru. Ley de sociedades mercantiles', or 'Argentina. Ley no. 20.744'. In the case of collections of laws, the country-name is followed by a *uniform title* such as 'Código civil', or (if the laws cover more than one code) even 'Laws, etc.' The title of the specific work then follows. Decrees may also have a uniform title, in the form of the official short or citation title, as 'Brazil. Lei da correção salarial', followed by the work's own title or decree number. Treaties, which previously were all to be found under the country followed by the form heading 'Treaties, etc.', now add to the heading the name of the other party and the date; thus 'Spain. Treaties, etc. Great Britain, 1713'. For presidential messages, look under the country, 'President', date and the president's name—as, for instance, 'Bolivia. President (1826–1828 : Sucre)'. Under earlier rules the format is not dissimilar, though some catalogues put such messages directly under the name of the president—'Sucre, Antonio José de, 1795–1830, Pres. Bolivia'. For congressional and parliamentary publications, no significant differences exist: the rule is still (1) country, (2) congress, (3) branch, (4) agency subdivision: 'Mexico. Congreso. Cámara de Senadores. Comisión Primera de Minas'.

Other jurisdictions, such as states (provinces, departments) and cities, work the same way. When a state and a city share the same name, the city will be distinguished by the addition, in parentheses, of just the country name; the state or province will be identified as such. Thus 'São Paulo (Brazil)' is the city; the state will be 'São Paulo (Brazil : State)'. Either heading will then be followed by subheadings for the appropriate agency and its subdivisions.

It will often be necessary to combine or augment an author search with a subject approach. Hints on this process are given in the chapter on LIBRARY CATALOGUES (pp. 37–39), but it must be emphasised again that the first step is to consult the appropriate thesaurus of terms used by your library. Using the *Library of Congress Subject Headings* (the most widespread of these), the basic legal subject heading is 'Law', which may be subdivided by process ('Codification', 'Interpretation and construction' and so forth), and/or by country or region. There are also main headings for specific legal branches ('Commercial law', 'Criminal law', 'Industrial laws and legislation'), which may be subdivided by country. In addition, the subdivision 'Law and legislation', further subdivided by country, may be added to many topical headings to give such composite headings as 'Divorce—Law and legislation—Argentina' or 'Political parties—Law and legislation—Nicaragua'. The help and advice of the specialist staff in your law library will be found invaluable here.

Bibliographies

The following general and specialised bibliographies will be of use:

Union List of Basic Latin American Legal Materials. Edited by Kate Wallach. South Hackensack, NJ: F. B. Rothman, 1971. Published by the Committee on Foreign and International Law of the American Association of Law Libraries, and updated by the following:

Basic Latin American Legal Materials, 1970–1975. Edited by Juan F. Aguilar and Armando E. González. South Hackensack, NJ: F. B. Rothman, 1977.

NAVARRO, Ricardo J. 'A Bibliography of Latin American Law: Primary and Secondary Sources in English.' *Texas International Law Journal* 19 (1984), pp. 319–334.

PATCHETT, Keith and Valerie JENKINS. *A Bibliographic Guide to Law in the Commonwealth Caribbean.* Mona, Jamaica: Institute of Social and Economic Research, University of the West Indies, 1973. Cites monographs, government documents and articles. An update is provided by the second part of:

NEWTON, Velma. *Commonwealth Caribbean Legal Literature: A Bibliography of All Primary Sources to Date and Secondary Sources for 1971–1985.* Cave Hill, Barbados: Faculty of Law Library, University of the West Indies, 1987. Provides access to legislation, constitutions and law reports.

RANK, Richard. *The Criminal Justice Systems of the Latin American Nations: A Bibliography of the Primary and Secondary Literature.* South Hackensack, NJ: F. B. Rothman, 1974. A country approach to the codes, statutes, law reports and cases, treatises and monographs devoted to all aspects of the judicial system, including criminal law, procedure, criminology, military criminal law and provincial coverage. A useful general section lists bibliographies, periodicals, encyclopaedias and dictionaries.

SNYDER, Frederick E. *Latin American Society and Legal Culture: A Bibliography.* Westport, CT: Greenwood Press, 1985. Contains bibliographies and indexes in law and political science, concentrating on English language material; cites works that bear on the economic, political and social evolution of Latin America.

VILLALÓN GALDAMÉS, Alberto. *Bibliografía jurídica de América Latina, 1810–1965.* Santiago: Editorial Jurídica de Chile, 1984—. In progress: volume 1 has a general introduction and materials on Argentina and Bolivia; volume 2 covers Brazil, Colombia, Costa Rica and Cuba. The first volume was originally published in 1969.

Index to Latin American Legislation, 1950–1960. 2 vols. Boston, MA: G. K. Hall, 1961. Compiled by the Hispanic Law Division of the Library of Congress, this index is alphabetically arranged by country: volume 1 covers Argentina to Cuba, and volume 2 the Dominican Republic to Venezuela. Three supplements have also appeared:

1961–1965. 2 vols. Boston, MA: G. K. Hall, 1970.
1966–1970. 2 vols. Boston, MA: G. K. Hall, 1973.
1971–1975. 2 vols. Boston, MA: G. K. Hall, 1978.

See also the section 'Specialized Research Collections: Latin American Legal Resources' in *Collection Development: Cooperation at the Local and National Levels: Papers* of SALALM XXIX, 1984. Madison, WI: SALALM, 1987, pp. 33–70. Contains excellent bibliographical articles by Rubens MEDINA, Selma CERVETTI DE RODRÍGUEZ, Ellen G. SCHAFFER and Igor I. KAVASS.

PTJ

Patents and Trade Marks

The patent, like copyright, is a form of intellectual property, but unlike copyright a patent protects the essential features of an invention rather than the form of expression of ideas. Patents are legal documents which confer a monopoly for the manufacture and sale of a new product or use of a new process; but they are, more fundamentally, a means of disseminating information: technological, commercial and economic. To enable patent protection to be obtained, the applicant has to produce a formal description of the invention, and this, the specification, is subsequently published. Trade marks are also a form of intellectual property which confer a monopoly, in this case enabling the goods and services of one manufacturer to be distinguished from another.

Patents as a Source of Information

An essential preliminary to the tackling of a new scientific or technical problem is to find out what other workers have already done in the same field. This information can be used to discover ways in which a problem has been approached in the past, and also to check whether a possible solution has already been developed. Patent specifications can be of greatest use here, as they frequently disclose technical information earlier than any other literature on the product. The use of patents and trade marks as legal means of protecting 'industrial property' varies from jurisdiction to jurisdiction, and, though there is some international harmonisation, procedures for the application and length of the patent term vary from country to country. Procedures in individual countries can be ascertained from the following works, all of which are in looseleaf format and are updated by supplements:

Manual for the Handling of Applications for Patents, Design and Trade Marks Throughout the World. Amsterdam: Manual of Industrial Property.

Trade Marks Throughout the World. 3rd ed. New York: Boardman, 1979.

Patents Throughout the World. 2nd ed. New York: Boardman, 1978.

GREENE, Anne Marie. *Designs and Utility Models Throughout the World.* New York: Boardman, 1983.

There is also a volume that covers all of Hispanic America:

Patents, Trade Marks and Designs in Central and South America. Buenos Aires: Obligado, 1984.

Patent and trade mark literature from over 40 countries (including Argentina, Brazil and Mexico) is discussed in:

RIMMER, B. M. *Guide to Official Industrial Property Publications.* London: British Library, 1985. Looseleaf, with updates.

The official patent and trade mark gazettes of 80 countries are listed, with details of their contents, in:

BARTON, H. M. *Industrial Property Literature: A Directory of Journals.* London: British Library, 1981.

Availability of Patent Literature

Major collections of patent literature are listed in:

World Directory of Sources of Patent Information. Geneva: World Intellectual Property Organization, 1985.

Inpadoc, the International Patent Documentation Center in Vienna, is an international coordinating body set up by agreement between national patent offices. It now receives and makes available, online and on microfiche, bibliographic information on the patents of 55 patenting authorities, including—from Latin America—Brazil, Argentina, Mexico and Cuba.

In the UK the only comprehensive collection of Latin American patent literature is held by the British Library's Science Reference and Information Service (SRIS), in the Chancery House Annex adjacent to the main reading room at 25 Southampton Buildings, Chancery Lane, London WC2A 1AW. Though SRIS's current intake from Latin America is restricted to the official journals of Mexico and the specifications of patent and utility model applications and official journals from Brazil, the collection contains extensive older material, including official journals, from many other Latin American countries. These materials are freely available without undue formality, and most of the holdings are on open access (though some older material is held at a remote store). Copies of patent specifications may be obtained 'while-you-wait', or by post or fax. A further collection of official journals, some of which include patent or trade mark information, is held in the Official Publications Library of the British Library in Great Russell Street.

The *World Directory*, cited above, lists no more extensive general collection of Latin American materials than SRIS, although some collections may be stronger on individual countries. The *Directory* does, however, omit the Registro de Propiedad Industrial (the Spanish patent office) in Madrid, which currently has extensive holdings of Spanish American patent materials, mostly dating from 1982–1983. See:

RIMMER, B. M. *Patent Information and Documentation in Western Europe: An Inventory of Sources Available to the Public.* 3rd ed. Munich: K. G. Saur for the Commission of the European Communities, 1988.

The following brief account of patent literature from Latin America is heavily based on the holdings of the SRIS.

Brazil

In sharp contrast to its neighbours, Brazil is of world importance in patent and trade mark literature. About 7,000 applications for patents, 2,200 applications for utility models ('petty patents') and 42,000 applications for trade and service marks were made in 1984—though more recently there has been a decline in these numbers. Brazilian patent, utility model, industrial model and industrial design specifications are published twice: first as the application, eighteen months after the priority (first application) date, and again after the patent is granted. Since 1972 the official patent journal has been the *Revista da Propiedade Industrial*, a continuation of section 3 of the *Diário Oficial*, which also includes trade marks. Regrettably, no cumulative indexes have so far been published.

The patents of Brazil are covered by online and hard-copy secondary abstracting services: *World Patent Index*, *World Patents Abstracts* and other services of Derwent Publications, Ltd., and in *Chemical Abstracts*. Brazil has also been covered since 1973 by the indexing service of Inpadoc, discussed at the beginning of this chapter,

Brazil is currently the only Latin American country to be a signatory to the Patent Cooperation Treaty, which provides for the filing and publication of international applications for patents in English, French, German, Russian or Japanese.

The SRIS holdings of Brazilian patent and trade mark information go back (under a variety of titles) to 1890. Full specifications of patents and utility models (petty patents) have been received since they began publication in 1971—although only the unexamined application, or 'pedido de privilégio', is received. SRIS also has a complete set of the *Revista da Propiedade Industrial*.

Other Latin American Countries

Argentina receives several thousand applications for patents each year but the full specifications are not published. The monthly *Patentes de Invención*, however, gives illustrated abstracts of all granted patents, with effect from number 18753. In addition, Argentine patents have been covered by Inpadoc since 1973. The trade mark journal *Marcas y Designaciones* has been published since the new trade mark law became effective in 1981. SRIS has an imperfect set of *Patentes de Invención* from 1923 to 1981, and the holdings of earlier Argentine patent publications go back to 1867.

For Colombia the principal source for patent information is the *Gaceta de la Propiedad Industrial*, published under various titles since 1930. It includes sections on patents (with abstracts or claims of applications), trade marks and industrial designs. SRIS has this periodical from 1958 to October 1983.

Since 1929, Mexico has also produced a monthly *Gaceta de la Propiedad Industrial*, with sections on patents, trade marks, slogans and trade names; the first section contains information on patents, inventors' certificates, designs and industrial models, and includes abstracts. SRIS has a complete set of this journal and its predecessors back to 1891. Inpadoc has included information on Mexican patents since 1981.

Venezuela publishes a quarterly *Boletín de la Propiedad Industrial* (1931—), of which SRIS has limited holdings to 1968. Most other Latin American countries publish details of patent applications and grants in their official journal (the title varies from country to country, but tends to be something like *Diario Oficial*, *Gaceta Oficial* or *Boletín Oficial*). More information about these will be found under

LAW AND LEGISLATION (p. 283). SRIS has limited holdings from Peru, Bolivia, Ecuador, Uruguay, Costa Rica, Guatemala, Panama, Cuba and the Dominican Republic.

DCN

Pressure Groups

A typology of pressure groups is suggested by:

> WILLETTS, Peter. *Pressure Groups in the International System: The Transnational Relations of Issue-Oriented Non-Government Organizations*. London: Frances Pinter, 1982.

Although the case studies in this work focus on agencies campaigning on, and working in pursuit of, global issues that are variably applicable to the contemporary Latin American scene, they prompt the approach adopted in this sketch of reference sources. In WILLETTS, the pressure groups are perceived as transnational actors, reflecting the critical, global urgency of the issues in which they are involved. Large numbers of pressure groups, however, operate more frequently at local levels to influence and change public policy or to supplant existing institutions, though increasingly they may associate in more or less formal networks transcending national boundaries.

For this reason, there is some sense in looking first at the global maps of institutions, many of which may be regarded as assuming the role and behaviour of pressure groups as one aspect of their corporate membership. The most extensive guide at the international level is:

> *Yearbook of International Organizations*. 23rd ed. Munich: K. G. Saur for the Union of International Associations, 1987. 3 vols. The historical series of this title can, with patience, be made to elicit the growth pattern of international bodies, subsuming as it does the large number of regional international organisations of Latin America and the Caribbean.

More specifically regional is:

> ROLLAND, Denis. *Amérique Latine: guide des organisations internationales et de leurs publications*. Paris: L'Harmattan/Publications de la Sorbonne, 1983. The 'Conclusion: pléthore et parcellisation' points to the increasing profusion and fragmentation of specialised interest groups the world over.

For national level organisations, the most extensive directory so far seen is:

> *Directorio latinoamericano: socio-económico, político, académico.* 4 vols. Quito: Ediciones de Información Económica Latinoamericana, 1985. 15,000 institutions are categorised country by country, giving names and addresses only; the four volumes cover, respectively, Mexico and Central America; the Caribbean and Brazil; the Andean Group countries; and the Southern Cone countries, including foreign and international organisations. Of the subject sections into which the institutions are grouped, the most relevant in the present context are 1.2 (Political representation), 2.2 (Trade unions and professional organisations) and 2.3 (Other social institutions including religious and women's groups).

More specialised coverage is given in:

> *Directory of Central American Organizations.* Austin, TX: Central America Resource Center, 1987. Lists over 1,000 US interest groups.

Political and Labour Movements

The most familiar category of pressure groups includes political parties and urban and rural labour movements. In the endemically unstable political scene of Latin America, identifying and keeping track of these movements is a complicated procedure. Several reference works are devoted to them or give them particular prominence; those published serially allow for comparisons over time. Two recent examples are:

> *Latin America and the Caribbean Contemporary Record.* New York: Holmes and Meier, 1983—. Annual.

> *South America, Central America and the Caribbean.* London: Europa Publications, 1985—. Biennial.

General reference works include:

> *Political Handbook of the World, 1986.* Binghamton, NJ: CSA Publications, 1986. The latest in a series which has appeared under varying editorial control since 1928.

> *Yearbook on International Communist Affairs.* Stanford, CA: Hoover Institution, 1966—. Annual.

HARPER, F. John. *Trade Unions of the World.* London: Longman, 1987.

KURIAN, George. *The Encyclopedia of the Third World.* 3rd ed. 3 vols. New York: Facts on File, 1987.

Ó MAOLÁIN, Ciarán. *The Radical Right: A World Directory.* London: Longman, 1987. Deals with neo-fascist, ultra-nationalist and racist parties, movements and groups.

DEGENHARDT, Henry W. *Revolutionary and Dissident Movements of the World: An International Guide.* London: Longman, 1987.

DELURY, George S. *The World Encyclopedia of Political Systems and Parties.* Rev. ed. New York: Facts on File, 1987.

A brief but useful comparative review, which includes comment on earlier editions of DEGENHARDT and DELURY, is:

BILES, Robert E. 'Recent Reference Works on Latin American Politics: A Neglected Area.' *Latin American Research Review* 20:3 (1985), pp. 268–272.

In a similar genre, but specific to the Americas, are:

ALEXANDER, Robert J. *Political Parties of the Americas: Canada, Latin America and the West Indies.* 2 vols. Westport, CT: Greenwood Press, 1982.

Ó MAOLÁIN, Ciarán. *Latin American Political Movements.* London: Longman, 1985.

RADU, Michael, and Vladimir TISMANEANU. *Revolutionary Organizations in Latin America.* Boulder, CO: Westview Press, 1987.

Other Pressure Groups

Many of the campaigning organisations in the private sector have a variety of objectives, making exclusive definition by category impossible. What they do have in common is an active involvement in the political process, whether from inside or outside their country of origin. The two most common overarching labels are 'Human Rights' and 'Development'. It would be impracticable here to do more than point to a number of focal organisations in these areas which produce continuing reference documentation and from which further information can be sought as required.

Human Rights

A major resource centre in this area is the Human Rights Internet, which is in the advanced stages of planning a database network. It has produced the principal directory in the field:

> *Human Rights Directory: Latin America, Asia, Africa.* Washington, DC: Human Rights Internet, 1981.

This is effectively supplemented by the bimonthly *Human Rights Internet Reporter* (Cambridge, MA, 1976—), whose reportage and bibliographical references provide a continuing commentary on the work of local organisations and their counterparts both in richer countries and in the international field. The areas monitored by the resource centre comprise the broad range of civil rights and fundamental freedoms, with subheadings for religious-oriented organisations; lawyers' associations and legal assistance groups; freedom of expression—in speech and in the media; political prisoners, the 'disappeared' and torture; workers', peasants' and labour rights; women's rights; children's rights; student and youth organisations; teachers' organisations; indigenous peoples; minorities; racial discrimination; refugees and exiles; housing and shelter; and health.

Amnesty International, based in London, produces reports on the condition of human rights in individual countries as well as the annual *Amnesty International Report* (1961—) which reviews, country by country, the year's progress or regress. An archive collection of Amnesty's publications, including country reports, is available on microfiche from the Inter Documentation Company of Leiden.

The Inter-American Commission on Human Rights, an agency of the Organization of American States, monitors the actions of member governments through a process of recommendations, followed by observers and fact-finding missions. It reports annually to the General Assembly of the OAS, and also on individual countries on an ad hoc basis. The reports can be found in the OAS Official Records (Series OEA/Ser.L/V).

Religious-Oriented Organisations

LADOC, or 'Latin America Documentation', originally a project of the Office of International Justice and Peace of the United States Catholic Conference and now based in Peru, publishes the bimonthly *LADOC* (Lima, 1970—), a bulletin of reportage. It has also started a New Keyhole Series (Lima, 1986—), which also appears six times a year, and focuses on themes of importance for the understanding of the

Church in Latin America, especially in its involvement in public concerns.

An extensive output of publications on church affairs in Central America comes from the Departamento Ecuménico de Investigaciones in San José, Costa Rica, while comparable documentation from outside the hemisphere can be found in the quarterly *Informes de Pro Mundi Vita, América Latina* (Brussels: Pro Mundi Vita, 1976—).

The extensive involvement of North American church organisations in the subcontinent is indicated in Appendix 2, 'Christian Churches with Latin American and Caribbean Offices' in:

> FENTON, Thomas P. and Mary J. HEFRON. *Latin America and the Caribbean: A Directory of Resources.* Maryknoll, NY: Orbis Books, and London: Zed Press, 1986.

Freedom of Expression

The most accessible international reportage can be found in *Index on Censorship* (London: Ormonde for Writers' and Scholars' International, 1972—), published ten times a year. A hard-copy index covering 1972–1985 is in preparation, and all articles are indexed in the PAIS International database. At the regional level there is the *IAPA News* (Miami, FL: Inter-American Press Association) now published twice a month. A more detailed overview of relevant concerns appears in the reports of the Inter-American Press Association's annual General Assembly meetings.

Women's Movements and Health

Of several resource centres, Isis International (with offices in Rome and Santiago, Chile) is particularly influential. It has produced what is probably the best starting point for investigation of the topic:

> *The Latin American Women's Movement: Reflections and Actions.* Rome: Isis International, 1986. Includes lists of twelve study centres for research and action, eight documentation centres and information services, 108 women's centres, groups and services and 56 regular publications, all in and from Latin America.

An important analysis, including a section on women's organisations, is:

> *Investigaciones sobre la mujer e investigación feminista: balance y perspectivas de la Década de la Mujer en América Latina.* 3 vols.

Montevideo: Grupo de Estudios sobre la Condición de la Mujer, 1984.

Periodic situation reports are published in the Organization of American States Official Records series (OEA/Ser.C/VII), as are the Final Acts of the Assembly of Delegates of the Inter-American Commission of Women.

An older directory still of some use is:

Integración de la mujer en el desarrollo de América Latina: directorio, instituciones, actividades, recursos humanos. Santiago: CEPAL/ CLADES, 1979.

More recently, for the Caribbean area, there is:

Guide to Resources in Women's Studies in the Caribbean. St. Augustine: University of the West Indies, 1986. Produced by the inaugural seminar 'Gender in Caribbean Development' of the UWI's Women and Development Studies Programme, Documentation Working Group. There is a list of organisations on pp. 14–18.

Complementary documentation on children comes from the Instituto Interamericano del Niño, and on health from the Pan American Health Organization. Insofar as family planning efforts are documented, the collection in the library of the International Planned Parenthood Federation in London is as comprehensive as any. Emergency and disaster relief at the international level is particularly the concern of the Office of the United Nations Disaster Relief Coordinator and the League of Red Cross and Red Crescent Societies.

Development Agencies

The largest number of these are listed in two works produced by the Technical Assistance Information Clearing House of the American Council of Voluntary Agencies for Foreign Service:

U.S. Non-Profit Organizations in Development Assistance Abroad: TAICH Directory, 1983. 8th ed. New York: TAICH, 1983.

Central America and the Caribbean: Development Assistance Abroad. New York: TAICH, 1983.

Similar listings are published from time to time by counterpart agencies in other rich donor countries. Much of this information is still collected by the Development Centre of the Organisation for Economic Cooperation and Development (OECD), whose own directory remains of use:

> *Directory of Non-Governmental Organisations in OECD Member Countries Active in Development Co-operation.* Paris: OECD, 1981. 2 vols.

The only comparable listing from Latin America would seem to be:

> *Catálogo de instituciones de desarrollo sin fines de lucro en América Latina, 1979.* Santo Domingo: Solidarios, Consejo de Fundaciones Americanas de Desarrollo, 1979. Updating information appears, not very systematically, in the quarterly publication *Solidarios* (Santo Domingo, 1977—).

Peace Movements

The International Peace Research Association in Rio de Janeiro publishes the quarterly *International Peace Research Newsletter* (Rio de Janeiro, 1963—), which is thorough and well-documented. The most current general directory is:

> DAY, Alan J. *Peace Movements of the World: An International Directory.* London: Longman, 1987. Lists over 1,000 peace and anti-nuclear movements.

MR

Statistics

'Reported hard facts from Latin America, and particularly statistics, are late, unreliable and inconsistent.'
>   (*Latin America Newsletters Special Reports* SR-85-06 (1985), p. 1)

'At the outset of the 1980s, there are policymakers who see little use in retaining older data resources, and others who have misplaced faith that data banks can resolve the qualitative problem of statistics. And some even question the very usefulness of statistical series.'
>   (*Statistical Abstract of Latin America* 22 (1983), p. 656)

The Producers

Central governments are the principal gatherers and diffusers of statistical information, but by no means all official data are collected and published by a country's national statistical office. Many other government agencies at national and sub-national levels engage in sectoral and local data collection and publication. Central banks invariably, and many private sector organisations also, collect and disseminate statistical data in their specialised fields. Many inter-governmental and international organisations assemble data from their members, and rework them according to their own systematic classifications and evaluative methodologies.

Increasingly, a significant proportion of the collected data is made available in machine-readable rather than printed form; this is partly because the physical volume of records is so extensive, and partly because statistical returns are nowadays regularly processed for machine storage, manipulation and retrieval.

Two good sources for identifying statistical databases are:

Directory of United Nations Databases and Information Systems, 1985. New York: UN Advisory Committee for the Coordination of Information Systems, 1984. The section on the Economic Commission for Latin America and the Caribbean is especially relevant.

RANDALL, Laura. 'Research Inventory on Holdings of Historical Statistics of Latin America.' *Latin American Research Review,*

13: 2 (1978), pp. 194–221. This updates *Data Banks and Archives for Social Science Research on Latin America* by William G. TYLER (Gainesville, FL: Consortium of Latin American Studies Programs, 1975).

General Sources

The best recent overview is:

'Where to Find What in Latin America.' *Latin America Newsletters Special Reports* SR-85-06 (December 1985), pp. 1–12. Quoted above. This is a twelve-page, briefly annotated country-by-country survey of 280 continuing sources of statistics and economic reportage, emanating from international, national, central, regional, governmental and private organisations and agencies. It presumably encompasses the sources to which the staff of Latin American Newsletters has regular access, but whether they are all accessible also to other researchers is left unclear.

A more detailed listing of statistical sources, effective up to the mid-1970s and giving locations in three major UK libraries, is:

HARVEY, Joan M. *Statistics America: Sources for Social, Economic and Market Research; North, Central, South America.* 2nd ed. Beckenham, Kent: CBD Research, 1980. Most items listed have locations in the Official Publications Library of the British Library in London, The Statistics and Market Intelligence Library in London and the library of the Institute of Development Studies at the University of Sussex.

This work is favourably reviewed in:

HARTNESS-KANE, Ann. 'Social Science Bibliographies on Latin America.' *Latin American Research Review* 20:1 (1985), pp. 232–243. A brief but useful discussion of the bibliographic control of Latin American statistical publications.

The principal compilations of current statistics are:

Anuario estadístico de América Latina/Statistical Yearbook for Latin America. Santiago: CEPAL, 1973—. Annual.

Statistical Abstract of Latin America. Edited by James W. Wilkie. Los Angeles, CA: UCLA Latin American Center, 1955—.

Annual, except for 1958 and 1959. Also publishes irregular
supplements on specific topics.

Latin American socio-economic performance in a global, comparative context is most usefully indicated in the reworked compilations
of the the International Bank for Reconstruction and Development
(IBRD), formerly known as the World Bank:

World Bank Atlas. Washington, DC: World Bank, 1966—. A
short, graphic and thematic annual presentation.

World Tables. 3rd ed. 2 vols. Baltimore, MD: Johns Hopkins
University Press for the World Bank, 1984. The volumes cover
economic and social data respectively.

Guides to Statistical Organisation

There are very few descriptive, let alone methodologically critical,
accounts of the statistical systems of individual countries; nor,
apparently, are there many catalogues of the publications of
individual national statistical offices. Recent examples of the latter
genre do, however, exist for Chile, Guatemala and Puerto Rico:

Catálogo de series estadísticas, 1983. Santiago: Instituto Nacional
de Estadística, 1983.

*Panorama de estadísticas producidas por la Dirección General de
Estadística.* Guatemala City: Dirección General de Estadística,
Consejo Nacional de Planificación Económica, 1980.

Directorio estadístico, 1979. San Juan, PR: Junta de Planificación,
1979. Covers all Puerto Rican government statistical agencies,
their organisation and their publications.

Catalogues or sales lists, such as those listed above, can be used in
conjunction with whatever explanatory indications appear in the
statistical publications themselves to keep a check on the statistical
methods employed. It is most important to watch out for information on changes in procedures of data collection, analysis and
presentation. When accessible published sources (including the
publications themselves) prove to be inadequate in this regard,
direct communication with the issuing agencies may be necessary.
Agency addresses can be found in many general and local
directories, or in:

Directory of Official Statistical Agencies. Voorburg, Netherlands: International Statistical Institute, 1983.

For an appreciation of the continuing international attempts to standardise and systematise statistical methodologies and practices, reference should be made to the United Nations Statistical Office's Studies in Methods (Series F), especially:

National Accounting Practises in Seventy Countries. Studies in Methods, Series F, no. 26 (ST/ESA/STAT/Ser.F/26). New York, 1979. Fourteen of the seventy countries are Latin American.

Handbook of Vital Statistics Systems and Methods. Vol. 2: Review of national practises. Studies in Methods, Series F, no. 35 (ST/ESA/STAT/Ser.F/35). New York, 1985.

An overview of one important aspect of statistical concern is:

McGranahan, Donald et al. *Measurement and Analysis of Socio-Economic Development.* UNRISD Report no. 85.5. Geneva: United Nations Research Institute for Social Development, 1985. Includes discussion of selected Latin American countries.

Still relevant, despite its age, is this broader-based study of statistical policy and objectives:

Wilkie, James W. *Statistics and National Policy.* Statistical Abstract of Latin America, Supplement 3. Los Angeles, CA: UCLA Latin American Center, 1974.

The same author has uncovered newer concerns in:

Wilkie, James W. 'Management and Mismanagement of National and International Statistical Resources in the Americas.' *Statistical Abstract of Latin America* 22 (1983), pp. 655–660.

Bibliographies

The best coverage is provided, consecutively, by:

Bibliography of Selected Statistical Sources of the American Nations... Washington, DC: Inter-American Statistical Institute, 1947. This is updated and complemented by the following two items:

Hostilio Montenegro, Tulio. 'Bibliografía anotada de las principales fuentes de estadísticas sobre América Latina.' *Handbook of Latin American Studies* 29 (1967), pp. 613–639.

JOHNSON, Charles W. *Indice de cuadros estadísticos socio-políticos sobre América Latina, 1946–1969.* Mexico City: UNAM, Instituto de Investigaciones Sociales, 1972.

For more recent years, one must rely on HARVEY's *Statistics America* (cited above) and the biennial *Planindex: resúmenes de documentacion sobre planificación* (Santiago: CEPAL/CLADES, 1980—), which is less well organised for the extraction of references to statistical sources.

The most general, regular tabulations gathered for each country may be fond in:

WESTFALL, Gloria. *Bibliography of Official Statistical Yearbooks and Bulletins.* Government Documents Bibliographies Series. Alexandria, VA: Chadwyck-Healey, 1986. Contains reliable information up to 1984 on the contents of national statistical yearbooks. The volume also includes information on microform and other reprint editions, which rarely go beyond the mid-1970s.

Population statistics are discussed in the chapter on CENSUSES (p. 276). Of particular note, however, is the bimonthly journal *Population Index* (Princeton, NJ: Office of Population Research, 1969—), which includes regular sections on the production of population statistics (section O) and on statistical publications (section S). The earlier volumes of the index have been cumulated as:

Population Index Bibliography: Cumulated, 1969–1981, by Authors and Geographical Areas. 4 vols. Boston, MA: G.K. Hall, 1984.

Better still is the semi-annual *DOCPAL: resúmenes sobre población en América Latina* (Santiago: Centro Latinoamericano de Demografia, 1977—). Both the *Population Index* and *DOCPAL* databases are searchable online.

Citation

Statistical publications present problems of citation (and of location in library catalogues and databases) similar to those of other government publications. See the section on Citation in the chapter, OFFICIAL PUBLICATIONS (pp. 199–200).

MR

Research and Career Development

Universities and Research Centres

Latin American Studies in the UK

Although significant British academic interest in Latin America began at least as long ago as the 1920s, the framework in which present-day research is organised is largely the result of the 1965 report of the Committee on Latin America, established by the University Grants Committee under the chairmanship of Dr. J. H. Parry. This report led to the creation of five 'Parry Centres' for Latin American studies at the Universities of Cambridge, Glasgow, Liverpool, London and Oxford; at the same time the then newly-founded University of Essex was building up what was virtually a sixth centre for the study of the region. (See also LIBRARY RESOURCES ON LATIN AMERICA, pp. 5–6)

The report also provided some stimulus for Latin American studies elsewhere, and the area has always formed a natural focus of interest for specialists such as economists, anthropologists, political scientists and Hispanists. As a result, despite a concentration of work at the six universities named, there is much activity elsewhere, some of it outstanding in particular fields (Amerindian linguistics at St. Andrews, for example). In addition, while the universities for the most part offer Latin American studies only at a postgraduate level, or as a special subject or option in first degree courses centred on a traditional discipline, some non-university institutions such as Wolverhampton and Portsmouth Polytechnics and the Ealing College of Higher Education have given a special place to Latin American studies as undergraduate degree courses.

Courses

Latin American courses are offered in some 32 universities and 18 polytechnics in the UK. The relevant syllabuses are outlined in:

Latin American Studies in the Universities and Polytechnics of the United Kingdom. Rev. ed. London: University of London, Institute of Latin American Studies, 1988. Future editions are to be published biennially.

Research Institutes in the UK

Latin American centres in the UK are listed below. It should be
noted that while some are active centres of research, others merely
centralise information about research on the region carried out
elsewhere in their universities.

University of Cambridge
Centre of Latin American Studies
History Faculty Building
West Road
Cambridge CB3 9DR

University of Essex
Latin American Centre
Wivenhoe Park
Colchester CO4 3SQ

University of Glasgow
Institute of Latin American Studies
3 University Gardens
Glasgow G12 8QT

University of Liverpool
Centre for Latin American Studies
P.O. Box 147
Liverpool L69 3BX

University of London
Institute of Latin American Studies
31 Tavistock Square
London WC1H 9HA

University of Oxford
Latin American Centre
Saint Antony's College
21 Winchester Road
Oxford OX2 6NA

Centres with a special interest in the Caribbean include:

University of Warwick
Institute of Caribbean Studies
Coventry CV4 7AL

University of London
Institute of Commonwealth Studies
27/28 Russell Square
London WC1B 5DS

Latin American Studies in the US

The growth of US academic interest in Latin America closely parallels the history of the discipline in the UK. Although important work was done on the region in the nineteenth and early twentieth centuries by pioneering scholars such as Hubert Howe Bancroft, Hiram Bingham, Herbert Bolton and others, it was only after the Second World War that formal area studies programmes began to appear on university campuses. Much of the impetus for the growth of these programmes came from the establishment in 1952 of the Ford Foundation Foreign Area Fellowship Program, which offered funds to individuals for advanced study and field research, and the passage in 1966 of the US Department of Education's National Defense Education Act (NDEA), which provided financial support for area studies programmes at selected academic institutions. The NDEA was later replaced by the Higher Education Act (HEA), under which funding for area studies programmes was incorporated as Title VI.

Thirteen universities and university consortia currently receive Title VI funds to support National Resource Centers for Latin American Studies which, in turn, administer degree programmes and other Latin America-related activities on their campuses. The funds are awarded on a competitive basis determined by the university's demonstrated commitment to the area. Consideration is given to such factors as the number of faculty members involved in Latin American studies, the number of relevant courses offered and students enrolled, the strength of language training and proficiency courses, the quality of library support for research, outreach programmes undertaken, conferences or lecture series presented and linkages established with other institutions. Open funding competitions are held every three years, and support levels for the funded institutions are reevaluated annually.

Courses

Given the rigorous competition for funds, it is not surprising that the Title VI-sponsored universities, listed below in the section on research institutes, support the best Latin American studies courses available in the US. Most of these institutions offer degrees at both undergraduate and Master's levels, and many (including UCLA and the University of Texas at Austin) have initiated joint degree programmes with one or more of the university's professional schools. These joint programmes, which enable the student to earn two Master's degrees simultaneously, are popular despite their gruelling requirements because they prepare one more fully for a career in a specific Latin American field (see CAREERS FOR LATIN AMERICANISTS, p. 352).

There are, in all, more than 100 universities and colleges in the US that offer degree courses in Latin American studies. A recent list of these institutions, a project of the Consortium of Latin American Studies Programs (CLASP), is available free of charge from the issuing body:

> BRAY, David B. and Richard E. GREENLEAF. *A Directory of Latin American Studies in the United States*. New Orleans, LA: Tulane University, Roger Thayer Stone Center for Latin American Studies, 1986. Identifies faculty members and courses by discipline, gives addresses and telephone numbers for each programme, and provides a brief description of supporting library collections.

Research Institutes in the US

Listed below are the National Resource Centers for Latin American Studies funded by the US Department of Education under Title VI of the Higher Education Act in 1988–1989. An asterisk indicates that the institution is funded as a centre for undergraduate studies only:

Individual Institutions

> University of California, Los Angeles
> Latin American Center
> 10343 Bunche Hall
> Los Angeles, CA 90024

> University of Florida
> Center for Latin American Studies
> 319 Grintner Hall
> Gainesville, FL 32611

*   Florida International University
     Latin American and Caribbean Center
     Tamiami Trail
     Miami, FL 33199

     University of Texas
     Institute of Latin American Studies
     Sid Richardson Hall
     Austin, TX 78712

     Tulane University
     Roger Thayer Stone Center for Latin American Studies
     New Orleans, LA 70118

Consortia

Columbia University	*with* New York University
Institute of Latin American Studies	Center for Latin American and
834 International Affairs	Caribbean Studies
New York, NY 10027	19 University Place
	New York, NY 10003

*University of Connecticut   *with* Brown University
Center for Latin American Studies   Center for Portuguese and
U 103   Brazilian Studies
Storrs, CT 06268   Box E
    Providence, RI 02912

and

University of Massachusetts
Program in Latin American Studies
Machmer Hall
Amherst, MA 01003

University of Illinois   *with* University of Chicago
Center for Latin American and   Center for Latin American Studies
   Caribbean Studies   Social Sciences 118
1208 W. California Avenue   1126 E. 59th Street
Urbana, IL 61801   Chicago, IL 60637

University of New Mexico   *with* New Mexico State University
Latin American Institute   Center for Latin American Studies
801 Yale N.E.   Las Cruces, NM 88003
Albuquerque, NM 87131

University of Pittsburgh   *with* Cornell University
Center for Latin American Studies   Latin American Studies Program
4E04 Forbes Quadrangle   190 Uris Hall
Pittsburgh, PA 15260   Ithaca, NY 14853

San Diego State University	*with*	University of California, San Diego
Center for Latin American Studies		Center for Iberian and Latin
San Diego, CA 92182		Studies
		102D Institute of the Americas
		La Jolla, CA 92093

Stanford University	*with*	University of California, Berkeley
Center for Latin American Studies		Center for Latin American Studies
Bolivar House		2334 Bowditch Street
582 Alvarado Row		Berkeley, CA 94720
Stanford, CA 94305		

University of Wisconsin-Madison	*with*	University of Wisconsin-
Ibero-American Studies Program		Milwaukee
1470 Van Hise Hall		Center for Latin America
1220 Linden Drive		Box 413
Madison, WI 53706		Milwaukee, WI 53201

A recent guide to other research centres in the US and Canada is:

Research Centers Directory. 8th ed. Edited by Mary Michelle Watkins and James A. Ruffner. Detroit, MI: Gale Research, 1983.

An older listing of Latin Americanist research can be found in:

HARO, Roberto P. *Latin Americana Research in the United States and Canada: A Guide and Directory*. Chicago, IL: American Library Association, 1971.

Other Research Institutes Abroad

The international counterpart of the *Research Centers Directory* is:

International Research Centers Directory, 1986–1987. Edited by Kay Gill and Darren L. Smith. Detroit, MI: Gale Research, 1986.

A select list of Latin American research centres worldwide is given in:

SABLE, Martin H. *The Latin American Studies Directory*. Detroit, MI: Blaine Ethridge, 1981. Research centres are listed on pp. 475–574.

European centres are listed in the following two volumes:

MESA-LAGO, Carmelo. *Latin American Studies in Europe*. Latin American Monograph and Document Series, 1. New York: Tinker Foundation, 1979.

Manual para las relaciones europeo-latinoamericanas: instituciones y organizaciones europeas y sus relaciones con América Latina y el Caribe. Edited by Brigitte Farenholtz and Wolfgang Grenz. Madrid: Instituto de Relaciones Europeo Latinoamericanas, 1987.

Centres in Japan, China and India are described in:

MESA-LAGO, Carmelo. *Latin American Studies in Asia*. Pittsburgh, PA: University of Pittsburgh, 1983.

and an account of centres and courses in Israel is given in:

AVNI, Haim and Yoram SHAPIRA. 'Teaching and Research on Latin America in Israel.' *Latin American Research Review* 9:3 (Fall 1974), pp. 39–51.

Research in Progress

Staff research in UK universities and polytechnics is listed in:

Research on Latin America in the Humanities and Social Sciences, Incorporating Theses Completed and in Progress. London: University of London, Institute of Latin American Studies, 1988. The latest to appear covers 1984–1988, and further biennial issues are planned.

An important source of information on current research being undertaken in the US, Europe and Latin America is the section 'Investigaciones en curso/Research in Progress' which has appeared twice a year since 1981 in the *Inter-American Review of Bibliography/ Revista Interamericana de Bibliografía* (Washington, DC: Organization of American States). Of more restricted coverage is the regular section 'Registro de estudios belgas y neerlandeses sobre América Latina', covering books and articles in progress, published regularly in the *Boletín de Estudios Latinoamericanos y del Caribe* (Amsterdam: Centrum voor Studie en Dokumentatie van Latijns Amerika, 1963—). For work on Brazil there is an irregular 'Research in Progress' section in the *Luso-Brazilian Review* (Madison, WI: University of Wisconsin, 1973—).

See also the chapter on THESES AND DISSERTATIONS (p. 221).

Information on Academics

Information about lecturers in the UK, arranged by academic institution, is given in *Research on Latin America in the Humanities and Social Sciences* (see above). Included are all academic staff members having Latin American interests, whether or not they teach courses in the subject, and information is given about their positions, status, degrees held, research interests and recent publications. A similar list covering academics in West Germany can be found in:

> FERNO, Renate and Wolfgang GRENZ. *Handbuch der deutschen Lateinamerika-Forschung.* Hamburg: Institut für Iberoamerika-Kunde, 1980. The listing occupies pp. 107–386, and pp. 27–100 of the *Ergänzung* (supplement) of 1981.

General alphabetical directories of Latin Americanists in Europe, the US and Canada are listed in the chapter HANDBOOKS, GUIDES AND DIRECTORIES (pp. 164–165).

There are also specialised lists of scholars in particular areas or disciplines. 1,577 researchers on Mexico in twelve different countries, together with full details of their research projects, are represented in:

> *Guía Internacional de investigaciones sobre México/International Guide to Research on Mexico.* Tijuana: El Colegio de la Frontera Norte, and La Jolla, CA: Center for US-Mexican Studies, 1986—. Annual. A merger of two listings previously published separately.

For the study of the Caribbean, there is:

> PERUSSE, Roland I. *Worldwide Directory of Caribbeanists, 1975.* Hato Rey, PR: Caribbean Studies Association, 1975.

Historians are listed in:

> *Guía de personas que cultivan la historia de América.* 2nd ed. Mexico City: Pan-American Institute of Geography and History, 1967. This may be supplemented by:

> MORALES PADRÓN, Francisco. 'Guía de profesores de historia de América en universidades iberoamericanas.' *Historiografía y Bibliografía Americanistas* 17 (1971), p. 45–79.

while for sociologists there is the older:

REMMLING, Gunter W. *South American Sociologists: A Directory.* Austin, TX: University of Texas, 1966.

See also:

Latin American Studies Association Handbook and Membership Directory, 1984–1985. Austin, TX: Latin American Studies Association, 1984.

Grants and Scholarships

Grants, bursaries and scholarships to attend colleges, universities and individual courses are available from many sources. This section attempts to list a few of them.

Reference Books

Every other year Unesco in Paris issues its *Study Abroad*, which includes information on sources of financial support. Arrangement is by country of study, subdivided by topic. A preliminary chapter covers international awards.

The British Council in London publishes annually a rather briefer *Scholarships Abroad*, which is intended exclusively for UK students who wish to study overseas.

The *Grants Register*, published biennially in London by Macmillan, lists awards available for postgraduate students and others who require further professional training. It is intended principally for English-speaking students, but some of the awards listed are international in scope, and so may be available to students from other parts of the world. Arrangement is alphabetical by grant-making body, and the subject index shows whether the award is tenable in particular regions and if it is restricted to citizens of particular countries.

Awards for study and research in Commonwealth countries are to be found in the following publications, all issued by the Association of Commonwealth Universities: *Financial Aid for First Degree Study at Commonwealth Universities*; *Scholarships Guide for Commonwealth Postgraduate Students*; and *Awards for Commonwealth University Academic Staff*.

Of occasional value is:

International Foundation Directory. Edited by H. V. Hodson. 3rd ed. London: Europa Publications, 1983. Contains information on some 800 foundations and trusts worldwide. Coverage includes seven Latin American countries, in addition to Spain and Portugal.

There are many publications dealing with funding for study in the US for home or overseas students. The following is a selection of the most useful of them.

Scholarships for International Students: A Complete Guide to Colleges and Universities in the United States. 1986–1988 ed. Edited by S. Manek and Anna Leider. Alexandria, VA: Octameron Associates, 1986. Intended for overseas students.

Scholarships and Grants for Study or Research in the USA: A Scholarship Handbook for Foreign Nationals. Edited by Walter Wickremasinghe. Houston, TX: American Collegiate Service, 1986.

The *Handbook on International Study* produced by the Institute of International Education in New York now appears in two parts: *Handbook on International Study for US Nationals*, with information on opportunities for study in the other American Republics, and *Handbook on US Study for Foreign Nationals*. Both parts contain information on funding and scholarships.

Produced irregularly as a series of leaflets are the *United States Government Grants under the Fulbright-Hays Act* (Washington, DC: Conference Board of Associated Research Councils, Committee on International Exchange of Persons).

The Foundation Center in New York provides comprehensive information on US foundations and the grants they award. Among their publications are *Foundation Directory* (11th ed. Edited by Loren Renz, 1987; with *Supplement* edited by Stanley Olson, 1988), *Foundation Grants Index* (currently edited by Ruth Kovacs) and *Foundation Grants to Individuals* (6th ed. Edited by Stanley Olson, 1988). The first two works are also available online via DIALOG (see below).

Other publications useful to both the US and international student or researcher are the annual *Directory of Research Grants* (Phoenix, AZ: Oryx Press), and:

COLEMAN, William E. *Grants in the Humanities: A Scholar's Guide to Funding Sources.* 2nd ed. New York: Neal-Schuman, 1984.

Fellowships in the Arts and Sciences (American Council on Education) gives sources outside the universities for postgraduate and postdoctoral research.

Online Databases

There are currently three online databases containing information on foundations and grants accessible via DIALOG: Foundation Directory and Foundation Grants Index (see above), and a database entitled Grants, compiled by the Oryx Press, which includes the *Directory of Research Grants* and *Grants in the Humanities* (see above).

Other Sources

Universities and research institutions in the UK and the US often have research funds available which they may not publicise, but which local scholarship offices and heads of Latin American centres and departments will know about. Information of this kind can often be uncovered by reviewing the newslatters of the major Latin American centres and associations. It is also worthwhile enquiring of the Department of Education and Science (DES) in London, The US Department of Education, research councils such as the Economic and Social Research Council and the National Endowment for the Humanities, and institutions such as the British Academy and the Ford Foundation.

The would-be researcher in a particular Latin American country would also do well to contact the cultural department of the appropriate embassy, consulate or high commission; there may be special restrictions or, sometimes, opportunities. Finally, some of the larger Latin American nations regularly award scholarships to foreign students, and these may be administered through the embassies.

CT/BGV/CY

Language Courses and Study Abroad

Prospective students of Latin America who have not learned Spanish or Portuguese at school or taken a first degree in these languages will usually require a short course to help them acquire the necessary language skills. Spanish and Portuguese may be studied on their own at all levels, or as part of a broader course including secretarial or business skills, or Latin American studies. Courses are taught at most times of day and for various lengths of time; they are given in a variety of colleges, by correspondence and through private study. This chapter will be limited to a discussion of language courses taken outside the traditional undergraduate university degree programme, for the individual who needs to improve or perfect previously acquired language skills or to learn a second foreign language. Most of the specific information given in this chapter applies to the United Kingdom and, to a lesser degree, the United States. The general principles, however, will be found to apply to most countries.

In Britain, Spanish and Portuguese are not widely taught in schools; but because the Iberian peninsula is a popular holiday destination there is an appreciable demand for language instruction at an adult level. There are two major sources of information on available courses, learning materials and examinations. The first is:

> Centre for Information on Language Teaching and Research (CILT)
> Regent's College
> Inner Circle
> Regent's Park
> London NW1 4NS
> (Telephone: 01–486 8221)

CILT publishes a series of language and culture guides for students of the less frequently studied languages: *Portuguese* (1982) is number 20 in the series. Unfortunately, CILT does not publish guides for the three most popular languages, of which Spanish is one. The other prominent coordinating organisation is:

Hispanic and Luso-Brazilian Council
Canning House
2 Belgrave Square
London SW1X 8PJ
(Telephone: 01–235 2303)

Canning House's Education Department maintains an information service on full-time, part-time and intensive Spanish and Portuguese courses in the UK and abroad. Its *Education Department Newsletter*, published three times a year, frequently carries details of new courses and publications. Another useful Canning House leaflet is *Commercial, Business and Secretarial Courses with Languages in London* (1986), which lists degree and diploma courses at 54 colleges.

Other publications that may be of use are the Institute of Linguists' *Schedule of Courses in Translating, Interpreting and Practical Linguistics and Degree-Level Courses in Languages Combined with Technical Subjects*, which is revised periodically; and *A Guide to Language Courses in Polytechnics and Similar Institutions*, published biennially for the Standing Conference of Heads of Modern Languages in Polytechnics and Other Colleges (SCHML). The latter lists full-time, part-time and sandwich degree and diploma courses in polytechnics, colleges of higher education and technical colleges, but unfortunately restricts its coverage to SCHML members.

Diploma Courses

In the UK, if you need to study full-time (though not to degree level), or wish to obtain a formal qualification, you should contact local colleges, and also enquire from your local education authority or local public reference library. The annual *Directory of Further Education* (Cambridge: Hobsons, 1968—) provides information on the full range of evening and day-release courses available in the UK. More detailed is a publication of the Careers Resource Advisory Centre (CRAC):

> TIGHT, Malcolm. *Part-Time Degrees, Diplomas and Certificates: A Guide to Part-Time Higher Education Courses* .... Cambridge: Hobsons, 1986. Tabulates the courses that can be studied part-time or by correspondence at UK universities, polytechnics and colleges.

Among other organisations that award vocational diplomas or proficiency certificates in languages are the Business and Technical

Education Council (BTEC), the London Chamber of Commerce and Industry (LCCI) and the Royal Society of Arts (RSA). Full addresses can be obtained from CILT (see above). BTEC offers a wide range of practical courses leading to a nationally-recognised diploma, which falls just short of first degree level; the courses last for two years full-time, or three years as a sandwich course. Spanish may be taken as part of business or technical courses, from scratch or from GCE 'A' level standard. LCCI offers a range of examinations in Spanish and Portuguese in its 'Foreign Language for Industry and Commerce' syllabus. Designed for any type of student, the examinations are entirely oral and primarily business-oriented. The Royal Society of Arts has also devised a number of vocationally-specific language examinations, though not to such a high level as BTEC: a typical qualification would be a Certificate in Spanish for the Office.

The Institute of Linguists (24a Highbury Grove, London N5 2EA; telephone: 01-359 7445) offers a wide range of routes to a language certificate, with evening classes available at all levels in Spanish and at a more basic level in Portuguese. In addition to conventional examinations, the Institute runs 'guided tests' in linguistic proficiency on the lines of those offered to people learning musical instruments. In 1990 a new syllabus will be introduced, based on practical exercises and using authentic materials (the language in context).

Individual private and public institutions for higher education have introduced their own diploma courses in languages, generally including Spanish and occasionally Portuguese. Courses are normally full-time, over one or two years, and typically involve an average of three to five hours per week language tuition. Some institutions, among them Brighton Polytechnic and the Edinburgh University's Institute for Applied Language Study, provide flexible language courses, tailored specially for individuals or companies. Full details will be found in the *Directory of Further Education* and in *A Guide to Language Courses in Polytechnics and Similar Institutions*, both cited above.

In the United States, virtually all language teaching leading to a qualification is carried out in the university or college context. Information about specific programmes can be obtained by contacting each school's Department of Modern Languages, or its equivalent. There are also several publications listing colleges and universities that offer degree courses in Spanish and/or Portuguese. Among them are:

The College Blue Book. New York: Macmillan, 1923—. Describes US colleges, universities and occupational schools, with lists of degrees offered. The section 'Degrees offered by College and Subject' is a subject index to programmes, divided geographically.

Directory of Master's Programs in Foreign Languages, Foreign Literature and Linguistics. New York: Modern Language Association of America, 1987. Indexed by language.

Peterson's Guide to Graduate Programs in the Humanities and Social Sciences, 1989. 23rd ed. Peterson's Annual Guides to Graduate Study, book 2. Princeton, NJ: Peterson's Guides, 1985. Arranged by field of study subdivided by institution. Gives information on programmes, number of students enrolled, size of faculty, requirements, expenses and financial aid.

Part-Time and Short Intensive Study Courses

If you wish to learn the language part-time, attending once or twice a week (or more often) at a local class, the first step should be to contact your local education authority, high school, community college or the Continuing Education division of a nearby university. In the UK a handy guide is the *Yearbook of Adult Continuing Education*, published annually by the National Institute of Adult Continuing Education.

British local education authorities conduct adult education evening classes; the courses are announced in August and commence (if the demand warrants) in September. Usually held on school or college premises, they are intended mainly for the amateur enthusiast, although there are some diploma or certificate courses. Each authority produces its own prospectus, generally supplied free of charge to residents in the area, and certainly available at public libraries. Some programmes are also advertised in the local press.

Similar classes are offered throughout the academic year by many US high schools. In addition, community colleges and university extension schools offer beginning and intermediate level language courses that may be taken on a part-time basis and credited, if desired, toward fulfilment of a degree programme.

Private language schools are to be found almost everywhere, and can be traced through the Yellow Pages of any telephone directory. They are, however, of variable quality and reliability. British colleges of this sort are monitored by the independent British

Accreditation Council for Independent Further and Higher Education and the Conference on Independent Further Education, though there is no compulsory registration system. Before embarking on a course (or paying any deposit required) it might be advisable to consult Gabbitas, Truman and Thring, a long-established private educational consultancy (6–8 Sackville Street, London W1; telephone 01–734 0161).

Many organisations and individuals offer flexible programmes of one-to-one and group instruction, all generally taught by native speakers of the language concerned. Some even provide residential accommodation in pleasant country surroundings. You can choose between private tuition; small-group teaching teams (popular with businessmen); intensive 'survival' courses; and 'total immersion' residential tuition, involving twelve hours or more of instruction every day for a week or two at a time. This type of teaching is, of course, likely to prove expensive. Consult *Part-Time and Intensive Language Study: A Guide for Adult Learners* (CILT Information Guide, 8; London: Centre for Information on Language Teaching, 1982), or *Time to Learn*, a guide to residential study breaks, summer schools and study tours, published twice a year by the National Institute of Adult and Continuing Education.

Frequently-overlooked centres for study in Spanish and Portuguese in Great Britain are the cultural associations and foundations established to promote good relations between the UK and the Hispanic nations. Canning House, already mentioned, organises its own evening classes in peninsular and Brazilian Portuguese. In addition, the following institutions provide part-time language courses and conversation classes, as well as advice on learning the language concerned:

Instituto de España (Spanish Institute)
102 Eaton Square
London SW1W 9AN
(Telephone: 01–235 1484)

Casa do Brasil (House of Brazil Foundation)
49 Lancaster Gate
London W2 3NA
(Telephone: 01–723 9648)

Latin American Cultural Centre
Priory House
Kingsgate Place
London NW6
(Telephone: 01–372 6573)

In the United States the Spanish Institute (684 Park Avenue, New York, NY 10021) aims to increase knowledge of the culture and life of Spain and Spanish-speaking countries, and provides language classes for adults and children, as well as special courses in business and medical Spanish. It also publishes a quarterly newsletter and various brochures.

Correspondence Courses and Self-Education

Many students find it easier and more convenient to work at home with a study kit, learning at their own speed, with or without the aid of a distant teacher. In the UK the Open University and the successful new Open College now provide extensive opportunities for distance learning for the committed part-time student. Linguaphone has two language centres (124–126 Brompton Road, London SW3; telephone 01–589 2422; and at The European Bookshop, 4 Regents Place, London W1) which stock a range of home-study courses in Castilian Spanish, Latin American Spanish, Portuguese and Brazilian Portuguese. Once again Canning House provides an advisory leaflet: *Spanish and Portuguese Home Study and Correspondence Courses* (1988).

A useful evaluation of some older course materials will be found in:

> WALFORD, A. J. *A Guide to Foreign Language Courses and Dictionaries.* 3rd ed. London: Library Association, 1977. A new edition is planned for 1990.

For more up-to-date information on books, cassettes, and home-study videos, there are two CILT leaflets: *Bookshops and Sources of Supply for Language Teaching Materials*, and *Some Commercially Available Foreign Language Courses and Supplementary Materials on Video.*

The British Broadcasting Corporation produces and broadcasts a number of beginners' and intermediate Spanish and Portuguese courses on both television and radio. It also regularly broadcasts foreign-language material for use by schools and colleges. BBC Education (London W5 2PA; telephone 01–991 8031) publishes an annual brochure, *Living Language*, listing the programmes and related resource materials for the coming year. CILT also produces an annual leaflet, *Broadcast Resources for Modern Languages*.

There are no programmes in the US equivalent to those provided by the BBC, but many correspondence and self-education courses are available. Publications that list them include the following:

JONES, John Harding. *The Correspondence Educational Directory and Alternative Educational Opportunities.* 3rd ed. Oxnard, CA: Racz, 1984.

Learning Independently: A Directory of Self-Instruction Resources ... Edited by Stephen Waserman et al. Detroit, MI: Gale Research, 1987.

The Macmillan Guide to Correspondence Study. 3rd ed. New York: Macmillan, 1988.

SMART, Joseph E. *College and University Correspondence Courses in the United States.* Rocheport, MO: Smartco, 1987.

Nor should new technologies be overlooked: software for computer-assisted language learning (CALL) is improving rapidly from simple vocabulary tests to far more sophisticated exercises. The UK National Centre for Computer-Assisted Language Learning is based at Ealing College of Higher Education (School of Language Studies, St Mary's Road, London W5 5RF; telephone 01–579 4111). *Hispania*, the journal published by the American Association of Teachers of Spanish and Portuguese, includes reviews of teaching materials such as computer software and video cassettes as well as textbooks.

Study, Work and Teaching Abroad

There are many universities and private language schools in Spain, Portugal and Latin America that offer a wide range of language courses for foreigners. Most operate during the summer months (July and August in the northern hemisphere), but many teach all the year round. Every level is catered to, and courses may last for any period from a week to nine months. Language teaching is often combined with general cultural and literary studies, and classes are nearly always taught in small groups of six or so. Accommodation —hotel, residential or homestay—may be provided, but students are normally encouraged to make their own arrangements.

The Instituto de España in London can provide a list of such courses in Spain, and the Education Department of Canning House produces annual leaflets on available courses in Spain, Portugal and Latin America. The Spanish and Portuguese departments of most US universities can also provide information about courses of study abroad. A useful international publication is:

Study Abroad: International Scholarships, International Courses. Paris: Unesco, 1948—. Biennial.

In addition to language courses abroad, there are possibilities for work abroad, volunteer work in Latin America, adventure holidays, homestays, archaeological digs, Amazon expeditions and the like. A coordinating body for educational exchanges in general is:

Central Bureau for Educational Visits and Exchanges
Seymour Mews House
Seymour Mews
Wigmore Street
London W1H 9PE
(Telephone: 01–486 5101)

The Central Bureau organises exchange programmes providing undergraduate study and course-related industrial, technical or commercial experience in another country and publishes a series of guides, including Study Holidays (1988), Working Holidays (1988), Home from Home (1987), and Volunteer Work (1986).

In the US the largest exchange agency for higher education is:

Institute of International Education (IIE)
809 United Nations Plaza
New York, NY 10017–3580

The IIE provides information on educational exchanges and assists with the administration of the Fulbright Program for graduates. Among its publications are Vacation Study Abroad (39th ed., 1989), Academic Year Abroad (17th ed., 1988) and Teaching Abroad (4th ed., 1988). The latter is a guide to opportunities worldwide for US teachers and university faculty.

Another body concerned with exchanges is:

Council on International Educational Exchange (CIEE)
205 E. 42nd Street
New York, NY 10017
(Telephone: (212) 661–1414)

The CIEE sponsors exchange programmes with Europe and Latin America, and provides services for US citizens on summer jobs abroad through its offices in London, Madrid and other foreign capitals. It also publishes the useful guide *Work, Study, Travel Abroad* (9th ed., 1988–1989; New York: St. Martin's Press, 1988).

Other important publications on the subject are:

> *Latin America: Notes on Opportunities for Employment and Travel for Foreigners and Students.* London: Hispanic and Luso-Brazilian Council, 1987. A pamphlet prepared by Canning House Education Department.

> *Summer Jobs Abroad, 1989.* 20th ed. Oxford: Vacation Work, 1989. Revised annually. Published in the US as *Directory of Overseas Summer Jobs* (Cincinnati, OH: Writer's Digest Books).

> *International Directory of Voluntary Work.* Oxford: Vacation Work, 1988.

> *A Year Off, A Year On.* Cambridge: Hobsons, 1985. Published for the Careers Resource Advisory Centre.

Translations

When faced with a document in an unknown language which there is no time to learn, one's only recourse is a translation service. There are numerous commercial translation agencies in the UK, some of which have been in business for a considerable time and have very good reputations. Unfortunately, no official body exists to set minimum standards of competence for the agencies and the staff they employ, and the quality of the translation work done can vary considerably from service to service. The Institute of Translation and Interpreting (318a Finchley Road, London NW3 5HT; telephone 01–794 9931) is attempting to improve the situation and publishes a twice-yearly directory of translators and interpreters in many languages. The Institute can also give guidelines on fees. In addition, the Institute of Linguists (see above) has 6,000 members, some of whom are professional translators into and from Spanish and Portuguese. It plans to publish a directory in 1989 which will include a full list of members and their areas of expertise.

The professional society of translators and interpreters in the US is the American Translators Association (109 Croton Avenue, Ossining, NY 10562). It publishes a list of translators and their qualifications accredited by the society:

Translation Services Directory. 6th ed. Laurel, MD: American Translators Association, 1986.

AB/PAS

Societies and Associations

Associations and professional societies are, in English-speaking countries at least, valuable adjuncts to research in a particular area or subject field. They can act as magnets, drawing together enthusiasts and interested businessmen as well as scholars from a variety of disciplines, and can also provide a forum for discussion or for the dissemination of information. More than this, they may sometimes provide more or less immediate access to highly qualified sources of information. 'Frequently a phone-call or letter ... produces more information—faster—than any amount of research in books, periodicals and other printed materials.' (*Encyclopedia of Associations*, 22nd ed., 1988; see below).

This chapter attempts to identify some of the major organisations in Europe and the Americas, commencing with North America, where the greatest concentration of them is to be found.

North America

Americans have a propensity to associate. No matter how arcane one's interests or area of professional specialisation, there is likely to be at least one association of like-minded enthusiasts, and probably several. Latin Americanists are no exception, and because there are so many ways that regional interests may be applied to subject specialities, professions and personal concerns, the number of associations having a Latin American focus is staggering. For this reason, the following discussion will, of necessity, be confined primarily to a sampling of US academic associations. Of these, the largest and most comprehensive is:

> Latin American Studies Association (LASA)
> Reid Reading, Executive Director
> William Pitt Union, 9th Floor
> University of Pittsburgh
> Pittsburgh, PA 15260
> Telephone: (412) 648–7929

LASA was formed in 1966 '... to provide a professional organization that will foster the concerns of all scholars interested in Latin American studies, that will encourage more effective training, teaching and research in connection with such studies, and that will provide a forum for dealing with matters of common interest to the scholarly professions and to other individuals concerned with Latin American studies.' (*LASA Constitution*. Article 2: 'Purposes'). LASA has more than 2,000 members, most of whom are university professors and academic librarians. Conferences are held every eighteen months in various US cities and , occasionally, abroad. The association publishes a quarterly newsletter, the *LASA Forum*, and the highly respected journal *Latin American Research Review*, which appears three times a year. LASA does not, however, publish its conference proceedings.

The institutional arm of LASA is the Consortium of Latin American Studies Programs (CLASP), which includes among its membership most of the US colleges and universities offering a significant number of courses in Latin American studies. CLASP also supports a strong publications programme of reference works and scholarly monographs.

Eight autonomous regional associations are very loosely affiliated with LASA. Varying considerably in terms of size, level of activity, publications and so forth, they reflect the scholarly interests of Latin Americanists in diverse parts of the country. They are:

Middle Atlantic Council of Latin American Studies (MACLAS)

Midwest Association for Latin American Studies (MALAS)

New England Council of Latin American Studies (NECLAS)

North Central Council of Latin Americanists (NCCLA)

Pacific Coast Council on Latin American Studies (PCCLAS) (Center for Latin American Studies, Arizona State University, Tempe, AZ 85281). Publishes a semi-annual journal, *Review of Latin American Studies*.

Rocky Mountain Council of Latin American Studies (RMCLAS)

Southeastern Council of Latin American Studies (SECOLAS)

Southwestern Council of Latin American Studies (SCOLAS)

Because few of these organisations support permanent secretariats, the addresses change each year with the President. It is therefore best (except where the address is given above) to contact the LASA Secretariat for current information.

LASA's counterpart in Canada is:

> Canadian Association of Latin American and Caribbean Studies/Association Canadienne des Etudes Latino-américaines et Caraïbes
> Serge Larose, Executive Secretary
> Centre de Recherches Caraïbes
> Université de Montréal
> C.P. 6128, Succ. 'A'
> Montréal H3C 3J7

Founded in 1969, the Association publishes the semi-annual *Canadian Journal of Latin American and Caribbean Studies*, a *Newsletter*, occasional directories and its conference proceedings.

The professional association of Latin Americanist librarians and bookmen is the Seminar on the Acquisition of Latin American Library Materials (SALALM). Founded in 1956 as a forum for US practitioners, SALALM now enjoys an international membership of nearly 500 individuals and institutions. Annual meetings are held in the US and abroad. The organisation supports an active publications programme that includes a Bibliography and Reference Series and a quarterly *Newsletter* as well as annual conference proceedings. (Suzanne Hodgman, Executive Secretary, Memorial Library, 728 State Street, University of Wisconsin, Madison, WI 53706).

Latin Americanists have also formed associations concerned with individual academic disciplines. Foremost among these is the Conference on Latin American History (CLAH), an independently chartered group of about 800 Latin American historians that meets annually at the conference of the American Historical Association (AHA), between Christmas and the New Year. CLAH sponsors the publication of the prestigious quarterly journal, the *Hispanic American Historical Review*, and a monograph series published by the University of Wisconsin Press. It also publishes a semi-annual *Newsletter*. (L. Ray Sadler, Executive Secretary, Center for Latin American Studies, New Mexico State University, Las Cruces, NM 88003).

The Business Association of Latin American Studies (BALAS) is a comparatively new organisation that focuses on the study of commerce and industry in Latin America and the Caribbean. Its 250 members include academics and managers of business firms and non-profit organisations. The association holds annual meetings, and publishes its conference proceedings as well as a periodic newsletter, *On Target with BALAS*. (Robert P. Vichas, Executive Secretary, P.O. Drawer 7638, Fort Lauderdale, FL 33338).

The Council of Latin American Geographers (CLAG) was founded in 1970, and meets annually in and out of Latin America. Numbering between 400 and 500 members, it cooperates closely with, but is fully independent of, the American Association of Geographers (AAG). CLAG publishes its annual conference proceedings and a quarterly newsletter, *CLAG Communication*. Within the AAG there is a speciality interest group 'Latin America', the officers of which are also the officers of CLAG. (Thomas Martinson, Executive Secretary, Department of Geography, Auburn University, Auburn, AL 36849).

Other Latin American interest groups function only as divisions or sections of larger organisations. For example:

Brazilian Literature, Latin American Literature, Portuguese and Portuguese-African Literature, Portuguese Language and Linguistics, Portuguese Development Group, Puerto Rican Literature, and Women in Luso-Brazilian Literature / Sections of the American Association of Teachers of Spanish and Portuguese (James R. Chatham, Executive Director, Mississippi State University, Lee Hall 218, P.O. Box 6349, Mississippi State, MS 39762–6349). Publishes *Hispania*.

Society for Latin American Anthropology / Section of the American Anthropological Association (Eugene L. Sterud, Executive Director, 1703 New Hampshire Avenue, N.W., Washington, DC 20009).

Hispanic Folklore Section / American Folklore Society (Timothy Lloyd, Executive Secretary/Treasurer, Ohio Arts Council, 727 E. Main Street, Columbus, OH 43205).

Latin American Literature to 1900, Contemporary Latin American Literature, and Luso-Brazilian Language and Literature / Divisions of the Modern Language Association of America (Phyllis Franklin, Executive Director, 10 Astor Place, New York, NY 10003). Publishes *PMLA*.

Latin America Studies Section / Western Social Science Association (William W. Ray, Executive Director, Texas Christian University, Fort Worth, TX 76129).

Still other organisations are devoted exclusively to ethnic or regional studies. Among these are:

> Association of Borderlands Scholars (James T. Peach, Department of Economics, Box 3CQ, New Mexico State University, Las Cruces, NM 88003). Meets annually with the Western Social Science Association. Publishes a newsletter, *La Frontera*, and the semi-annual *Journal of Borderlands Studies*.

> Association of Caribbean Studies (O. R. Dathorne, P.O. Box 22202, Lexington, KY 40522–2202). Publishes *Journal of Caribbean Studies*.

> North American Association of Colombianists (James J. Alstrum, Department of Foreign Languages, Illinois State University, Normal, IL 61761). Publishes *Revista de Estudios Colombianos*.

> Consortium of US Research Programs for Mexico: PROFMEX (James W. Wilkie, Department of History, University of California, Los Angeles, CA 90024). Publishes a quarterly newsletter, *Mexico Policy News*.

> Latin American Jewish Studies Association (Judith Laiken Elkin, 2104 Georgetown Boulevard, Ann Arbor, MI 48105).

> University of California Consortium on Mexico and the United States: UC MEXUS (Arturo Gómez-Pompa, 1141 Watkins Hall, University of California, Riverside, CA 92521). Publishes an irregular newsletter, *UC MEXUS News*.

In addition to academic associations, a plethora of private, non-profit organisations function at national, regional and local levels to promote a variety of commercial, cultural, ecological, educational, political, philanthropical, social and other interests. The best way to identify these organisations is to refer to one of the following works:

> *Encyclopedia of Associations*. 3 vols. Detroit, MI: Gale Research, annual. Has a useful Name/Keyword Index (volume 1, part 3). Volumes 1 and 2 list US organisations, while volume 3 identifies international and regional organisations outside the US. Supplements are published between editions, listing new associations.

> *National Trade and Professional Associations of the United States*. Washington, DC: Columbia Books, 1982—. Annual.

There are also countless inter-American cultural support groups, such as the Argentine Association of Los Angeles (3160 Glendale Boulevard); these are often too small to be included in the *Encylopedia of Associations* and can be found only by consulting the telephone directories of major US cities.

Finally, many international organisations concerned with Latin America are based in the US, including most notably the United Nations and the Organization of American States. Information about these organisations, their sub-agencies, and many other international groups having Latin American interests can be found in:

> *Yearbook of International Organizations.* 3 vols. Munich: K. G. Saur. Annual.

Great Britain

While the United Kingdon cannot offer such a wealth of Latin Americanist organisations as the US, the field is, nevertheless, well covered. The major academic association, and the direct equivalent of LASA, is:

> Society for Latin American Studies (SLAS)
> John Dickenson
> Department of Geography
> University of Liverpool
> P.O. Box 47
> Liverpool L69 3BX

SLAS holds annual meetings (though their proceedings are not published) and publishes the prestigious *Bulletin of Latin American Research*. It acts to some extent as a coordinating body for Latin American studies in the UK, with representatives on the committees of most other organisations concerned with the area.

Two other academic associations are devoted primarily to the study of Hispanic languages and literatures; they maintain, however, links with the Latin Americanist community. These are:

> Association of Hispanists of Great Britain and Ireland
> Department of Hispanic Studies
> University of Birmingham
> P O Box 363
> Birmingham B15 2TT

Association of Teachers of Spanish and Portuguese (ATSP)
Gillian Mathie, Honorary Secretary
32 Gledhow Lane
Leeds LS8 1SA

The Association of Hispanists produces an annual list of *Research in Progress on Hispanic Subjects*, and the ATSP publishes its own journal, *Vida Hispánica*, three times a year.

The coordinating body for libraries and librarians in the Latin American field is a subgroup of the Britain's Standing Conference of National and University Libraries (SCONUL). Its full name is:

Advisory Committee on Latin American Materials (ACOLAM)
SCONUL Headquarters
102 Euston Street
London NW1 2HA

While the members of ACOLAM are appointed by SCONUL, the Committee holds an annual Meeting of Consultation, open to representatives from all UK libraries having significant Latin American collections; it also sponsors the publication of reference works on the area (including this one), and produces an annual *ACOLAM Newsletter*.

The leading non-academic centre of Latin American interest and culture in the UK is:

The Hispanic and Luso-Brazilian Council
Canning House
2 Belgrave Square
London SW1X 8PJ
Telephone: 01–235 2303

Generally known as 'Canning House', after its imposing premises in Belgravia, this organisation exists to promote cultural and commercial relations between Britain on the one hand and Latin America, Spain and Portugal on the other. It supports a fine library, open to the public, and issues the twice-yearly *British Bulletin of Publications on Latin America, the Caribbean, Portugal and Spain*. The Education Department organises exhibitions and lectures, monitors and promotes the teaching of Spanish and Portuguese in UK schools, and publishes a regular *Newsletter*. Canning House also acts as an unofficial centre for the activities of the independent 'friendship' societies, founded to encourage links with individual Latin

American nations. As a result of Britain's commercial ties with the region, the UK has a plethora of these, running the alphabetical gamut from the Anglo-Argentine Society (2, Belgrave Square, London SW1) to the Anglo-Venezuelan Society (50a Primrose Mansions, Prince of Wales Drive, London SW11). Full details and addresses can be obtained from Canning House.

Canning House also plays host to the Latin American Trade Advisory Group (LATAG), a government-sponsored organisation founded to promote commercial and business relations with the Latin American countries.

An organisation with more overtly political aims is:

> Latin America Bureau
> 1 Amwell Street
> London EC1R 1UL

Established in 1977, this is an independent, non-profit organisation, whose purpose is to raise public awareness of social, economic, political and human rights issues in Latin America, and to support Latin American movements against injustice and exploitation. Among its publications was the annual review, *Great Britain and Latin America*, which commenced in 1978, and in 1980 changed its name to *Europe and Latin America*. Nothing has been heard of this publication for several years.

A group similar to Canning House, though with a narrower focus, is:

> The West India Committee
> 48 Albemarle Street
> London W1X 4AR

The committee was organised to promote trade, investment and friendship between the UK and the Caribbean. It publishes *Insight: A Monthly Bulletin on the Caribbean*.

As is the case with the US, there are many societies and associations in the UK concerned to a greater or lesser degree with Latin America whose major focus is elsewhere. They may be traced by means of:

Directory of British Associations and Associations in Ireland. Edited by G. P. Henderson and S. P. A. Henderson. 9th ed. Beckenham, Kent: CBD Research, 1988. This may be supplemented by the same publisher's *Councils, Committees and Boards* (6th ed., 1984).

Europe and Elsewhere

It would probably be true to say that outside the English-speaking
nations voluntary societies and associations play a less important role
in academic study and research on Latin America. Nonetheless,
numerous Latin Americanist organisations exist in both Eastern and
Western Europe. A good approach to these is through one of the
two major trans-national organisations. The senior, based in Vienna,
is:

> Consejo Europeo de Investigaciones Sociales sobre América
>   Latina
> Österreichische Lateinamerika Institut
> Schmerlingplatz 8
> 1010 Wien
> Austria

This council, generally known as CEISAL, was founded in 1973,
and serves to coordinate Latin American studies in the social
sciences throughout Europe. Annual meetings are held in Vienna.

   A more recent foundation, working mainly in the EEC countries,
is:

> Instituto   de   Relaciones   Europeo   Latinoamericanas
>   (IRELA)
> Pedro de Valdivia 10, 3
> 28006 Madrid
> Spain
>   (Postal address: Apartado de Correos 2600, 28002 Madrid)

IRELA was founded in 1984 to foster and strengthen relations
between Europe and Latin America on a practical, interregional
level. It furthers these aims through international conferences and
meetings, and also publishes the invaluable and bilingual:

> *Manual para las relaciones europeo-latinoamericanas: instituciones y*
> *organizaciones europeas y sus relaciones con América Latina y el Caribe.*
> Edited by Brigitte Farenholtz and Wolfgang Grenz. Madrid:
> IRELA, 1987. In English and Spanish; lists the major
> European Latin Americanist organisations.

Finally, mention should be made of the principal international
organisation for the academic study of all aspects of Latin America.
This is the International Congress of Americanists, known in

Spanish as the Congreso Internacional de Americanistas. Confusingly, the congress's official name is in fact the French form:

Congrès International des Américanistes
David J. Fox, Secretary General
University of Manchester
School of Geography
Manchester M13 9PL
England

Congresses are held every three years, alternately in the Old World and the New, and the proceedings are published in a variety of formats.

Conferences and Meetings

Conferences and meetings present two major problems to the researcher: first, how to find out about them in advance, in case they are worth attending, and secondly, how to trace their published proceedings after the event.

Announcements

The *Hispanic American Historical Review* and *Latin American Research Review*, both of which used to have a regular section announcing future conferences, seem to have dropped this useful feature. Two journals which still provide such information are the *Informationsdienst* of the Arbeitsgemeinschaft Deutsche Lateinamerika-Forschung (quarterly since 1966) and *Latinskaya Amerika* (bimonthly since 1969), published in Moscow by the Institut Latinskoi Ameriki of the Academy of Sciences of the USSR. Otherwise, the best available sources of news about forthcoming meetings are the newsletters of Latin Americanist associations, many of which regularly announce the conferences of other organisations as well as their own. The names and addresses of some of the more important sponsors of conferences are given in the preceding section of this chapter.

There are also some general sources of conference information to which one can refer: the quarterly *Forthcoming International Scientific and Technical Conferences* (London: Association of Special Libraries and Information Bureaux, 1951—; previously published by the Department of Education and Science) and the annual *International*

Congress Calendar (Brussels: Union of International Associations, 1961—).

Published Proceedings

Published conference papers can usually be found in library catalogues under their collective title, under the editor's name, and also under the official name of the conference; unfortunately, it is often difficult to discover what any of these were. Some library catalogues try to help by grouping papers under one heading, such as 'Conference' or 'International Conference', or by consistently using the English form of the conference name. When in difficulty, try checking the catalogue under (in turn) the name of the sponsoring organisation, the editor of the published papers, and the name of any prominent contributor—preferably the one named first on the title-page, or the author of the first paper published. In desperation, try the subject catalogue, if the subject can be defined precisely enough.

The British Library Document Supply Centre in Boston Spa has produced since 1964 a regular keyword *Index of Conference Proceedings Received* (previously the *BLL Conference Index*). It appears monthly with annual and longer-term cumulations: there is now a cumulation from 1964 to 1981 on microfiche. This work indexes conferences, but not the individual papers. Another listing is the *Bibliographic Guide to Conference Publications* (previously *Conference Publications Guide*; Boston, MA: G. K. Hall, 1975—), which includes conference proceedings acquired by the Library of Congress from late 1973; the proceedings are listed by 'author' (the name of the conference or its sponsor), by title (of the proceedings as published), and by subject; all material of Latin American interest can be found in the 'Area Studies' section under 'Latin America'. There is also the bi-monthly *Proceedings in Print* (Arlington, VA, October 1964—), and the *Conference Paper Index* (originally *Current Programs*, Louisville, KY: Data Center, 1973—), which is a cumulating monthly index to papers presented. Some organisations, such as SALALM, publish indexes to their own proceedings (*Index to the SALALM Papers, 1956–1980*; Madison, WI: SALALM, 1984, and *Supplement, 1980–1985*, 1989).

A special case is the twice-yearly journal *Lateinamerika* (Rostock: Wilhelm-Pieck-Universität, Lateinamerika-Institut, 1965—), which publishes details of relevant papers presented at conferences, particularly in Eastern Europe—information which may be difficult to come by in any other source.

A word of caution is due at this point: many conference papers cited in bibliographies have never in fact achieved publication. To locate the information in instances such as these the researcher may need to contact the author directly in the hope of receiving a typescript. Authors of papers on Latin American studies may be traced through the directories of academics in the field cited in the chapter, UNIVERSITIES AND RESEARCH CENTRES (p. 314).

BGV/NT/RAM/LH

Contacts with Latin America

One of the great advantages accruing to the Latin Americanist is the increased possibility of direct contact with Central and South America and the Caribbean. This section covers the two principal methods of contact that the foreign researcher is likely to employ: travel in and correspondence with the region.

Travel

Latin America is one of the most spectacular regions of the world, and opportunities to spend time south of the Rio Grande are on no account to be missed. It is difficult to overestimate the value of the increased familiarity with local current events and patterns of thought that will result from your trip, or the beneficial effects on any research project you may be engaged in; besides which, you will almost certainly have a wonderful time. Of course, you are likely to encounter differences in manners, customs and general lifestyle from those you are accustomed to in Europe or North America: this is one of the great pleasures of foreign travel. And for a historical, social or literary researcher, there is really no substitute for a first-hand experience of the cultures being studied.

Guidebooks

Indispensable for any travel to Latin America and the Caribbean is the *South American Handbook* (1923—), published annually by Trade and Travel Publications of Bath and edited until 1989 by the late John Brooks, which (despite its title) covers the entire region. Its contents are essential reading whatever the traveller's socio-economic level and whatever the reasons for his or her trip. The advice ranges from how to travel in the Andes with a new-born child to how and when to bribe a policeman; on which side of which frontier to change your currency; and what spare parts to take on a cycling-tour in Patagonia. The introductory pages are particularly vital reading.

Eugene Fodor's Modern Guides, although considerably less reliable, are also revised annually, and now include volumes on *Mexico, The Caribbean and the Bahamas, Central America* and *Brazil.* There are also special *Budget Mexico* and *Budget Caribbean* volumes, and a guide covering just *Mexico City and Acapulco.* The publishers are Hodder in the UK and McKay in the US.

The Swiss publisher Nagel's Encyclopedic Guides include volumes for *Mexico* (1974), *Central America* (1979), *Brazil* (5th ed., 1979), *Peru* (1979) and *Bolivia* (1980), but these are revised much less frequently.

The New York firm of Frommer-Pasmantier publishes the annually revised *South America on Thirty Dollars a Day* (by Arnold and Harriet GREENBERG) and *Mexico on Twenty Dollars a Day* (by Tom BROSNAHAN). The difference in daily expenditure is instructive; when the first editions appeared twenty years ago the rate was just five dollars.

Editions Berlitz of Lausanne (distributed in the UK by Cassell of London and in the US by Macmillan of New York) have published guides to *Bermuda* (1982), the *French West Indies* (1978), *Jamaica* (1982), *Mexico City* (1978), *Rio de Janeiro* (1981), the *Southern Caribbean* (1981) and the *Virgin Islands* (1977). There are also Pelican Guides (from Penguin Books) to the *Bahamas* (1983) and the *Virgin Islands* (1986), both by James E. MOORE.

An excellent Michelin-style guide to Brazil is Editora Abril's annual *Guia Quatro Rodas.* And a locally-produced series of guides to Mexico is that of Editorial Trillas: their colourful *Guía Trillas de la Ciudad de México* was first published in 1986. For further titles see:

HEISE, Jon O. with Denis O'REILLY. *The Travel Book: Guide to the Travel Guides.* New York: Bowker, 1981.

In the UK, a collection of Latin American city plans and street maps has been built up at the library of the University of London Institute of Latin American Studies.

Documents

Passports are always essential, and visas are frequently so. Generally, the poorer the country, the more anxious it will be to welcome tourists with the minimum of formality. Some states (Brazil, for instance), simply insist on visas from nationals of countries that require visas from their own countrymen. So, as of 1987, Americans need visas to enter Brazil, while Britons do not. And when relations

between two countries are unhappy, extra red tape is an easy way to
ensure that the poor visitor is reminded of this: UK passport-holders
can expect extra formalities to get into Argentina, Guatemala or
Venezuela (boundary disputes); South Africans may expect them in
the Commonwealth Caribbean (apartheid), and so on. Even when
tourists are admitted without fuss, a student doing research might be
regarded as coming on business, and thus require a special entry
permit.

The local consulate of the country you are visiting should be the
best source of up-to-date information. Consular addresses can
usually be found in the telephone yellow pages, but always telephone
before you go; opening hours are usually limited. You may find that
the smaller consulates do not have all the information you require. If
you have any queries, and especially if your situation puts your case
in any way outside of the run-of-the-mill routine, double check with
others in a similar situation, or with the appropriate government
department in the country itself. The alternative is simply to find a
travel agent you can trust, and rely on him or her.

Many documents (educational qualifications, birth and marriage
certificates, driving licences and so on) may have no validity abroad
unless legalised and accompanied by a translation done by an
officially appointed translator of the country you are going to.
Legalising an English university degree parchment, for instance,
involves getting a certificate from the Department of Education and
Science (DES) in London attesting to the University Registrar's
signature, another from the Foreign and Commonwealth Office
attesting to the Department's certificate of authenticity, and an
Apostille from the appropriate Latin American consulate as evidence
that the Foreign Office stamp is itself genuine. American consulates
and other State Department agencies only attest to the authenticity
of documents issued by the federal government; state government
documents (marriage certificates, for example) have to be attested
by a state official known to the local Latin American consulate. So
start the process in plenty of time!

Even unlegalised documents, however, are well worth having in
order to impress officialdom, particularly those that attest to
academic status and *bona fides*. A letter of introduction (preferably
in Spanish or Portuguese) from the head of your department is a
good idea—one from the Vice Chancellor or Dean an even better
one. Printed, personal business cards are virtually a *sine qua non*; if
you cannot manage to acquire them, then at least be able to produce
an international student's card.

Cut-Price International Flights

Firms in the UK that specialise in cut-price air tickets are listed in the opening pages of the *South American Handbook*. For similar firms in the US consult the ads in the 'Travel' section of the Sunday edition of the *New York Times, Los Angeles Times* or similar major paper. The discounts are tremendous, but unfortunately the efficiency of such firms is sometimes not as great; if you have any reason for concern, telephone the airline to verify that their reservation records correspond to yours and to confirm your flight.

Internal Travel in Latin America

Airlines sell tickets to residents of Latin America on the instalment plan at an interest below the inflation rate; they manage this by fixing an excessively high cash price in the local currency. It may, therefore, be cheaper to buy tickets for all your intended internal flights in hard currency before you leave. If your travel is likely to be extensive, you may find the unlimited mileage tickets which some Latin American airlines sell to tourists abroad to be a bargain. In any case, book well in advance, especially for journeys at holiday times (December–March and July–August).

Long distance bus services are often remarkably good, especially the Brazilian *leito* type buses with fully reclining seats. These, like airlines, make a policy of overbooking, with priority given to the passengers who book first. So take your seat early, and if problems arise insist quietly but firmly on your rights.

Taxis are usually not expensive, but large cabs are often allowed to charge at a higher rate than the ubiquitous VW 'Beetles'. Several countries have a system of 'route taxis' or 'jitneys,' which function like buses for both in-town and cross-country journeys. In some areas (Trinidad, for instance), officialdom is ashamed of this system as a symptom of underdevelopment, and, even though everyone uses it, refuses to acknowledge its existence. Boarding points are therefore unmarked, and you will have to enquire of the local inhabitants.

Rail travel is seldom very satisfactory outside the Southern Cone.

Luggage

Before you decide that sending luggage in advance by international air freight will save paying money for excess baggage, remember that you will need to employ a despachante or other agent at your destination to clear the freight through customs, and that this can prove expensive. As they used to say at Harrods, 'The parcel you take with you arrives today,' and with a minimum of formality.

Money

Small denomination US dollar bills are best, if you can keep them in a safe place. Banks, even in large cities, may sometimes be suspicious of travellers' cheques: apparently if you exchange them and immediately report them stolen, the cashing bank has to bear the loss. (We do not recommend this method of financing your travel!) When banks do accept them, their commission may run as high as 20%; ask before you sign. The simplest and fairest place to exchange travellers' cheques is often a branch of the government's own bank (the Banco do Brasil, for example). Most of the larger cities also have American Express offices which will cash their own travellers' cheques free of charge, change currency, and even cash personal cheques for cardholders. In any such transaction, keep the receipt; it will be useful if you want to change the money back later.

Official attitudes to black market currency dealings vary from country to country and over time, but basically they are tolerated just so long as the black market (or 'parallel') rate does not get too far out of line—perhaps more than 10% better than the official rate. This means in effect that you can only get away with it when it is hardly worth the trouble involved (considering the amounts you are likely to be dealing in, that is).

Try not to have to rely on having money sent to you. A cable may take much longer than you expected, even when nothing goes wrong. Again, an American Express card is an excellent standby, and can be relied on for a fair exchange rate. You can also buy goods in the larger cities with Visa or Mastercard; the exchange rate will usually be fair, though never better than the official rate, if there is one.

Be sure to report any theft of documents, traveller's cheques or large sums of cash; the police may well do nothing, but you will need to prove that the incident was reported to secure replacements or to make insurance claims. Having a recent photocopy of your passport (and other important documents) in a safe place may help you to cope better with loss or theft. In some countries, Peru and Brazil among them, no report can be made to the police without first paying a small fee into the police authority's bank account. So try to secrete a small reserve fund somewhere, and endeavour not to be robbed outside banking hours!

Health and Personal Safety

Recent cut-backs in government expenditure resulting from the debt crisis have seriously compromised public health programmes in much of Latin America. Mosquito-borne diseases, polio and tuberculosis are among the diseases whose incidence is increasing as a consequence, and the spread of AIDS will enlarge the potential host population for these and many other diseases. This need not affect your trip too much, but the health advice given in the *South American Handbook* should be read with particular attention, and followed implicitly.

On the matter of personal safety, it is apposite to quote the words of Patricia Noble, Latin American librarian at the University of London Library, who wrote a personal account of book-buying trips to the region for the papers of SALALM XXIX: 'I have been asked on occasion if I have ever had any fears for my personal safety on these tours. On the contrary, in my experience people everywhere are unfailingly kind, helpful and sometimes even overly protective, particularly to the lone traveller. I should like to think that Latin American visitors to the United Kingdom meet with as much courtesy and kindness as I found in their countries.' ('Book Collecting Trips: A British View.' In *Collection Development: Co-operation at the Local and National Levels: Papers* of SALALM XXIX, 1984. Madison, WI: SALALM Secretariat, 1987, p. 103).

Correspondence

If you can't get to Latin America in person you can still keep in touch. This section deals with the various methods of communicating with Latin America from a distance: by mail, telephone and telex.

Mail

Surface mail can be inordinately slow, and should only be used for heavy packages; six months to reach London from, say, Quito is quite common, and eight months to Recife from Hamburg is not unknown. Air mail can generally guarantee delivery in a matter of days or, at worst, weeks, but is prohibitively expensive for heavier items. Anything which is valuable (or looks as if it is) should be registered, but this is no total guarantee of safe delivery, and compensation for lost international mail is limited. The best way to

ensure safe delivery of valuable mail is to entrust it to a friend
visiting the country.

Air Freight

Air freight should be considered for valuable items, particularly any
that cannot easily be replaced, such as legal documents. It is,
however, expensive—and the expense falls mainly on the recipient,
who will probably have to engage an agent to clear the package
through customs (a procedure seldom needed for parcel post), and
also to see to carriage from the airport to the final destination.

Addresses

Ensure that all communications are fully and accurately addressed,
or they may be returned as undeliverable, or maybe even lost simply
because the addressee's office has moved to another floor in the same
building. Whenever there is a chance that an address may be
outdated, it should be checked in a telephone or other recent
directory. Remember, too, to save incoming envelopes: many Latin
Americans put their return address there and not on the letter itself.

Spanish American and Brazilian addresses give the building
number after the street name, but the numeric postcode where it
exists comes before the name of the town; thus, 'Rua Martins
Ferreira 32, 22271 Rio de Janeiro'. *Edifício* or *Ed.* is 'building'; 'floor'
is *piso* (Portuguese *andar*); 'room' or 'office' is *oficina* (Portuguese *sala*
or *s/*); 'suite' is *conjunto* or *conj.*; and *sobreloja* (*s/l*) is common in Brazil
to denote the floor above a shop. *Sin* (or *sem*) *número* (*s/n*) means that
the building has no street number.

Some countries have their own special practices: in Argentina,
Brazil and Mexico town names should always be qualified by the
department or state. Argentine provincial names are written in full,
with the city of Buenos Aires designated 'Buenos Aires (Capital
Federal)' to distinguish it from the province. Mexican addresses also
require the appropriate state name, properly abbreviated. Brazilian
states and territories require not only official abbreviations but also
postcodes, which should never be omitted; when the exact postcode
is unknown, it is better to include the general state code rather than
to omit it altogether. In Brazil, mail for delivery in the town where it
is posted is usually addressed 'nesta' (in this [same city]). The
recognised abbreviations of Mexican and Brazilian states, together
with Brazilian postcodes, are given in Appendix I, below.

Other recognised abbreviations of Latin American and Caribbean relevance include BVI (British Virgin Islands), CA (Central America), CR (Costa Rica), DE (Distrito Especial; i.e., Bogotá), PR (Puerto Rico), RA (República Argentina), RD (República Dominicana), ROU (República Oriental del Uruguay), SA (South America), USVI (United States Virgin Islands), WI (West Indies) and ZC (Zona Central).

'Post Office Box number' is *apartado (postal)*, variously abbreviated, in most Hispanic countries. Colombia, where air and surface mail are separately administered, has separate *apartados aéreos* for air mail. In the Southern Cone countries of Argentina, Bolivia, Chile and Uruguay (but not Paraguay) the expression is *casilla de correo(s)* (*C/C*). Peru uses both terms interchangeably. The equivalent in Portuguese is *caixa postal*; this should never be abbreviated, lest it be read as *código postal* (postcode).

Style

The language of your correspondence is a matter of personal taste and/or capability. Writing in Spanish or Portuguese, however, is frequently the only way to gain a response from some Latin American correspondents, and there are several useful guides to letter writing in both languages, with specimen letters. Examples (which require a basic knowledge of the language concerned) are:

JACKSON, Mary H. *Guide to Correspondence in Spanish*. Lincolnwood, IL: National Textbook Co., 1978, and London: Thorne, 1981.

PEET, Terry C. and Marta Stiefel AYALA. *A Guide to Spanish Correspondence for Acquisitions Librarians*. Bibliography and Reference Series, 18. Madison, WI: SALALM Secretariat, 1987. Has a usefulness by no means restricted to the library profession.

If you are composing your own letter in Spanish or Portuguese, be careful (even in the most routine, formal business context) to conform to the traditional pattern, with definite opening and closing paragraphs. The latter in particular should be elaborate and almost flowery by contemporary Anglo-American standards; a mere translation of what would be appropriate in an English language context may well strike the reader as abrupt, cold, and possibly even rude.

Telephone Calls

Now that direct dialling is possible to all major Latin American cities, telephoning is recommendable as a practical means of communicating, even from abroad, if your language skills are equal to it. Try to call when rates are lowest—late evening from Europe, early morning from the western United States. Information on some dialling codes is given in Appendix II, below.

The word for 'extension number' is *extensión* in Spanish and *ramal* in Portuguese. When giving numbers digit-by-digit in Portuguese, it is usual to substitute *meia* (half [a dozen]) for *seis* (six), for greater phonetic clarity.

When planning a phone call do not forget to take public holidays and time differences into account. The back pages of the *South American Handbook* give basic time zone information. And remember to allow for Daylight Saving Time in the South American summer—even in tropical Brazil.

Telex

International phone calls from Latin America should be made with caution; rates in some countries (Brazil, Mexico and Uruguay, for instance) are still exorbitant. Many Latin American institutions prefer telex for this reason, and there are telex stations available to the general public in many cities. If you are in a position to receive telex messages, therefore, always let your Latin American correspondents know your telex number.

LH

Appendix I

Brazilian State Abbreviations and Postcodes

Acre AC 69.900 (and up)
Alagoas AL 57.000...
Amapá AP 68.900...
Amazonas AM 69.000...
Bahia BA 40.000...
Ceará CE 60.000...
Espírito Santo ES 29.000...
Fernando de Noronha FN
Goiás GO 74.000...
Maranhão MA 65.000...
Mato Grosso MT 78.000...
Mato Grosso do Sul MS
Minas Gerais MG 30.000...

Paraíba PB 58.000...
Pará PR 80.000...
Pernambuco PE 50.000...
Piauí PI 64.000...
Rio de Janeiro RJ 20.000...
Rio Grande do Norte RN
    59.000...
Rio Grande do Sul RS 90.000...
Rondônia RO 78.900...
Roraima RR 69.300...
Santa Catarina SC 88.000...
Sergipe SE 49.000

Brasília (Distrito Federal) is DF 70.000... and São Paulo has three different codes: for central São Paulo city SP 01.000..., for the rest of the city and greater São Paulo SP 02.000-09.000 and for other parts of the state SP 10.000... Letters to São Paulo city are usually addressed 'São Paulo (capital)'.

Mexican State Abbreviations

Aguascalientes—Ags.
Baja California (N)—B.C.
Baja California (S)—B.C.S.
Campeche—Camp.
Chihuahua—Chih.
Chiapas—Chis.
Coahuila—Coah.
Colima—Col.
Durango—Dgo.
Guanajuato—Gto.
Guerrero—Gro.
Hidalgo—Hgo.
Jalisco—Jal.
México—Edo. de Mex.
Michoacan—Mich.

Morelos—Mor.
Nayarit—Nay.
Nuevo León—N.L.
Oaxaca—Oax.
Puebla—Pue.
Querétaro—Qro.
Quintana Roo—Q.R.
San Luis Potosí—S.L.P.
Sinaloa—Sin.
Sonora—Son.
Tabasco—Tab.
Tamaulipas—Tamps.
Tlaxcala—Tlax.
Veracruz—Ver.
Zacatecas—Zac.

'Mexico City (Distrito Federal)' is 'México, DF'. New two-letter codes are being considered, but have as yet to come into general use.

Appendix II

Telephone Dialling Codes

The access code for direct dialling abroad is 00 from most countries; the exceptions include Australia (0011), North America and most of the Caribbean (011), Portugal (07), Spain (07, then wait for dial tone) and the UK (010). This should be followed by the country code, then by the area code (omitting any initial zero) and then by the subscriber's number. Relevant country codes (and some combined country and area codes) are as follows:

Argentina 54 (Buenos Aires 541, Córdoba 5451, La Plata 5421, Rosario 5441)

Belize 501 (Belize City 5012, Orange Walk 5013)

Bolivia 591 (Cochabamba 59142, La Paz 5912, Sucre 59164)

Brazil 55 (Belem 5591, Belo Horizonte 5531, Brasília 5561, Fortaleza 5585, Petrópolis 55242, Porto Alegre 55512, Recife 5581, Rio de Janeiro 5521, Salvador 5571, São Paulo 5511)

Canada 1 (Montreal 1514, Ottawa 1613, Toronto 1416, Winnipeg 1204)

Chile 56 (Concepción 5642, Santiago 562, Valparaíso 5631)

Colombia 57 (Barranquilla 575, Bogotá 571, Cali 573, Medellín 574)

Commonwealth Caribbean Islands all 1809 (no area codes)

Costa Rica 506 (no area codes)

Cuba 53 (Havana 537) [NB No direct dialling from the US]

Dominican Republic 1809 (no area codes)

Ecuador 593 (Cuenca 5937, Guayaquil 5934, Quito 5932)

El Salvador 503 (no area codes)

France 33 (no area codes)

Guadeloupe 590 (no area codes)

Guatemala 502 (Guatemala City 5022)

Guyana 592 (Georgetown 59202)

Haiti 509 (Port-au-Prince 5091)

Irish Republic 353 (Dublin 3531)

Martinique 596 (no area codes)

Mexico 52 (Acapulco 52748, Guadalajara 5236, León 52471, Mérida 52992, Mexico City 525, Monterrey 5283, Puebla 5222, Veracruz 52293)

Netherlands Antilles 599 (Aruba 5998, Bonaire 5997, Curaçao 5999)

Nicaragua 505 (León 50531, Managua 5052)

Panama 507 (no area codes)

Paraguay 595 (Asunción 59521, Concepción 59531)

Peru 51 (Arequipa 5154, Callao and Lima 5114)

Portugal 351 (Braga 35153, Coimbra 35139, Lisbon 3511, Oporto 3512)

Puerto Rico 1809 (no area codes)

Spain 34 (Barcelona 343, Bilbao 344, Madrid 341, Seville 3454)

Surinam 597 (no area codes)

United Kingdom 44 (Cambridge 44223, Colchester 44206, Glasgow 4441, Liverpool 4451, London 441, Oxford 44865)

United States 1 (Los Angeles 1213, New York City 1212, Washington DC 1202)

Uruguay 598 (Montevideo 5982)

Venezuela 58 (Caracas 582, Maracaibo 5861, Mérida 5874, Valencia 5841)

Virgin Islands 1809 (no area codes)

Careers for Latin Americanists

Career opportunities for work involving Latin America are almost unlimited—particularly for those Latin Americanists who combine area studies specialisation with appropriate language skills and training in a specific subject discipline or profession. This can apply to jobs both in one's own country and abroad. A well-planned undergraduate curriculum may, in some instances suffice to obtain an entry-level position related to the field. More commonly, however, postgraduate study is necessary to obtain all the skills required for a professional career. Information about the range of courses available is given in the chapter, UNIVERSITIES AND RESEARCH CENTRES (pp. 307–313).

While the Foreign Service is an obvious choice for an area studies specialist, it must be remembered that—at least at the junior levels—one has little choice of posting; a Latin Americanist may well have to spend years in Bulgaria or Zimbabwe or Indonesia before reaching the South American subcontinent. But even bearing this in mind, the countless research, administrative and field work opportunities available in the Diplomatic Corps and the Intelligence Agencies certainly merit consideration.

University teaching is a clear option for Latin Americanists who pursue their education through the research degree or doctoral level, but there are also many opportunities for those with less impressive academic credentials. Most professional skills can be applied to positions in either the public or the private sector; in non-profit development, philanthropic, religious, relief or research organisations; or in one of the myriad international agencies involved in work with Latin America.

For specialists interested in working with Latin Americans in the US, the opportunities are even greater. In the last ten years the national demographic composition of the United States has changed to such an extent that Spanish-speaking populations now constitute a large percentage of several major metropolitan areas. As a consequence, the influence of the Hispanic market has grown tremendously, and this has in turn generated a strong demand for skilled professionals having a background in Latin American studies in almost every field.

Listed below are just a few of the kinds of careers outside the Foreign Service and the academic world that are open to Latin Americanists.

Arts. Management or specialist work in a museum or art collection concerned with Latin American materials; photojournalism.

Business. Management, sales or consulting position with a multinational firm doing business in Latin America, or with an international airline carrier or shipping company; international banking; development banking with a private firm or international financial organisation; economist; management or purchasing for an import/export firm.

Communications. Foreign correspondent or regional specialist for a newspaper, magazine or television network; producer or director of documentary films; foreign distributor of Latin American films or television; sales or management position with an international communications firm; editor for an academic or commercial press publishing Latin American materials.

Data processing. Software developer for Latin American applications in private or public sector concerns; technical or sales position with a hardware or software firm doing business with Latin America.

Education. Teaching English as a second language; teaching abroad; bilingual education programme management; educational development consultancy for an international agency or Latin American government-sponsored programme.

Engineering. Technical, consulting, research or management position with a multinational firm, international agency or Latin American government-sponsored programme in the areas of civil, mechanical, petrochemical or geotechnical engineering.

Language. Teaching Spanish or Portuguese in the school system or to business people at home or abroad; translation for a commercial firm, publishing company, government agency or international organisation.

Law. International territorial law; international aspects of such fields as corporate, trade or copyright law; immigration law.

Librarianship. Latin American cataloguing, reference or collection development in an academic or government library; management position in a government-sponsored library abroad or in the library of an international agency; Latin American database searching or management.

Public Health. Field work, research or management job in a non-profit group, international agency or government-sponsored health programme; research or management position with a pharmaceutical or health care firm doing business with Latin America.

Social Work. Organiser, coordinator or fund-raiser for a voluntary programme for local Latin American populations; mental health or public welfare counsellor; field work or management position for an international relief agency.

Urban Planning. Field work, research or management position in an international development agency or Latin American government-sponsored programme involved in community development, regional planning, demography or public services.

As will be seen, this is by no means an exhaustive list; it is merely an attempt to enable the student to visualise his or her own aspirations or interests in a Latin American context.

For specific information about employers of Latin American specialists, there is an excellent directory listing the names, addresses and some activities of business firms active in Latin America, planning and research organisations, specialised language and translation services, government agencies, international development organisations and bilingual schools in Latin America and the Caribbean. Although the book cites mainly US employers, it can also be used to identify similar kinds of firms and agencies operating in the UK and elsewhere:

> KREGAR, Shirley A. et al. *After Latin American Studies: A Guide to Employment for Latinamericanists.* Latin American Monograph and Document Series, 10. Pittsburgh, PA: University of Pittsburgh, Center for Latin American Studies, 1987.

BGV

Acronyms and Indexes

Acronyms and Abbreviations

Authors and publishers delight in the use of acronyms and abbreviations, but frequently fail to provide any explanation or glossary. New examples are continually appearing, and the student may find the need to keep a personal file of those relevant to his or her field of interest. Hearteningly, it is no longer always essential to know the full name of an organisation in order to trace its publications in library catalogues: by the latest *Anglo-American Cataloguing Rules* (AACR2), a corporate body is listed under the most common form of its name, not necessarily the fullest form. This means that UNESCO (or Unesco) may be a catalogue heading in its own right, and the researcher will not be forced to hunt around under 'United Nations Educational, Scientific and Cultural Organization'. Not all libraries have adopted the new rules, however, and it will still help considerably to know the full name of the required organisation. Dictionaries of abbreviations, such as those listed below, can help with the better-established and commoner examples.

The two major international works are:

BUTTRESS, F. A. *World Guide to Abbreviations of Organizations*. 8th ed. Revised by H. J. Heaney. Glasgow: Blackie, 1988.

Acronyms, Initialisms and Abbreviations Dictionary. Edited by Julie E. Towell and Helen E. Sheppard. 12th ed. 3 vols. Detroit, MI: Gale Research, 1987. Volume 1, in three parts, is the dictionary proper; volume 2 an 'Interedition Supplement' of additions. Volume 3 is a reverse dictionary, also in three parts, referring from the organisation name to the abbreviation.

A much shorter Spanish language dictionary is:

MARTÍNEZ DE SOUSA, José. *Diccionario internacional de siglas y acrónimos*. Madrid: Pirámide, 1984.

The principal source for abbreviations of Latin American regional and national organisations was prepared by the United Nations Economic Commission for Latin America (CEPAL in Spanish):

Lista de siglas latinoamericanas/Latin American Initialisms and Acronyms, with English Translations. Edited by Delia Barbosa. New ed. Santiago: Biblioteca de la CEPAL, 1978. The translations given are the official ones. The first edition (1970) was reprinted in the United States (Detroit, MI: Blaine Ethridge, 1974).

There are also many dictionaries of abbreviations and acronyms used in particular countries or for particular subjects.

If all else fails, there is an index of abbreviations and acronyms maintained in a card file at the Institute of Latin American Studies of the University of London (31 Tavistock Square, London WC1H 9HA; telephone 01-387 4055), and the staff there can help with enquiries.

The principal abbreviations and acronyms used in this book are listed below (most are explained in the text at their first appearance). Excluded are the two-letter postal code abbreviations for the states of the US that appear in the citations of North American works.

AACR2	*Anglo-American Cataloguing Rules.* 2nd ed.
AAG	American Association of Geography
AATSP	American Association of Teachers of Spanish and Portuguese
ACOLAM	Advisory Committee on Latin American Materials (UK)
ACURIL	Association of Caribbean University and Research Libraries
AGN	Archivo General de la Nación
AGRINTER	Inter-American Information System for Agricultural Science
AHA	American Historical Association
AIBDA	Asociación Interamericana de Bibliotecarios y Documentalistas Agrícolas
ANH	Academia Nacional de la Historia (Venezuela)
ARL	Association of Research Libraries (US)
ATSP	Association of Teachers of Spanish and Portuguese (UK)
BALAS	Business Association of Latin American Studies (US)
BBC	British Broadcasting Corporation
BLAISE	British Library Automated Information Service
BLDSC	British Library Document Supply Centre, Boston Spa
BLOWS	British Library of Wildlife Sounds
BLPES	British Library of Political and Economic Science
BN	Bibliothèque Nationale, Paris
BNB	British National Bibliography
BTEC	Business and Technical Education Council (UK)

BUCLA	British Union Catalogue of Latin Americana
BUCOP	*British Union Catalogue of Periodicals*
BVI	British Virgin Islands
CA	Central America
CALL	Computer-assisted language learning
CAMINO	Central America Information Office
CARICOM	Caribbean Community
CBP	*Catálogo Brasileiro de Publicações*
CCC	Centrale Catalogus Caraibiana
CCT	Computer-compatible tape
CD-ROM	Compact disc—read-only memory
CEDLA	Centro de Estudios y Documentación Latinoamericanos/ Centrum voor Studie en Documentatie van Latijns Amerika (Netherlands)
CEISAL	Consejo Europeo de Investigaciones Sociales sobre América Latina, Vienna
CELADE	Centro Latinoamericano de Demografía
CENECA	Centro de Indagación y Expresión Cultural y Artística
CEPAL	Comisión Económica para América Latina/United Nations Economic Commission for Latin America (and the Caribbean)
CIAT	Centro Interamericano de Agricultura Tropical
CICH	Centro de Información Científica y Humanística, UNAM
CIDIA	Centro Interamericano de Documentación e Información Agrícola
CIDOC	Centro Intercultural de Documentación, Cuernavaca
CIEE	Council on International Educational Exchange (US)
CILT	Centre for Information on Language Teaching and Research (UK)
CIMMYT	Centro Internacional de Mejoramiento de Maíz y Trigo
CIS	Congressional Information Service (US)
CLACSO	Consejo Latinoamericano de Ciencias Sociales
CLADES	Centro Latinoamericano de Documentación Económica y Social
CLAG	Council of Latin American Geographers (US)
CLAH	Conference on Latin American History (US)
CLASP	Consortium of Latin America Studies Programs (US)
CNRS	Centre National de la Recherche Scientifique (France)
COHA	Council on Hemispheric Affairs (US)
COLA	Committee on Latin America (UK)
COM	Computer output microform
CR	Costa Rica
CRAC	Careers Resource Advisory Centre, London
CRL	Center for Research Libraries, Chicago, Illinois
CURL	Consortium of University and Research Libraries (UK)
DDR	Deutsche Demokratische Republik/German Democratic Republic

DE	Distrito Especial
DES	Department of Education and Science (UK)
EEC	European Economic Community
EEHA	Escuela de Estudios Hispano-Americanos, Seville
EOSAT	Earth Information Satellite Company
EUDEBA	Editorial Universitaria de Buenos Aires
EUI	*Enciclopedia Universal Ilustrada Europeo-Americana*
FAO	United Nations Food and Agriculture Organization
FBIS	Foreign Broadcast Information Service (US)
GCE	General Certificate of Education (UK)
HAPI	*Hispanic American Periodicals Index*
HEA	Higher Education Act (US)
HLAS	*Handbook of Latin American Studies*
HMSO	Her Majesty's Stationery Office (UK)
IADB	Inter-American Development Bank
IBGE	Instituto Brasileira de Geografia e Estatística
IBRD	International Bank for Reconstruction and Development
ICA	International Council of Archives
IDB	Inter-American Development Bank
IDC	Inter Documentation Company
IEE	Institute of International Education
IFLA	International Federation of Library Associations and Institutions
IICA	Instituto Interamericano de Cooperación para la Agricultura
IIE	Institute of International Education (US)
ILAS	Institute of Latin American Studies, University of London
INDEC	Instituto Nacional de Estadística y Censos (Argentina)
INIDEF	Instituto Interamericano de Etnomusicología y Folklore
Inpadoc	International Patent Documentation Center, Vienna
IPS	Inter Press Service (Italy)
IRELA	Instituto de Relaciones Europeo Latinoamericanos
ISBN	International Standard Book Number
ISSN	International Standard Serial Number
IUPERJ	Instituto Universitário de Pesquisas do Rio de Janeiro
JANET	Joint Academic Network (UK)
JLP	Jamaican Labour Party
KIT	Koninklijk Instituut voor Taal-, Land- en Volkerkunde, Leiden
LACAP	Latin American Cooperative Acquisition Plan (US)
LADOC	Latin America Documentation (Peru)
LAMP	Latin American Microforms Project (US)
LASA	Latin American Studies Association (US)

LATAG	Latin American Trade Advisory Group (UK)
LC	Library of Congress (US)
LCCI	London Chamber of Commerce and Industry
LCMARC	Library of Congress Machine-Readable Catalog
MACLAS	Middle Atlantic Council of Latin American Studies (US)
MALAS	Midwest Association for Latin American Studies (US)
MLA	Modern Language Association of America
NCCLA	North Central Council of Latin Americanists (US)
NCIP	North American Collections Inventory Program
NDEA	National Defense Education Act (US)
NECLAS	New England Council on Latin American Studies
NFT	National Film Theatre, London
NPAC	National Program for Acquisition and Cataloging (US)
NRMM	*National Register of Microform Masters* (US)
NSA	National Sound Archive (UK)
NST	*New Serial Titles*
NUC	*National Union Catalog* (US)
NYPL	New York Public Library
OAS	Organization of American States
OCLC	Online Computer Library Center (US)
OECD	Organisation for Economic Cooperation and Development
OPS	Organización Panamericana de la Salud/Pan American Health Organization
OSD	Overseas Survey Directorate (UK)
PAHO	Pan-American Health Organization
PAIGH	Pan-American Institute of Geography and History
PAIS	Public Affairs Information Service (US)
PCCLAS	Pacific Coast Council on Latin American Studies
PNM	Peoples' National Movement (Trinidad)
PR	Puerto Rico
PRI	Partido Revolucionario Institucional (Mexico)
RA	República Argentina
RD	República Dominicana
RILA	*Répertoire International de la Littérature de l'Art*
RILM	*Répertoire International de la Littérature Musicale*
RLIN	Research Libraries Information Network (US)
RMCLAS	Rocky Mountain Council on Latin American Studies
ROU	República Oriental del Uruguay
RPM	Register of Preservation Microforms (UK)
RSA	Royal Society of Arts (UK)
SA	South America
SALALM	Seminar on the Acquisition of Latin American Library Materials

SCHML	Standing Conference of Heads of Modern Languages in Polytechnics (UK)
SCOLAS	Southwestern Council on Latin American Studies (US)
SCONUL	Standing Conference of National and University Libraries (UK)
SECOLAS	Southeastern Council on Latin American Studies (US)
SLA	Special Library Association (US)
SLAS	Society for Latin American Studies (UK)
SRIS	Science Reference and Information Service, British Library
TAICH	Technical Assistance Information Clearing House, American Council of Voluntary Agencies for Foreign Service
UCB	University of California, Berkeley
UCLA	University of California, Los Angeles
UDC	Universal Decimal Classification
UK	United Kingdom of Great Britain and Northern Ireland
ULS	*Union List of Serials in the United States and Canada*
UMI	University Microfilms International
UN	United Nations
UNAM	Universidad Nacional Autónoma de México
Unesco	United Nations Educational, Scientific and Cultural Organization
UNRISD	United Nations Research Institute for Social Development
US	United States of America
USVI	United States Virgin Islands
UTEHA	Union Tipográfica Editorial Hispanoamerica (Mexico)
UWI	University of the West Indies
WI	West Indies
ZC	Zona Central

GS/BGV

Subject Index

Reference Source Index

Morales, Enrique L.
  'Estado actual de los archivos en Latinoamérica', 27
Morales Padrón, Francisco
  'Cartografía sobre Puerto Rico', 182
  'Guía de profesores de historia de América en universidades ibero-
  americanos', 314
  Mapas, planos y dibujos sobre Venezuela ..., 182
Morel Solaeche, R.E.
  Bibliografía de obras paraguayas, 60
Morínigo, Marcos Augusto
  Diccionario de americanismos, 170
Mörner, Magnus
  Fuentes para la historia de Ibero-América, 25
Mosier, John
  'Film', 259
Moss, S.G.
  Books on the West Indies or by West Indian Writers ..., 58
  'El movimiento de musica folklórica en México: apuntes para su estudio',
  247
Mraz, John
  'Particularidad y nostalgia', 257
*Muestras de errores y defectos del 'Diccionario biográfico de Chile' de José Toribio
  Medina*, 270
Mundo Lo, Sara de
  Colombian Serial Publications in the University of Illinois Library, 215
  The Falklands/Malvinas Islands, 131
  Index to Spanish American Collective Biography, 144, **269**
Museo-Biblioteca de Ultramar en Madrid: catálogo de la biblioteca, 56
*Music from Latin America Available at Indiana University: Scores, Tapes and
  Records*, 250
Music in Latin America: An Introduction, 113
Music Index, 114
Music of Many Cultures: An Introduction, 247
La música de México, 114
Musso Ambrosi, Luis Alberto
  Bibliografía de bibliografías uruguayas, 119

La Nación (Argentina), 186
La Nación (Chile), 187
La Nación (Costa Rica), 187
Nacional (Mexico), 188, 189
El Nacional (Venezuela), 188, 196
NACLA Report on the Americas, 194
Nadurille, Ramon
  *Catálogo colectivo de publicaciones periódicas existentes en las bibliotecas de la
  República Mexicana*, 214
Naef, Weston J.
  Pioneer Photographers of Brazil, 256

About the Contributors

Alan BIGGINS (*AB*) is Librarian of the Institute of Latin American Studies, University of London; his research interests include Argentine librarianship and bibliography.

Chris CLARK (*CC*) is Jazz Curator for the British Library National Sound Archive. His ambit extends to the urban popular music of South America.

Harold COLSON (*HC*) is Public Services/Collection Development Librarian at the International Relations and Pacific Studies Library, University of California, San Diego. His research interests centre on online databases for Latin American studies.

Tim CONNELL (*TC*) is Principal Lecturer in Spanish at Ealing College of Higher Education in London. He is co-author of a dozen books and some twenty-four articles on a wide range of Hispanic themes.

Paula Ann Hattox COVINGTON (*PAC*) is Latin American and Iberian Bibliographer at Vanderbilt University Library, Nashville, Tennessee. She is the author of *Indexed Journals: A Guide to Latin American Serials* and editor of the forthcoming *Latin American and Caribbean Studies: A Critical Guide to Research Sources*.

Hilda CUTHELL (*HMC*) was until 1987 Head of the British Library London Lending Unit.

Martha DAVIDSON (*MD*) is a consultant on Latin American picture resources and presently works at the Fogg Art Museum, Harvard University, Cambridge, Massachusetts. She is the author of *Picture Collections: Mexico*.

Carl W. DEAL (*CWD*) is Director of Library Collections, Universit, of Illinois at Urbana-Champaign.

John EAST (*JE*) has worked for the British Library Science Reference and Information Service, London.

James ELLIOT (*JDE*) is a Curator in the British Library Map Library, and is responsible for cataloguing, automation and exhibitions. He recently published *The City in Maps: Urban Mapping to 1900*.

Betty D. FATHERS (*BDF*) is in Map Curator and Superintendent of the Map Section of the Bodleian Library, Oxford. She compiled the 'Recent Maps and Atlases' article in *The Cartographic Journal* from 1964 to 1987.

Gillian FURLONG (*GF*) is Archivist in the Library of University College London.

Paul GOULDER (*PG*) is Director of the Centre for Advanced Learning Technology and Lecturer in Latin American Studies at the City Polytechnic, London. He is author of *Brazil: The Business Future*.

Laurence HALLEWELL (*LH*) is Ibero-American Bibliographer at the University of Minnesota Libraries. He is the author of *Books in Brazil* (1982) and the editor of *Latin American Bibliography* (1978), the first edition of this book.

Brigid M. HARRINGTON (*BMH*) was until 1979 Librarian of the Institute of Latin American Studies, University of London. She is currently Librarian at the Latymer School, Edmonton, London, and has contributed over a number of years to the *Hispanic American Periodicals Index*.

Margaret JOHNSON (*MJ*) is Head of the Hispanic Section, British Library, Humanities and Social Sciences. She is the current compiler of 'Theses in Hispanic Studies Approved for Higher Degrees by British and Irish Universities', published regularly in the *Bulletin of Hispanic Studies*.

Peter T. JOHNSON (*PTJ*) is the Princeton University's Bibliographer for Latin America, Spain and Portugal and also a Lecturer in the Program in Latin American Studies. His research interests concern the different forms of resistance ranging from revolutionary movements to questions of censorship and publishing.

Peter Ward JONES (*PWJ*) is Music Librarian at the Bodleian Library, Oxford.

Sara E. JOYNES (*SEJ*) was formerly Senior Assistant Librarian at the Institute of Commonwealth Studies, University of London, where she was responsible for maintaining the catalogue of theses completed or in progress in Commonwealth Studies.

Roger MACDONALD (*RRM*) is Languages and Area Studies Librarian at Portsmouth Polytechnic. He is co-author of *Libraries and Special Collections on Latin America and the Caribbean: A Directory of European Resources*.

Robert A. McNEIL (*RAM*) is the head of the Hispanic Section at the Bodleian Library, Oxford.

David NEWTON (*DCN*) is Head of Patents Information at the British Library Science Reference and Information Service, London.

John PINFOLD (*JRP*) is Reference Librarian at the British Library of Political and Economic Science, London School of Economics. He is the compiler of *African Population Census Reports: A Bibliography and Checklist*.

Barbara J. ROBINSON (*BJR*) is Curator of the Boeckmann Center for Iberian and Latin American Studies at the Doheny Library, University of Southern California, Los Angeles. She is co-author of *The Mexican American: A Critical Guide to Research Aids*.

Michael ROGERS (*MR*) was until the end of 1987 Librarian of the Institute of Development Studies at the University of Sussex.

Patricia A. SEMPLE (*PAS*) is Head of the Education Department of the Hispanic and Luso-Brazilian Council, Canning House, London, and editor of the Department's *Newsletter*.

Gillian SHAW (*GS*) was until 1988 Assistant Librarian at the Institute of Latin American Studies, University of London.

Carole TRAVIS (*CT*) was Librarian of the Institute of Latin American Studies, University of London from 1979 to 1988. She is co-author of *Libraries and Special Collections on Latin America and the Caribbean: A Directory of European Resources* and editor of *Guide to Latin American and West Indian Census Materials*.

Noel TREACY (*NT*) is the Librarian of the Hispanic and Luso-Brazilian Council at Canning House, London. He also edits the *British Bulletin of Publications on Latin America, the Caribbean, Portugal and Spain*.

Barbara G. VALK (*BGV*) is Coordinator of Bibliographic Development at the Latin American Center, University of California, Los

Angeles. She is editor of the *Hispanic American Periodicals Index* and *BorderLine*.

Ann WADE (*AEW*) is a Curator in the Hispanic Section of the British Library (Humanities and Social Sciences) in London. She is the Secretary of the SCONUL Advisory Committee on Latin American Materials.

John WAINWRIGHT (*JW*) is in charge of Spanish and Portuguese materials at the Taylor Institution Library, Oxford. He is the author of numerous bibliographies.

Purabi WARD (*PW*) was until recently Curator of the Agricultural and General Life Sciences collections of the Science Reference and Information Service, which forms part of the Science, Technology and Industry Division of the British Library. She has been involved in developing the collections of scientific literature published in Spanish and Portuguese.

Geoffrey WEST (*GW*) is a Curator in the Hispanic Section of the British Library (Humanities and Social Sciences) in London. He has taught Spanish language at the University of Essex and Spanish American literature at the University of Birmingham.

Gayle A. WILLIAMS (*GAW*) is Assistant Curator of Latin American Collections at the University of New Mexico, Albuquerque.

Christine YOUNGER (*CY*) is an Information Officer at the British Council, London. She has previously worked as Librarian at Canning House, London (where she edited the *British Bulletin of Publications on Latin America* from 1981 to 1984) and in the Hispanic Section of the British Library.